High Upon A Hill
A History of Bellarmine College

High Upon A Hill
A History of Bellarmine College

Wade Hall

Bellarmine College Press * Louisville * 1999

Photo credits:
Photographs and other illustrations in this book are from the Bellarmine College archives, unless otherwise indicated.

Early view of the Newburg Road entrance.

Dedicated to

Archbishop John A. Floersh
The Founding Fathers
and
The Pioneer Class of Bellarmine College

You gambled and won!

You are the light of the world. A city set on a hill cannot be hidden. Men do not light a lamp and then put it under a bushel basket. They set it on a stand where it gives light to all in the house. In the same way, your light must shine before men so that they may see goodness in your acts and give praise to your heavenly Father.

—Matthew 5:14-16, Catholic Biblical Association of America, 1970

———————————

. . . wee shall finde that the God of Israell is among us, when ten of us shall be able to resist a thousand of our enemies, when hee shall make us a praise and glory, that men shall say of succeeding plantations: the Lord make it like that of New England: for wee must Consider that wee shall be as a Citty upon a Hill [and] the eyes of all people are uppon us. . . .

—John Winthrop (1588-1649), Governor, Massachusetts Bay Colony; from *A Model of Christian Charity*, c. 1640

———————————

In the City of the Falls, high upon a hill,
Stands Alma Mater Bellarmine, the pride of Louisville.
Her scarlet, silver colors true shine brightly in the sun
And warm our hearts and memories, your daughters and sons.

The hopes and dreams and values born in our Kentucky home
Will stir our hearts and minds and lives wherever we may roam.
And as we grow, dear Bellarmine, in the love of truth,
Alma Mater Bellarmine, so grows our love for you.

—Joseph J. McGowan, Jr., "Bellarmine College Alma Mater," 1992

Contents

Preface

It is Tuesday, October 3, 1950, and a new college is opening its doors. Pioneer Class member John Wernert remembered, somewhat dramatically, that it was a quiet and warm day. "Autumn had hardly made its presence felt," he wrote. "Summer foliage hung to the trees as if reluctant to even begin its final coloration and disintegration. From every part of the City of Louisville, individuals were converging on a certain point—individuals intent on one purpose. They came singly, in small groups of two or three, by bus, car, or hitchhiker's thumb, some halfheartedly, some timidly, some with utmost confidence. And as they came, the one thought uppermost in each mind was just what this assembly point held in store for each of them."

Indeed, this is assembly day for some 115 eager, nervous freshmen (an additional 113 men and women enrolled in night classes would bring the first year's total to 228) who are enrolling in a new Catholic men's college called Bellarmine, a college envisioned and called into existence in Louisville, Kentucky, by Archbishop John Alexander Floersh and built by Fr. Alfred Horrigan, Fr. Raymond J. Treece and hundreds of supporters. Twenty-two years later, during brief remarks made at his final graduation ceremony as president, Fr. Horrigan noted that his mandate from the Archbishop had been to create "an excellent college."

By 1972 this "excellent college" had become a reality. But in 1950 it is still a distant dream. One building has been completed—almost. While some workmen are painting and installing furniture and equipment in the single building, others are laying sod and planting shrubs along the covered walkway.

Students walk in shirt sleeves, ties and coats to their first orientation, where with the assistance of registrar Fr. John Loftus and members of the faculty, they fill out enrollment and schedule cards.

Officially, the school year begins the following morning with a Solemn High Mass at the Cathedral of the Assumption in downtown Louisville in the presence of the Archbishop. At 9:15 a.m. students from Louisville's three Catholic colleges—Ursuline, Nazareth and Bellarmine—enter in procession. At 9:30 the Mass begins, celebrated by the Very Rev. Wenceslaus Hertvik, Provincial of the Franciscan Friars Minor Conventual (called Black Franciscans), and assisted by the Rev. Alfred Horrigan, Bellarmine's president, and the Rev. Raymond J. Treece, vice president. The Mass is sung by the Archdiocesan priests' choir. The sermon is delivered by the Very Rev. James F. Maguire, S.J., President of Xavier University some 125 miles upriver in Cincinnati. He stresses the historical importance of religion in American eduation and calls St. Robert Bellarmine, the college namesake, "the ideal patron" for the new school. Father Maguire cites the desperate need for Christian education in a nation, he says, "becoming spiritually bankrupt from year to year." While the world is begging American leaders to lead the way to "spiritual heights," he says, "the only goal many of these well-meaning but confused leaders can point to is the purely materialistic one of a higher standard of living."

Following the service at the cathedral, students report to Bellarmine's new campus for the college's first convocation. The students are pensive and excited as they hear the Archbishop tell his first student body that they are in the vanguard in the fight against secularism. "Today," he tells them in an address being carried by radio stations WAVE and WHAS, "is the day of the lay apostolate." Looking to the future of his new college, he concludes, "We are looking forward to the day when the college ranks with the great colleges of our country."

Finally, after a week of orientation, on Monday, October 9, 1950, classes begin and school organizations are formed. The first is the Student Council, with David Wallace Baird III, the first student to seek admission, president, Paul J. Davin, vice president, John Anthony Korfhage, secretary, and Alvin Irvin Cassidy, treasurer. Except for Davin, a graduate of Flaget High School, they are all St. Xavier alumni.

Everyone is ready for the great adventure to begin. Three years later an unsigned article in the student newspaper, *The Concord,* presumably by editor Ray Tillman, recalls their pioneer days: "Ah, those were the days! Box lunches, cold but tasty, were available. And before long the cafeteria was opened, supervised and operated by one woman. Real home cooked meals. And then there was the ceiling. Like the Henny Penny of Fairyland the sky was falling. Because the glue used to hold the celotex ceiling blocks in place was not yet dry, the students were subjected to the perils of falling ceiling. It was not uncommon to have a block fall during any class.

"Chiggers were an intimate part of that class. Due to the head-high weeds which surrounded the building, hide and seek was a wonderful game for lunch time. The only trouble was some of the fellows couldn't blaze their way back to class on time. With this thought in mind, Fr. Treece gave the much awaited command, 'The weeds must go.' And so they went and in their stead shrubbery and grass were planted.

"Ever wonder why many call the classrooms by color rather than by number? Well, in the early days, numbers weren't on yet. In fact, all the [exterior] doors weren't on yet either. Nature lovers had a field day when a gust of wind blew leaves through the halls.

"Perhaps the most memorable event was the day the steam roller chugged back and forth across the roof. Heaven felt mighty close when it thundered overhead."

So begins the history of Bellarmine College. The rest of the story is the subject of this book.

Acknowledgements and a Personal Note

In the fall of 1950 I enrolled as a 16-year-old freshman at Troy State Teachers College in Alabama. At the same time some 450 miles to the north other freshmen were enrolling at a new school in Louisville, Kentucky, called Bellarmine College. It would be almost twenty years before our paths would cross. During those years I earned bachelor's, master's and doctor's degrees from Troy, the University of Alabama and the University of Illinois—with a two-year hiatus for service in the U.S. Army. I would teach at all three schools as well as one year in a public school in south Alabama and almost two years at the University of Florida, which I left in December of 1962 to join the faculty of another new school called Kentucky Southern College in Louisville.

Like its slightly older sister institution in the same city, it was a church-related school, but unlike Bellarmine its tenure was short-lived. During the seven years of its existence, however, its predominantly Baptist faculty became close colleagues with the predominantly Catholic faculty at Bellarmine. While I was teaching at Kentucky Southern, I had become greatly attached to Louisville and to Kentucky and had developed much respect and admiration for Bellarmine, its faculty, students and administration. Finally, when financial pressures forced Kentucky Southern to close, I was reluctant to leave Kentucky and gladly accepted an invitation to join the English faculty at Bellarmine.

I already knew many of the faculty and administration and did not feel that I would be going into a strange new world at all. Indeed, I had served on committees and projects with Dr. Kathleen Lyons and Sr. Clarita Felhoelter and had even taught Dr. Joan Brittain—all of the English department—and I had worked closely with Dr. Jude Dougherty of the philosophy faculty on the Book-A-Semester program. I had also developed great admiration for the moral leadership provided by Fr. Alfred Horrigan and Fr. John Loftus of the Bellarmine administration for the Louisville community. Indeed, the first day of my research in the college archives I pulled from the shelf volume one of a series of scrapbooks labeled "Bellarmine College News Clippings." In one of the first news accounts of Bellarmine, I read of a momentous decision by Bellarmine, Ursuline and Nazareth (now Spalding University), to be the first predominantly white Kentucky and Southern colleges to open their doors to African-Americans. What a firm foundation on which to build! Small wonder that Bellarmine College has thrived.

It seemed to me an auspicious match—as indeed it proved to be. It was so successful that I stayed at Bellarmine for the remainder of my teaching career, some 27 years. When Dr. Joseph McGowan approached me about writing the history of Bellarmine as a part of the college's 50th anniversary celebration, I quickly said yes. After all, I have spent most of my teaching career at this institution and have lived all its history except for the first nineteen years. I have known all three presidents, most of its other administrators and faculty, many of its trustees and other supporters, and most importantly I have taught hundreds—even thousands—of the students who have passed through its halls since 1969, when I joined the faculty as a professor of English. The writing of this history has been the capstone and conclusion of my academic career.

Moreover, it has been a pleasure and sometimes a revelation to research and write this history of the institution that I have come to know intimately and love as an alma mater. During the two years of research and writing, I came across many interesting pieces of information, including some that pertain to my own career at Bellarmine that I had completely forgotten. This note in the daily calendar of *The Louisville Times* of May 31, 1972, for example, was quite a puzzle: "Parents Without Partners. Wade Hall, chairman of the English Department at Bellarmine College, to speak to East Division. Zachary Taylor Post, 4610 Shelbyville Road. 8:30 p.m." As a bachelor member of the faculty, I cannot recall a single word I had to say to those "Parents Without Partners."

A history of this magnitude is necessarily selective. I have tried, however, to include details of people and events that are representative and will open up the exciting story that is Bellarmine's history. Furthermore, this is not merely a book of facts and statistics, although they can be cited to show how successful we have been. Recent statistics show a 100 per cent placement rate for nursing and education graduates; that 90 per cent of pre-med students have been admitted to medical school; that 25 per cent of the professional staff in Louisville's major accounting firms are Bellarmine graduates; that, according to *Money* magazine and *The New York Times*, Bellarmine stands as one of the ten best private colleges and universities in the region; that our cost is 25 per cent below the national average for private colleges; that more than 80 per cent of the full-time faculty have Ph. D.s or other terminal degrees. But that is only one way to tell the story.

Bellarmine is surely one of the best documented colleges in history. Few institutions have been so well recorded by the religious and secular media. Because of its youth and the good custodial habits of its founders, I have had a wealth of documentation on which to base this history. I have used three main sources: college files and publications, external newspaper and magazine references, and interviews with faculty, students and alumni. In addition, my 27 years on the faculty (1969-1996) have played no small part in this book.

The most valuable college sources are the complete sets of *The Concord,* the college newspaper, and *The Lance,* the college yearbook. In addition, the annual reports of the various college departments and offices, academic and nonacademic, from the 1950s through the 1990s contain a chronicle of the inner workings of the college by those who were on the daily firing line and reported it as they saw it. Although most of the reports are predictably optimistic and defensive, a careful reading will show the ups and downs of the component parts of the college, from the presidents' annual reports to the faculty's yearly self-profiles. Other useful college sources include such printed reports as Fr. Horrigan's *Roots of a Catholic College* (1955) and *The First Decade, 1950-1960* (1960).

Other Louisville printed sources include publications at Ursuline and Nazareth as well as the following periodicals: *The Courier-Journal, The Louisville Times, The Louisville Defender, Business First, The Kentucky Standard, Louisville Magazine, The Voice of the Highlands, The Voice-Jeffersonian* and *The Kentucky Jewish Post.* The best single source was the Archdiocesan paper, *The Record,* which has covered the college accurately and in-depth from its beginnings.

In 1970 the college began using a clipping service and began receiving clippings from numerous out-of-town periodicals from throughout Kentucky as well as out of state. Although most of the articles are sports-related, they profile the expanding outreach of Bellarmine beyond Louisville. In-state sources used include: *The Lexington Herald-Leader, Kentucky Sports World, The LaRue County Herald News, The Elizabethtown News Enterprise, Kentucky Business Ledger, The Owensboro Messenger & Inquirer, The Park City News* (Bowling Green), *The Henderson Gleaner & Journal, The Kentucky Standard* (Bardstown), *The Glasgow Times, The Madisonville Messenger, The Corbin Sunday Times, The Frankfort State Journal,* and *The Danville Advocate-Messenger.* Out-of-state sources include: *The Cincinnati Enquirer (Kentucky Edition), The Evansville Courier (Kentucky Edition), The Nashville Tennessean, The Indiana Catholic and Record, The Jeffersonville Post, The Jeffersonville Evening News* and *The New Albany Tribune.* Bellarmine has also received

considerable coverage in the national press, including *The Wall Street Journal, U.S. News and World Report, Time* and *The New York Times.* I am indebted to many people for help in writing this history, but first of all, to Dr. McGowan and the College History Committee, who entrusted this awesome responsibility to me. I thank the dozens of faculty and staff members, past and present, as well as students and alumni who shared with me their experiences and impressions of their college. Their contributions have given this history a vital human dimension. A special thanks is reserved for Miss Alma Schuler, whose sense of the historic mission of Bellarmine College motivated her to run a one-woman clipping service that chronicles more than two decades of college history. My thanks also to all those people who continued to keep scrapbooks of college events after Miss Schuler left her office as secretary to the president, Fr. Horrigan. Thanks to Michael Steinmacher, who spent many hours organizing the college archives and made my job much easier, and to the late Dr. Robert Daggy, curator of the Merton Collection and College Archivist, who gave me easy access to the college papers.

My grateful appreciation goes to the following people of Bellarmine College who read this history in draft form and offered numerous suggestions for its betterment. If there are errors and omissions that we all missed (and I'm sure there are), I will take full responsibility. Thanks to Dr. Margaret Mahoney, Mr. William J. Stewart, Professor David O'Toole, Mr. John O. Kampschaefer, Fr. Clyde Crews, Dr. Susan J. Hockenberger Davis, Dr. Fred Rhodes, Dr. Joseph J. McGowan, Mr. Jimmy Ford and especially to Mrs. Holly Gathright, who made certain that this book would be as readable and as accurate as we could make it.

Another special thanks to Jack Kampschaefer, who has been associated with this school as student and administrator for almost all of its history and knows it as well as anyone. After I began work on the project, he would remind me of my deadline with this admonition: "I hope you finish the book before I'm gone." One day I said, "Jack, someone used the term, 'struggle and progress,' to describe a difficult period in the college's history, but it seems to me that it could be the theme of its entire existence. Do you agree?" As the long-time supervisor of finances for the college under many different titles, he agreed. I am also grateful to my friend Gregg Swem, who has served as copy editor and adviser on editorial matters and has thus made this book more reader friendly.

Finally, I want to thank the seven members of the Pioneer Class who met with me at a dinner party on December 6, 1995, at the home of Al and Barbara Cassidy in Louisville, and reminisced about their Bellarmine experiences. From John Ford, Jerry Denny, Ed Seitz, Ted Henle, Bob O'Connor, Hank Ellert and Al Cassidy I received not only new information about the early years of the college—their initial misgivings about attending a new school with a name that hardly anyone could pronounce, a school with almost no campus facilities—even the lack of doors on its one building—the cafeteria food, the "casino," the going-away parties for their classmates leaving for service, student high jinks and capers, their colorful faculty (even more colorful and outrageous in retrospect)—but most of all, their universal agreement that they would not exchange their Bellarmine education for one anywhere else. They rounded out my research and gave human faces to it. Thanks most importantly to the hundreds of students from my own classes who are indelibly imprinted on my memory, a list much too long to compile. You know who you are.

Facts and events are milestones in the history of an institution, but they can be boring. I have, therefore, tried to celebrate the Bellarmine pioneers in a dignified but lively fashion. I have tried to make them come alive in words spoken by the trailblazers themselves and in words written by others at the time to describe the events. A reporter for *The Record* or *The Louisville Times* who covered the first graduation or the first ball game is an eyewitness to history-in-the-

making. I have shamelessly borrowed from such news accounts wherever possible, and my thanks to those reporters who were perhaps unaware that they were also historians-in-the-making.

If, as the poet says, there are 10,000 ways of looking at a single blackbird, there are at least a million ways of looking at a college. In the researching, organizing, interpreting and writing of this history my challenge has been to take an overwhelming amount of material and present it in a meaningful and readable form. I have tried to leaven the facts with real people who have lived the history of this college—people who have worked and talked and sometimes argued—but all with the spirit of academic fellowship dedicated to the betterment of a young, vibrant and thriving institution.

This book has been written for everyone who has been touched by Bellarmine College, but especially for the students who have made the school possible and necessary. For you I hope this book will bring back memories of the school that you lived with for perhaps four years and will present the full picture of what happened here before and after you were here.

Fr. John Loftus, Bellarmine's beloved dean, in a memo to the students two months before his death in November of 1968, gave this description of Bellarmine in a poetic shorthand: "A wondrous world/ of wit/ wrath/ folly/ fun/ affection/ growth/ agony/ wisdom wending." What follows are the people of this college—the three presidents, the deans, the financial officers and supporters, the faculty and staff, the students and alumni—and "the wondrous world" they built into Bellarmine College.

In The Beginning . . .

In 1949 Archbishop John A. Floersh selected Fr. Alfred F. Horrigan and Fr. Raymond J. Treece, who were associate editors of *The Record*, the Louisville Archdiocesan newspaper, and also associate pastors at the Cathedral of the Assumption, to start a Catholic men's college in Louisville. Neither man wanted what they both knew would be a daunting job. But, as Fr. Treece said at his retirement 33 years later, when the Archbishop speaks, you jump. So they invented a college, including its philosophy and curriculum, following the model of Catholic University, with its core curriculum of history, literature, philosophy and theology, and collected a faculty and student body.

In an interview following his retirement, Fr. Horrigan recalled the origins of the college. "I think Archbishop Floersh had the college in his mind for a long time before he approached Fr. Treece and me in 1949—perhaps as far back as 1929, when St. Mary's College, the only Catholic college for men in the Louisville Archdiocese closed—but because of the Depression and World War II, he had to delay his plans. In the 1940s, Louisville was probably the largest city in the United States without a Catholic men's college. To complete the Catholic education system in his Archdiocese, the Archbishop wanted this college.

"The Archbishop had hoped to get a religious community to be the main staffers of the college. As early as 1948 he had been in discussions with the Oblate Fathers, a Marist Order in Canada, and even had a tentative agreement with them, but a new provincial was elected who was opposed to the idea, and the plans were dropped. Then he talked to the Franciscan Conventual Fathers at Mt. St. Francis about staffing the college. They said they didn't have sufficient manpower to do it alone but agreed to cooperate with the Archdiocese. That's why the Archbishop went ahead and made Bellarmine an Archdiocesan college, which is a relatively rare American Catholic phenomenon. In this country parishes are considered responsible for basic education through the eighth grade—which was the most education that most Catholics could afford or needed in the 19th and early 20th centuries—so colleges were left to religious communities.

"It was one day in October of 1949 when the Archbishop called Fr. Treece and me aside and asked us if we'd like to be a part of the new college he was starting. He said we could think about it for a week. Well, I was happy doing what I was doing. In addition to my work at *The Record* and at the Cathedral, I was also teaching part-time at Nazareth and at the University of Louisville. We talked about it and agreed that working at the new school didn't interest us. When we went back to see the Archbishop, he asked, 'So what did you decide?' I said, 'Neither of us thinks we'd like to get involved with the new college.' He said, 'Well, in that case, I'll give the job to both of you.' I think what he had in mind originally was that one of us would get the job. I enjoyed teaching very much but administration was the last thing I wanted to do. In fact, I've since decided never to trust anyone who wants to be an administrator. A good administrator needs to be drafted for the job. I don't know how good I turned out to be, but I was certainly drafted for the job. After we got over the shock of our new appointment, we asked, 'When do you want the new college to open?' He said, 'How about next September?'

"Our meeting with the Archbishop was in the midafternoon. After we left him, we hurried out to inspect the location of the school we were told we would build. I was acquainted with the property because it had been the site of an old orphanage and seminary and, more recently, the annual Corpus Christi procession. But I hadn't actually been on the site for many years. We parked our car just off Newburg Road. The old road that ran through the property was closed at the Newburg Road entrance by a barbed wire fence. We climbed over the fence and walked toward where the administration building—recently named Horrigan Hall—now stands. I remember that we passed cows grazing in the field where the baseball diamond is now. The Archdiocese was renting the pastureland to several people in the neighborhood who owned cattle.

"When we reached the top where I could see the ruins of the old seminary and orphanage building, I closed my eyes and tried to imagine what the site would look like 50 years into the future. Without claiming any special gifts of foresight, I believe I came close to imagining a college not unlike what Bellarmine is today. Even in a state of neglect it was a beautiful place, with rolling fields, trees and pastureland.

"We knew we had a lot of work to do to transform that abandoned property into a college in less than a year. My first act as president, however, was to develop a bad case of the flu and spend a week in the hospital. When I recovered Fr. Treece and I went around the country to talk with officials at Catholic colleges, especially the new ones, to get advice on how we should begin ours. We traveled from Notre Dame and Catholic University, our official adviser, to Scranton University in Pennsylvania and St. Thomas in Houston. We received a lot of good advice, especially on the importance of a liberal arts core requirement. Everyone agreed that we had to be a good college before we could be a good Catholic college. One administrator said to me, 'You'll make a lot of mistakes in your new job, but don't worry about them. You'll live most of them down. There are,

however, two mistakes you'll never get over, starting a football team and a medical school. You can redeem any mistakes but these. So beware of them.'

"But we were young and optimistic. I was 35 and one of the youngest college presidents in the country. I took stock of the pluses and they looked promising. The economy was fairly good. The Archdiocese could use a men's college. There seemed to be good financial support for it. We already had a campus owned by the Archdiocese out on Newburg Road where we could build our new school. It was a beautiful location and ideally situated for a college. In fact, the University of Louisville had tried some years before to buy the property from the Archbishop for a new campus. And, of crucial importance, Floersh was our Archbishop; and he wanted the college.

"I don't know what a feasibility study would have shown, but we didn't have one made to find out. I suppose there is sometimes an advantage in not knowing too much about what you're doing. That way, you don't know what can't be done. I like the story of Roger Bannister, the first man to run the 4-minute mile, a feat that scientists had said no human would ever be capable of doing. Fortunately, he hadn't read the scientific reports and didn't know it was impossible. So he went out and did it.

"I believe if I had taken stock of my abilities and if we'd conducted a market survey, we would have been so discouraged, we would have tried to call it off before we started. If a feasibility study had come up and bitten us on the street, we wouldn't have known one. Fortunately, like Roger Bannister, we didn't do any of those things to see if we could start a college like Bellarmine and make a success of it. Our experience may lend credence to the oft-repeated line from Alexander Pope: 'Where ignorance is bliss, 'tis folly to be wise.' Maybe it was also my innocence and ignorance that led me to put a small plastic sign on my desk that read: 'Let's Think of a Few Reasons Why It Can Be Done.'

"Yes, I suppose we were just too young to be apprehensive about our chances for success. So we set about building the college. We had $200,000 from the Archdiocese to begin with, and we could borrow additional funds from the Archdiocese as we needed them. The $200,000 had been raised in an earlier capital fund drive and earmarked for the college. Two capital fund drives gave us enough money to build what is now Pasteur Hall—that is, the old part of Pasteur Hall—which cost about $500,000, and the administration building, which cost about a million and a half. The Archbishop said he would do what was necessary to support the college, and he did. Indeed, we had to live on borrowed money from the Archdiocese for the first several years until we could build up a student body

Opening day at Bellarmine — October 3, 1950.

and the tuition income. Tuition, however, didn't bring in a great amount of money. We set our first tuition at $150 a semester so that it would not be more than the University of Louisville.

"Until the beginning of the first semester of classes in October of 1950, the official address of the college was 1801 Harvard Drive, Louisville 5, Kentucky. The single college phone number was HIghland 4887. Until Pasteur Hall opened in the fall, this address served as both college office and residence for Fr. Treece and me. It's where we moved in early 1950 and set up housekeeping. A house shower given us on March 5 by the Catholic Parent-Teachers Association at least partially solved the problem of furnishing our new home. Hubbuch Brothers, an interior design firm, donated bedroom furniture; and

Office Equipment Company provided office furniture. In its May 1950 issue, the Nazareth College periodical *The Stub* commented: 'Although the two main officers of the new college will have had sufficient experience in the field, no home economics will be offered next fall when the first term begins.' Indeed, in those days an all-male school would have had no need for such a course in its curriculum.

"Nearby, at 1804 Princeton Drive, was the first faculty residence, the Franciscan House, in which the first Franciscan faculty lived—Fr. John Loftus, Fr. Killian Speckner, Fr. Jeremiah Smith, Fr. Hilary Gottbrath and two Franciscan brothers.

"By the time classes began in October of 1950, our official address was 2000 Norris Place, which it remained until the administration of Eugene Petrik, who turned the campus around and made the more spacious thoroughfare of Newburg Road the main entrance.

"Ground had been broken on December 31, 1949, for the first campus building, which would be called Pasteur Hall. The first year the college was open my office was at the Norris Place entrance of Pasteur. Of course, we didn't call it Pasteur Hall then. It was just Bellarmine College. That one small building had the whole college in it: the offices, the classrooms, the cafeteria, the chapel—everything!

"When classes started, we had everything we thought we absolutely needed—except for a front door, which I believe was installed the second week. Of course, work was continuing on the building as we began to use it. Our first convocation was held in a large classroom located near the entrance because the science theater, our large lecture room, was still without seats. In addition to the Archbishop, I also welcomed the students and tried to impress them with the challenge and fun of being pioneers, blazing our own trails and making our own traditions. Fr. Treece also spoke briefly, as did Fr. John Loftus, who was serving as registrar and dean of students. For the first year I served as president and dean. When Fr. Hilary Gottbrath arrived the second year to become dean of students, Fr. John took over as dean and continued as registrar. Of course, we didn't have many students to register in the early years. Fortunately, however, enough students showed up the first year to start our college."

The Pioneer Class

To Bellarmine's first students, dubbed The Pioneer Class, the college owes a huge debt of gratitude. The first issue of *The Lance* put it succinctly: "Bellarmine College life is different because there are no long-standing traditions to imitate or precedents to follow. We are pioneers in a unique undertaking. We are helping to build Bellarmine College." Let the record show, therefore, that the pioneers below signed on to an adventure without knowing where it would lead. They were risk-takers whose daring paid off.

Beckman, William J.
Birkel, Paul E.
Blandford, James R.
Bobzien, Don C.
Bowling, Paul D.
Brennan, John A.
Burke, Joseph C.
Carr, Alfred J.
Cassidy, Alvin I.
Crist, Allen C., Jr.
Davin, Paul J.
Denny, David J.
Ellert, Henry G.
Engle, Robert H.
Erskine, Bernard G.

Ewing, Willis B.
Ford, John J.
Forst, William H.
Garry, John R.
Graham, Larry E.
Henle, Theodore A.
Kaelin, Lawrence J.
Kampschaefer, John O.
Kiefer, Edward P.
Korfhage, John A.
Korfhage, Raymond E.
Lincoln, Robert W.
Lutes, Thomas L.
Merrifield, George B.
O'Connor, Robert R.
O'Regan, John P.
Richart, William L.
Rieber, Joseph W.
Schlegel, Earl J.
Seitz, Edward H., Jr.
Simon, Paul F.
Sinkhorn, Lloyd J.
Stetter, Irvin J.
Sullivan, Norton R.
Thompson, Cuthbert L.
Weber, Thomas L.
Wernert, John J., Jr.

Indeed, these young men were fully conscious that they were pioneers, doing everything for the first time. They knew they were writing the first pages of a new history. John Ford recalled 45 years later: "It was a wonderful community. We were true pioneers. We had no rules. We made them as we went along." Of course, without many prescribed rules and regulations, college life was simpler. John O'Regan recalls how he enrolled at the new college: "One day I went over to the corner of Harvard and Sewanee and knocked on the door. A young Msgr. Treece let me in and enrolled me on a 5 x 7 index card."

Why would 42 bright youngsters put their faith in an untested institution? O'Regan, an English major, now a retired executive from CSX transportation company, remembers distinctly why he chose Bellarmine. "I wanted a good Catholic education. Furthermore, I have always thrived on challenges, and I knew a new school would be a challenge."

In fact, most of the first students chose Bellarmine because it was a Catholic college. Al Cassidy says it succinctly: "It was Catholic and that was important." Like most of the students, he was a product of the Catholic school system from the first grade through high school, and he wanted to stay with the system through college. Cassidy, who became an executive with the Anaconda Corporation and later director of planned giving at St. Meinrad Seminary, also knew the first president. "Father Horrigan had been an associate pastor at Holy Spirit Church for one year, and he became a kind of folk hero to us boys because he got an athletic program started," he remembered.

Indeed, before Fr. Horrigan could become a real college president, he had to recruit students. This is the way he did it: "Close to 90 per cent of our first students were from St. Xavier, Flaget and Trinity. Fr. Treece and I were given free access to the students and we did our best to recruit them to our new college that had no reputation or track record. All we had, in the words of Arthur Miller's *Death of a Salesman*, was 'a shoestring and a smile.' I'm sure we lost most of the top students who were offered scholarships to schools like Notre Dame, Xavier and St. Louis University. But we did manage to attract many highly motivated, bright students, who compiled an impressive record at Bellarmine and beyond. They became a class of achievers. From that class came prominent businessmen, lawyers, doctors, educators. With no upperclassmen over them, they were seniors for four years."

The late Fr. Killian Speckner, who taught English, remembered that students in the first class were very

good students. "I recall many of them very well. One of the best students I ever taught was Paul Birkel, who went on to become a university library director in California. He and I had something in common too: Both our families were in the hardware business in Louisville." Like many of Bellarmine's early students, John Ford was a pioneer in two ways. The youngest of eight children born of Irish immigrant parents in Louisville, he was not only in Bellarmine's first class, but "I was the first of my family to see the inside of a college."

Intelligent, well-prepared, highly motivated—Bellarmine's first students were college achievers and career achievers. John Ford: "All the students of that first class were outstanding, and they all had outstanding careers after they graduated." Cassidy echoes his classmate: "Every one of the students stands out. We were a close knit class then and we still are. Many of my best friends to this day were from the Pioneer Class. We did everything together, and like the faculty and administration, we all wore many hats. With so few students, for example, we didn't have to be outstanding to participate in sports—and even earn a letter." Fr. Horrigan remembers that "the students were positive and excited."

As soon as the school opened, it seemed it might have to close for lack of students. Almost one-half of the class was lost to the Korean War by the second semester, with full-time enrollment dropping from 115 to 65. "There were two things that worried us most," says Al Cassidy, "studying and the draft." Fortunately, new students were found for the day school and for the evening division, which brought in dozens of part-time, working students.

There were other downsides for the first class, but pioneers get used to roughing it. John O'Regan remembers that "not only did we not have doors for the first two weeks of class but we had to hold class in odd places. I remember an English class taught by Fr. Killian at 7 a.m. in Msgr. Horrigan's office. We had to

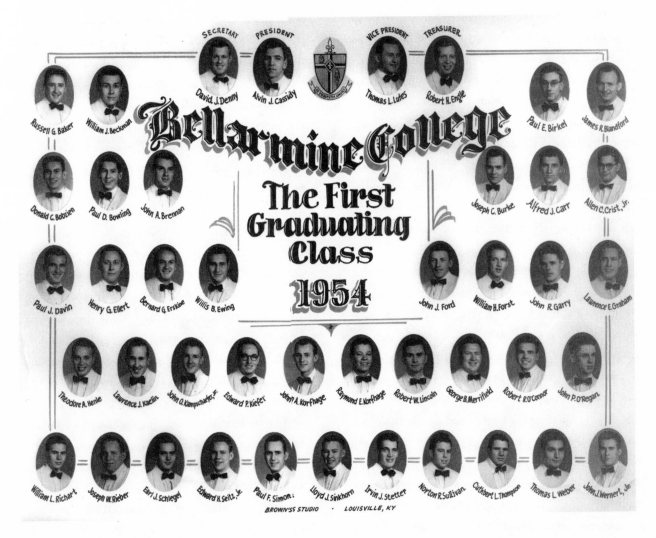

be out by the time he arrived at 8." Jack Kampschaefer summarizes their cramped facilities: "During that first year, we had half of an unfinished building."

Indeed, the Pioneer Class was lacking in everything but determination and imagination. Soon there was a lively menu of student activities. The first social activity was a mixer early in the first semester. On Thanksgiving Eve the first Pioneer Dance was held at the old Knights of Columbus Hall in downtown Louisville. Al Cassidy remembers the excitement of the challenges: "Our class was a class of firsts: the first Dance of the Roses, the first *Concord,* the first *Lance,* the first student council, the first religious groups, such as the Militia of Mary and III Order of St. Francis." An intramural sports program was soon in operation. John O'Regan remembers

playing softball at nearby Highland Junior High School on weekends.

Indeed, the first class studied hard and acquired the tools and attitudes to succeed professionally, but it was not all work and no play. And if students couldn't find what they wanted to play on campus, they engaged in extramural activities. Ed Seitz, a vice president at Meidinger & Associates, an actuarial consulting firm in Louisville, says, "If you want to look at track records, from an economic point of view, we've done very, very well as a class. But I have to admit that some of us spent more time than we should at hangouts like Kentucky Tavern, Air Devil's Inn, Brady's Bar, and El Rancho on Cane Run Road."

Nevertheless, the Pioneer Class and Bellarmine College were pointed toward success. John O'Regan says it well: "From the first day there seemed to be a magical rapport between faculty and students. All the pieces seemed to fit." John Ford, who has been involved with Bellarmine since 1950 as student, part-time instructor, alumni president and college attorney for more than a quarter of a century, says, "Our liberal arts education at Bellarmine prepared us to compete. Whether in law school or army intelligence school, where we had mostly students from the elite Ivy League schools, I never had to take a back seat to anyone. In fact, out of our small class, four of us ended up as special agents in the Army Intelligence Corps."

Finally, the Pioneer Class became the first senior class, with the following class officers: Alvin Cassidy, president; Thomas L. Lutes, vice president; David J. Denny, secretary; and Robert H. Engle, treasurer. By June of 1954 a class which had grown by transfers to 42 was ready to graduate. By attending summer school, 14 seniors had completed their work one semester early. The first graduating class was feted by the Board of Overseers with a dinner in the Flag Room of the old Kentucky Hotel on May 10, 1954. The dinner was designed to give the new graduates a head start in fitting themselves into the business and professional life of the area. Board chairman Bernard J. Lenihan said the occasion would mark "the formal introduction of the college as a supplier of men trained for community leadership." The speaker was Atomic Energy Commissioner Thomas E. Murray, whose topic was "Living in the Atomic Age." Greetings were brought by Mayor Andrew Broaddus, by Archibald P. Cochran, president of the Louisville Chamber of Commerce, by Joseph A. Getzow, president of the Kentucky Chamber of Commerce, and by a representative of the governor's office.

There were three days of graduation ceremonies, beginning on Saturday, June 19, with a baccalaureate Mass at St. Francis of Assisi Church, conducted by Joseph E. Ritter, Archbishop (later Cardinal) of St. Louis. The baccalaureate sermon was delivered by the rector of the Catholic University of America, Bishop

Bryan J. McEntegart. The service was followed by a luncheon in the college lounge and at 2:30 p.m. with the dedication of the new administration building. Using his ceremonial censer, Archbishop Floersh blessed each room of the building. The dedication address was given by the Very Rev. Paul C. Reinert, S. J., president of St. Louis University, who said, "Bellarmine College has dedicated herself first, to the preservation of truth, secondly, to the discovery of truth, and thirdly, to the teaching of truth." An academic convocation and symposium on "The Catholic College and Contemporary American Society" were held on Sunday at 8 p.m. in the college auditorium, followed at 9:30 by a Board of Overseers reception.

The commencement exercises reached a climax the next day, Monday, June 21, 1954, at 6:30 p.m. on the Administration Building lawn facing Newburg Road, when Bellarmine College awarded its first diplomas—all Bachelor of Arts degrees—to the 42 men in the Pioneer Class. The speaker, Karl J. Alter, Archbishop of Cincinnati and chairman of the National Catholic Welfare Conference, told the audience that college graduates were "an intellectual aristocracy based on privilege" and that they, therefore, must follow the motto, "Noblesse Oblige: Nobility Has Its Obligations." Taking part in all the graduation ceremonies were three archbishops, two bishops, one abbot, one college president, five prominent laymen and scores of priests. To top off the celebration, the Pope sent his paternal Apostolic Blessing.

The three top graduates were Paul Birkel, John Wernert and Henry Ellert. English concentrator Birkel came close to having a perfect academic record, with a grade point average of 2.978 out of a possible 3.0. He won a Knights of Columbus fellowship to Catholic University to study library science. Others graduating with Latin honors were John Brennan and Joseph Burke. Cash awards from the Bellarmine Parents Association went to Thomas Lutes, Norton R. Sullivan and David J. Denny as the students who made the best use of their four years of college. Five of the 14 graduates who had completed their academic work in January—Alfred Carr, Bernard Erskine, Lawrence Graham, Irvin Stetter and Cuthbert Thompson—were already in military service.

One of the most inspiring stories to come out of the first graduation was that of 23-year-old Thomas Lutes, a sociology major from Bardstown. Legally blind, he had only light perception in his left eye and "travel vision" in his right eye, but he commuted every day by bus from Bardstown to Bellarmine and graduated with a grade point average of 2.52.

Thus ended a remarkable series of ceremonies celebrating the completion of Bellarmine's pioneer cycle. Of the first commencement, *The Courier-Journal* said: "Bellarmine College has flowered magnificently in the brief time since ground was broken on New Year's Eve of 1949. It has come to fruition while the growing process keeps on." Indeed.

But a graduation is a commencement, not an ending. It was now time for Bellarmine's first graduates to prove the worth of their newly minted degrees. In his graduation address to the class of '54, Fr. Horrigan had already sounded the theme: "Today you stand as the first graduating class of Bellarmine College. You have done a difficult job with distinction. During these past four years, you have shared with us of the faculty a pioneer venture. What we see in you today assures us the venture has been a success.

"Some of you will now move on to positions in business and industry; some will proceed to fulfill your obligations in the armed forces of your country; others will continue your education in professional and graduate schools. In each instance, you will carry into some situation for the first time the title of a graduate of Bellarmine College. Generations of future Bellarmine graduates have a stake in the manner in which you will discharge this high responsibility. As our motto proclaims,

Bellarmine College has been founded 'In the Love of Truth.' Foster this love."

The graduates took their mission to heart. Al Cassidy says it straightforwardly: "We knew a lot was expected of us, and I think we pretty much lived up to expectations." Or in the words of financial officer and statistician Jack Kampschaefer, who has spent most of his professional career reading the "bottom line" at Bellarmine College and measuring inputs vs. outcomes: "The proof of the quality of a college is in its outcomes. Our outcomes have been first-rate from the first class. Look at their achievements." It is a lesson in quantifying quality. By any measure, however, the Pioneer Class built an impressive legacy.

After some 40 years, this is how the scoreboard read: From those first 42 graduates, 12 had earned advanced degrees; 24 had risen to senior management positions, 3 of which were president and 11 were vice president; four owned their own businesses; two had become medical doctors and one a dentist; three were attorneys; two were certified public accountants; three were licensed professionals in other areas; one had become a college president and one a vice president; and one alumnus was a director of libraries at a large university. Two other statistics are also significant: 30 members of the first class were still living in the

Al Cassidy and Hank Ellert, members of the 1954 Pioneer Class.

Louisville area and 11 had second-generation Bellarmine graduates in the family.

Members of the Pioneer Class were guests of honor at the Bellarmine 26th commencement in May of 1979. The speaker was Pioneer Class member Alvin Cassidy, vice president and general manager of Anaconda's Aluminum Division in Miami Lakes, Florida. He recalled his Bellarmine days with great fondness and a bit of fear—fear of being drafted for the Korean War. "War," he said, "tends to improve a fellow's grade point average because each year the lower one-fourth to one-third got drafted. But the survivors who graduated were a very talented bunch of men." It was high-achieving men like Cassidy and Ellert and Wernert and Birkel who put Bellarmine on the academic map. Louisville psychiatrist Bob O'Connor remembered that in 1950 people were mispronouncing Bellarmine as "Bell-er-RAME-ee" or "Bell-AR-mine" or "Bell-er-mine-ee." These first graduates helped to get Bellarmine's name before the public and taught them how to pronounce it correctly.

A Narrative History

Getting Started...

President Joseph J. McGowan in his inaugural address on October 12, 1990, quoted an unnamed faculty member who told him that "while Bellarmine is very young, it has had a long history." He was right, the new president agreed, because "the history of Bellarmine and therefore my vision for the institution goes back well past its mere 40 years of existence, past my distinguished and youthful predecessors, all of whom, marvelously, share the dais with me this afternoon; past the Jesuits who left a college in St. Mary, Kentucky, in the 1840s to staff and develop Fordham

Dr. Eugene V. Petrik, J.O. Kampschaefer, Dr. Steve Permuth, Hon. Wilson W. Wyatt and Dr. Joseph J. McGowan, Jr. at the 1990 Inauguration.

University, which this year celebrates its 150th year— past the brilliant and controversial Roberto Bellarmino, and all the way back to those identified in Professor Wade Hall's beautiful and commemorative poem—to Aristotle and Thomas and Homer."

Indeed, from its beginning Bellarmine has been seen as yet another link in a long chain of Catholic education that extended back to the early days of settlement of Kentucky. Its deep roots in Kentucky history were evident in an editorial published in *The Record* on November 19, 1949:

"A century ago when our Diocese was considered mission territory and hardly removed from the pioneer era, scholarly work was being done by missionaries in log structures and one Catholic school after another was being established in our State. . . . Thus we can say that while Bellarmine College will be, strictly speaking, a new venture, it will not be lacking in tradition. Its roots will be sunk deep in the past— not merely in the past of the Church itself, which has always been the Mother of Learning and Universities, but also in the past of our own State and Archdiocese."

As noted by President McGowan, education has always had a high priority with Kentucky Catholics, from primary grades through graduate and seminary training. While Kentucky was still being settled, a number of schools were opened to give young people a formal education underpinned by religion and morality. When Bellarmine opened in 1950, it was the only men's college in the Louisville Archdiocese, but as Fr. Horrigan has said, the college is actually "continuing, after a 20-year lapse, a 150-year-old tradition of higher education for Catholic young men in this Archdiocese."

In fact, Bellarmine can trace its ancestry in Kentucky back to St. Thomas of Aquin, a college for young men in the Diocese, founded by the Dominican Fathers at St. Rose, Kentucky, in 1806, with classes in a log cabin and an enrollment of 12 students. Other colleges included St. Joseph's, established at Bardstown in 1819, St. Aloysius College in Louisville in 1849, and St. Mary's College at St. Mary, Kentucky, begun in an abandoned distillery in 1821 and continued until it became a seminary in 1929.

Moreover, through its Ursuline ancestry, Bellarmine can trace its history back to 1921, when the Ursuline Sisters began Sacred Heart Junior College, which in 1938 became a four-year school and renamed Ursuline College until it was merged with Bellarmine in 1968. Bellarmine College was, therefore, building on a rich tradition not only in Europe and the older Eastern states but in Kentucky. It was not created out of nothing in 1950. It came out of a rich tradition of Catholic higher education, with an emphasis on teaching, the liberal arts and sciences, concern for the whole person and a focus on value-centered education.

Bellarmine's immediate origins may have had impeccable credentials. According to a much-repeated story, Bellarmine's foundation may have been ordered by Pope Pius XII, who directed Archbishop Floersh to start a men's college for the Diocese. Whatever his motivation, it is known that the Archbishop had long wanted such a college; but his plans were thwarted, first by the Great Depression of the 1930s and then by the Second World War. Finally, when he revealed his plans to Fr. Horrigan and Fr. Treece in October of 1949, the time was ripe for the college to be built. Throughout the country, the Catholic school system at all levels was expanding, caused by a huge pent-up demand delayed by the depression and the war and made possible by post-war prosperity. In the 1950s secondary schools for Catholic young men were opening throughout Louisville—Trinity High School, de Sales, Bishop David and Catholic Country Day. When they graduated their first students, Bellarmine College was ready to enroll them.

Other than fathers Horrigan and Treece, very few people in Louisville had even heard about the proposed new college until the Archbishop's first public announcement in November of 1949. That news brought an outpouring of good wishes from throughout the Catholic community as well as from many local and national dignitaries, ranging from Louisville's mayor, Charles P. Farnsley, to John W. Taylor, president of the University of Louisivlle, who noted that the college "will round out the Catholic school system in Louisville." Congratulations also came from Kentucky's Lt. Gov. Lawrence W. Wetherby and from Msgr. Fulton J. Sheen of the Catholic University of America, who, echoing the words of St. Augustine, expressed his delight that at yet another school young men would be educated in "the great truth that man is made for God and restless until he rests in Him."

The early history of an institution is a chronicle of "firsts"—the first president, the first chancellor, the first board of trustees, the first day of school, the first convocation, the first graduation, the first basketball game, the first building. As Bellarmine's first President, Fr. Horrigan, remembered more than forty years later, "It was exciting to do so many things for the first time."

The man who was Bellarmine's first chancellor was the eighth Bishop (and first Archbishop) of Louisville, John Alexander Floersh, who was born the son of a cigar manufacturer in Nashville, Tennessee, in 1886. From 1924 until his resignation in 1967 at the age of 80, he was Archbishop of Louisville, serving for 43 years as spiritual leader of more than 200,000 Roman Catholics in 121 parishes and 23 mission churches in thirty-seven central Kentucky counties. He was preceded by Bishop Denis O'Donoaghue and was followed by the Most Rev. Thomas Joseph McDonough, who had previously served as Bishop of Savannah.

The patron of the college is St. Robert Bellarmine. In 1949, when this new college bearing his name was announced, people all over Louisville and beyond—Catholics and non-Catholics alike—were asking, "Who is this Robert Bellarmine?" First, he was a saint and Fr. Horrigan said that's what was

St. Robert Bellarmine, engraving by Valdor of Liége.

needed: "Things need patron saints, practically all kinds of things—countries, cities, dioceses, parishes, guilds, institutions, and movements. We need patron saints because they help us to keep things headed in the absolutely right direction."

But St. Robert Bellarmine was especially appropriate for Bellarmine College because of the high place he holds in the spiritual and intellectual history of the Roman Catholic Church. He was a distinguished Jesuit writer, teacher, theologian, philosopher, patron of the sciences and spiritual director. His writings in political philosophy were even said to have influenced, at least indirectly, Thomas Jefferson's concepts of democracy.

For anyone wanting to learn more about the college patron, it was easy enough to read the outline of his life in almost any encyclopedia. He was born at Montepulciano, Italy, in 1542, admitted to the Society of Jesus in 1560 and ordained to the priesthood at Louvain about 1570. In 1576 he was called to fill the Chair of Controversies at the Roman College and while there wrote *De Controversiis,* a compendium of contemporary controversies. In 1592 he was made rector of the Roman College and in 1599 was elevated to Cardinal by Pope Clement VIII, who stated that "the Church of God has not his equal in learning." He died on September 17, 1621, and was canonized in 1931. His feast day is May 13, later moved to September 17.

An editorial in *The Record* of November 19, 1949—probably written by Fr. Horrigan—praised him in these words: "With logic and precision Bellarmine set forth the philosophical foundations of true political democracy. Leaving aside all arguments as to how direct an influence his writings may have exerted on the Founding Fathers of our republic, there is no doubt that the genuine principles of American democracy are based on exactly the premises he so brilliantly defended against the arrogant proponents of the 'Divine Right of Kings.' . . . St. Robert Bellarmine was completely contemporary, too, in his perceptions of the significance and value of the physical sciences. His calm insistence that all truth is from God and that there is no possibility of genuine conflict between science and religion would have prevented many an ill-conceived and bitterly waged controversy during these past centuries if it had been more carefully heeded."

Because not many people were familiar with the saint, in the same issue of *The Record* a pronunciation guide was given: "The Saint's name is usually pronounced Bell-ar-min, with the accent on the first syllable." In the spring 1960 issue of the national Jesuit weekly, *America,* Fr. Horrigan published another article on the saint, entitled "Patron of Intellectual Life," in which he suggested that Catholic educators and intellectuals in the United States would do well to take him as their patron and study to imitate him.

In a bulletin issued by the college before the first formal catalogue was published, the patron was described as belonging "to the intellectual world of modern times." Bellarmine's time was like America at midcentury, the article continued, a period of intellectual turmoil, of protracted, bitter controversies. In the midst of such confusion and ill will, Bellarmine became known for his calmness, courtesy and devotion to truth. Furthermore, to everyone, friend and foe alike, he was gracious and considerate and exercised Christian justice and charity.

Once people began to find out about Bellarmine, most of them agreed that the college was aptly named. At the October 4, 1950 Solemn High Mass at the Cathedral of the Assumption, Fr. Maguire said: "It is peculiarly appropriate that a college, which, in its philosophy, fits foursquare with the Declaration of Independence and the Constitution of the United States, should be named in honor of Robert Bellarmine. . . . Robert Bellarmine was the first to systematize and defend a very old, but uncodified Christian conviction, the conviction that political power comes to the ruler from God through the people themselves." Fr. Maguire labeled Bellarmine, therefore, "the ideal patron for a college in which the basic principles of Americanism will be stoutly defended in this day when they are so universally attacked. . . . Today Bellarmine College enters the lists to contend with the giant forces of secularism." He concluded, "And from this day it is our prayer that the strong grip of the deadly secularist philosophy will be notably weakened as the spiritual impact of generations trained in Bellarmine's halls makes itself felt in the world." On Bellarmine's feast day, May 13, 1954, the Rev. James Brodrick called him "a perfect type of fully-educated Christian man."

There was, however, a controversial side to Robert Bellarmine. On his feast day in 1950 *The Record*

Dr. Don R. Osborn

called Bellarmine a Prince of the Church, a catechist, a patron of the arts and sciences, a controversialist and "one of the brightest lights and glories of the Church in the chaotic sixteenth century." The editorial writer (again, probably Fr. Horrigan) then added: "He was unavoidably engaged in controversy almost all his life. His exposition of Catholic doctrine was as uncompromisingly clear and firm as the ringing blows of a great hammer on bedrock. But his patience and charity and sweetness of manner were as conspicuous as his orthodoxy and brilliance."

As Professor Don Osborn of the Bellarmine psychology faculty pointed out in an article in the September 15, 1978 *Concord,* "Saint Robert Bellarmine is perhaps best known for his role in persuading Galileo to repudiate the theory that the sun is the center of the universe." Bellarmine was a friend and admirer of Galileo and interested in his scientific discoveries and theories. As a consultor of the Holy Office, however, he had a leading role in the first examination of Galileo's papers and concluded that Galileo had not sufficiently proved that the earth revolves around the sun. He did not absolutely deny the Copernican heliocentric view, but he rather advanced the claim, now part of routine scientific procedure, that it should be presented merely as an hypothesis until given scientific demonstration.

In 1955 Giorgio de Santillana in his *Crime of Galileo* said of Bellarmine: "His name is now almost forgotten in our countries, but it was once a name to conjure with." In discussing his reputation for controversy, he quoted a doggerel couplet: "First to breakfast, then to dine,/ Is to conquer Bellarmine." He also notes that "Bellarmine" is the name commonly given "to certain paunchy jugs used for liquor, whose neck was in the grotesque effigy of a bearded man." Don Osborn's evaluation of Bellarmine as a controversialist is evenhanded and positive. "Bellarmine argued from accepted scientific rules," he wrote in his *Concord* article, "that the weight of the evidence was in favor of the conventional view that the earth was the center of the universe. Because Bellarmine was later shown to be wrong, he is somewhat unjustly made the 'fool' in this cosmological dispute." However, as Osborn continued, "Further research has in fact indicated that Galileo was also incorrect—the sun is merely a star in the outlying regions of the universe and the naming of any one point as the center of the universe is seen to be quite problematic in a universe which is literally exploding." Therefore, he labeled "the dispute between heliocentrics and geocentrics . . . a pseudo-argument." In other words, scientific "fact" is always based on limited knowledge and subject to revision.

Indeed, with his keen and active mind, Robert Bellarmine was often involved in disputes in many areas. He sometimes displeased his popes. For example, he incurred the displeasure of Sixtus V when he suggested in the first volume of his *De Controversiis* that the Holy See had limited power over temporal matters. According to Fr. Horrigan, it was this work that places St. Robert among the first thinkers to formulate the philosophical principles of democracy.

Bellarmine's "controversies," in fact, make him an even more attractive patron for a school like Bellarmine College, whose motto is "In the Love of Truth." As the editorial headed "Our New College" in the November 19, 1949 *Record* makes clear, Bellarmine is the model for the "struggle and growth" anticipated for the new school: "Under the patronage of the great saint and scholar our new college takes its place among American institutions of higher learning. Before it lies the period of struggle and growth through which every new college must pass. But its struggle will be in the cause of God and His Church. What greater assurance of vigorous growth could anyone ask?"

In fact, Bellarmine College has been served well by being under the watchcare of its namesake and all the other patrons claimed by the college. In December of 1961 the college published a 65-page booklet of essays, which claimed additional patrons. The five essays, written by college faculty, were on St. Robert Bellarmine, St. Bonaventure, Henry Cardinal Newman, Louis Pasteur and concluded with an essay on Christian chivalry, which inspired the name for the gymnasium, Knights Hall, and the college athletic teams.

In 1953 a statue of St. Robert was placed in the lobby of Horrigan Hall, where it still stands as Bellarmine completes its first half century. A more direct connection to the saint is found in a letter written by Bellarmine purchased by the college for $1,000 in September of 1990. Although it is a business letter with little substantive content, it is an intimate connection across almost 400 years. It joins a recently acquired pair of Bellarmine relics, tiny pieces of the

Norris Place entrance in the mid 1960's.

saint's bones, which, for many people, form a spiritual bridge to the saint. The rich fruits of the association of the college with the saint are suggested in words spoken recently by Fr. Horrigan: "St. Robert

Bellarmine took us under his protecting wing and gave us good care."

From Idea to Institution to Maturity. . .

The history of Bellarmine College is the story of steady, sometimes dramatic, progress. Occasional periods of marking time and retrenchments have been mere blips on a graph that points ever upward. It is not unlike the short "corrections" that have characterized the American stock market in the '90s.

Bellarmine's dramatic progress is seen in a quick summary. In the 1950s the college was founded and grounded in the Roman Catholic tradition of higher education by the Archbishop of Louisville, John A. Floersh, and his hand-picked administrators, Fr. Alfred Horrigan and Fr. Raymond J. Treece, who served as President and vice president, respectively. The campus was developed, programs expanded and faculty increased. Pasteur Hall and the administration building were constructed. Enrollment rose from an initial 115 in 1950 to 1,033 in 1959.

In the '60s expansion continued, with six new buildings—Knights Hall, Kennedy Hall, Newman Hall, Lenihan Hall, Bonaventure Hall, an addition to Pasteur Hall and a small Student Activities Building. The most dramatic change was brought on by the merger with Ursuline College in 1968, which made the college fully co-educational. By the fall of 1968 enrollment had reached 2,020.

During the decade of the '70s the college welcomed its second president when Msgr. Horrigan resigned in 1972 and Dr. Eugene V. Petrik was appointed as Bellarmine's first lay President in 1973. (Fr. Treece served as interim President for one year.) Dr. Petrik landed in Louisville from California and quickly began to revitalize the college with new programs and directions, adding the first graduate program—a master's degree in business administration in 1975—and rebuilding enrollment back above 2,000 after it had fallen to a low of 1,306 in 1973.

Another decade of growth followed in the 1980s, with a record enrollment of more than 2,800 in 1983, and the opening of five new buildings: the Brown Activities Building, Wyatt Hall, Alumni Hall, the Norton Fine Arts and Music Buildings. At the May 1989 commencement exercises, a bold new five-year $20 million capital campaign was announced to propel the college into the 1990s.

Indeed, the '90s were to become a capstone decade for a college that has been steadily building its campus, faculty, students, financial base and reputation for half a century. With the retirement of Petrik, the college welcomed its third President, Dr. Joseph J. McGowan, Jr., who has built aggressively and imaginatively on the achievements of Petrik and Horrigan, with bold new programs and initiatives to meet the needs of the final decade of the century and to prepare the college for its mission in the 21st century. Appropriately, he paid homage to his precedessors by naming the newly completed coed dormitory Petrik Hall and the administration building Horrigan Hall.

An Upclose Look at Details and Milestones. . .

The Record of November 19, 1949, reported plans for a new college in terse headline style: "On Thursday of this week Archbishop John A. Floersh announced the establishment of a Catholic college for men in Louisville. The college will accept its first class of students in the fall of 1950. The Archbishop named the Rev. Alfred F. Horrigan, Ph.D., President of the college, and the Rev. Raymond J. Treece, M.A., vice-president and finance officer.

"The new school will be called Bellarmine College in honor of the famous 16th century Jesuit Cardinal, philosopher, and Doctor of the Church, St. Robert Bellarmine. It will be located on the former site of St. Thomas Orphanage, a 100-acre tract of land lying between Newburg Road and Norris Place. According to Archbishop Floersh's announcement, the long-range plans for Bellarmine College call for a plant estimated to cost approximately $2,500,000. Construction work on a $400,000 science building will be begun around the first of the year. The college will be under Archdiocesan control and will be staffed by Archdiocesan priests, Franciscan Conventuals, and lay professors. Through arrangements negotiated with Dr. Roy J. Deferrari, Secretary General of the Catholic University of America, it will be affiliated immediately with the Catholic University. . . .

"The college will be begun as a "day school" and no facilities for boarding students on the campus are contemplated at this time. Bellarmine College will be the only exclusively men's college under Catholic direction in Kentucky. The only other institution in the state offering at present a general college program open to men students is the co-educational Villa Madonna College [now Thomas More College] at Covington."

Thus the college began. With the Korean War making young men vulnerable to the military draft, it was not an auspicious time to begin a new college for males. Classes began on October 9, 1950, with an enrollment of 115 freshmen. Only 68 returned for second semester classes. A rumor had reached *The Courier-Journal* that the new college was closing its doors.

The headline in Bellarmine's new college newspaper, *The Concord,* was also ominous: "Bellarmine's Enrollment Drops as Sixteen Enter Armed Forces." The rumored closing was, however, discounted and "A Letter from the Dean" sought to reassure students that the college would continue: "Bellarmine, together with all the other colleges in our country at the present time, faces an uncertain future. It is simply impossible at this time to predict what the exact impact of the national emergency upon these institutions will be. I should like to say, however, with all possible clarity and emphasis that there is no question in the minds of the administrators of Bellarmine College that it will carry on its work without interruption during these trying times. . . . Under God's

Providence, Bellarmine College has had its beginnings in these dark and uncertain days. It has a mission to fulfill now and in the immediate future. We have a serene confidence that God will see to it that nothing will interfere with the fulfillment of this mission."

Despite the enrollment drop, the college looked to the future. Eleven new courses were offered for the second semester, including a political science course on American foreign policy, courses on the Russian language and history and logic. In addition, Fr. Horrigan offered a free course on "the vocation of marriage," with lectures by priests, a physician, a psychiatrist and a married couple.

Another event signaled the permanence of the new college. The blessing and dedication of Bellarmine College took place on Sunday, February 18, 1951, as the second semester was just getting under way. The ceremony was performed by Archbishop Floersh, who blessed the outside of the single yellow brick building and then went to the front hall where he blessed the crucifix, which was later hung over the bulletin board. An open house and reception was attended by a large crowd. Bellarmine students served as acolytes at the blessing and as ushers during the reception.

Finally, the first year came to an end; and *The Concord* summed up the highlights: "Remember the first assembly on October 3 . . . the address of Archbishop Floersh . . . Mass the following morning at the Cathedral . . . the confusion of those first few days . . . the election of our first student council . . . the Pioneer Dance . . . Bellarmine's first basketball team . . . intra-mural basketball inaugurated . . . first of *The Concord* . . . that long cold winter . . . Bellarmine losing its first students to the Armed Forces . . . Mid-Year Ball on January 26 . . . Vivid memories of the blessing of the College on February 18 by Archbishop Floersh . . the Archbishop celebrating the first Mass in the Bellarmine Chapel . . . inauguration of the daily Rosary . . . commemoration of the Feast of St. Thomas on March 7 . . . the silence of our first retreat and Father Raymond . . . the feast of St. Robert Bellarmine . . .

the draft was the number one item on everyone's mind . . . recall the anxiety . . . Father Horrigan's assurances and steadying influence." It was an impressionistic chronicle that seemed to say, "This is just the beginning of an institution that will be around a long, long time."

The second school year got an early start when a full progam of two semesters was offered during the first summer school of 12 weeks starting on June 25. Courses were offered for recent high-school graduates as well as Bellarmine's sophomores. No night classes were held.

As the opening of the fall semester approached, there were new problems with the draft. A headline in *The Courier-Journal* of August 19, 1951, read: "New Draft Rules to End Deferments for Thousands." The new Military Training and Service Act provided that married men without children were subject to the draft and the draft age was reduced from nineteen to eighteen and a half. A spokesman for the Kentucky Selective Service headquarters spoke to Bellarmine students on August 29 to explain the new regulations. Anyone who stayed in the upper half of his class, he said, and made above 70 on recent draft exemption tests would probably be able to complete another academic year.

The new semester opened with an enrollment of 160 students, 90 freshmen and 70 sophomores. A full program of freshman and sophomore courses in commerce, science and the liberal arts was offered. Credit courses and noncredit adult education courses were offered in the evening school. The second school year was officially opened with Mass at the Cathedral of the Assumption for Bellarmine, Ursuline and Nazareth. Fr. John D. Mahon from the Dominican House of Philosophy at St. Rose Priory in Springfield, Kentucky, delivered a sermon on the "sacred task" of Catholic education.

Two of the new Franciscan professors were Fr. Hilary Gottbrath and Fr. Jeremiah Smith. Fr. Hilary, a native of Louisville, held a master's degree in mathematics from De Paul University and did

additional graduate work at Catholic University. He had served as math professor and athletic coach at Mount St. Francis before coming to Bellarmine. Fr. Jeremiah, a native of Jersey City, New Jersey, was ordained in 1944. His master's and doctorate in history were from Catholic University.

Bellarmine even went international during its second year, with a new professor of languages, Leonard Latkovski, from Latvia and a new student from Austria. The student was 17-year-old Walter Wernhart from the Russian Sector of Vienna, who lived as an exchange student on a Fulbright scholarship with the Louis D. Coady family on Eastern Parkway. His mother was killed in an air raid during the war, and he was almost suffocated in the debris before rescue by his father. At Bellarmine he studied English, American history, sociology and psychology. According to a news report he liked canasta, raking leaves, fencing and suspenders. He wasn't very fond of cabbage, carrots, baseball or football. But, of course, he was a newcomer to America and to Bellarmine; and he would learn a lot during his first school year. More importantly, however, at the start of its second year Bellarmine was granted provisional membership in the Kentucky Association of Colleges and Secondary Schools, with full membership to be extended following a routine inspection of the new college.

During its first three years Bellarmine was making modest but steady progress. By the fall of 1952 enrollment had climbed to 225 full-time students, with ages ranging from 17 to 53. Most of the students came from the 41 Louisville parishes of the Archdiocese, with the largest number, 17, coming from St. Columba. In the May 7, 1953 issue of the University of Louisville's student newspaper, *The Cardinal,* an unnamed columnist lamented the lack of facilities on its Belknap Campus, then added: "A couple of weeks ago Bellarmine defeated the University of Louisville in baseball. It was their first win over the U of L, but at the rate things are going, it won't be their last. The University has been in reverse gear, and

Bellarmine appears to have slipped into high. If the situation is not considered seriously by more people at the University, I'm afraid Bellarmine will become the principal college in Louisville." In its third year of classes Bellarmine offered courses for freshmen, sophomores and juniors.

Fall semester of 1953 enrollment rose to 320 full-time students, despite continuing losses to the draft. Bob Cooper was drafted out of Bellarmine in late 1953, and in December of that year wrote his impressions for *The Concord* from basic training at Fort Knox, where he spoke of harassment, bewilderment and boredom. In the transformation of "Joe College to G.I. Joe" the army is different from college, especially, he said, in "the profanity, the lack of freedom, the neatness and the rigorous physical training." Freshman enrollment increased 34 per cent. Nineteen high schools, including one in Spokane, Washington, were represented among the 142 freshmen. Flaget and St. Xavier together, however, accounted for 75 per cent of the first year class. Total enrollment, including evening classes, was 517 students, who represented 62 parishes of the Archdiocese. Sixty-six veterans were in the full-time student body. And for the first time Bellarmine had a senior class.

One wing of the new administration building was occupied at the start of the second semester on February 8, 1954, and the student lounge, library and administrative offices were ready by Easter. The building, designed by Thomas J. Nolan & Sons contained a carillon room and two apartments for faculty members. June 20, 1954, was a day long awaited by Bellarmine. It was the graduation of the first class,

the class of '54, the Pioneer Class. The formal announcement of Bellarmine's accreditation by the Southern Association of Colleges and Secondary Schools was made in December of 1956.

An article by staff writer James S. Pope, Jr. in *The Louisville Times* on April 29, 1957 served as a review of Bellarmine's progress and a preview of what was to come. Headlined "Collegiate Success Story: Bellarmine," the story pronounces the first seven years

Mrs. Josephine Allgeier, receptionist, welcomes new students.

a grand success. And, he wrote, "with the three classic traits of success in America—youth, beauty and money—plus energy and ambition, it seems destined for still greater achievement." The article concluded with the words of Archbishop Floersh to the freshman class in the fall of 1950: "We are looking forward to the day when the college ranks with the great colleges of our country." Pope concluded: "If that day has not dawned, it may not be too far in the future."

After serving as Bellarmine's mentor for more than nine years, J. M. Campbell of Catholic University wrote Fr. Horrigan in February of 1959: "Of the many affiliated institutions with which I have been associated in the last quarter-century, none has given me greater satisfaction than my association with Bellarmine. The college has been so successful that there is a natural temptation to exaggerate the significance of one's role." In the November 27 issue of *The Record* later that year, the college presented its ten-year report. Among the achievements noted: full accreditation; enrollment growth from under 200 to 1,578 students; increase of academic departments to 18; a total of 410 alumni; a faculty total of 86, of whom 60 were full-time and 23 were priests; half of the full-time faculty held doctorates; campus buildings consisted of the administration and science buildings, with a dormitory and gym under construction.

At the beginning of its second decade, Fr. Horrigan spoke at a special convocation on Foundation Day, October 3, 1960. "Ten years ago," he said, "we were just finishing our first building. Today four buildings are complete, and work is soon to begin on two additional ones. In 1950 we had about 200 students in both the day and evening divisions. Today, the total number of students carrying credit courses at the college is 1,276. Ten years ago our faculty consisted of 11 priests and six laymen. Today the make-up of the faculty is as follows: 23 priests, 36 laymen on full-time status, and 25 laymen on part-time status, for a total of 84 faculty members." Despite big problems facing independent schools, he said, "speaking for our own young institution and our own small place in the affairs of men, let me proclaim, as the college now expresses its thanksgiving for its first decade of growth, an optimistic view for what lies ahead."

Enrollments continued to climb in the early '60s. The student total reached a record 1,441 by the fall of 1962, a 4.3 per cent increase over the previous year. By the fall of 1963 Bellarmine had an enrollment of 1,526, the largest of any of the Kentucky independent colleges. Although nearly 80 per cent of the student body still came from the Louisville Archdiocese, there were students from 17 states and two foreign countries.

And although nearly 85 per cent of college alumni lived and worked within a 150-mile radius of Louisville, graduates were also living in 33 states and on four continents.

In June of 1964 the college's largest class to date of 163 received their bachelor's degrees. For the first time Bellarmine alumni crossed the 1,000 mark, when Marvin J. Hanka, a psychology major from Louisville, received his degree. Also honored at the ceremony was Louisville accountant Donald C. Bobzien, who received the first Bellarmine degree in 1954. The commencement speaker was attorney John J. Ford, another member of the Pioneer Class and the first alumnus to address a graduating class. Ford said: "The 859 graduates who have gone before you have proved to the nation there is something special about Bellarmine. These men are making their mark in all fields of business and in all walks of life." At the 1966 graduation diplomas were written for the first time in English rather than Latin, which had been used for the previous 11 graduations.

A milestone in campus communication was reached in 1968 when Bellarmine installed its first computer. In the beginning it was a mixed blessing. For three years the computer system was infested with gremlins and glitches. In the fall of 1971 registrar Donald Baron admitted, "It's really screwed up." He said it would probably take four years to straighten out the system. Soon the system was again up and going and its temporary derailment was merely a frustrating memory. But other problems were more life-threatening.

By the end of the decade private higher education was in trouble. Even the '69 *Lance* reflected the bleak mood of the period in its barbed description of the '69 graduation: "[County Judge Marlow] Cook was political, the diplomas were fake, [Father] John was missing, and the pomp was circumstantial." Independent colleges were indeed fighting for their survival because of reduced contributions, growing inflation and fewer students. In Louisville, Kentucky

Southern College, founded in 1962, fought gallantly for survival but succumbed in 1969, when the University of Louisville took over the college campus and closed down the college.

Bellarmine's struggle was articulated with eloquence as faculty, administration and students defended its reason-for-being. Robert J. Desmond, vice president for development and planning, summed up the arguments for Bellarmine in an article in *The Record* on February 20, 1969. Headed "Making a Case for Catholic Colleges," the article presents a concise overview and history of Catholic higher education; then it zeroes in on Bellarmine-Ursuline College and its mission, particularly to the Louisville Archdiocese. College accomplishments are detailed: its quality program, its merger with Ursuline College, its dedicated faculty, its successful students and alumni and its special programs designed to serve a spectrum of educational needs. These messages were spread widely in the print and electronic media as well as in frequent addresses to church and civic groups. Bellarmine partisans were determined that the college would survive and prosper. And so it did.

Reforms were already underway in the early '70s. Despite the economic crunch, Bellarmine finished the 1970-71 academic year in the black. A new academic structure that grouped 23 traditional departments into five divisions was implemented. Some programs and faculty were discontinued. An experimental program was begun in the fall of 1971 which allowed honor students in local Catholic high schools to complete their freshman year while still in high school.

In the fall of 1970 Fr. Horrigan quit his office and moved to a new location on campus to devote his full time to college problems. Fr. Treece assumed the routine duties of the presidency while Horrigan worked on student recruitment, fund raising and long-range planning. He immediately began work on a "'70s Development Program," with a goal of raising more than $20 million. By November of 1970 he was able to announce that more than one million dollars had

been pledged toward the first phase of the ten-year program.

In May of 1971 Fr. Horrigan issued a status report in which he explained the changes that had occurred since Ursuline's founding in 1938 and Bellarmine's opening in 1950. One of the major changes at Bellarmine, he said, was the composition and authority of the board of trustees, now made up of "various publics" served by the college plus *ex officio* trustees that included the Archbishop of Louisville and representatives from the Ursuline Sisters and the Franciscan Conventual Fathers. Such changes, he said, had produced "a new type of Catholic college, representing the open, progressive, ecumenical and experimental spirit of Vatican II, and an American society in a state of transition."

The report also covered student life, fund raising, religious life, curriculum and student awards. In the last category he listed 14 Woodrow Wilson Fellowships, seven National Science Foundation Fellowships, three Fulbrights, two Danforths and two East-West Fellowships. Such honors, he noted, were the results of Bellarmine's commitment to excellence. He emphasized that many of the changes had placed more responsibility on the student. He said: "The Catholic college does not protect its students. Its challenge to them, its question—Is your faith important to you?— places the burden on the student." Then he promised: "This very loyalty to original inspiration serves today as a compelling incentive to build upon the past in order to meet the exciting new demands which God has set before us at this time."

In 1975 Bellarmine College celebrated its Silver Anniversary. After 25 years it was a good time for the college to take stock of itself, to see where it had come, where it was headed and where it was at the 25th milestone. The Louisville higher education scene had changed radically in the 25 years since Bellarmine was founded. Two new successful colleges were founded. Two others had been merged out of existence, Ursuline and Kentucky Southern. The University of Louisville had grown from a 6,000-student city university to a state university of 14,000. The Baptist and Presbyterian seminaries had celebrated centennials. An extension center of Indiana University in Jeffersonville had developed into a regional university. At Bellarmine Eugene Petrik had assumed the presidency in 1973 and had instituted many reforms, but there were still serious problems, particularly in financial support and student enrollment.

But there were bright spots as well. In 1975 Jack Kampschaefer described for a *Courier-Journal* reporter the differences between the Bellarmine he knew as a member of the Pioneer Class in 1950 and the Bellarmine 25 years later. "It was predominantly run by priests then," he said, "where now it's predominantly run by laymen." That did not mean, however, that the religious dimension was less important. Fr. Clyde Crews, who had returned to teach at his alma mater, also said in 1975: "The religious influence is stronger now than when I was here as a student." In fact, attendance at religious services boomed in the early '70s and in 1972 the city fire marshal informed the college that too many people were crowding into the chapel on Sundays for Mass. By 1975 two more Masses had been added for students and the public.

Indeed, for several years some Bellarmine supporters had criticized the college for underplaying its Catholicity. By 1975 Fr. Treece could say: "There was a time when we tried to put our Catholic identity at a lower profile because of some faulty public relations advice we'd gotten. We were going into a major fund-raising campaign, and we were told that if we went downtown and paraded the fact that we were Catholic, we would not get community support. We feel now that we would have been better off to have said unashamedly that we *are* Catholic."

In fact, by 1975 President Petrik was calling Bellarmine's Catholicism a major asset. He told a *Courier-Journal* reporter in April of 1975: "If a person cannot see any difference between Jefferson Community College and Bellarmine, or the University

of Louisville and Bellarmine, then it would be absurd for him to want to come here." A new "statement of purpose," crafted by faculty, students and administrators, also came out of the 25th anniversary celebrations. In March of 1976 the revised version of the statement written when the college opened was approved and published. It began: "The college insists upon giving first attention to the obligation of teaching its students how to live and how to die in the light of eternal truths." That was the difference that caused students to come and pay a premium price for a Bellarmine education.

There was, indeed, much to celebrate after 25 years; and the celebrations lasted all year. In January of 1975 the college held an open house featuring mini-classes, information on financial aid, sports exhibits, Mass, a faculty musical concert and a jazz/rock program called "Switched On" performed by the Charles Mahronic Sextet.

On January 16 Archbishop Thomas J. McDonough wrote an open letter acclaiming the college's 25th anniversary. "This institution can pause with good reason to offer its gratitude to God for the blessings that have brought so many accomplishments in its first 25 years: some 4,000 alumni with an impressive list of credentials, honors and careers." He singled out the recently established Center for Community Education for taking educational instruction "to office areas, apartment complexes and wherever there is an educational need." He also noted The Thomas Merton Studies Center, which "is becoming a focal point for the religious dimensions of the College" and called the campus St. Thomas Center "a house of information for the seminarians of our Archdiocese who take regular courses at Bellarmine."

During the year Dennis Riggs, director of development, launched "Operation Awareness," a ten-part program to make people in the Louisville area aware of the college and its contributions to the region's culture and economy. It included print and television advertising, on-campus receptions for civic leaders and the public, college fairs, visits of high-school students to the campus, open houses and direct mailings.

A Spring Fling was held on Sunday, April 20 and included various booths, an auction of used furniture and equipment and a 25th anniversary birthday party with free ice cream and cake. One of the most widely publicized events in Bellarmine's history occurred during the Spring Fling. It was a "Tater Toss," which involved the throwing of mashed potatoes dyed pink at J. Courson, the housing coordinator. For a quarter a person could throw a wad of potatoes at the hapless target and usually hit him. A *Courier-Journal* photograph showing Courson being splattered with pink potatoes was carried by the Associated Press and widely reprinted in newspapers around the country and globe. Not everyone, however, thought it a good sport. In a letter to *The Courier-Journal* a reader in Princeton, Kentucky, suggested that Bellarmine students were wasting food when so many people in the world were hungry. "Next time," he said, "they should try mud."

During Bellarmine's first quarter century the institutions of higher learning in the Louisville area had learned they had to adapt to changing conditions and needs. Spalding became more responsive to the inner-city. Ursuline focused on childhood education in its laboratory schools. The Southern Baptist Theological Seminary added the Schools of Church Music and Religious Education to its School of Theology and in 1963 absorbed the Carver School of Missions and Social Work to provide a broader spectrum of church-related vocations. The Louisville Presbyterian Theological Seminary began to emphasize field ministries in hospitals and social agencies and in 1963 moved to a spacious new campus on Alta Vista Road. Its old campus on Broadway was occupied by the Jefferson Community College, which by 1975 had its own branch in southwest Jefferson County and a total of more than 4,600 students. After its merger

with Ursuline in 1968 Bellarmine had become co-educational.

So how did Bellarmine fare during this period of the changing face of higher education in Louisville? With deep roots in Catholic education, a solid foundation in the liberal arts and sciences and a recognition that people must be educated for careers, Bellarmine had come a long way. As Fr. Treece once said, Bellarmine College has tried "to career-orient people within the humanizing liberal arts framework." Furthermore, Bellarmine officials have always been aware of the financial "bottom line." As Kentucky Southern officials discovered too late, a good academic program does not ensure permanence. From the beginning, college leaders, led by Fr. Horrigan, knew the books had to be balanced; and they did what was necessary to do it—by raising money from college constituencies, from annual and special Diocesan drives, from corporations and individuals, from foundations and government sources—indeed, from anywhere there was honest money to be had. Bellarmine had learned how to develop a quality program and pay for it.

The college received kudos and congratulations on its success throughout its 25th year. An editorial in *The Record* of February 13, 1975, however, was one of the best tributes: "The measure of a center of higher learning is not its endowment, or the number of its graduates, or other quantifiable factors. When all is said, a college is to be judged on its contributions to the quality of life of a community. On this basis, we heartily congratulate Bellarmine now celebrating twenty-five years in the love of truth."

As the college entered the '80s, the lean times had become better times. The school's permanence seemed assured. In the fall of 1980 the college seemed old and stable enough to merit a historical marker in front of the administration building, sponsored by the Bellarmine Alumni Association and supervised by the college historian-in-residence, Fr. Clyde Crews. By the early '80s the college was even old enough to look back to an earlier "golden age," when campus life was simpler, motives were purer and students were more conscientious. Or at least that's the way it seemed in hindsight. Or as *The Concord* editorialized in September of 1983, "times change—and not necessarily for the better." Some faculty and students complained that the college had sold its soul for a mess of pottage— or at least for too many professional and vocational programs, to the neglect of the liberal arts.

But life and college had changed in the 30 years since Bellarmine was founded. The college had lived through the Cold War, a Presidential assassination, the Vietnam War, racial unrest, the resignation of a U. S. President, a major energy crisis, a revolution in gender and sexuality and other mind-boggling events and trends. One of the fun events of the 30th anniversary celebrations in October of 1980 was a "Fabulous Fifties Fashion Show" in the college cafeteria. Narrated by Ruth Wagoner and Bob Daggy, it featured faculty models Jerry Rodgers, Bill Stewart, Joan Brittain, Bernie Thiemann and Jim Spalding wearing the old-fashioned garb of Bellarmine's founding years. We had come a long way from "that," Baby....

As the decade lengthened, new buildings were built and occupied; and Bellarmine's students were finally getting the physical facilities of a first-class college. The ever-popular cafeteria moved into its new location in the west wing of the Brown Activities Building, along with student activities offices and the campus book store. Named for George G. Brown, the founder of Brown-Forman, Inc., the building also included Amelia Brown Frazier Hall, a multi-purpose space for public lectures, dinners and social events.

In September of 1984 Frazier Hall was the site of a giant celebration of Bellarmine's 35th academic year and a christening of the new facilities. On that occasion Bellarmine celebrated its motto and paid homage to a dozen saints, scientists, artists, social activists and philosophers who had lived "in the love of truth." At the dinner attended by more than 300 people, a large portrait of each honoree was unveiled:

St. Francis of Assisi, the founder of the religious order whose members had contributed so vitally to Bellarmine's success; St. Angela Merici, founder of the Ursuline Sisters, who had become vital members of the college community since the merger with Ursuline College in 1968; Hillel the Elder, one of the great teachers of Judaism; St. Robert Bellarmine, the college's namesake; Louis Pasteur, the French scientist after whom Bellarmine's first building was named; Mary Breckinridge, the founder of the Frontier Nursing Service in the Kentucky mountains; and Mary Anderson, the acclaimed 19th century Louisville actress.

Also honored were Thomas Merton, the Trappist monk and author; John Howard Griffin, the author, photographer and close friend of Merton; Karl Rahner, the eminent 20th century theologian; Benedict Joseph Flaget, the first Bishop of Bardstown; and Thomas Jefferson, who, in the late 18th century was governor of the western territory of Virginia called Kentucky. Indeed, these role models and forebears were as diverse as Bellarmine itself had become in its fourth decade. The opening ceremonies also included an original musical composition, *The Feast of Love*, with words by Wade Hall and music by Doug Starr. As the decade drew to a close, the growth and diversity of the college caused serious discussion regarding whether Bellarmine College should become Bellarmine University. The consensus held, however, that Bellarmine should *be* a university before it *called* itself one.

And now the '90s, which are still unfolding. The college has a new state-of-the-art library. The campus is wired with fiber optic cable lines. Guided by three successive technology advisory committees—Tech 10, the Technology Advisory Group and *bellarmine.edu*— a three-year plan for the installation and implementation of state-of-the-art information services technology was accomplished. The guiding principle throughout was that technology should be designed to support teaching, learning and communication. Bellarmine now has its own homepage, *www.bellarmine.edu.*

Led by its energetic, forward-looking President McGowan, Bellarmine is poised to greet the new century in its own language. Nevertheless, the old language of faith is still spoken, as the college gathers funds to build a freestanding chapel that will not only accommodate worshippers but serve as a symbol of the rock on which the college is built. Groundbreaking for the chapel, Our Lady of the Woods, was held in June of 1998. Completion is expected in 2000, in time for the chapel to serve as a focus for the celebration of the 50th anniversary of Bellarmine's founding.

The world of 1950 was very different from the world 50 years later as we approach the new millennium. A quick perusal of the most recent *Student Handbook* will show how different the college is today from what it was half a century ago. Now there is a "smoking policy," with smoking restricted to certain areas. Now there is a policy on the use of illicit drugs. Now there is a "statement on sexual harassment." But its mission remains the same as stated in the first issue of *The Lance:* "The College recognizes and seeks to discharge completely its obligation to teach young men how to earn a livelihood in the complex twentieth-century world. But it insists upon giving first attention to the obligation of teaching its students, in the light of eternal truths, how to live." While the mission of the founders has remained, its scope has broadened. Now the college seeks to teach men *and* women of *all* ages.

The Campus: Location and Buildings

Rome was not built in a day, and neither was Bellarmine College. First came the idea, then the location, then the buildings. It was a sometimes slow but always deliberate progression.

On December 31, 1949, ground was broken for the first building of what would become Bellarmine College. It was a prime spot. The 100-plus acre campus between Newburg Road and Norris Place some seven miles east of downtown Louisville consisted of rolling farm and grassland in one of the most desirable locations in the entire area. In early 1950 it consisted of woods, weeds and briars, and traces of cornfields and pastures. Although new subdivisions were being built to the east, it was close to established and choice neighborhoods in Louisville's hilly Highlands.

Yet the campus was undeveloped and rural, even bucolic, and motorists driving along Newburg Road could expect to see occasional cows, rabbits and other animals dotting the land. In May of 1992, however, motorists did not expect to see a 400-lb. Holstein calf grazing serenely on the campus. In point of fact, it was not a mirage. The calf had escaped from the Ursuline-Pitt School fund-raiser barbecue at nearby St. Agnes School and found refuge on the Bellarmine campus. The calf had been borrowed for the festival's "Cow Chip game," the object of which was to guess where the calf would

drop a "chip." Campus sightings continued for several weeks and then stopped.

The land has been hospitable to a large variety of animals and people and institutions, stretching back before the American Revolution to James McCorkle, who received it as part of a royal land grant from King George III for his service in the French and Indian War. Indeed, before then, prehistoric Native Americans had in all probability hunted and camped on its premises. Before the Civil War the land had

Preston Park Seminary, St. Thomas Orphanage, and Bishop McCloskey's home.

passed into the hands of the Griffin family, who were impoverished by the war and sold it to the Archbishop of Louisville, William George McCloskey, in 1870 for

36

$17,000—"a frightful waste of money," so said many of the faithful. The estate house, variously called "Preston's Folly" and "Griffin's Folly," was begun as a summer home for the Griffin family, abandoned at the outbreak of the war, then converted into a military hospital during the war.

Bishop McCloskey completed the partially built Victorian Gothic house, which served as the Bishop's country residence and as the major seminary for the Diocese from 1870 until his death in 1909. St. Thomas Seminary, which was founded in 1811 as the first Catholic seminary west of the Alleghenies, was transferred from Bardstown to Louisville. It was renamed Preston Park Seminary and stood where the present administration building, Horrigan Hall, now stands. The site also served as St. Vincent's Orphanage for girls between 1892 and 1901 and as the St. Thomas Orphanage for boys between 1910 and 1938—both staffed by the Sisters of Charity of Nazareth. In 1938 the two orphanages were merged and moved to the present location in Anchorage. The Preston Park site was abandoned except for the annual summer Corpus Christi procession, which was held on the grounds until the early 1940s. For almost seven decades before Bellarmine College was founded, therefore, the campus was the location of educational and philanthropic institutions—all links in an historical chain. For many years the oaks that had lined the driveway to the Bishop's home still stood on campus.

According to Bellarmine professor of mathematics David O'Toole, Bellarmine College almost didn't get its present location. "In the mid to late forties," he recalls, "Archbishop Floersh contacted my father, William O'Toole, who was an architect, about drawing up some plans for a couple of properties owned by the Archdiocese. One became the location of Bellarmine College. The other became the site of St. Thomas Seminary on Highway 22. At that time the Archbishop wanted a college and a seminary, perhaps combined in a single institution. He even considered building a subdivision on the Newburg Road property. As it turned out, St. Thomas and Bellarmine became separate institutions on separate campuses (although St. Thomas Seminary would eventually be moved to Bellarmine), and the subdivision was not built."

Indeed, under the leadership of its three Presidents—Fr. Alfred Horrigan, Dr. Eugene Petrik and Dr. Joseph McGowan—Bellarmine College would not only survive but prosper. In the early 1990s, several years following his retirement, Fr. Horrigan recalled a 1949 visit to the property that he was to turn into an "excellent college." He said, "As I walked up the hill on that particular afternoon, picking my way through the briars and bushes and dodging stones and potholes, I closed my eyes and tried to look ahead to those future years when a great college would be spread across the hills and rolling fields."

Not only was the 100-acre site in the Highlands of Louisville an ideal spot for the new college but also its location in Louisville was fortuitous. The urban environment has always been one of the college's major assets—a host city of some one million people in its metropolitan area. It is a stable, arts-minded, good-government, progressive city that is attractive to faculty and students alike. In the second half of the 20th century it has become a commercial, industrial, medical and educational center where numerous internships and employment opportunities have been available to students and graduates. It has been a major factor in attracting a quality faculty with credentials and work experience at world-class colleges and universities. Academic Vice President David House, now president of St. Joseph's College in Maine, said it was a major plus when he and his family decided to leave Johns Hopkins University for a new position at Bellarmine.

In the beginning it was estimated that the price tag for the new college, "when completed," would be an astounding two and one-half million dollars. Needless to say, that amount was grossly understated. As the college aged, the price tag kept getting larger, and that's the main reason for the delays. The science building was first, in 1950, followed by the administration building in 1953. Then came two residences for the clerical faculty, a dormitory and the gymnasium in 1960 and 1961. Kennedy Hall, another student residence, was built in 1964. The campus grew in 1968 with the modest addition of the Student Activities Building and the more impressive addition to the science building. After a long hiatus, a number of new buildings created the quadrangle and remade the campus in 1984 with the opening of Wyatt Hall spaces for drama, art exhibits, lectures and a chapel; the Norton buildings for art and music; Alumni Hall for humanities; the Brown Activities Building for student activities, food services and large public events. These buildings have been followed by Petrik Hall in 1990, Miles Hall in 1993, which is a remake of the old Student Activities Building, and the W. L. Lyons Brown Library in 1997.

Many of the buildings were not initially named. They were called simply "the science building" or "the administration building" or "the gym." On January 15, 1961, five of the college's six principal structures were finally labeled as part of the 10th anniversary celebration of the college. The science building became Pasteur Hall, for Louis Pasteur, the French Catholic chemist. The auditorium-gymnasium became Knights Hall, after the college's athletic teams and to suggest the Christian tradition of chivalry and manly honor. The residence hall became Newman Hall, to honor John Henry Newman, the British philosopher, author and cardinal. The Diocesan priests' residence became Lenihan Hall, after the late Bernard J. Lenihan, the first chairman of Bellarmine's Board of Overseers, and his brother Frank P. Lenihan. The Franciscan Conventual Fathers' residence became Bonaventure Hall, after the 13th century Franciscan scholar and minister general of the Franciscan Order who was canonized in 1482. Although the east wing of the administration-library building had been named Horrigan Hall in 1987 during the Petrik administration

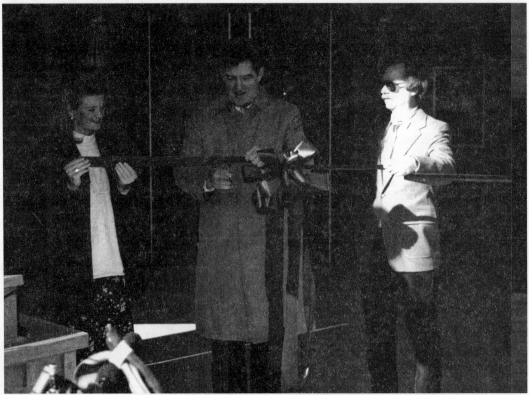

Christa Spalding, S.G.A. President, Dr. Joseph J. McGowan, Jr., and David Chatham, Library Director, at the campus ribbon cutting for the W. L. Lyons Brown Library, January 7, 1997.

to honor the founding father and first president, the entire building became Horrigan Hall early in the McGowan administration.

In March 1965 Bellarmine unveiled an $8 million master plan for the campus that would add 11 new buildings to the campus over the following 20 years, including a student union, a library, a classroom building, a residence hall, a chapel, a field house and an amphitheater. Some of them became reality within the time frame, but most did not. Some have yet to be built. A library was dreamed and planned for several decades before it became a reality in 1997. A separate college chapel was on the master plan from the start, and by 1999 some $3 million had been raised to make that dream a reality and a chapel was underway.

Campus expansion has never been hampered by lack of space. The only major threat to the integrity of the campus was avoided in 1966, when the City-County Planning and Zoning Commission refused to approve a proposed Newburg by-pass that would have divided the campus into three pieces. For almost fifty years two of Bellarmine's principal selling points have been its size and location. One advantage to Bellarmine's spacious, uncrowded campus has been the availability of convenient parking spaces for faculty, students and visitors—at minimal cost. At least, the space has been available, even if parking lots sometimes lagged behind the enrollment increases. In September of 1965 *The Concord* published an explanation of the "parking bill," which the Student Senate had recently passed. At that time, students were required to buy parking stickers and park during class hours in their assigned lots—A lot for seniors, B lot for underclassmen, and R lot for students living in the residence halls. The junior class had the responsibility for giving out tickets for violations, and the usual fine was two dollars. In 1970, when parking decals for students went from 50 cents up to $5, one student commented, "Heck, inflation hasn't gone up that much!"

Seldom, however, has anyone with business on campus ever had to search on neighborhood sidestreets for a place to park. Sue Hockenberger Davis, dean of the Lansing School of Nursing, says that one of the attractive features of the college for her students, especially in the evening, is the parking and safety of the campus.

With the completion of the W. L. Lyons Brown Library in 1997, Bellarmine College could at last boast that it had the buildings and facilities needed for a first-class liberal arts college. For most of its history, therefore, there were large gaps—no separate library building, inadequate dormitories, substandard accommodations for social activities, athletics, dramatics, concerts and just about any other academic and nonacademic activity. Bellarmine students and faculty, however, learned to accept and make the most of what was available.

In the early years college dances were usually held in downtown hotels, and athletic contests took place at someone else's playing field or gym. Big dinners and banquets had to be spread off campus. Even the first alumni dances were held in the Bellarmine parking lot. James Sohan, '59, remembers that during his four years at Bellarmine there were only two campus buildings, Pasteur and Horrigan Hall, and except for residences for the religious faculty, no new buildings were built. A history of Bellarmine College is also, therefore, a study in campus development.

The Land...

First, the land area grew. To the original 100-plus acres were added two important pieces of property—one on the southside of Richmond Drive and the other across Newburg Road. On March 28, 1955, Archbishop Floersh announced that the Archdiocese had bought the property of the Bonnycastle Club, one of the city's oldest athletic clubs, for $85,000 for college expansion. The property, which was located on about 2 3/4 acres between the campus and Richmond Drive, included a dressing room, clubhouse, concession stands, two tennis courts and a softball diamond. Bellarmine took possession on September 6, 1955.

In May of 1960 the college added another 40 acres to the campus when Archbishop Floersh paid $225,000 to Mrs. Bess H. Collings for property on the west side of Newburg Road south of Our Lady of Peace Hospital with 1,000 feet of frontage on Newburg Road. Located across the road from the college's athletic field, the property, according to Fr. Horrigan, would be held for future expansion. At the time he said the college's full-time enrollment of 650 students was expected to double by 1970. Around 1980 the Archdiocese sold the 40 acres of land.

Bellarmine had also obtained an option to buy the remaining 83 acres of the Collings estate, and in November of 1965 the college decided to exercise the option—despite plans by the city of Louisville to buy the land for a municipal park. Mayor-elect Kenneth Schmied reminded the college that the city had the power to condemn the land for public use but agreed to work with Fr. Horrigan on a compromise that would allow both sides to share the property. On December 31, 1965, Bellarmine bought the property for $597,500 from the executors for the estate of Mrs. Collings, who had died on October 22.

Following negotiations between the college and the city, Mayor Schmied, acting for the city, paid Bellarmine $596,000 for 68 acres of the Collings estate in November of 1966 and agreed to erect a fence between the college property and the city property whenever the college wanted it. According to the mayor, the city purchased the land for park use and as the possible site of a natural history museum. Fr. Horrigan announced that the remaining 15 acres— which had cost the college only $1,500— plus the 40 acres purchased from the estate in 1960, would be held for future expansion. Some years later the

By December 31, 1949, construction was underway for Pasteur Hall, Bellarmine's first building. Designed by Thomas J. Nolan & Sons; Al J. Schneider was general contractor.

Louisville and Jefferson County Parks Department moved its administrative offices into the three-story Georgian-style mansion on the estate.

Pasteur Hall...

In early January of 1950, ground was broken for Bellarmine's first construction, a science building, later to be named Pasteur Hall, designed by the architectural firm of Thomas J. Nolan & Sons and acclaimed as "the last word in modern design and equipment." The first spade of earth was turned by the Very Rev. Wenceslaus Hertvik, O.F.M. Conv., Provincial of the Black Franciscan Fathers. Of the $400,000 cost, half the amount was paid from funds raised during the 1942 Archdiocesan drive, which had taken in over $1 million for various Diocesan projects. The general contractor was Al J. Schneider, an active Catholic layman who took special pride in building the first buildings on the campus.

On Sunday, July 30, 1950, at 2:30 in the afternoon—after most of the exterior work on the building was completed—Archbishop Floersh blessed the building at the cornerstone-laying ceremony. He was assisted by the Rev. Edward Link, pastor of St. Francis of Assisi, and the Rev. John Loftus, the college registrar and English professor. In his address the Right Rev. Msgr. Felix N. Pitt, secretary of the Catholic School Board, said: "In Bellarmine, the students will not be given truth and error and allowed to choose. Here the teachers will teach the truth of which they are convinced." Furthermore, he said, "There will be no conflict between science and religion because God is the Author of both and God is truth." Thomas J. Nolan, Jr. presented the copper box which was placed in the cornerstone. Inside the box were newspapers carrying the news of Bellarmine's beginnings as well as a crucifix and religious medals.

The science building was built first, according to the founding fathers, to give more emphasis to science in a Catholic liberal arts curriculum than was customary; however it had to contain the entire college until the administration building opened in the fall of 1954. For four years it housed offices for the administrative staff and faculty, a library and bookstore, the science laboratories and a science theater, a cafeteria, a chapel, seven classrooms, a seminar room, a student lounge, a boiler room and several storage areas.

An ad in the May 7, 1950 *Courier-Journal* called the science building "strikingly beautiful," noting that it was equipped with aluminum sashes and gutters and downspouts made of copper and "topped with a built-up composition roof, gravel coated." Its "prepossessing" exterior was buff colored of rough-texture brick with limestone trim. The ceilings featured acoustically treated tile. All the interior trim as well as the cabinets and worktables were made of red oak. The classrooms and laboratories were said to be airy and well lighted and had floors of asphalt tile. The other floors were made of terrazzo.

Even an article in the winter 1951 *Louisville* magazine sounded like a commercial. "The day of antiquated, murky colored classrooms," the magazine announced, "is gone for the students of the new Bellarmine College." One classroom was described as having chartreuse walls, a damson plum ceiling and a turquoise blackboard. The library was painted in hunter's green and equipped with vivid yellow chairs. Why, even the chemistry lab had "robin's egg blue walls and a green blackboard"! Students attending this college certainly seemed to be having great fun in their colorful environment.

A more moderate endorsement of the contemporary architecture and daring decor came from F. W. Woolsey in an article on President Petrik in *The Courier-Journal Sunday Magazine* of August 15, 1976. While acknowledging that the overall campus was one of the handsomest in the city, he wrote: "The utilitarian architecture on the Bellarmine campus makes it easy to imagine that people inside the buildings are making soap or plastic furniture or breakfast cereal, rather than studying." Such a

Pasteur Hall, from an early Bellarmine postcard.

commentary is not surprising from a man who never had the advantage of an education at this newfangled college.

Although the college's dominant campus architectural style has been often lampooned as "yellow Catholic brick," it was intentionally chosen to embody a philosophy of education. To explain the style chosen for the buildings, Fr. Horrigan wrote a series of articles in *The Record* in May and June of 1950 and in 1955 expanded on it for *Catholic Building and Maintenance* in its May-June issue. He said that he had instructed the architects to use modern or contemporary design rather than the traditional Gothic or "pseudo-Gothic," with its false buttresses and high-pitched roofs for good reason. Whereas in the past architecture had been limited by construction materials, he said, "Today there is no need to erect college buildings which look like halfhearted imitations of Roman temples, Gothic churches or colonial meeting houses." Furthermore, he added, "In deliberately selecting the strictly contemporary style of architecture for Bellarmine College, the administrators feel that they are expressing the role which a Catholic college must play in the world today. The Church belongs both to time and to eternity. Catholic education, rooted in eternal truths, must deal with real problems and conditions of the world as it exists today at any given moment in human history."

Such architecture would embody and project the Church's mission: "The Catholic college takes its tools and its techniques from the present moment, while its

philosophy is fashioned under the aspect of eternity. In the simple and rhythmic sweep of the contemporary lines which will mark the buildings of the campus of Bellarmine College will be expressed the conviction that Catholic truth is ever old, yet ever new."

When the first building was opened, a writer for *The Concord* observed approvingly: "The Cross is affixed to the modern walls of the college and it appears not strange at all. Nor does it seem strange to attend the celebration of the Mass in a chapel not far from the science lecture hall and the well-equipped chemistry labs." Moreover, he noted that the 150 periodicals in the college library were as diverse as the *Journal of the American Chemical Society* and *The New Scholasticism*. The college was obviously trying to practice what its architecture preached.

Some 12 years later the science facilities doubled. In the spring of 1962, Fr. Horrigan announced a science development program to build a new wing to Pasteur Hall, adding new labs and equipment. As a part of the development program, he announced the appointment of two new science professors: Dr. James J. Dyar, a plant physiologist at Brown & Williamson Tobacco Corporation, with a doctorate in biology from Ohio State University, and Dr. John R. Roberts, a 1957 Bellarmine graduate with a degree in chemistry from Notre Dame.

In December of 1966, with the considerable aid of chemistry professor Dr. Jack Daly, Bellarmine was awarded a $222,000 grant from the U.S. Office of Education to pay about one-third of the cost of building an addition to Pasteur Hall. The addition would contain 11 labs, nine offices, a classroom and a 300-seat auditorium, later to be named the New Science Theater. (The first science lecture hall was renamed the Old Science Theater.) Finally, in the fall of 1969 the new science wing was opened. The science faculty has generally been well pleased with the facilities, according to Dr. Daly: "Actually, not many schools had much more in the way of facilities when I came to Bellarmine in those early years. We were usually able to get National Science Foundation and private grants to add equipment as we needed it."

The Administration Building: Horrigan Hall

In January of 1953 Archbishop Floersh announced the Archdiocesan Education Campaign to raise $2,500,000 for several building projects, including the construction of a new Archdiocesan high school for boys, the completion of St. Thomas Seminary and the construction of a one million dollar administration building for Bellarmine. In a letter which was read in the churches of the Archdiocese, he stated that there were no funds available for such capital improvements. "You may have heard reports concerning the large holdings of the Diocese in securities and real estate," he wrote. "In addition to the fact that those holdings are greatly exaggerated, it must be observed that the few assets which the Diocese does own are in the nature of trust funds, the principal of which . . . cannot be spent." Therefore, he concluded, some 8,000 Catholic

Msgr. Horrigan, Cardinal Stritch, Fr. Treece, and Archbishop Floersh at the 1953 groundbreaking for the Administration Building, later named Horrigan Hall.

men would carry the appeal to each Catholic home in the Archdiocese.

Fr. Horrigan was very active in the six-week campaign, frequently speaking at fund-raising dinners and meetings and writing promotional articles and essays. At a dinner in the Henry Clay Hotel, he reminded donors of their religious obligation to support the drive. "We believe in God-centered education," he said. "We believe it intolerant for our God to walk the side streets of Louisville."

In a column in *The Record* of February 22, 1953 headed "Sacrifice and Success," Fr. Horrigan noted the appropriateness of the campaign during Lent because "Lent means sacrifice, and everyone knows that sacrifice must be the basis of the success the

Entrance to the Administration Building in 1954.

campaign will achieve." Furthermore, drawing on his knowledge of church history, he added, "Not the least impressive of the miraculous accomplishments of the Church in its history has been the development of the Catholic school system in the United States. It is a unique kind of thing. Probably it stands unparalleled as a completely nontax supported system built and supported entirely from the freewill donations of a religious group."

He reminded his readers that most of their Catholic ancestors were "simple people, plain people, mostly quite poor people" who had come to America "to work out a new life in a land of opportunity." Although they had little opportunity for formal education, "Through sacrifices which would seem scandalous in this air-foam age, they built the parochial schools and academies which were the foundations of our Catholic school system." Thus the president of Bellarmine was again connecting the college with the roots of Catholic education in the United States and in Kentucky.

So hopeful were the Archbishop and the college adminstration of the campaign's success that construction of the administration building began during the drive. Groundbreaking for the new building was held in February of 1953 with Samuel Cardinal Stritch, Archbishop of Chicago, presiding and turning the first spadeful of earth. The principal speaker was the Rev. John H. Murphy, vice president of the University of Notre Dame.

Although the building was unfinished, a cornerstone blessing ceremony was planned for May 17, 1953, which had to be postponed a week because rain had turned the construction area into a quagmire of mud. On the following Sunday, May 24, some 250 people gathered at the site for the services, with addresses by the Rev. John F. Murphy, dean of Villa Madonna College in Covington, Kentucky, Mayor Charles Farnsley of Louisville and Archbishop Floersh. The cornerstone featured three inscribed fleurs-de-lis, in commemoration of the 175th anniversary of the city's founding. Inside the cornerstone were placed a medal of St. Robert Bellarmine, a list of current students, copies of the college catalogue, a student manual, a college brochure and a map of Louisville.

The new building was designed to match the architecture of Pasteur Hall. Thomas J. Nolan & Sons was again the architect, and the Al J. Schneider Company was again the general contractor. Again the exterior was of buff-colored, rough texture brick with limestone trim. The floors of the halls and lounge were made of terrazzo. The three-story building was intended to crown the top of the hill and featured a six-story tower.

Because the new building contained most of the college facilities, it quickly became the center of campus life. The ground floor housed a 300-person cafeteria,

a kitchen, snack bar, soda fountain, faculty dining area, student lounge, game room, athletic locker room, library storage rooms and service entrance. A large lecture room seating 150 called The Cardinal Room was also on this floor. At the rear of the student lounge were offices for student activities, student publications, the student senate and the orchestra. While the cafeteria was still in Pasteur Hall, it was run on the honor system—until one student protested by eating a large chicken dinner and not paying for it. Complaints about high cost and low quality have been constant since the first day of service. Responses by food service vendors have met with only temporary success. But try they do. In a letter to *The Concord* on December 15, 1961, food service director John W. Mahoney, Sr., announced reductions on certain items, with a barbecue sandwich dropping from 25 to 20 cents—or two for 35 cents.

The first or main floor was occupied by a spacious lobby, the library, faculty offices, seven classrooms and five seminar rooms. The top or second floor contained the book store and ten administrative offices. The chapel featured three altars and seated 350. A roofed walkway was built to connect the new building with the science building.

Through the years the administration building has been remodeled and upgraded. The college showed that it was on the cutting edge of new technology when in December of 1961 it turned on a centrally controlled sound system for broadcasting music, announcements and educational programs throughout the building. In the '70s central air conditioning was added. A facelift in 1986-87 included the installation of an elevator and a new entrance onto Newburg Road. Needless to say, changes in programs and personnel have meant extensive rearranging of spaces for administrators on the second floor.

In ads and promotional brochures the new building was touted as the latest in modern architecture and furnishings. It was featured in several national trade publications in ads sponsored by Armstrong

Acoustical Materials. The classrooms, lobby and cafeteria were pictured for their use of the noise-absorbing ceiling tile. A double-page spread showing the new administration building was featured in the November 1955 issue of *Scenic South*.

As part of the new Master Plan for the campus approved by the Board of Trustees in October, 1998, plans have been drawn and fund raising is underway for a new Campus Center to be located in the space once occupied by the old library. It has been designed as a place to bring together traditional and nontraditional students, faculty and staff in informal surroundings, and will feature a cafe, lounge areas, multipurpose spaces, offices and meeting rooms for student government and student organizations and an expanded bookstore.

and was to house not only athletic events but lectures, plays, concerts, retreats, commencement and baccalaureate services. For sporting events the seating capacity was 3,500. Roll-away seats on both sides of the playing court could be folded back to allow for two regular-sized basketball courts for intramural games. Opposite the lobby was a stage with a 50-foot proscenium opening. With folding chairs the facility could be transformed into an auditorium seating 11,000 people. On the second floor were several classrooms, athletic offices and other athletic facilities. Showers, athletic lockers and supply rooms were located on the lower level.

Cornerstone-laying was held May 19, 1960, with Archbishop Floersh presiding.

Knights Hall . . .

When Fr. Horrigan announced on February 1, 1955, plans to build a $350,000 auditorium-gym, he said, "The need of Bellarmine College and the Catholic high schools in the city is urgent at this time." It was, however, a long time in coming. Ground-breaking for the new building was delayed until May 10, 1957. The cost had escalated to $700,000 and was finally made possible by the Archdiocesan Educational Development Campaign of 1957. The ceremony included a concert by the St. Xavier High School band and an address by Brother Thomas More, who was principal of the school. Also participating was a 4-year-old youngster, Robert Bellarmine Mackey, whose father and mother had named him to honor the school and its patron. Master Robert used a junior-sized spade.

The multipurpose building was intended for use not only by the college but by the entire Archdiocese

Knights Hall construction, 1960.

Bellarmine had had an athletic program from its first year, and with the appointment of Alex Groza as basketball coach in 1959 it signaled its intention to enter intercollegiate sports seriously. Indeed, the college entered the big-time basketball arena for the first time in December 1960, when it met undefeated University of Louisville in a game that christened the new gym. The occasion was a public relations success, with Lt.

Kennedy and Newman Residence Halls.

Lifting Championships. In March of 1962, two members of the U.S. Davis Cup Team—Chris Crawford and Jon Douglas—played an exhibition tennis match at the gym. For more than 40 years Knights Hall provided Bellarmine with an alternative site for commencement when the weather prevented the outdoor ceremony on the south side of the administration building. Since 1995 the ceremony has been held exclusively in Knights Hall. Many local public and private high schools also have held their graduation exercises in the gym.

In addition to accommodating large audiences for popular guests ranging from Alex Haley to Mother Teresa, the auditorium has been the site of a number of religious and secular conferences. On May 30, 1972, some 3,000 mostly elderly people crowded into Knights Hall to attend the Governor's Conference on Aging, a Kentucky follow-up to the White House Conference on Aging. Speakers included Gov. Wendell Ford and Dr. Arthur H. Flemming, the President's adviser on aging. Indeed, with orchestra concerts, including performances by Al Hirt, the U.S. Air Force Band and other groups, dance and music recitals, rock concerts and a host of other programs, Knights Hall has become a community center.

Student and Faculty Housing . . .

Original plans for the college called for student and faculty housing, but not upon the opening of school in the fall of 1950. Local students were expected to live with their parents or relatives. Students from places like Bardstown or Springfield or Cincinnati either lived with relatives or roomed in approved houses near

Gov. Wilson Wyatt and President Philip Davidson of the University of Louisville in attendance. Bellarmine was not so successful on the basketball court. Coach Groza hoped for a reversal of recent misfortunes. The Bellarmine Knights had played three games that season and lost three. But, as the coach noted, the team had improved since it lost to Xavier University 106-69. The improvement wasn't enough. U of L won 79-52. Trying to put a happy face on the loss many years later, alumnus Robert Pfaadt commented, "The game with U of L wasn't a complete wash-out, even though we lost."

Knights Hall has, however, been a great success as a multipurpose building. In addition to serving as a popular site for a variety of sports activities for local high schools, for Bellarmine and other colleges, it served in the early '70s as a training camp for the Kentucky Colonels professional basketball team. In the '70s and '80s it was also the scene of the annual Mr. Louisville contest and has also served as the stage for the Mr. Teen-Ager Weightlifting and Physique Contest and the Ohio Valley Physique and Weight the campus. Sometimes they made other fortunate arrangements. Fr. Horrigan's secretary, Alma Schuler, recalls a special case: "On the first day of classes a boy showed up in the office from somewhere in Western Kentucky. He said he had no place to stay. At that time Fr. John was doing some radio programs on WHAS and he knew the manager, Vic Sholis, with whom he placed the boy as a live-in baby sitter. They got along so well that he stayed with the Sholis family all four years he was at Bellarmine. We found out that one reason he was such a good baby sitter was that he was the oldest of 10 children and had had a lot of practice."

In March of 1958 the college received a $725,000, 40-year, 3 per cent government loan from the Community Facilities Administration to aid in building student and faculty living quarters on campus. At that time in addition to students who lived with relatives, about 70 boarded off campus.

A decade after the school opened the first student residence hall was opened. Students moved into the new 108-student dormitory, named Newman Hall after Cardinal Newman, during the Christmas holidays of 1959, but the first "residence program" didn't get underway until February 1, 1960. One of the two faculty apartments was occupied by the director of the dorm, the Rev. William E. Hogan of the sociology department. The other apartment was the residence of the college chaplain, the Rev. J. Howard French. There were 54 double rooms, containing twin beds, two built-in wooden desks and two wardrobes. The building also had a chapel, a recreation room, guidance office, an infirmary, a kitchenette, laundry and small barber shop, and a lobby and lounge for students and visitors. The class of '59 had declared May 4, 1959, as "Senior Giving Day" and raised more than $1,200 to furnish the recreation room. Student mailboxes were in the lobby. Within a year the dorm was home to 102 young men from 13 states.

Residence hall rules were more restrictive than today and included an 11 o'clock curfew on week nights

and a midnight limit on weekends. Room rental was $115 per semester, plus an additional $255 for board.

The new facility was almost immediately inadequate for the demand. In the fall of 1961, at least a dozen freshmen were denied admission because of the lack of on-campus housing. At that time the college required that unmarried freshmen and

Eunice Kennedy Shriver at the conerstone laying for Kennedy Hall, April 9, 1964.

sophomores from outside the Louisville area live on campus. The rule for sophomores was temporarily suspended. In his annual report Fr. Horrigan urged that top priority be given to a new dorm. A second student residence hall was announced in the spring of 1963, with completion by the fall of 1964. Another

housing crisis erupted, however, in the fall of 1963, when 20 per cent of the college enrollment was from outside the Louisville area. The overflow was accommodated in private homes.

Originally, the new dorm was to have been named for Bishop John Lancaster Spalding, a native of Lebanon, Kentucky, a founder of Catholic University of America and founder, in 1869, and pastor of St. Augustine Church, the first parish in Louisville for black Catholics. In January of 1964, however, Fr. Horrigan announced that it would instead be called Kennedy Hall "as a memorial to the name and ideals of President Kennedy." Said Fr. Horrigan: "He added important new dimensions to the world in which college students of today and tomorrow will live and work. For the American Catholic community in particular, he opened great new vistas of opportunity and—more importantly—public responsibility." With a capacity of 150, the dormitory had been begun several weeks before the assassination. Located adjacent to Newman Hall, the building was designed and built by

Robert Nolan and Al Schneider, the architect and contractor for all the previous buildings.

Ceremonies for Kennedy Hall were held in April 1964, with Mrs. R. Sargent Shriver, sister of the late President, helping to seal the cornerstone.   In November the new building was dedicated, and a bust of Kennedy donated by the Office Staff Association was unveiled. The speaker was former Congressman Frank Burke, who had served in the House of Representatives during the Kennedy Administration, which he labeled as one with "a new sense of youth and vitality."

Following the merger with Ursuline in 1968, provision was made for women's housing on campus. Kennedy Hall was remodeled for women, and in February of 1970 the old Newman Chapel in Newman Hall was converted to a study hall and a new chapel was opened in converted space in the administration building. Its old altar and pews were donated to the Jefferson County Jail for a nondenominational chapel. In the early '90s, a third dormitory, Petrik Hall, joined Newman and Kennedy halls following a grant of $1.5 million from the James Graham Brown Foundation.

At the beginning secular priests lived in a house on Harvard, and the Franciscan priests lived on Princeton. In the fall of 1953 the Franciscan Friary moved to the convent at the old site of Holy Trinity parish on Frankfort Avenue. The new residence housed seven Franciscan priests on the Bellarmine faculty and three lay brothers. Thirteen faculty members were parish priests and lived in their parishes. Later, diocesan priests moved into Lenihan Hall and the Franciscans into Bonaventure Hall.

Because the number of priests on the faculty had dwindled, in the late '70s the remaining ones moved into other housing and both faculty residences were turned into other uses. Bonaventure was renovated to offer small conference facilities for business and professional groups. Its facilities, which included meeting and lounge areas and rooms for up to 32 overnight guests, soon began to accommodate

such clients as General Electric, First National Bank of Louisville, United Parcel Service (UPS) and Meidinger & Associates. Soon, Lenihan was made over into classrooms and offices for the Lansing School of Nursing. In 1997 Lenihan Hall was converted into a dormitory for honors students. To accommodate the growing demand for student housing on campus, in 1998 Bonaventure was also converted into student housing. In the fall of 1998 a record 455 students lived in residence halls. Additional residence halls are included in the campus Master Plan. No permanent housing for lay faculty has ever been built on campus.

Facilities for Student Activities . . .

Until the opening of the George G. Brown Activities Building in 1984, the student activities area was woefully underserved. Throughout the '50s, '60s and '70s Bellarmine students made do with recreational and social facilities that were designed for other functions.   In the '50s student leaders began urging the administration to provide adequate spaces for activities outside the classroom, but it wasn't until the

Student Activities Building.

early '60s that concrete plans were laid. In November of 1964 the annual Student Fund Drive was directed at raising money toward building a student union building. The following year almost $3,500 was raised by the drive for the facility.

Finally, in the fall of 1969 a boxlike, smallish $115,000 structure to be known as the Student Activities Building (SAB, for short) was opened downhill on the east side of the administration building. It was soon very obvious that it was too little too late. It contained modest recreation space, a lounge, several offices, a snack bar—where students 21 and over could stop by for a beer—but it was never popular with students and by its fourth year it was hardly ever used. In October of 1973 *The Concord* described it as "a little cubical building on the hillside between the dorms and the Administration Building." Students and faculty with a penchant for numbers called it "a $100,000 white elephant." Renovation in the spring of 1979 brought in new furnishings and a 25-inch color television set, but students still stayed away in droves.

In the fall of 1980 student Dave Spoelker editorialized in *The Concord* that students deserved a real activities building, not the present "Student UNactivity Building." Finally, in November of 1981 William J. Stewart, dean of students, wrote a case statement for a real student center, in which he said the space crunch had reached crisis proportions. "There are 2,585 Bellarmine students," he wrote, "who have no campus facility, except the cafeteria, designed primarily for their outside-of-classroom needs."

At the same time, increased enrollment and an expanded curriculum were straining the academic facilities, and the SAB was converted into the Student Art Building, with temporary classrooms and faculty offices for the art department. Student activities were evicted and scattered all over the campus, from Knights Hall to the cafeteria. Meanwhile, students were pressuring for a student union. As student Joseph A. Cassidy put it in a letter to *The Concord* in October of

1981, "Bellarmine does need a student union building or room if for no other purpose but to set it apart from high schools who have 'sock hops' in cafeterias and gyms." Finally, three years later the dream became a reality. What became of the SAB? It's still on campus but hidden under the sparkling new Miles Building, which encloses it.

Maurice D.S. Johnson Quadrangle, 1999 view.

The Maurice D. S. Johnson Quadrangle Buildings . . .

During the administration of Eugene Petrik, the campus finally developed a center, the Maurice D.S. Johnson Quadrangle, when Horrigan Hall and Pasteur Hall were joined by the Brown Activities Center, the Norton art and music buildings, Alumni Hall and Wyatt Hall.

When space problems hit crisis proportions in the early '80s, Bellarmine launched its first major building campaign since 1967—and, at that time, the largest one in its history. A major expansion was announced in the fall of 1982 and the Louisville firm of Grossman-Martin-Chapman Architects, Inc. was chosen to design a 40,000-square-foot College

Curtis W. Miles Hall

Petrik Hall

Wilson W. Wyatt Lecture–Recital Hall

George G. Brown Activities Center

Activities Center and Fine Arts-Humanities Complex, with a price tag of $4.5 million. When construction began in the summer of 1983, the project had grown to five buildings with a cost of over $5 million—a figure that would eventually rise to $6.5 million, which was raised under the leadership of President Petrik and Board of Trustees Chairman Maurice D.S. Johnson and former chairman, Wilson W. Wyatt, Sr. The new buildings increased campus facilities by approximately 20 per cent.

The George G. Brown Activities Center was named for the late founder of Brown-Forman Corporation. It was designed to house a cafeteria (later named the Florence and Fred Koster Commons, after the business and community leader and her late husband), an 8,000-square-foot assembly hall to seat 700 (the Amelia Brown Frazier Hall), a bookstore, student government offices, offices of the dean of students, a student lounge, and offices for student publications. Also new were 500 parking spaces and 200 trees that replaced 13 diseased giant catalpa trees which had been removed from the entrance driveway.

Also opening were the George W. Norton Fine Arts Complex, consisting of two buildings with facilities for art and music, including piano studios and the Catherine B. Lenihan Rehearsal Room; Alumni Hall, with offices for humanities faculty and including the Grace and Joshua Everett Memorial Conference Room, and the Wilson W. Wyatt, Sr. Lecture-Recital Hall, which included the Mr. and Mrs. Edward L. McGrath Art Gallery, St. Robert's Chapel and the Amy Cralle Theatre. At the January 1985 dedication of Wyatt Hall, Maurice Johnson, who was instrumental in raising the funds for its construction, described the new building as "a gift from the friends of Wilson W. Wyatt, Sr. in recognition of his contribution to our community and in recognition of the contribution which Bellarmine College is making to the community." Donors included a who's-who of Louisville: Barry Bingham, Sr., Wendell Cherry, David A. Jones, David

Grissom, Samuel H. Klein, Bruce L. Ferguson and Edward J. McGrath.

Another fund drive, the $20 million Partnership for Progress campaign, which grew to $36 million, resulted in additional buildings in the 1990s. The first product of the campaign was the $2.7 million student residence named after Bellarmine's second president. At the dedication ceremonies on October 11, 1990, the recently retired Eugene V. Petrik called it "the greatest honor that you could bestow." The new dormitory was arranged in suites that accommodated eight students for a total capacity of 134. In addition to sleeping and bathroom facilities, each suite included a study room, a computer and a cable television hook-up. Elsewhere in the building were a game room, a laundry room, and a reception area with a large screen television and a microwave oven.

In 1993 Miles Hall was opened, followed in 1997 by the W. L. Lyons Brown Library, with state-of-the-art design and technology. With the completion of these two structures Bellarmine College had finally housed its programs in first-class accommodations. In addition to the Campus Center in Horrigan Hall, new residence halls and a new chapel, the new Master Plan also calls for expansion and renovation of Pasteur Hall, an Academic Resource Center in the unfinished ground floor of the Brown Library, more parking and, in time, a new Wellness and Recreation Center. At last the college is acquiring a physical plant that will match the quality of its curriculum and instruction.

Other Campus Structures and Landmarks . . .

In addition to buildings with thousands of square feet of covered space, a campus is also made of smaller structures and points of interest. Appropriately, one of the first campus landmarks was a wood carving of St. Robert Bellarmine, now located on a wall pedestal in the lobby of Horrigan Hall. It was acquired in August of 1953 and installed and blessed on the feast day of St. Robert, May 13, 1954, in connection with the official opening and dedication of the new college chapel and the dedication of the college athletic fields. The statue was purchased at a modest price because of a mistake made at a German art center. It was carved at the Archabbey of Bueron, an art center in the Danube Valley of Germany near the Swiss border, and a leader in the movement to revive religious art.

Sometime in 1952 the archabbey received an inquiry from a Jesuit institution in California regarding a statue of Bellarmine. The letter of inquiry was mistranslated as a commission to carve a statue. The sculptor, A. Hertnagel, had almost finished the work before the mistake was discovered. At a spring meeting of an educational group meeting in Atlantic City, Fr. Horrigan and Fr. Treece learned that the statue was for sale. They contacted the archabbey and obtained the statue for half its original price of $500, and placed it in the administration building upon its completion a few months later. The form of the saint's name on the statue is Bellarmin, the Italian spelling.

Another early landmark is the flagpole on the Newburg Road side of Horrigan Hall. It was presented to the college on June 6, 1955, by a local Knights of Columbus unit, the Fourth Degree Knights of Monsignor Bouchet Council. Marking the Newburg Road entrance to the college are two stone columns erected in 1956 by Louisville attorney Arthur J. Deindoerfer as a memorial to his mother, Rose R. Deindoerfer.

Finally, the best-known landmark, the Bell Tower, has been a prominent part of the Bellarmine landscape since 1953, when it was constructed as a part of the administration building. For several years it was used as apartments for priest members of the faculty, and at

one time it was home to *The Concord*. Since it was determined to be in violation of fire codes (it has only one stairway), it has been used mainly as a storage area. A student writing in *The Concord* in November of 1978 suggested, mock-seriously, that a restaurant be located there and called Top of the Tower.

In 1962, Al J. Schneider, a member of the Bellarmine Foundation and the owner of the construction company that built the college's first structures, donated the steel cross that is located between Bonaventure and Lenihan halls. In the summer of 1963 he also donated a life-sized figure of St. Francis of Assisi. Originally stationed in a wooded area near Bonaventure Hall, when it was the friary of the Conventual Franciscan Fathers who teach at Bellarmine, it is now located on a grassy knoll between Pasteur and Horrigan halls.

In February of 1970 a piece of environmental sculpture called "a fragmented or exploded cube" was installed in front of the new science building. The four-ton, $10,000 cube, which was built with federal

"Exploded Cube," created by Eric O. Swab of G.E.'s Appliance Park with federal funds obtained by Chemistry Professor Dr. Jack Daly.

Community mural conceived by Art Professor Bob Lockhart, with over 50 students, faculty and staff contributing to the 1975 mural.

funds obtained with the aid of chemistry professor Dr. Jack Daly, was intended to symbolize the reunification of fragmented knowledge. Industrial designer Eric O. Swab of General Electric's Appliance Park conceived the fragmented shape as having the potential for achieving its original unity. Shaped like an angled arch soaring some 10 feet into the air, the figure could be reassembled as a cube, thus returning the fragmented mass to its original shape. *The Courier-Journal* art critic called it "a striking addition to the campus and to the city's face as well." The exploded cube has been the site of many campus gatherings, planned and unplanned, including a sunrise service which kicked off Town and Gown Week in November of 1970.

An addendum to Pasteur Hall on the east side is the greenhouse, built with a donation of $10,000 from the national Fraternal Order of Eagles and the St. Matthews unit. Dedicated in May of 1971, it was designed as a research facility for the botanical study of possible connections between tobacco and cancer.

In 1973 the college formed a partnership with certain alumni and friends of the college to build the College Tennis Club.

In the spring of 1975 another campus "sight" had its debut in the bookstore corridor (now the home of the campus print shop). On the corridor walls art professor Bob Lockhart conceived and developed a colorful community mural to which some 50 students, faculty and staff contributed figures, words, names and art. The mural is now hidden by a wall covering outside the print shop in Horrigan Hall.

In addition to the administration wall painting cooperative, Lockhart and 16 of his students installed a 20-foot-long, 8-foot-high beige jigsaw puzzle or wall sculpture in 1977 opposite the entrance to the Old Science Theater in Pasteur Hall. Called simply "The Wall," it consisted of several hundred "jigs" sawed by the students, styrofoam faces, egg crates, a rubber bird, shells, feathers, finials, driftwood, string, letters of the alphabet, a plastic crab, a cow horn, balls, toy pistols, auto parts and nameless other objects. It was another way of confronting students with art. Of course, these two more-or-less formal art projects were not the first wall art to grace the Bellarmine campus, as attested to by a student who wrote this anonymous letter to *The Concord* in the fall of 1958 regarding the state of restroom graffiti: "I'm not an English major, but I wish those guys who write on the rest-room walls (first floor, administration building) would learn how to spell."

Indeed, the Bellarmine campus of today looks very little like the empty, almost abandoned property that the newly appointed administrators saw when they parked on Newburg Road and climbed the hill through briars and weeds, dodging holes and stones, and tried to imagine what a college would look like on the hill. The facilities that you see before you now could hardly have been envisioned by the newly anointed president and vice president.

The only constant has been change—from the sprouting of new buildings to the rerouting of campus roads, from the turning around of the campus from Norris Place to Newburg Road. What Cecil Mingus of the maintenance staff said about the restructuring of interior space—"We were always building walls that we later had to take down and put somewhere else"— applies to all the campus spaces.

Bellarmine as a Good Neighbor. . .

Bellarmine College exists in a specific location in the Highlands of Louisville, Kentucky. Its campus, its buildings and its activities are located in a larger neighborhood. Bellarmine has always tried to be a caring college in its relationship to its immediate community and the community outside.

Although Bellarmine's 100-acre-plus campus provides a useful buffer between the college and the immediate residential areas, the college has tried to be sensitive to the way it impacts on its neighbors, working with them on traffic control, consulting them about new construction and opening its campus to joggers and walkers. From the beginning the college has related itself closely with the local community, offering free courses, lectures, readings, even the use of the library to the public. After the doors were opened Bellarmine became a flurry of activity, not only in its classrooms and laboratories but in the community at large. Hardly a stone was left unturned to involve the college, its faculty and students in the religious, civic and professional life of the larger Louisville community. In July of 1956 the position of community relations director was created and Fr. Henry B. Schuhmann was named to fill it.

One of the most visible evidences of Bellarmine's outreach to the local community— especially for anyone driving along Newburg Road— has been the college cinder track, where dozens of people can be spotted running, jogging, walking—and sometimes huffing and puffing—along. In fact, many people assume that it is a public track. For almost half a century it has been a popular campus and community spot, with runners, joggers and walkers who crowd the track almost 24 hours a day—in sunshine and rain, summer and winter, in shorts and sweat suits, alone or accompanied by friends or children or dogs. It is where town and gown meet daily.

Many community groups have held meetings and festivals on campus, from a planning group for a Youth Speaks workshop in February of 1955 to the first Louisville Fest, a celebration of Irish dancing and culture, which took place in June of 1997. In May of 1966 a Louisville chapter of the Ancient Order of Hibernians, limited to men of Irish descent, was formed on campus with a membership of 100. For the past eight years, Bellarmine has been host to the Irish Family Fest, bringing thousands to the campus.

Bellarmine has opened her doors to immigrants in need. In 1975 the college donated classroom space for English language courses for Vietnamese refugees; and in the late '70s the college sponsored the Trans, a Vietnamese family who settled in Louisville.

Dozens of professional groups have been welcomed to the campus, including a conference in industrial management sponsored by the Kentuckiana Council of National Management Association Clubs. In March of 1966 Bellarmine, assisted by the C.I.T. Financial Corporation, hosted the nation's first community Interdependence Day, a daylong discussion of opportunities for closer partnership between business and higher education. Participating in the conference were local business leaders as well as college presidents and officers and trustees from 14 area colleges and universities.

An unusual example of Bellarmine's involvement with the local community occurred in December of 1971, when the Louisville Police Department, under a federal grant, opened an experimental substation on campus in a trailer. In a special referendum in November of 1970 almost 80 per cent of students voting approved the installation of the substation trailer, which remained on campus for almost a year and a half. During its operation many Bellarmine students developed a more positive view of law enforcement as they took advantage of the opportunity to ride with police officers on their beats. Another innovative program was begun in the fall of 1997, when students in several of Gail Henson's classes, nicknamed the "Bellarmine Buddies," tutored and mentored students at nearby Highland Middle School.

Cultural events of the 1996-97 academic year free and open to the community included art exhibits, lectures on subjects ranging from social justice to the ceramic arts of China, prominent speakers like James M. Burns and Peter Matthiessen, faculty and student music recitals and plays, and a host of other activities. Such events not only enriched the college's instructional program but also served as effective public relations. As President McGowan wrote in a brochure inviting the community to the college, these events are a way

The Bellarmine Knight, commissioned by Owsley Brown Frazier and created by Professor Bob Lockhart, 1998, overlooks the W. L. Lyons Brown Library.

"to give back to our city" something in return for the social, cultural and recreational resources that the community provides for the college.

The W. L. Lyons Brown Library

The quality of a college is determined in large part by its library. Despite limited resources and facilities, from the start Bellarmine students have been fortunate to have had a good library and competent librarians. In the beginning the Bellarmine library was called simply "the library." It wasn't until January of 1997 that the library got its own building and name and became the W. L. Lyons Brown Library. But that is the end of the story.

This is the beginning: In the summer of 1950 there was Betty Delius, the director of the library until 1980, sitting at a table in the temporary college office on Harvard Drive and planning the library. She had joined Alma Schuler the previous summer as the second woman on the staff. There were already a few books, mostly donated by friends of the college. On February 11, 1950, *The Record* had announced that Fr. Horrigan would review the best-selling novel, *The Cardinal,* by H. Morton Robinson, at the forthcoming local meeting of the International Federation of Catholic Alumnae at Nazareth College. Members and friends were invited to attend the tea and make contributions to the library fund. More than $1,100 was raised.

When the college opened in Pasteur Hall in the fall of 1950, the library was given space on the second floor. The few hundred books became a few thousand, augmented with selected reference works and periodicals. The collection barely supported research

Dr. Joseph J. McGowan, Jr. and Mrs. W. L. Lyons Brown.

papers, and students often went book-hunting in high-school libraries and the public library. But the makeshift library was serviceable for the school's pioneers, who already knew they would have to make do with few resources and amenities.

Betty Delius set a high standard for hard work and efficiency. As the sole librarian in a new college, she worked countless hours building the library collection and serving the needs of dozens of desperately seeking students. John J. Ford, a member of the first class, calls her a brave library pioneer but admits that "a lot of us students did our best to drive her crazy." Rosalie Baker, who began her service to the college as a clerk in the president's office in 1951 and became assistant to Delius the following year, remembers her as "an intense and dedicated librarian who spent long hours day and night doing the work of the library." Marquita Breit, who joined the library faculty in 1967, calls Delius "a woman of high ethical standards, a procrastinator who, once she makes up her mind to do something, is impossible to stop. She's like a cobra in a corner." Joan Wettig, who was appointed director in 1980 when Delius became circulation librarian, calls her predecessor "knowledgeable and dedicated." Like most of Bellarmine's first leaders, Betty Delius was the right person in the right place at the right time.

When the new administration building was completed in 1954, the library moved into quarters on the east side of the first floor, where it remained for

43 years. Its vacated space in Pasteur Hall became a freshman chemistry laboratory. The move into the new building was a marvel of human engineering, and the local media covered it as a news event. Classes were dismissed for three hours and a book brigade or human chain was formed of students and faculty, who passed books from hand to hand from the old library into the new one.

One of the first big public events in the new library was the celebration of Catholic Book Week in February of 1955, with an open house, which featured displays of outstanding Catholic books published in

Reading Room in the W. L. Lyons Brown Library.

1954. The displays were divided into three sections: juvenile, high school and adult. Although its shelves were not filled, the new space had a capacity for 60,000 volumes. The speaker for the occasion was Notre Dame professor of English and author Richard Sullivan. There was also a display of comic books selected under the direction of Fr. Horrigan, who discussed the decency code recently adopted by the Comics Magazine Association of America.

Although it was soon cramped for space, the library was convenient to students, who took most of their classes in the building. There were student-accessible stacks (an open stacks policy which has continued down to the present), a spacious reference room, a fiction room-lounge with a fireplace, a periodicals room, and an audio-visual room. There was also a locked, prohibited-books room that held books on the Index of Prohibited Books, such as the *Communist Manifesto*. These books were available to faculty and students but were not in open circulation. Needless to say, the room is no longer in use.

Rosalie Baker

Joan Wettig

Marquita Breit

By the fall of 1959 the library collection totaled some 25,000 books. The following year the number had grown to 30,000, with subscriptions to 324 periodicals, 1,000 recordings, 200 film strips; and the professional staff had increased to four. In October of 1964 a turnstile was installed to prevent loss of books. By 1984 the library contained approximately 100,000 volumes.

According to Joan Wettig, the new library was a "lovely showcase" with decor designed by Hubbuchs of Kentucky. Tours were brought through all the time, including patients from Our Lady of Peace Hospital. Library patrons who had roughed it in the old Pasteur location found themselves at last in a lovely, reader-friendly, comfortable setting. Marquita Breit remembers the beautiful open courtyard—later to become the storage area for bound periodicals—which each December had a large Christmas tree, "decorated with gorgeous ornaments and lights and sometimes covered with real snow and ice." Library hours, however, were still limited to an 8 a.m. to 5 p.m. schedule, with no weekend hours.

Library hours and other services improved through the years. With the advent of computers and massive information databases, Bellarmine became a pioneer on the Information Highway, with a computerized card catalogue, on-line searches and other marvels of information storage and retrieval. It was a long time coming. Rosalie Baker reflects on the plans and delays: "We had talked about a new building from the time I joined the staff in 1952. In 1968 we were seriously planning a building." In 1969 a library building committee took a field trip to Covington, Kentucky, to see Villa Madonna's new library and get ideas to take back to Bellarmine. Then after the merger with Ursuline money became scarce, government support dropped, the college had its own financial crisis, and all plans were put on hold until the early '90s.

John Boyd and Martha Reed Perry, moving into the new library.

It wasn't until March 1995, when ground was broken for the long-awaited W. L. Lyons Brown Library, that Bellarmine took a giant step foward into the future. The literal move would not be more than a few yards northwest to the open space between Alumni Hall and Horrigan Hall, but the new building would signal Bellarmine's maturity as a college. A recently minted authority on the new technology, David Chatham, had accepted the directorship of the library the previous August and was overseeing the building's design to make sure that it was a good fit for Bellarmine's present and future requirements.

Unforeseen difficulties and delays hampered construction through 1995 and much of 1996. Faculty, students and interested visitors watched as the library began to take shape. Jack Kampschaefer, vice president for administration and finance, kept the college community informed with periodic "library updates." A member of the college's Pioneer Class and a long-serving administrator, he had waited a long time to see this capstone building completed. Indeed, the usually staid, no-nonsense, bottom-line man-of-facts became a one-man cheering squad as the library rose above the campus. Finally, in a memo dated April 23, 1996, and headed "GOOD NEWS!," he pulled out all the stops and waxed with more eloquence than anyone would have supposed possible from an accountant. For the first time, he writes, we can "get a sense of what the library will really look like." After describing some of the more pedestrian work being completed on the exterior walls, tower and roof, he continues:

"We begin to get a sense of the beautiful arches and other wall relief and soffit work inside which will add so much class to the finished work. We also begin to get a sense of the wonderful openness created by the many windows and beautiful skylights. A space in the tower for an impressive clock and the several arched ceilings on the interior will be stunning. The spacious main stairway with its large windows to the exterior will offer a beautiful view of the rolling hills of our campus. The view from the upper level into the two-story periodical room will be breathtaking. Many of the limestone accents to the brick work have been placed and, hopefully, will help make it an award-winning building. . . .

"This has been an exciting time. For me, personally, it's the culmination of the project of longest duration the college has ever had. The new library was first discussed in the mid 1950s, and the first rough plans were begun in the early '70s. Serious plans were actually considered in the early '80s and had to be shelved due to lack of funding. We can now thank God for the delays because the earlier plans would have been inadequate at this time had the construction taken place earlier. We will soon occupy a beautiful, modern, state-of-the-art library. It will truly be the jewel in the crown of the Bellarmine College campus."

The library opened in January of 1997 and it was, indeed, a state-of-the-art library. Designed by the Hillier Group of Princeton, N. J., working with Michael Koch and Associates of Louisville, the 70,000-square-foot library has facilities for more than 150,000 books,

Mrs. W. L. Lyons Brown and Mr. Owsley Brown Frazier at the Dedication of the W. L. Lyons Brown Library on April 7, 1997.

800 magazines and 5,000 videos and compact discs. It also includes a reference center with Internet access, a technology lab with 18 computers, 400 Internet outlets spaced throughout the building, a study lounge open 24 hours a day, a listening-viewing room, two multimedia classrooms, numerous study carrels,

research rooms, group study rooms, the Owsley Brown Frazier Board Room and spacious facilities for the Thomas Merton Studies Center. Three challenge grants of $750,000 each from the James Graham Brown Foundation supported the installation of a campus-wide computer network centered in the library.

Named for the late civic leader and chairman of Brown-Forman Corporation, W. L. Lyons Brown, the library's completion and dedication during the week of April 7, 1997, was a highlight of Joseph J. McGowan's six years as President of Bellarmine College. The weeklong celebration included a liturgy presided over by Dom Timothy Kelly, O.C.S.O., Abbot of Gethsemani, poetry and dramatic readings, musical concerts, poems by Thomas Merton read by monks from the Abbey of Gethsemani and a public dedication presided over by President McGowan. Speakers included Louisville Mayor Jerry Abramson, Jefferson County Judge-Executive David Armstrong, Mrs. W. L. Lyons Brown, widow of the building's namesake, and Louisville Archbishop Thomas Kelly, who gave a blessing for the $10 million building.

Speaking for the faculty, history professor Dr. Margaret Mahoney noted that St. Robert Bellarmine built a library for the Roman College in 1593 and as rector issued an ordinance "for the conservation and advancement of mathematical studies for the great glory of God, our Lord." Furthermore, she said, Bellarmine himself used the library, even during the cold winter months in an unheated building. She concluded: "It is a long way in time and space from the Library of Alexandria, built by the Ptolemys out of worm-eaten fragments of Aristotle's library in the third century B.C., through the Benedictine *scriptoria* and cathedral schools of the Middle Ages and on to that library built by Robert

Bellarmine at the Roman College to the Library of Congress established as the great public institution guaranteeing the preservation of freedom of thought in the United States to this dedication of the W. L. Lyons Brown Library with its state-of-the-art technological innovations. But all of these institutions had in common the collecting of the wisdom of the past and present."

Indeed, Bellarmine's own library has come a long way since 1950. As late as 1962 being on the cutting edge meant setting up an exhibit in the library entitled "Atoms in Action" from the Atomic Energy Commission. To Marquita Breit the biggest changes in libraries have been in technology. Bellarmine's leap into computer technology, she says, began in 1976, "when the library received a Kellogg grant and we got our first OCLC terminal and we began to do orders, searches and interlibrary loans through the system." The library is now a member of the Library Council of Kentuckiana Metroversity, which allows students access to materials in other Louisville area institutions, and a member of Solinet (Southeastern Library Network), through which the library accesses OCLC, the largest bibliographic network database in the world.

Other librarians echo the revolutionary changes wrought by computers. Rosalind Parnes explains the information revolution she has witnessed this way: "I took not one course in computers when I was in library school, and now we are in an era of on-line database searching, national networking, national databases and CD-ROMS—all terms that I would not have understood then. In many ways Bellarmine has been a leader in the change to the new technology. We have taken workshops, courses, seminars to bring us up to date. I can't say that computers have made our job easier, but they have made it easier for us to be efficient; and they have made it easier for us to be accepted by students as faculty members, as teachers."

Joan Wettig's view is even longer and broader: "When I became a librarian, we were doing things pretty much the way they had been done for

generations; then the computer came on the scene and revolutionized the way libraries operate. Insofar as our resources permitted, we at Bellarmine were pioneers in adopting the new technology. In the 1970s Betty Delius started bringing Bellarmine College into the Information Age, and in 1977 we began cataloguing on-line. In fact, we have been ahead of most institutions in this area. Now all our books are in the on-line database. We no longer have a card catalog."

A–V Room, Horrigan Hall Library. Librarian Joan Wettig with painting.

Before the era of computer retrieval of information, however, professional librarians had to be masters of hands-on service; and Bellarmine has been fortunate to have had a cadre of hard-working, knowledgeable librarians. Following Betty Delius as library director in 1980 was Joan Wettig, who joined the library faculty in 1957 and spent her entire library career at Bellarmine, as she says, "without regrets." Before she came to Bellarmine, she had spent several years teaching in parochial elementary and high schools, finally "fleeing" a fifth grade classroom of 50 students and a mountain of stress.

She was appointed to be audio-visual librarian at a gross salary of $350 a month. She reported to work to find one audio-visual room, decorated in black and white and yellow, one record player, three Bell & Howell 16 mm. thread-it-yourself projectors, one reel-to-reel tape recorder, "which weighed a ton," two filmstrip projectors, and one old-fashioned slide projector, which was used by an art history professor with slides borrowed from the University of Louisville. "That," she says, "was the a–v department."

Rosalind Parnes

Another stalwart of the library faculty is Marquita Breit, who came to Bellarmine as assistant circulation director in May of 1967 after three years in the Louisville public library system. Before she joined the faculty, she had been a library volunteer. In her words: "I think Betty Delius had me volunteering for a full year before I got my position." At Bellarmine she has headed just about every department, from cataloguing and acquisitions to audio-visual. Despite a heavy workload, she has found time to compile the standard Thomas Merton bibliography, which is used by Merton scholars around the world.

Another librarian who is an indelible part of Bellarmine's history is Rosalind Parnes. After almost 30 years at Bellarmine, she can still affirm: "There have been three big watershed events or defining relationships in my life that I feel very fortunate to have had: first, my parents; second, a personal friendship; and third, my coming to Bellarmine. There's not a library job that I know of in Louisville that would tempt me away from this school." It is a mutual admiration. As reference librarian, Parnes has probably worked more directly with more students than any other member of the faculty. She remembers in good humor a question that Betty Delius asked her during her interview in 1970. "She asked me if I was planning on getting married and pregnant. I knew it was a crucial question because she had just lost two librarians to men and babies. I told her not to worry." What she says about the faculty in general and their loyalty to Bellarmine surely applies to her: "I've been very impressed by their dedication to their disciplines, but their love of Bellarmine is unsurpassed."

Although until recently all of Bellarmine's library faculty—except for one—have been women, men and libraries can sometimes be a good mix. The first male librarian was a member of the Pioneer Class, Paul Birkel, who earned a graduate degree in library science at Catholic University and returned to serve as assistant director of Bellarmine's library for several years. The second male librarian is the present director of the Brown Library, David Chatham, who joined the faculty in the fall of 1994. With degrees from Drew University, Colorado State University and the University of Washington and with special expertise in information systems and library technology, he arrived on campus just in time to oversee the transition into the new library.

The library faculty in the waning years of the 20th century is made up of a suitable mix of men and women. In addition to Chatham, Breit and Parnes, the professional staff includes Martha Reed Perry and John Boyd, both in the reference department. The professional librarians have been well assisted by a support staff, ranging from temporary student assistants and community volunteers to clerical assistants like Rosalie Baker, one of the longest-serving members of the college staff. In June of 1951 she became an assistant in the president's office, serving Fr. Horrigan and Fr. John Loftus, and the following year she transferred to the library to assist Betty Delius. From then until her retirement in the spring of 1996, she did most of the jobs of the library, from ordering to cataloguing to her final position as administrative assistant to the director of the library. Indeed, the entire library system—from circulation to cataloguing—is still ably supported by a staff that includes Dustin Strong, Bob Haarz, Nancy Zanone, Linda Lally, Jeanne Catalano, Ken Lundgren and Jim Laval, who serves as director of information services for the college.

The W. L. Lyons Brown Library

An indication of the central role played by the Bellarmine library in the college academic program is the fact that librarians long had faculty status, a position that was rather unusual when Betty Delius joined the faculty in 1950. According to director emeritus Wettig, "Betty established the tradition that all professional librarians at Bellarmine would be members of the faculty with faculty rank. We have always believed that we deserve faculty status because we consider ourselves a vital part of the academic, teaching function of the college. In fact, our faculty status at Bellarmine has lighted the way for other colleagues, including librarians at the University of Louisville, who have pointed to us as examples."

While pleased that Bellarmine librarians are members of the faculty, Marquita Breit admits that their academic role is different from that of classroom professors. "We've had generally good relations with the faculty and administration," she says, "and although we have faculty status, our positions and problems are unique to us. We are somewhat autonomous. Our

work schedules are different, and our academic mission is different." In recognition of his unique status as an administrator, David Chatham was appointed library director in 1994 without faculty rank.

Special Collections and Services...

Many of the first books in Bellarmine's library were donated by well-meaning supporters who had little understanding of the books appropriate for a college collection. Indeed, many of those donated books then, as well as now, cannot be kept and are returned or sold in the annual Bellarmine Women's Council's book sale, which raises money for student scholarships. Rosalie Baker remembers how books were sometimes acquired at the beginning: "Fr. Treece came to visit my husband and me shortly after his appointment as vice president and said, 'Now, we'll have a library, of course, so we'll be glad to take any old books you want to give us.'"

Now, with more than 125,000 carefully selected books, periodicals and nonprint materials as well as computer on-line access, the library has the research materials and technology to support a varied curriculum and growing student body. The collection quality is ensured by faculty input in the selection of library materials. All courses of instruction, according to Breit, are adequately supported, but she points to the humanities as an especially strong area. Indeed, she says, among the heavy-user departments are English, history, theology and philosophy.

In addition, special collections add depth to the library's general holdings. Special collections, which are usually acquired by donation, include the Raymond Riebel Collection of English and American Literature and Fine Press Books; the Ursuline-Monsignor Felix N. Pitt Collection of Early Kentuckiana, which was acquired from the Ursuline Sisters in 1991; the Eleanor Mercein Kelly Collection, consisting of fiction and nonfiction and printed and manuscript items by the late Louisville-based author; the Sister Therese Lentfoehr Photograph Collection; the Harry Miles Civil War Collection; and Data Courier, a business information service, which, beginning in 1977, for almost 20 years provided articles from some 1,800 periodicals to hundreds of companies in the United States and worldwide. This important library outreach was based on one of the most comprehensive collections of business-based periodicals in the United States.

Mrs. Margaret Maloney, who headed the Data Courier service, described the service and what it meant to Bellarmine College. "In 1978 the collection of periodicals was housed in what had been the Thomas Merton Room behind the audio-visual area. I felt that it was a special place because it was where Thomas Merton had a small office when he was on campus. I was recruited for the job by my first cousin, Fr. Raymond Treece, who assured me that it was an easy, sit-down job. Well, it was not as easy as he had said, but I loved the work from the very first day. The collection was brought to Bellarmine from *The Courier-Journal* through the efforts of Doris Batliner, who was *The Courier-Journal* librarian, and a friend of Joan Wettig. The removal to Bellarmine was approved by Jack Kampschaefer, our finance officer, provided it didn't cost the college anything. Through the years it has grown to be an important instructional asset for the college as well as a moneymaker. Our staff peaked at 13 employees and usually stands around

10 full-time and part-time members. We like to say that we touch the Fortune 500 companies every day and have never missed a deadline." In 1997 the college took over the collection and continues to maintain the periodicals most used by the business faculty and students.

Bellarmine's Adopted Son: The Thomas Merton Collection and Studies Center . . .

Pre-eminently, however, the collection that has given the college an international reputation is the unrivaled Thomas Merton Collection of The Thomas Merton Studies Center, including such support collections as the William Habich Collection of Mertoniana and the Owen Merton Collection. Named for the Trappist monk and author Thomas Merton, the collection was established in the Bellarmine library and the Thomas Merton Room was formally dedicated on November 8, 1964, when more than 600 items went on display, including manuscripts, letters, essays and lectures by Merton and a notebook kept by his mother giving a detailed account of his life from birth to his second birthday. The room was a gift to the college from Dr. and Mrs. Irvin Abell, Jr. and Mr. and Mrs. Cornelius Hubbuch. Speaker for the occasion was Dr. Daniel Walsh, a close friend and former teacher of Merton at Columbia University, who named him

"Bellarmine's adopted son" and discussed "The Relevance of Thomas Merton's Writings to the 20th Century World." Fr. John Loftus, the chairman of the Merton Committee, said the college intended to become an international center for Merton studies. On November 9, 1969, the Thomas Merton Studies Center was formally established, with John Howard Griffin, author of *Black Like Me* and close friend of Merton, as speaker.

In the 1970s the Merton Center was moved to Bonaventure Hall, where it remained until 1997, when it was moved into special quarters in the Brown Library. Its mission is the same as it was when it opened: To preserve the Merton Collection, to promote the spiritual, contemplative and humanistic values central to Merton as revealed in his life and writings and to manifest in a special way the religious character of Bellarmine College. By the mid-'90s it contained more than 40,000 items in more than 28 languages and included works by and about Merton. Using the resources of the Merton Center, scholars have produced more than 60 books, 125 theses and dissertations and hundreds of articles and essays.

According to Fr. Horrigan, it was Fr. John Loftus who provided the initiative for the Merton Center. In the early '60s Fr. Loftus, who was a close friend of Merton, asked the monk if he would consider donating his papers to Bellarmine College. Merton agreed. "Fr. John's rationale was that Merton was a member of the Louisville Archdiocese and Bellarmine was the Archdiocesan college, thus the logical depository for his papers," says Fr. Horrigan. "He also saw Merton as a role model for students with his broad intellectual interests and his support of universal human rights. I quickly agreed that Bellarmine would be a good location for such a center. John was afraid that Merton would disperse his manuscripts and papers to the four winds, certainly to anyone who asked for them. He had already given the manuscript for *The Seven Storey Mountain* to a nun in Illinois whom he did not know simply because she asked for it."

As Fr. Horrigan details the procedure: "With John's urgings, then, I went through the proper channels and received the permission of the Archbishop, the abbot of

Gethsemani and finally Merton for the establishment of the Thomas Merton Studies Center. He was somewhat embarrassed about having a center for collecting his papers, but he finally agreed and, in fact, with a hyperbolical flourish decided to leave Bellarmine College his entire collection of papers. The Merton Legacy Trust had already been established to supervise the publication of his works and to serve as the depository for royalties."

Merton drew up a will some 13 months before his death on December 10, 1968, which specified Bellarmine as the principal depository of his papers. These included hundreds of unpublished works, including manuscripts, tape recordings, notes, calligraphy, drawings, journals, letters and photographs. His letters ranged from correspondence with ordinary people to a diverse assortment of famous people, including Pope Paul VI, Mrs. Robert F. Kennedy, Joan Baez, James Baldwin, Boris Pasternak, Martin Luther King and Henry Miller. After Merton's death the papers were sent to Bellarmine from the Abbey of Gethsemani, where he had lived for the last 27 years of his life.

His will also provided that all of his unpublished works be assigned to the Merton Legacy Trust, consisting then of three trustees: Naomi Burton Stone, his literary agent; his publisher James Laughlin of New Directions; and a close friend, Mrs. Frank (Tommie) O'Callaghan III. In an interview several months after his death, Mrs. O'Callaghan spoke of her family's close relationship with him. "When he had to come to Louisville to see doctors, as he often did for bursitis treatment, he always stopped by for a sandwich or a drink, depending on the time of day." He also helped her children with their homework. They called him Uncle Tom and were surprised when they discovered shortly before his death that he was a famous man. "Sometimes he'd call from Gethsemani and say, 'Tommie, so-and-so is coming in from New York today and I want you and Frank to meet him. Why don't you pack us a picnic lunch and drive down.' And we would."

The trust was given the power to copyright the works, publish them and set policy for the use of the collection. All income from his papers would go to the abbey. The will also stipulated that Bellarmine must never sell, give or dispose of any part of the donated materials. If so, the items would revert to the abbey. Some of the personal papers were to be restricted for 25 years, though they could be made available to a competent biographer. The will further stated that none of the autobiographical materials could ever be used for a film, radio or television dramatization. The will also gave to the trustees the literary rights to the materials he had already given away, but ownership would remain with the recipients.

Bellarmine's personal connections with Merton and the Abbey of Gethsemani go back to the college's early years, when a program of cooperation and sharing between the college and abbey was started. For example, as early as the fall of 1955 British sculptor Peter Watts, who was at Gethsemani to install a commissioned series of stations of the cross, lectured to Bellarmine students on Christian art and its significance to the Church.

Bellarmine's relationship with Merton goes back to the mid-'50s, when he was retreat master for the faculty at Gethsemani. Fr. Horrigan recalls his friendship with Merton: "Following our retreat at Gethsemani, I got to know Fr. Louis largely through my service as chaplain for the Carmelite Sisters. Frequently when Merton was in Louisville to see his doctor he would say Mass at the Carmelite Monastery a few blocks from the campus and we would have breakfast together. He had a great gift for making every person he spoke to feel special and important. He also had a wonderful smile and a kind of impish sense of humor. One morning at breakfast at Carmel, as he was telling me about the novices that he worked with as novice master at Gethsemani, he said, 'You know that in the traditional instruction in spirituality, novices are urged to learn to curb and control their passions; but I wish to God we'd get some novices that had passions that need to be curbed!'"

A number of other Bellarmine faculty have developed ties to the abbey and to Merton. Fr. Clyde Crews remembers fondly his encounter with Merton: "In the summer of 1968, when I was home from graduate school at Fordham, Fr. John Loftus invited me to dinner with Merton at the old Embers Restaurant on Shelbyville Road. The time I spent with Merton and John became even more special after both their deaths a few months later." When he was a Bellarmine student, Fr. George Kilcourse saw Merton several times in the library: "Then I met him the summer before his death. He asked me to go into the stacks and get him some books on James Joyce. What I remember about him physically is that he was shorter than I thought and that his sky-blue eyes were mesmerizing." Kilcourse, like Fr. Crews, is a member of the Bellarmine theology faculty, a Merton scholar and the author of *Ace of Freedoms: Thomas Merton's Christ*, which won an award from the International Thomas Merton Society in 1995.

Fr. Eugene Zoeller, also of the theology faculty, has had a close, warm relationship with the abbey and its monks. "In addition to lectures and seminars I have done there," he says, "I use it as my place of refuge. It is where I go to unburden myself and pray. Like my relationship to Bellarmine, it has been a grace." He remembers a special meeting with Merton on February 29, 1964, at the abbey. "My chalice had been stolen, and I commissioned a new one by a very good artist living in Switzerland. When it arrived, I realized that it was so nontraditional that our Archbishop would never consecrate it for me. But I knew of an old abbot from Belgium in residence at Gethsemani who delighted in doing rather offbeat things. I contacted him and, sure enough, he agreed to consecrate my chalice. During the ceremony Thomas Merton came in and stood beside me, obviously amused by the trappings of the abbot, who was dressed like a medieval bishop, and the elaborateness of the procedings. At the end he introduced himself to me and asked, 'Why did you bring it down here?' When I told him, he laughed and said, 'This is a splendid piece of liturgical art,' and showed me several pieces the abbey had by the same artist."

Ron Seitz

Ron Seitz, a poet and long-time professor of English at Bellarmine, had an especially close and warm friendship with Merton. In addition to a lengthy correspondence, Seitz and his wife Sally made frequent trips to visit Merton at Gethsemani, and Merton often spent time with them when he was in Louisville. In fact, Merton spent his last evening in Kentucky with them before he boarded the plane the next morning for the conference in Bangkok, from which he never returned. An article in *The Record* in June of 1972 quotes Seitz as saying that his close friendship with both Merton and John Howard Griffin "helped me away from the idea that I have to justify my existence by what I produce."

Griffin, the renowned author of *Black Like Me,* which was based on a seven-week tour of the Deep South in 1960 with the author disguised as a black man, was designated by the Merton Legacy trustees in 1969 to write Merton's official biography. In 1962, the year after the publication of *Black Like Me,* Griffin , a native of Texas, had met Merton during a visit to Gethsemani, and the two men had become good friends. Griffin had already achieved considerable fame as a fiction writer. A battle wound during World War II had left him blind for 11 years, but following brain surgery in 1957 he regained his sight and saw his wife and two children for the first time.

In 1973 he told a reporter for *The Record* that he had been spending about one week a month working at Merton's Hermitage at Gethsemani. He said that he had complete access to all of Merton's works and papers and estimated that he had completed one-third of the final draft and expected the book to be published the following fall. He had just published *A Hidden*

Wholeness: The Visual World of Thomas Merton, which featured drawings and photographs by Merton as well as photographs by Griffin. While he was on campus at Bellarmine in January and February of 1973 he conducted two short courses: "Thomas Merton: Man as Believer" and "Racism: 1973." Unfortunately, ill health prevented him from completing his book, and Michael Mott published the authorized biography, *The Seven Mountains of Thomas Merton,* in 1984.

Who was this man whose rich legacy is now so important a part of Bellarmine's identity? The biographical facts chronicle an odyssey of the spirit that began in Prades, France, where he was born on January 31, 1915, the son of Ruth Jenkins Merton, an American-born artist-designer, and her husband, Owen Merton, a New Zealand-born painter. It was a journey that led eventually to his final vocation as a Trappist monk in Kentucky. After his mother's death when he was six, Merton lived with his father, as well as other relatives and family friends, in Europe and America. He was educated in the United States, Bermuda, France and England, where he was graduated from Oakham School in 1933. He attended Clare College, Cambridge University, and received degrees from Columbia University, including an M. A. in English in 1938.

After several years of a bohemian lifestyle, he converted to Roman Catholicism in 1938. He applied for admission to the Franciscan order but was rejected. In 1939-40 he taught English at St. Bonaventure University in New York state; then on December 10, 1941, he joined the Order of Cistercians of the Strict Observance (the Trappists) and entered the Abbey of Our Lady of Gethsemani, near Bardstown, Kentucky, beginning a life based on prayer, silence and work. He was ordained a priest on May 26, 1949, assuming the religious name of Fr. Louis, and became a U. S. citizen at Louisville in 1951.

A writer before he became a Trappist, he continued to write as a part of his monastic vocation. His best-known book is his spiritual autobiography, *The Seven Storey Mountain,* 1948, which became an international best seller. In the 1960s he wrote on many topics of social justice, including racial conflict, genocide, nuclear armament, the Vietnam War, and The Third World. In 1965 he received permission to move into a small block cabin (called "The Hermitage") away from the main monastery buildings and live a life of solitude. His interest in non-Christian religions and cultures finally led him to attend a Buddhist-Christian conference on monasticism in 1968 near Bangkok, Thailand, where he died an accidental death by electrocution on December 10, when he touched an electric fan with faulty wiring. After hearing of Merton's death, Fr. John Loftus told a reporter for *The Courier-Journal* that meeting Merton at a luncheon in 1958 was "the beginning of one of the richest experiences of my life." He added, "I've spent most of my time since I heard of Merton's death drying the tears of kids around the college." Sadly, in less than a month Fr. John also died. Merton's body was returned and buried at the Abbey of Gethsemani.

The Merton Studies Center has had six directors since the appointment in 1970 of Fr. Alfred Pooler as part-time director. In 1972 the Rev. Raymond Bailey, a Baptist minister and professor of communication arts at the college, became the first full-time director. Fr. Treece became temporary acting director in the fall of 1973. He was followed in September of 1974 by Fr. Gervase Beyer, who served as acting director, and Dr. Robert Daggy, with degrees from Yale, Columbia and Wisconsin, as curator of the Merton Collection. In June of 1976 Fr. Clyde Crews became director and Daggy associate director and later director. During his tenure Daggy was instrumental in spreading the Merton legacy to an ever wider audience. Following his death in December of 1997, Dr. Theresa Sandok, a professor of philosophy and dean of the College of Arts and Sciences, was appointed director. She was followed in 1998 by Jonathan Montaldo, an editor of Thomas Merton's private journals. In the same year Robert G. Toth was appointed executive director of The Thomas Merton Studies Center Foundation.

Except for a short period when they reported to the director of the library, the Merton Center directors have reported directly to the academic vice president.

Since its foundation the Merton Center has sponsored classes, seminars, exhibits, lectures, workshops, readings and conferences related to Merton and Merton-based subjects. During the spring of 1967, for example, a six-week seminar on Merton as artist, philosopher and poet was held on campus, with lectures by Dr. Daniel Walsh, Dr. John Ford and *Courier-Journal* art critic Sarah Lansdell. In November 1968 *Courier-Journal* critic Jean Dietrich called a campus performance of the "John Jacob Niles-Thomas Merton Song Cycle" an "inspired collaboration." To honor Merton's birthday in February of 1971 the Center sponsored an exhibit of works by Louisville artist Ulfert Wilke which were inspired, he said, by his friendship with Merton.

Throughout the '70s and '80s there were ecumenical workshops and lectures featuring representatives from Catholic, Protestant and Jewish groups on topics ranging from spirituality and human rights to alcoholism and drug addiction. On the 10th anniversary of Merton's death in December of 1978, a week of commemoration included a lecture by the priest-sociologist Fr. Andrew Greeley. Other center-sponsored lecturers included novelist Guy Owen, author Rollo May, and Rabbi Marc Tannenbaum. In 1987 the center formed the International Thomas Merton Society, and in 1989 hosted its first meeting on campus for some 300 scholars and admirers from around the world.

Under the leadership of directors Daggy and Sandok and, now, Montaldo, activities of the Merton Center during the '90s have been innovative and varied. The 1993-94 academic year was designated "The Merton Year" to commemorate the 25th anniversary of his death. Events included seminars, liturgies, lectures and a final conference at Bellarmine in the spring entitled "The Human Way Out," which attracted an international group of scholars from the United States, Canada, Europe and Asia. To encourage student

Dr. Robert Daggy, Curator of the Thomas Merton Center.

awareness of the Merton legacy, the college sponsored a series of Merton weekend retreats at Gethsemani in 1994, 1996 and 1997. Elderhostel "Weeks with Thomas Merton" offer guests from throughout the United States an opportunity to read and study the legacy of Merton. The center publishes a widely circulated quarterly review, *The Merton Seasonal,* as well as occasional papers. Daggy edited and prefaced numerous books related to Merton and gave countless talks before scholarly, religious and civic groups. Sandok added more dimensions to the center's activities, including the Thomas Merton Poetry Competition, which invites submissions of sacred poetry for an annual prize. The Gethsemani connection for the project is Br. Paul Quenon, a poet who had been a novice under Merton in the 1960s.

And yet there is much to be done to exploit the full potential of Merton's legacy to Bellarmine College. When he arrived on campus in the early '90s, former academic vice president David House said that "one of the things that attracted me to Bellarmine was the Merton Center," but, he said, much needed to be done to exploit its potential. "I certainly don't think that Bellarmine should build a shrine to Thomas Merton, but I do think the college should take his ideas and interests and develop them into programs that carry

forward his legacy. We should be doing conferences on such topics as interchurch families and peace in the post-Cold War world. We should have a Merton chair that would bring scholars to campus for a semester or two each year. We should offer courses that capitalize on Merton's broad, interdisciplinary interests. We could have courses like the history of the spiritual autobiography from Augustine to Merton, culminating with students writing their own self-narrative."

Fr. Kilcourse echoes many of Dr. House's concerns. "We are always in jeopardy of fostering a cult of Merton and not doing what we should be doing, that is, pursuing his interests in a kind of Post-Merton era—interests such as peacemaking, spirituality, ecumenism, East-West relations. I think the center should be a place not only for scholars to do research but where scholars can come and work through questions and establish positions on topics and issues. And we must always remember the danger that Bellarmine will simply exploit our connection with Merton. We should, instead, seek to be a cultural lightning rod. With more and more imagination we will realize more and more of the Merton Center's great potential."

Former philosophy professor and former Metroversity director Jack Ford calls the Center "a tremendous resource for Bellarmine College" but one that "has been underutilized" and in need of "a much broader scope." That scope would probably not have included renaming the college for Thomas Merton, as was seriously proposed in the early '70s during discussions of a permanent name for what was then Bellarmine-Ursuline College. "Had Merton been alive and consulted," Ford opines, "I think he would have allowed it, but I think his first reaction would have been to laugh."

Indeed, in the several years since Dr. House, Fr. Kilcourse and Dr. Ford voiced their opinions, the Merton Center under Dr. Sandok and Mr. Montaldo has broadened its scope, become more imaginative, and with its handsome new quarters in the Brown

Library, at last it has a home worthy of its calling and its mission. In fact, the college statement read at the center's dedication in 1969 has been on target all the time: "The purpose of the center is not to build a Merton cult; rather it is to continue his work in a special way. By bringing knowledgeable people together; by allowing them to share ideas, perspectives and experiences, the center seeks new directions and reaffirms enduring values for contemporary man . . . in the light of Merton's vision." It is one of the jewels in the Bellarmine crown.

In Conclusion. . .

Bellarmine College has truly been blessed by the quality of its library services from the first day of the first semester of the first year of classes on October 3, 1950. The library has grown, along with the college, from its small space in Pasteur Hall to a larger space in Horrigan Hall to its grand space in the sparkling new W. L. Lyons Brown Library. It also has grown in beauty, in comfort, in efficiency. But there is still work to be done—more collection building, additional periodicals, additional professional staff.

Like everyone else today, librarians know they will have to run to stay caught up with the future. Joan Wettig, now retired and able to view past and present with some objectivity, looks toward the future with hope and humanity: "Library forecasters say that librarians of the future will no longer brag about how many people come into the library. Instead, they will brag about how many people don't have to come into the library to find information they want. I don't especially like our new designation as 'information specialists,' but I am excited about the information accessibility made possible by the new technology. I hope, however, that nothing will ever replace the excitement of opening and reading an old-fashioned book." Indeed, as we all know, some pleasures are not determined by time or place or technology. Some pleasures are eternal.

THOMAS MERTON

A Retreat at Gethsemani

sponsored by
BELLARMINE COLLEGE

'The Human Way Out'

A Thomas Merton Conference

Selections with an introduction by George A. Kilcourse, Jr.

Support Groups

Shortly after resigning the presidency of Bellarmine College in 1972, Fr. Alfred Horrigan published an article in the Sunday *Courier-Journal & Times* in which he surveyed the financial problems of his tenure. First, he recounted an article that appeared in *The New York Times* the first week of October in 1949, "the same week I was appointed President of Bellarmine College. The main conclusions of the article were that many American colleges and universities were in serious financial straits, with some 20 per cent of private institutions operating on a deficit, and that many of them would have to do severe retrenching, discharging faculty members and eliminating courses."

Despite the negative forecast for higher education, however, Fr. Horrigan headed into his new venture with confidence and optimism. While many older and better financed institutions faltered along the rocky way, Bellarmine College managed to survive and thrive. "The point is that the good independent colleges," he wrote with the hindsight of his 23-year tenure as President, "through good years and bad, have proved themselves among the most sturdy of all social institutions. They have coped. They have confronted problems and solved them. In the face of the variety of crises that the revolving seasons have brought, they have grown and enhanced the value of their distinctive contribution to American society."

Although funds for the college have come from different sources and some have been earmarked for special projects such as scholarships and building construction, they are all part of the same package that has kept the college open and solvent for half a

century. The major financial sources include tuition and fees, funds for capital projects, funds raised for endowment, endowment income, government grants and loans, subsidiary enterprises, annual giving and funds raised by special support groups.

From the beginning administrators realized that the college could not be supported by tuition alone. An article in *The Record* in May of 1952 reported that the first building on campus, the science building (later to become Pasteur Hall), had cost more than $375,000. The report also stated that the average cost per student for the previous academic year was $530, while the average income from each student for tuition and fees was $350. A 1960 college fact sheet updated the support statistics. At that time student tuition and fees accounted for 61 per cent of college revenue, with the remainder coming from such sources as corporations and foundations, the Kentucky Independent College Foundation (KICF), the Archdiocesan Advent Collection, the Bellarmine Parents Fund, the Alumni Endowment Fund, the United Student Fund, the Bellarmine Foundation and the College Athletic Association. In addition, the contributed services of the priest members of the faculty represented 14.9 per cent of college income. In other words, the 33 per cent deficit between income from students and college expenses in 1951-52 had risen to almost 40 per cent in eight years. It was a percentage that would continue to rise and an amount that had to be made up from other sources.

At a planning conference following the cornerstone-laying ceremonies for the new auditorium-gymnasism (now Knights Hall) on May 19, 1960, Fr.

Horrigan suggested a plan for a unified fund drive for operational support under which various college groups would launch their fund drives at the same time. He set an optimistic goal of $168,200. Gift income, said the President, was absolutely necessary to keep

the college open. There was already a development office in operation. Opened in the fall of 1956 and headed by the Rev. Henry B. Schuhmann, it was an umbrella office for five college operations: public and community relations, publicity, alumni, student recruitment and placement and fund

The Rev. Henry B. Schuhmann

raising. By 1961 the most important gift channels included the following: the Bellarmine Foundation, whose members donated $100 or more annually; the Bellarmine Foundation Associates, whose members contributed from $10 to $100 each; the Annual Parish Collection, which was taken throughout the Archdiocese to aid Bellarmine and the Catholic University of America; the Alumni Association, which was begun following the first graduation in 1954; the Bellarmine Parents Fund, which was begun in 1959 and the Student Fund, which started in 1957. Meanwhile, the operations budget was growing and for the first time topped one million dollars for the 1961-62 budget year. By the fall of 1963 the full-time faculty included 40 laypersons and 25 priests, whose contributed services were worth $134,000. Nevertheless, according to Fr. Horrigan, the college had to raise some $177,000 for the 1963-64 academic year in order to balance the operating budget. By the next budget year the budget had risen to more than $1,750,000. Small wonder that Fr. Horrigan told a *Louisville Times* reporter in April of 1965 that money-raising was "a very central and a very grim factor" of his job as President.

  As the '60s progressed and the '70s began, especially during the seven years following the merger

Dr. J. Duffy Hancock, chair, Board of Overseers, Msgr. Alfred F. Horrigan, Bellarmine President, and Mr. Bart A. Brown, Sr., Foundation Committee chair, December 1958.

with Ursuline College in 1968, declining enrollments and a growing deficit meant financial crises which meant extensive budget cuts which meant program and faculty reductions. It was an exhausted President who said in an interview in *The Record*, just after he had announced his resignation in May of 1972, that for 23 years he had been "ringing doorbells, in one form or another."

  The task of turning Bellarmine around and putting it on solid fiscal ground was placed on the shoulders of Eugene Petrik, who became President in 1973. To help eliminate budget deficits from the three previous years, in the fall of 1975 tuition was raised from $50 to $60 per semester hour; and all forms of fund raising were accelerated. The results were striking and little short of miraculous. Operating budgets were soon balanced, and by the fall of 1981 the college endowment had grown to more than $2,300,000. The financial picture would get brighter as Petrik's administration lengthened to 17 years. In 1990 Joseph J. McGowan took over the presidency of a college with a bright future but with challenges and problems enough to keep him ringing doorbells as his two predecessors had done. By the mid-'90s the college's financial base was becoming strong, as the debt-to-equity ratio dipped to a very modest eight percent and net assets climbed to more than $36 million. The 1994-95 fiscal year ended with an operations surplus of more than $960,000, which was used for much-needed capital purchases and debt retirement.

Not only have independent colleges like Bellarmine coped and survived because of their unique place in American education but because they have had the generous patronage of groups and individuals. Indeed, the support groups for Bellarmine College range from the Archdiocese and the Board of Overseers to the Women's Council, the President's Civic Council and, after the first graduating class, an active and faithful alumni association. Surely, few colleges can boast greater loyalty among its constituency. Starting with no endowment at its founding in 1950, Bellarmine College ranked, as of June 30, 1999, with an endowment of almost $18 million, 15th among Kentucky and Indiana colleges and universities and 444th nationally.

Bellarmine's financial solvency has been made possible not only by its generous supporters but by its careful and efficient use of its resources. Although a comparison of costs per student at different institutions is a bit like comparing apples and bananas, Bellarmine has a proven track record of judicious spending. A letter to *The Courier-Journal* in 1979 noted that during the previous academic year at the University of Louisville the cost per student was about $9,500 while at Bellarmine the cost was only $1,600. "Maybe it's time to bus some Belknap campus managers [to Bellarmine] for an in-depth study in practical education management and tender loving care of taxpayers' dollars," wrote Emil A. Graeser of Louisville. Perhaps the administration's close watch on the bottom line helps to explain the consistently low rate of student loan defaults among Bellarmine students and alumni—usually the lowest of any college in Kentucky.

Another factor in Bellarmine's slow but generally steady progress toward financial stability has been the contributed services by members of religious communities, usually in the form of priests and nuns who served as faculty members, particularly during the first quarter of the college's history. The early support of the Franciscans was vital to Bellarmine. One could hardly imagine the college without the presence of Franciscan administrators and faculty like Fr. John Loftus, Fr. Killian Speckner, Fr. Hilary Gottbrath and Fr. Jeremiah Smith. Financial officer Jack Kampschaefer emphasized the early advantage of such support: "In the early years almost all of the full-time faculty were priests; and with their contributed services the cost was considerably below that of lay faculty, 25 to 35 per cent less. As the percentage of priests declined and the lay faculty grew, our cost of instruction went up tremendously."

Nevertheless, the financial history of Bellarmine has been one of constant struggle, near disaster and slow progress. The college had the advantage of founding fathers who were realists and believed that the Lord would provide for those who work hard. In a statement published in November of 1949 in *The Record*, Fathers Horrigan and Treece described the prospects for the new college in these bold words: "To launch a new college at this time is to undertake a project involving the most formidable difficulties. The serene optimism which we entertain for the future of Bellarmine College does not derive from any lack of realism about the magnitude of these difficulties. Rather, it is based on our confidence in the loyal and unstinted support of our people which we know will be given to the college."

Here is a closer look at the groups who have provided vital support to Bellarmine over its first half century. When Bellarmine opened in 1950, it had no alumni and no endowment and stopgap measures had to be taken to keep the college afloat until a permanent financial cushion could be built. Funds raised in Archdiocesan capital fund drives could be used only

Robert Fitzpatrick and Fr. Raymond Treece

for construction, not day-to-day expenses. Founded in the fall of 1958 by the Board of Overseers to provide additional operating funds, the Bellarmine Foundation took as its first goal to raise a sum equivalent to the income from a $1 million endowment. This was achieved when 375 charter members donated some $40,000 for Bellarmine's immediate use. Chaired by Bart A. Brown, who was assisted by Louis A. Arru, Cornelius E. Hubbuch and George M. Goetz, the foundation provided funds for faculty salaries, scholarships, student loans as well as library and science equipment. By 1963 the foundation was raising some $68,000 a year.

Smaller groups from inside and outside the college have made significant contributions to the college's financial well-being, usually targeting particular programs and projects. Grants and awards have come from dozens, perhaps hundreds, of sources, ranging from the the local James Graham Brown Foundation and the Humana Foundation to DeRance, Inc., a Wisconsin private foundation, which awarded the Thomas Merton Studies Center $8,000 in 1973 for operational expenses. During the '50s the college received modest grants from such private foundations as the Esso Education Foundation in New York and the Union Carbide Corporation, each of which gave

the college $2,000 in the fall of 1959. In the early '50s an award of $5,000 was made from the Time Finance Company of Louisville to support the business program, and the D. J. Maloney family gave $500 to the College Athletic Fund. Some Louisville businesses—Office Equipment Company, the Tafel Electric & Supply Company and Hubbuch in Kentucky—made donations of badly needed equipment and furnishings.

Throughout the '50s and '60s such support filled gaps in college funding. Frequent small grants, ranging from $1,000 to $20,000, came from such giant corporations as Gulf Oil, the Kresge Company, the United States Steel Corporation, International Harvester, Texaco, Sears, Roebuck & Company and such local businesses as the Brown-Forman Distillers Corporation, Standard Oil of Kentucky and WAVE Radio. In 1956 the Keeneland Foundation of Lexington, with proceeds from races and sales of Thoroughbred horses, made a gift of $1,000. In 1958 the Raskob Foundation of Wilmington, Delaware, provided $10,000 for the purchase of lab equipment to expand the physics program. The college has also been the frequent beneficiary of estate bequests, such as $2,000 from the estate of Miss Eleanor M. Lenihan, whose brothers had founded Time Finance Company.

One of the most unusual gifts came in April of 1953 from Truck Drivers Local 89, which voted to give Bellarmine $25,000 to establish a program in labor relations as a memorial to the late head of the A.F. of L. local, Pat Ansboury. At that time it was the largest private donation to the college. The grant designated $15,000 for books in the field of labor relations and $10,000 for a labor relations classroom to be located in the administration building then under construction. In February of 1955 the Patrick Ansboury Memorial Classroom was duly dedicated.

In the '70s and '80s such miscellaneous grants increased in number and amounts, though small grants, such as $500 from the Kentucky Arts Council to the *Kentucky Poetry Review*, published at Bellarmine, were still welcome. In May of 1970 the college received a $10,000 grant from the Southeastern Region of the Fraternal Order of Eagles for cancer research and the construction of a greenhouse. In the early '70s the W. K. Kellogg Foundation provided a grant of $5,000 to support environmental studies, and the International Harvester Foundation gave an unrestricted grant of $5,000. In 1976 the college received an award of $150,000 from the James Graham Brown Foundation, and in the fall of 1982 the Capital Holding Corporation donated $250,000 to support the computer science program.

A generous donation from Wilson W. Wyatt, Sr. in the late '70s supported the Wyatt Fellowship of Academic Excellence, which recognized one student and one faculty member each year with a cash award. In the mid-'70s Col. Harland Sanders underwrote a number of academic scholarships. With support from several sources, a two-year Associate of Arts degree of computer science was begun in 1974 and a four-year program in 1980. By 1982 there were 150 students in the computer science program.

Louisville corporations and business and professional people were especially generous to the Bellarmine business programs. In November of 1982 the Brown & Williamson Tobacco Corporation made a $200,000 grant to establish the Brown & Williamson Chair of Business Administration in the Rubel School of Business. To honor an early supporter of the college, the business school was named the W. Fielding Rubel School of Business. Rubel, who served the college as a trustee, a fund raiser and donor, performed the first open-heart surgery in Kentucky in 1960. He died in April of 1983 at age 58 of coronary disease. In the fall of 1983 the First National Bank made a grant of $125,000 to the Small Business Development Center.

The generosity of the business and professional community has continued into the '90s. In the fall of 1991 the Knight Foundation provided $250,000 for faculty development, and for several years Philip Morris

USA has given large grants for minority scholarships. Philanthropy by individuals is well represented by the Jayne L. and Arthur N. BecVar Endowed Nursing Scholarships, established in 1996 by the former Bellarmine Women's Council president and her husband, a retired executive at General Electric.

In recent years foundations and individuals have been especially generous to the college and made possible the reshaping of the campus. The new library was made possible by the W. L. Lyons Brown Foundation and the Brown and Frazier families. Major gifts have been received from David and Betty Jones and the Humana Foundation for library and faculty development. The James Graham Brown Foundation has made three recent gifts of $750,000 each for technology support and an additional gift for the Campus Center. The Paul Ogle Foundation has made significant contributions to the library, to improvements in technology and to the Campus Center. Gifts also have been received recently from the Cralle Foundation and Kresge Foundation. Earlier gifts from the Norton family made possible the construction of the arts complex. Several anonymous gifts have been made for the construction of the new chapel.

College-related groups have been faithful donors to campus programs and projects. During the first academic year, the Bellarmine Parents Association was formed and remained for many years a strong financial and public supporter of the college. Parents Weekend provided special opportunities for parents and their sons and daughters to enjoy a weekend on campus together. Activities in the fall of 1977 included an afternoon at the races, a cocktail party, a banquet and a Parents Mass. The tradition has been revived and strengthened during the McGowan administration.

Even students were tapped for contributions during the annual Student Fund Drives in the '50s and '60s. Students contributed more than $1,500 in cash for building the college gym. Almost all of the students—more than 95.5 per cent—participated. The kickoff for the drive was held in the college cafeteria and sweetened by a 50-pound cake sent as a gift by Cornelius E. Hubbuch, chairman of the special gifts division. In January of 1964 the Student Fund Drive announced it had received pledges of $3,500, with 86 per cent of the student body participating and an average of $4.25 per student.

Campus enterprises also provided funds for designated programs. In December of 1964 calligraphic drawings by Thomas Merton (he called the spontaneous ink drawings "signatures") were exhibited at Catherine Spalding College and sold to benefit scholarships at Spalding and Bellarmine. By 1975 the Bellarmine College Singers were holding spaghetti dinners in the college cafeteria to raise money for their annual tours. By the fall of 1979 almost 60 per cent of campus athletic expenses were being paid for by profits from weekly bingo games held in Knights Hall.

In November of 1983 Joshua B. "Uncle Josh" Everett was awarded an honorary Doctor of Letters degree by the college and received the accolades of dozens of Bellarmine alumni who had benefited from the summer scholarships program to British universities sponsored by the Kentucky Branch of the English-Speaking Union, which he headed for many years. Melanie L. Votaw, who had studied at the University of London, wrote from her home in New York, "Thanks to Uncle Josh, I was able in 1981 to experience something I would never have been able to do on my own."

Since 1975 the department of education at Bellarmine has received generous grants from the WHAS Crusade for Children for use in curriculum development, scholarships and other needs of the program for exceptional children.

Support groups, of course, have done much more than raise money for Bellarmine. They have, sometimes more importantly, raised Bellarmine's name in the community in a positive way. The Bellarmine College Faculty Wives Association, which was very active in the '60s, not only supported campus projects but spread out to support the cultural life of the community. In January of 1965, for example, some 60 wives and their husbands—plus about 50 Bellarmine students—attended a special performance of Actors Theatre of Louisville's *The Glass Menagerie* and a cast party afterwards.

One of the most crucial support groups is the ever-growing alumni, now numbering more than 10,000, many of whom work for their alma mater through the Bellarmine Alumni Association. For almost 50 years they have helped raise hundreds of thousands of dollars—either directly or indirectly—and they have influenced thousands of young people to attend Bellarmine. In Louisville they have helped create a Bellarmine-friendly community.

For their size their fund-raising success has been impressive. During the '50s the alumni fund drives usually yielded in the low thousands of dollars. By the mid-'60s the annual yield was above $10,000. In 1964 in the second annual Louisville-area alumni fund drive, Bellarmine's alumni raised more than $12,000, second only to Centre's $13,000. Chaired by George Brinkhaus, '65, in 1966 the drive netted some $18,000 from over 1,200 alumni in 40 states and nine foreign countries. Three years later the goal had risen to $30,000. By the '80s students were joining alumni in the annual Phon-A-Thon, raising more than $265,000 in 1983 in a special campaign.

In February of 1952 Bellarmine joined with seven other Kentucky independent colleges to form the Kentucky Independent College Foundation (KICF), a nonprofit corporation to raise funds from private business and industry. The foundation's mission was to seek annual large gifts to be distributed to its member institutions, while allowing them to pursue their own channels of fund raising. The foundation used a number of appeals in seeking funds from the private sector: the quality of their education, their concentration on the individual, their role as laboratories for new educational development, their values-oriented emphasis and their independence from government control.

The initial fund-raising goals were modest. During the first year the foundation raised $56,000 for the eight member colleges. In 1958 the total had reached $68,000. By 1960 the foundation had raised more than $100,000 from some 600 Kentucky businesses and industries. But the foundation aided its members in other ways. In 1958, for example, it published a job placement directory to acquaint prospective employers with the work qualifications of the seniors graduating from the independent schools. Moreover, the KICF has become a lobbying influence during legislative sessions in Frankfort, particularly when legislation affecting higher education is offered.

Perhaps its most important influence has been to make the public aware of the role played by independent colleges in American society. Throughout his presidency at Bellarmine, Fr. Horrigan made persuasive appeals before business and professional clubs, women's clubs, religious groups and in public statements for support of Kentucky's independent colleges. At the request of the KICF numerous business and professional people have become spokesmen for the member colleges. Thomas A. Ballantine, president of the Louisville Taxicab and Transfer Company, wrote in June 1953 a supporting apologia: "The years have proven the worth of these independent, liberal-arts colleges whose graduates have become a large part of the leadership of our state's economic, political and religious life," with, he said, approximately half of the leadership of the state coming from these colleges. "It is not a matter of charity," he concluded. "It is a matter of investment." That was just the message that Kentucky's independent colleges wanted to get across.

Without the support of the Archdiocese of Louisville and its Archbishops Floersh, McDonough and Kelly, there would have been no Bellarmine College founded in 1950 and there would be no Bellarmine College today. Throughout his tenure as President,

Fr. Horrigan emphasized that the founding, nurture and progress of Bellarmine had been made possible by the generous support of the Archbishops and the people of the Archdiocese.

Indeed, like Catholic schools at all levels, from elementary grades through graduate school, Bellarmine College has benefited from the support of the faithful—through donations, scholarships, and most importantly, the contributed services of religious teachers. In the November 1955 issue of the college newsletter, Fr. Horrigan wrote: "The real secret of the successful financial operation of the gigantic . . . Catholic school system in the United States has been the religious teacher. The priests, brothers and sisters have consecrated themselves to a permanent life of poverty, chastity and obedience."

Through annual donations and special fund drives, the Archdiocese of Louisville, especially during its first two decades, sustained the college and made it possible for the fledging institution to become strong and gradually self-supporting. In fact, the first funds raised for the college were part of a general Archdiocesan effort conducted in 1942, more than seven years before ground was broken for the first building. One of the most visible examples of early Archdiocesan support was the First Sunday in Advent Collection for Catholic University and Bellarmine College. In an open letter to the Catholic community dated November 21, 1951, Archbishop Floersh announced that the proceeds of a special collection to be taken up in all Archdiocesan churches on December 2 would go as usual to Catholic University as well as "our own Bellarmine College." That year Phillip Hall was about 13 and a member of the Holy Name Society at St. Benedict's Church in Louisville's West End. "I was given about 10 pledge cards and assigned to solicit pledges from members of the parish on Kentucky Street between 22nd and 25th," he recalls. "I only got two pledges, but everyone agreed that a Catholic college for boys in Louisville was a good idea."

By 1954 the annual donation for Bellarmine had reached $16,500. In his annual Advent letter in 1959 soliciting educational funds, Archbishop Floersh wrote: "Bellarmine College, now in its tenth year, is still a very young school. Yet it has filled a very great need in the local school picture. By your sacrifices you have made it a success up to this point. The benefits which

(L to R) Mrs. Cornelius Hubbuch, Mrs. Kenneth Barker, Mrs. Robert Nolan and Mr. Cornelius Hubbuch at the first Designers' Show House, the Lemon Estate.

it brings to the Catholic community are such that it deserves the support of all the faithful." Although the necessity of such support would eventually wane as Bellarmine was able to tap other donors, Archbishops McDonough and Kelly continued the Advent offering for higher education, with Spalding College and St. Catharine College joining the beneficiaries by the early '80s.

In the 1950s the Archdiocese enabled much of the campus construction through the Archbishop's Educational Program. In November of 1956 he called an educational development conference at the fairgrounds coliseum with more than 1,000 laymen and priests present. Its purpose, according to the letter of

invitation, was to consider problems and challenges in the burgeoning Catholic school system. At the conference the Archbishop announced plans for a fund drive to raise $3,500,000 for capital improvements at Bellarmine College and at Catholic boys high schools in the Archdiocese. Bellarmine's share in the amount of $1,650,000 would be used to build an auditorium-gymnasium, student dormitories, additional classroom space and faculty living quarters as well as payments on the college debt and funds for scholarships and faculty salaries. In applauding work at Bellarmine, the Archbishop said, "It is a miracle that small Catholic colleges like Bellarmine accomplish so much on so little, since they frequently operate on a shoestring, on shoes that are not paid for."

Campaign chairman was B. J. Lenihan, assisted by T. V. Hartnett and Cornelius Hubbuch, who headed special divisions of the drive. The campaign headquarters were at Bellarmine, where various "sales sessions" for fund raisers were held. The salesmanship, the appeals and the strategy paid off. In May of 1957 Archbishop Floersh announced that with the aid of more than 7,500 lay volunteers, the Educational Development Program had topped its goal and raised more than $3,650,000. At the same time Bellarmine's own Educational Development Campaign had raised more than half a million dollars from industrial and business donors in Louisville.

In addition, the Archdiocese made a number of construction loans to the college. The value of Archdiocesan support, however, cannot be measured simply in terms of dollars. The very existence of the college was justified by its relationship to the Archdiocese. As the college has grown, it has become a source of great pride for all the faithful. In its early days whenever a distinguished visitor came to town to visit Archbishop Floersh, the Archbishop brought him out to see his new college, then hardly more than a handful of students, a dozen or so faculty and one small building. Imagine what delight he would take in a visit today to the handsome campus that has grown from the seed he planted.

No little support has been provided by the governing boards and committees of the college. The original bylaws provided for a Board of Visitors of 11 members selected from the Archdiocesan clergy. The Board of Visitors was charged with the responsibility for the college as a corporate entity, the determination of the general educational policies of the college and the financial matters, including annual budgets.

The Board of Overseers was organized on March 4, 1954, as an advisory and fund-raising body appointed by the Archbishop. Its first chairman was Bernard J. Lenihan, a Chicago native who moved to Louisville in 1940 and founded Time Finance Company, a chain of 70 loan offices in seven states. Early on, he took a special interest in Bellarmine and helped bring the college through its early formative years. Serving as board chairman for six years, he headed a dedicated group of men that included Paul Tafel, Cyril J. Deutsch, Robert T. Burke, Jr., William P. Kelly, Bart A. Brown, Sr., David Erle Maloney, J. Gordon Baquie, John F. Oertel and George Goetz—all of whom gave their

money and their time to ensure that the college would survive.

Other leading Louisville businessmen who have headed the Board of Overseers include Timothy V. Hartnett, J. Duffy Hancock, Louis A. Arru and James K. Booher. Originally made up of men only, women began to join the board in the '70s and in the early '80s women like Marty Dryer Guarnaschelli and Louisa Mapother were valuable members. The help of such business and community leaders was essential to the college because, as Fr. Horrigan recalls, "We had no great Catholic wealth in Louisville that we could draw on for major support. We had no million dollar donors." One of the principal Board of Overseers outreaches has been its sponsorship of the Bellarmine Medal Award and Dinner, which has brought world-class visitors to campus since its inception in 1955.

According to Fr. Horrigan, in the early days major policy decisions were made by an executive committee of the administration. Actually, says Fr. Treece, that "executive committee" usually consisted of him and Fr. Horrigan in consultation with the Archbishop. Indeed, Fr. Horrigan said, "For the first six years the college was not independently incorporated. Rather, we were a part of the corporation of the Archdiocese of Louisville. As we approached the time for our accreditation study, however, I suggested to the Archbishop that the accreditation committee might look upon us with more favor if we had a separate corporate identity; and he agreed. At that time the Board of Visitors became the governing body.

Following Vatican II, laymen were named to the Board of Visitors for the first time. In accord with the council's decrees on the expanded role of the laity in the Church and its institutions, in July of 1965 the Board of

First Board of Overseers, 1954.

Mr. Maurice D. S. Johnson

*Three former chairs of the
Bellarmine College Board of Trustees*

Mr. & Mrs. Kenneth Barker

Hon. Wilson W. Wyatt

Overseers elected two members, George Goetz and Cornelius Hubbuch, to serve with voting powers on the Board of Visitors. Later in the same year, Ursuline named Kenneth A. Barker, Jr., president of Louisville Asphalt Company, and James L. Meagher, president of Stratton & Terstegge Company, to its Board of Trustees. Both men would serve the newly merged Bellarmine-Ursuline College after the 1968 merger. In June of 1967 laymen were given majority representation on the Board of Visitors, which was soon renamed the Board of Trustees, and in May of 1969 Kenneth A. Barker, Jr. became the first layman to serve as chairman of the board. Mr. Bart A. Brown, Sr. had been elected interim chairman at the organizational meeting of the Board on May 13, 1968 and served until May 31 when Archbishop McDonough was elected chairman. At the same time David L. Chervenak became the first alumnus to serve as a trustee. Also elected was Maurice D. S. Johnson, president of Citizens Fidelity Bank & Trust Company and a non-Catholic, who later became board chairman.

Five years later Louisville attorney and former mayor Wilson W. Wyatt, Sr. was elected to the board. During the administration of Presidents Petrik and McGowan board membership was expanded to include the elite of Louisville's business and professional leadership. Board chairman Owsley Brown Frazier said

that from the start Petrik's intention was to build a Board of Trustees that would rival that of any other college. By the fall of 1996, it was done. At that time Frazier said, "We have the cream of the crop of Louisville's leaders associated with the college," and pointed to the presidents of the city's four largest banks, the CEOs of several major corporations and the heads of the three leading law firms as examples of the success.

Indeed, Bellarmine College has always been fortunate in the support it has received from the business and professional community. Men and women have served tirelessly on its boards and councils and committees and fund drives. In the fall of 1968, during the lean years following the Bellarmine and Ursuline merger, Cornelius E. Hubbuch headed the President's Society drive to raise $85,000 to help defray expenses during the first year of the new institution. At the same time James K. Booher headed the Bellarmine-Ursuline Foundation, which raised some $100,000.

Fortunately, when the merger occurred in 1968, one of the college's most visible, imaginative and hardest-working support groups was already in place. In April of 1963 the Bellarmine Women's Council had been organized to serve as a medium of contact between the college and the community, to advise and assist in the promotion of its cultural activities, to support the library and, added later, to raise funds for student scholarships. Mrs. Kenneth A. Barker, the first president, led an impressive roster of directors, including Mrs. B. J. Lenihan, Mrs. Emmett A. Ratterman, Mrs. L. A. Arru, Mrs. C. E. Hubbuch, Mrs. Fred J. Karem and Mrs. James U. Smith, Jr. The first five Women's Council presidents remain active in college life today. The "fearsome five" include: Mrs. Bunny Barker, Mrs. Marge Smith, Mrs. Barbara Montgomery, Mrs. Jayne BecVar, and Mrs. Rose Lenihan. Their first major gift to the college was a 52-cup silver coffee urn and tray to be used for formal occasions. It was first put to use at a Christmas reception in 1964. A year later the council gave the college a pair of silver candelabra to complement the earlier gift. This was only the beginning of their service to Bellarmine.

To fulfill its pledge to be a bridge between college and community, in November of 1963 the council sponsored its first Town and Gown Week, which included public lectures, an art exhibit, a performance by the College Glee Club, films and various exhibits. A feature of the week was a lecture by Louisville Chief of Police C. J. Hyde on prostitution, which he said he opposed legalizing. The special weeks continued into the '70s. In 1970 the Town and Gown Week theme was "Education: Bridge to Brotherhood" and featured a production of *A Raisin in the Sun* by African-American playwright Lorraine Hansberry. The cast, which included local television personalities Faith Lyles and Cara Lewis, was itself a bridge between college and community. The week also featured the premiere performance of Don Murray's *Seeds of Contemplation,* based on a text by Thomas Merton.

The council has also provided dozens of volunteer library aides, co-sponsored a benefit performance (with the Walden School) of the Peking Opera Theatre at Memorial Auditorium in 1980; and their annual book fairs, Halloween haunted houses and designer show houses have provided over a million

dollars for the library and student scholarships. Since the annual book fair began in 1973, donations and library discards of books, recordings, magazines and art works have been recycled into student, faculty and community collections.

The council's first fund-raising project, however, was a spine-tingling haunted house, which opened during the Halloween season in 1969 in an old barn on the former Collings estate near the Louisville Zoo. More than 25,000 people toured Louisville's "original haunted house," leaving behind first year profits of $11,150. The second year brought in some 40,000 daredevils and reaped a profit of $17,000. Exhibits included hair-raising monsters, witches, ghosts, black cats, werewolves, as well as Puff the Magic Dragon, The Green Scaly Monster and The Spider, designed by artist Walter Pitt and created by Mrs. George Dumstorf and Mrs. Robert L. Dentinger.

In 1971 the Halloween theme was "Spooks in Space" and featured robot spooks, a space chicken and Frankenstein in a space helmet. The luncheon menu consisted of Witches Brew with Tombstone Garnish (actually, tomato soup with cayenne, sour cream and a sprinkle of parsley), Frankenstein Mix (salted and toasted cereals), Ghoulish Goulash, Loch Ness Seaweed, Macabre Cake with Hard Sauce Spooks and Spider Cider. Profits that year rose to $40,000. By 1972, however, when the exhibit theme was "Creepy Castle Creatures," the council's monstrous success had spawned competition from at least 15 other Louisville-area haunted houses and revenues began to drop. Because of the fierce competition and because the Collings estate barn burned in 1973, that year was the final haunted house sponsored by the council. Instead, they went in search of other ways to earn money for student scholarships.

In 1974 they again proved themselves pioneer fund raisers when they opened Louisville's first Decorators' Show House in the home of Mr. and Mrs. Louis Arru on Decatur Drive. It was an instant financial and artistic success. The concept was simple.

Designers' Show House 1990

ABRAHAM L. WILLIAMS HOUSE

BELLARMINE COLLEGE WOMEN'S COUNCIL   LOUISVILLE, KENTUCKY

A local home would be selected by a committee from the Women's Council and local interior designers would be invited to decorate and furnish house areas assigned to them. By 1982 the project was earning $40,000. One of the most popular and profitable showhouses was held on the 20th floor of 1400 Willow in May of 1980, when more than 12,000 paying customers visited the condominium home.

Another very successful event was held in the fall of 1988, when the Italianate home of Lawrence H. Butterfield, Jr. in Cherokee Gardens was the site of the show house. That year 29 areas were redecorated and furnished by designers ranging from London House and Scorpio Interiors to E. S. Tichenor Company, Miller's Fancy Bath and General Electric. In 1996 the Bray Place on Bashford Manor Lane was the show house site, and the interior designers participating included Bittners, Hubbuch & Company, Pride Tile and Wakefield-Scearce Galleries. In addition to house and garden tours, visitors could attend lectures, demonstrations and style shows and patronize

the cafe and boutique. In the fall of 1997 the 24th Annual Designer's Show House, chaired by Ellen Mellinger, was held at The Cherokee Road Mansion at 1508 and featured Gatsby-like decorations and furnishings.

A problem developed in April of 1983 when the new owner of a house the council was preparing for that year's show house filed suit charging that Bellarmine was using the property without her consent. The house, which had been built by C. Edwin and Mary Jo Gheens on Longview Lane off River Road, belonged to the Southern Baptist Theological Seminary, which had given the council permission to

Jean Dentinger, Helen Petrik and Rosemary Barth
Bellarmine Women's Council.

renovate and redecorate the house and then sold it before the show house event was held. A circuit court judge, however, ruled that the renovation could continue and that the original contract between the college and the seminary was valid. Despite occasional problems, by the end of 1996 the various ventures of the Bellarmine Women's Council had netted the college well over a million dollars.

The credit for such largess is shared by all the hundreds of women who have worked unstintingly for more than 35 years to support Bellarmine College, but special kudos are due to the council presidents and the other officers, who in 1997 were Patricia A. Damron, president; Mary Ellen Gunterman, first vice president; Peg Bergamini, second vice president; Margaret M. Reinhart, secretary and Joan Hedges, treasurer. Other presidents have provided imaginative leadership, including Mrs. James U. Smith, Jr., Jane Duerr and Sara Schuler.

The President's Society also has provided financial support and advice to the college since its founding in 1967. It is composed of members who contribute a minimum of $1,000 annually for special projects chosen by the President. After President Petrik revived the Society, chairman Maurice J. Buchart, Jr., who was director of advertising for *The Courier-Journal,* led the group in raising more than $110,000 in less than five months early in 1974. The President announced that the funds would be allocated this way: $21,000 for general operating expenses; $54,000 for student aid; $10,000 for campus renovation; $5,000 for campus vehicles; and $20,000 for a public relations campaign, which would include testimonials from Bellarmine alumni. The first alumni spokesman was John MacLeod, head coach of the Phoenix Suns professional basketball team.

College officials have frequently used innovative ventures to augment other sources of support. In June of 1973, for example, the college announced plans to build a half-million-dollar 12-court tennis center that would accommodate some 600 members of a Campus Tennis Club with six courts indoors and six outdoors. It was one of Fr. Horrigan's final fund-raising projects. He suggested the project to several friends and alumni of the college, who formed a limited partnership with the college as a general partner. The partnership, which leased 4.4 acres on the campus behind Knights Hall, included two alumni, Dr. Robert R. O'Connor, a psychiatrist, and Dr. John A. Schaefer, a dentist. Other partners were Mr. and Mrs. Kenneth A. Barker, Jr., Margaret S. Dumstorf, James L. Meagher, Raymond E. Montgomery, Mr. and Mrs. Robert Nolan, John L. Plamp, William J. Hennessy and Robert L. Jones.

Another innovative support venture sparked some opposition. In September of 1997 when the Seneca Gardens City Commission voted to sponsor a $420,000 bond issue for lighting improvements at the college, there was some opposition from residents because of Bellarmine's historical association with the Archdiocese of Louisville. Ed Kanis, public relations director at Bellarmine, pointed out that such an arrangement was legal and had been used many times by local governments to support community projects. In fact, he said, in 1996 Bellarmine had worked out a similar bond arrangement with Strathmoor Manor for $750,000 to help with the construction of a new library. Furthermore, he said, the sponsor incurred no legal or financial obligations.

Jack Kampschaefer, the college finance officer, has led the college in other creative ways of supplementing college income. In 1972, for example, the college began renting dormitory rooms each summer for visitors to special campus events. Knights Hall has often been rented for special events, such as professional wrestling and weightlifting competitions. In the early '80s at Kampschaefer's recommendation the college decided it could make more money by owning rather than renting campus vending machines. In 1976 the Bellarmine College Conference Center was created when Bonaventure Hall was renovated to be used for educational, religious and business retreats that could accommodate more than 30 overnight guests.

Another significant source of support for Bellarmine has been various forms of aid from state and federal governments. In the '50s and '60s government aid to private colleges was controversial, and Fr. Horrigan made frequent addresses on the subject. Indeed, in the President's Letter of December 1954 he was cautiously positioning the college for receiving federal aid when he wrote: "Bellarmine College is a 'public' college in terms of the service which it renders. It is 'private' in terms of sources of support." Four years later, in a speech to members of the National Catholic Educational Association in Philadelphia, his position had shifted toward government aid even more when he said that "opposition to federal aid is negative and meaningless unless it is accompanied by generous voluntary support." He warned, however, that government aid could not be a panacea: "I express the hope that our Catholic colleges and universities will continue to regard any prospective federal aid program as a quite secondary and supplementary adjunct to their own efforts to balance their budgets, take care of the bright but needy students, and improve the quality of their programs of instruction."

By December of 1961 Fr. Horrigan had become a defender of federal aid, which, he said, doesn't necessarily mean federal control. Speaking before the annual Conference of Church-Related Colleges in the South meeting at Miami Beach, he proclaimed the contributions of independent schools to higher education: "The church-related colleges of America for generations have produced almost incredible results on the most meager resources." Five years later Bellarmine's dean, Fr. John Loftus, was even more assertive. During a panel discussion of federal aid to church schools in February of 1966, he said: "My position is this—that education is the concern of the state" and concluded, therefore, that "the United States cannot afford mediocrity in any form of education." Bellarmine was ready to show how much it could do with a small amount of federal aid.

In February of 1965 Bellarmine announced that it had received the first antipoverty grant in Jefferson County under the new Economic Opportunity Act. The $7,500 grant would provide support for some 34 work-study students whose parents earned less than $3,000 a year. Morever, for the next academic year, 1965-66, Bellarmine was the only Louisville college to receive federal EOA grants, which totaled almost $45,000. The following year the work-study grant totaled more than $108,000. Administered by the U.S. Department of Health, Education and Welfare, the program grant of $125,000 (plus a 20 per cent match by the college) in 1970-71 benefited more than 400

Bellarmine students. By the fall of 1972 some 75 per cent of Bellarmine's students were receiving some form of financial aid, with 246 participating in the work-study program.

Other federal programs provided more aid for Bellarmine. In the fall of 1966 a federal grant of $6,500 supported a program to develop community leaders in West Louisville. An $8,000 grant from the National Science Foundation made possible a summer program in science for high-school students. A much larger grant was received by Bellarmine in March of 1969, when the National Science Foundation awarded the college $161,000 to improve the science program, with $35,000 earmarked for a nuclear spectrometer and the remainder for a closed-circuit television system.

Getting federal grants, however, was not easy for independent schools. In the fall of 1965, with campus science classes bursting with students, Fr. Horrigan lamented that Bellarmine had twice been turned down for a federal grant that would have provided about one-third of the construction cost of an addition to the science building. After only one private college, Villa Madonna in Covington, had received a grant of the nine awarded by the state Commission on Higher Education, he said, "We feel Kentucky's system is weighted in favor of larger institutions, and that means public institutions." He added, "I respectfully but candidly suggest that we have need for a more imaginative and discerning exercise of educational statesmanship which will take into consideration the needs and distinctive contributions of all of our colleges and universities, large and small, tax-supported and independent." His plea was apparently heard by the state panel. In December of 1965 the Commission on Higher Education voted to revise the formula for distributing federal funds, thus allowing more support for fast-growing smaller schools like Bellarmine.

As federal dollars became more available, Bellarmine took advantage of various federally sponsored programs. In the summer of 1966 the college participated in the first national Upward Bound project with a $63,000 grant for an eight-week program to help prepare 50 disadvantaged 11th grade students for college work. The students lived in college dormitories and took courses, as needed, in math, science, English and reading improvement. They also participated in organized recreation and attended cultural events. A surprise visitor during the summer program was Sargent Shriver, federal director of the War on Poverty. Under the direction of Fr. Joseph H. Voor, the project was so successful the grant was renewed for the following summer, when 60 students attended.

Bellarmine has also participated in various federal student loan programs, beginning with the G.I. Bill of Rights for World War II veterans and later the Korean and Vietnam programs. In the summer of 1956, 91 Korean veterans were enrolled at Bellarmine. The largest dollar amounts of federal support would eventually be awarded as grants and loans for campus construction.

State support has been more meager and harder to get. In July of 1971 the college posted a large notice at the Norris Place entrance, proclaiming "This College Saves Kentucky Taxpayers Approximately $2,250,000 Each Year." Through the Council of Independent Colleges and Universities, Kentucky's independent schools made constant appeals to the General Assembly for scholarship money to be made available to students attending their schools. It was merely a request for fairness, said the member schools, noting that Kentuckians attending state colleges were already receiving various forms of subsidized education. Finally, in March of 1972 Gov. Wendell Ford signed into law a bill which provided tuition grants to needy students in the state's private schools. It was funded after being lobbied by former Gov. Bert Combs, who had been recruited by Bellarmine supporters Wilson W. Wyatt, Eugene Petrik and James Patterson. By 1976 annual state grants to students in private colleges totaled $1.3 million. More than 220 Bellarmine students benefited. In 1974 the General Assembly approved a new student loan program, which made funds available to students in all Kentucky colleges who could not obtain loans from private lenders.

One of the most persuasive and eloquent justifications for state support of independent colleges was made by Michael F. Adams, president of Centre College, in the March 23, 1997 issue of *The Courier-Journal*. First, he said, private schools are not adversaries of the public institutions. "Over the years," he wrote, "the public and private schools have developed a symbiotic relationship." Each sector of higher education has a stake in the health of the other. Noting that the state subsidizes the state schools to the point of keeping tuition artificially low, he concluded that the grants to private school students are "the best bargains in Kentucky today," with the program saving the state over $90 million a year.

Another argument for government aid to students in independent schools is their high pay-back rate for loans. According to a report on defaults on students loans from the U.S. Office of Education in March of 1979, more than 17 per cent of students nationally and more than 14 per cent of students in Kentucky who had received government loans had defaulted. Bellarmine College, at 2.9 per cent, had the lowest default rate in Kentucky and one of the lowest in the nation.

During the past quarter century Bellarmine has conducted a number of successful capital construction campaigns, largely from private donors, which have remade the campus. When Wilson W. Wyatt, Sr. took over as chairman of the Board of Trustees in 1979, he announced that he would not be a part of another fund-raising campaign because after raising millions for several community projects, he was embarrassed to go begging his friends for more. But a month after he took over the chairmanship, the James Graham Brown Foundation offered Bellarmine $1 million if the school could raise $2 million by December 1981. Surely he couldn't let $1 million slip away, he said, so he and other Bellarmine fund raisers hit the streets

and offices again and met the challenge a full year before the deadline. According to Wyatt, they were successful because of the progress the college had made the previous five years under Petrik. Enrollment had grown 73 per cent. The college budget had been balanced for all five years. The school had the positive presence of its President. Said Wyatt of the entire college community, "Their heads are just a little higher."

The way was being prepared for the largest capital campaign in Bellarmine's history. On May 1989 President Petrik announced the kickoff of Partnership for Progress, a $20 million campaign to raise money to build four new buildings—a residence hall, a library, a nursing-education building and a student recreation center. Although the building schedule was modified and despite consultants' warnings that such a goal would be difficult to meet, under the chairmanship of Owsley Brown Frazier, the campaign raised some $30 million.

Mention should be made of sacrificial gifts by numerous college supporters throughout the college's

first 50 years. The list is too long for even representative names of people who unselfishly gave the school amounts ranging from a few dollars to hundreds of thousands of dollars—occasionally, even millions. Let, therefore, one man represent everyone. Early in Dr. Petrik's tenure James A. Patterson, president of PATTCO, Inc., surprised Petrik with a gift of $100,000 at a time when the college was desperate for help. He never stopped making significant gifts, for a total of some $2 million through 1997. Such generosity and others like his have made possible the campus, faculty and programs now in place for the 21st century.

The administration of President Joseph J. McGowan has built handsomely on the fund-raising foundations laid by his two predecessors. By the mid-'90s financial support for the college reached an all-time high. Ambitious fund-raising efforts yielded for the first time private gifts of over $6 million in 1995. By the end of the 1994-95 fiscal year, the library campaign had yielded $8,770,000. The Annual Fund for support of operations had its best year ever in 1994-95, with more than $1,265,000 raised from alumni, parents, the President's Society (with a record membership of 390) and the Corporate and Foundation Circle. Indeed, improvements were made in all phases of support, from planned giving to

1989 Partnership for Progress Campaign leaders, James A. Patterson, general chairperson, Ina B. Bond, vice chairperson, and Owsley Brown Frazier, general chairperson.

strengthened alumni loyalty. In 1990 the Heritage Society was created to recognize individuals who had made a planned gift to support the college, and increase its endowment. Because Bellarmine is a young institution, Dr. McGowan recognized the need to lay the foundation for future sustained support. Under the direction of Mrs. Joan Riggert, the Heritage Society has grown to 76 members, representing over $4 million in planned gifts by 1998. In 1996 Bellarmine College won the Circle of Excellence Award for exemplary work in fund raising from the Council for the Advancement and Support of Education. A very special gift to the college was made in 1998, when Dr. Allan Lansing, former Board chair, and his wife Donna, after whom the Lansing School of Nursing is named, donated a 130-year-old house and 3.2 acres in Glenview for renovation as the President's home. After it is renovated, Dr. and Mrs. McGowan will move into the Colonial Revival-style home. For the first time, Bellarmine College will have an official President's home.

These successes in fund raising were made possible by the dynamic, personable leadership of President McGowan, who was fortunate in having hard-working governing and support groups, such as the Board of Trustees, led by such men as Richard D. Thurman, Owsley Brown Frazier, Michael N. Harreld and C. Edward Glasscock; the indefatigable Women's Council; the loyal Booster Club; the faithful Alumni Board, led by Donald S. Mucci, Greg DeMuth and Jeffrey G. Blain; and an outstanding Board of Overseers. Altogether, they were a team that dreamed big dreams and brought them to reality.

In a January 1955 issue of *Commonweal,* the lay Catholic weekly, Fr. Horrigan asked the question, "Can the Small College Survive?" and defended his new small college while admitting that its survival was at stake. "The average Catholic college," he wrote, "is going to have to take a deep breath, say a fervent prayer, and prepare to do in fifteen years an expansion and reorganization job which normally would be a

Owsley Brown Frazier

Bellarmine College Board of Trustees Chairs

Michael N. Harreld

formidable undertaking even if spread over a full century." Because of their tiny endowments, lack of long-range planning and fund raising and modest public relations programs, he said, it would seem to be an impossible task. Fortunately, Bellarmine College was able to meet the challenges. Al Cassidy, a member of the Pioneer Class of 1954, suggests why Bellarmine has been so well supported: "I am convinced that people give from the heart, not from the head. Bellarmine has been able to assure donors that here was a college worthy to be supported."

The Administration:
The Presidents Horrigan, Petrik and McGowan

College administrators are charged with the responsibility of seeing that students and professors are brought together in an environment that is conducive to learning. From presidents to office assistants, they perform a vital and necessary function for the contemporary college. They recruit qualified students and faculty, provide comfortable facilities and implement sound procedures for the smooth operation of the college.

According to the philosopher-poet Emerson, an institution is the lengthened shadow of one person. In the case of Bellarmine College, the institution is the lengthened shadow of three men: the Rev. Alfred Frederic Horrigan, president, 1949-72; Dr. Eugene Vincent Petrik, president, 1973-90; and Dr. Joseph J. McGowan, Jr., president since 1990—plus the Rev. Raymond J. Treece, who served as Interim President in 1972-73, and Dr. John Oppelt, who served as Acting President during President McGowan's sabbatical in the spring of 1999. These men have determined the character and shape of Bellarmine College.

As most Bellarmine observers will testify, the college has been fortunate in its Presidents. Alumnus and chief financial officer Jack Kampschaefer describes their tenures in these words: "I've served under all three Presidents. Each one was the right person for his time." Another member of the Pioneer Class, John O'Regan, says that "each president has taken the college to a higher level." Marilyn Staples, a long-time member of the student activities staff, puts it another way: "I don't think either President would have been successful if he had served at any other time." Fr. Horrigan was the founding father who set a high moral, spiritual and intellectual standard. Dr. Petrik took this solid foundation and reinforced it with a business orientation and sound fiscal policies. Dr. McGowan has broadened and strengthened the vision of his predecessors and prepared the college for the amazing challenges and opportunities of the new century.

The Rt. Rev. Msgr. Alfred F. Horrigan

The Founding Father: Alfred F. Horrigan

Central casting could not have found a better founding President for Bellarmine College than 35-year-old Alfred Horrigan. *The Louisville Times* editorialized prophetically on November 19, 1949 that the leadership of the new college "insures that it will become an important community asset, cultural and civic." Born in Wilmington, Delaware, on December 9, 1914, to the William Horrigans, he moved with his parents to Louisville in 1923, where his father set up practice as a civil engineer. After attending parochial school in St. James parish, the young priest-in-the-making completed high school and junior college at St. Joseph's College in Rensselaer, Indiana. In college he served as editor of the student magazine, won two varsity letters in basketball and was active in dramatics. He later earned graduate degrees in philosophy from Catholic University, the M.A. in 1942 and the Ph.D. in 1944.

Horrigan did his seminary work at St. Meinrad's Major Seminary in Indiana, and after his ordination in 1940 he was appointed to Holy Spirit Church in Louisville. In 1944 he was appointed assistant pastor at the Cathedral of the Assumption and began teaching algebra and religion at Flaget High School. Later he served as chairman of the department of philosophy at Nazareth College and also taught philosophy at Ursuline College and the University of Louisville. In 1946 he was appointed editor of *The Record,* the official Diocesan newspaper. At the same time Fr. Raymond J. Treece, who would later become Bellarmine's vice president, was named the newspaper's business manager. In September of 1955 both men were recognized for their work in education when Pope Pius XII elevated them to monsignors. Fr. Horrigan was designated a Domestic Prelate, with the title of Right Reverend Monsignor, and Fr. Treece was designated Papal Chamberlain, with the title of Very Reverend Monsignor.

A college president is many things—policymaker, image maker, mediator, cheerleader, fund raiser, student recruiter—and Horrigan has held these jobs and more. He has also been an ardent defender of the independent liberal arts college and an effective spokesman for Catholic education at all levels, locally and nationally. Speaking in Dallas on December 6, 1956, before the Southern unit of the National Catholic Education Association in ceremonies marking the founding of the University of Dallas, which had just opened under the auspices of the Diocese of Dallas-Fort Worth, he asserted that the preservation of free enterprise in economic and political areas depends upon the preservation of free enterprise in American higher education. "Our privately supported and our tax-supported colleges are, and must remain, friendly and co-operative partners in the scheme of American education," he said, and added the caveat that "the thought of a single, completely state-controlled system of higher education is a thoroughly frightening one."

Throughout his career in education, Horrigan preached the partnership of church school and public school in a complete educational system. Furthermore, he acclaimed the remarkable contributions of private education to American history. On "Look Up and Live," a national TV public affairs program on CBS in June of 1962, he reminded viewers of the pioneer role played by church-related colleges in American higher education. All signers of the Declaration of Independence, he said, were educated in such schools. In a graduation speech to the seniors at Flaget High School in May of 1952, he responded to an attack on the Catholic school system by Dr. James B. Conant, president of Harvard University, who maintained that so many private schools tend to divide American society. Horrigan reminded public educators that they should be grateful for the relief they receive from Catholic parents who educate their own children.

Fr. Horrigan practiced what he preached and worked for quality in both public and private arenas. His support of public education was signaled in December of 1966, when Kentucky Gov. Edward T. Breathitt named him to a seven-member advisory board for the proposed Jefferson Community College, scheduled to open in 1968.

Horrigan's outreach and influence in the community and beyond was significant and pervasive, ranging from service on nonprofit boards to his voice as speaker and writer on a host of topics with a spiritual dimension. Many of his presentations were, of course, before religious groups, ranging from the Carmelite Sisters monastery on Newburg Road to the popular Living Rosary Presentations in the '50s and '60s. In the fall of 1959 he spoke before the Jefferson County Medical Society in opposition to so-called mercy killings, and on WHAS-TV he discussed Cardinal John Newman's *Idea of a University*. In a '50s Labor Day sermon at the Cathedral of the Immaculate Conception in Fort Wayne, Indiana, he asserted the dignity and value of human labor. "As Christians we believe that work is sacred and meaningful," he said, "because it is a share in, and an imitation of, the creativeness of God Himself."

In a series of speeches in Kentucky and elsewhere he became a spokesman against the rise of secularism in education and posited religious schools as a bulwark about it. He also opposed the popular notion of educating students to "fit in" with the prevailing cultural norms. He was a popular speaker before business and professional groups and women's clubs, and probably made more commencement speeches than any other half-dozen people in Louisville. He was the principal speaker for the 1954 kickoff luncheon of the Louisville Fund, which he described as "an intellectual slum-clearance program." As a board member of this forerunner of the Greater Louisville Fund for the Arts, he often cited the need to democratize the arts and bring them to all the people. In one speech he suggested that "long-haired culture" be given a crew cut to show that it is "not a finishing school oddity for future debutantes."

By the spring of 1955 his activities included the Louisville Chamber of Commerce, the American Red Cross, the Governor's Commission on Adult Education and the Community Chest, whose workers he called "an aristocracy of those who care." In 1973 he was appointed chairman of Jefferson County's Obscenity Commission, which conducted a yearlong study of

local views on obscenity. Despite all these involvements, Fr. Horrigan was seen frequently at social gatherings around Louisville and written up in the society pages of the local papers.

Msgr. Horrigan, Mrs. Kenneth Barker, Louisville Mayor and Mrs. Frank Burke.

His scholarly outreach as author and editor included such anthologies as *A Treasury of Catholic Thinking,* to which he contributed an essay, "Catholics on the Right and Left." Even after he assumed the presidency of Bellarmine College, he continued to write editorials for *The Record* on subjects ranging from the right of Catholic sisters to wear religious habits while teaching in public schools to the obligations of parents to provide their children with a religious education.

He was also a frequent contributor to the pages of *The Courier-Journal* and *The Louisville Times.* In December of 1952, for example, *The Courier-Journal* ran his article on "Christmas in the Atomic Age." Like a latter-day Jonathan Edwards, he attempted to show the continued relevance of religion in an age of science. "With trembling we now realize that progress and power in themselves," he wrote, "are neither good nor bad; that the knowledge of how to split the atom is a curse and not a blessing unless it is coupled with the worship of the Power which keeps the atom together." Finally, he asserted that "Christmas and its ideal of the brotherhood of all men under the fatherhood of God are not pretty and fragile little dreams, but the only values that are sturdy enough to operate in a world of harsh realities."

Neither was his writing limited to religious and educational subjects. In June of 1958 he wrote letters to the local papers urging business leaders to hire college students for summer work so that they could afford to return to school in the fall. His letter ended with the number of the Bellarmine Placement Office.

Horrigan's professional outreach included frequent trips around the United States and abroad. In the spring of 1955 he spent two months in Europe on a business trip for Bellarmine. He visited eight countries still recovering from the ravages of World War II, which, he said, reminded him that St. Robert Bellarmine is the model of the peacemaker in an age of violence and controversy. His trip included a visit to the 16th century home of Bellarmine in Rome. In a speech at the International Center of the University of Louisville, he noted that America is now "the showcase of the world" and must be careful of its reputation abroad. Sprinkling his presentation with impressions and anecdotes, he told of seeing a man drive up to Speakers Corner in London's Hyde Park and stop to listen to the ravings of an anarchist until a policeman politely asked him to turn off his motor lest he disturb the speaker. "If the British are going to have a revolution," the American visitor concluded, "they are going to have an orderly revolution." Even in Rome he observed an example of civility as two men argued over a parking space. "They decided to settle the dispute with a contest," Horrigan recalled. "They agreed to race each other to a selected spot, and the first one back got to park his car."

In the summer of 1960 he led a European tour sponsored by the Catholic Travel League of New York. The tour included a performance of the Passion Play at Oberammergau and an audience with Pope John XXIII.

What were the traits that made Alfred Horrigan the ideal founding father for Bellarmine College? How was he able to maintain close, amicable relations with Bellarmine students and faculty despite his heavy schedule on and off campus?   As a hands-on administrator he was knowledgeable about and involved in all aspects of college life, from student government to faculty teaching loads. A memo to Fr. Hilary Gottbrath, dated July 28, 1960, for example, includes this observation on a particular student activity: "I gather from your annual report that our orchestra still includes nonstudent members. Do you feel that this is creating a grave and perhaps criticized feature from the view of basic policy on student activities?" It is obvious that the President felt that it did!

Perhaps Horrigan's most characteristic and qualifying trait as Bellarmine's first President was his deep love of learning, a trait that he exemplified in a speech before a gathering of the Cincinnati Medievalists in June of 1957. After calling for "the traditional Catholic love of learning to flourish in America," he looked forward to "a Catholic who can write the great American novel." Unfortunately, as he admitted, Americans generally are indifferent to intellectualism. "When a European passes an intellectual on the street," he said, "he tips his hat. An American taps his head." The father in every family should set the standard as "one who loves and seeks the truth, one who is interested in the world of ideas as well as the world of action." In fact, he was also describing the kind of graduate he wanted Bellarmine to produce.

Those who knew him best—the faculty, fellow administrators, and students—list his traits as those of all good leaders. He was diplomatic and tactful, they say, a good listener, a good communicator and an indefatigable worker. Pioneer Class member Jack Kampschaefer describes him: "He had a solid philosophical base, and he had the support of people to build on that base. He was a community leader and a civil rights leader. On campus we students were in awe of him." The words that come to Ruth Wagoner's mind are "charming and welcoming." Margaret Mahoney calls him "a class act, a man of vision who always did everything well. He made me proud that I came to Bellarmine and stayed." According to William Stewart, "It was very much like a family, with Fr. Horrigan as its head. He never forgot a name— even the names of wives and children."

Miss Alma Schuler

As Alma Schuler, his secretary of 23 years, can attest, he was a considerate, modest man who made all who worked for him feel important. This is her account of how her relationship with him and the college began. "I was taking a class from Fr. Horrigan at Nazareth when we heard the announcement about the new college. I knew it was going to be a men's school, and I thought maybe they wouldn't want a female secretary. But I was working for a downtown law firm as a secretary and decided to apply for the position anyway. So I had an interview with him on December 6, 1949—I remember the date very well— but I didn't think he was much impressed with me. Well, maybe he was because I went to work for him at the college office, which was also his and Fr. Treece's residence, at the corner of Sewanee and Harvard Drive on March 6, 1950.

"On that first day of work he said to me, 'Now Miss Schuler, this is my first time to have a secretary, and I don't really know how to work with one; so I'd appreciate any suggestions you may have about how we can work together.' I said, 'Of course, I don't care where you go, but it would be helpful if you would let me know where you're going when you leave the office and when you'll be back.' That was my first suggestion. Through the 23 years I was his secretary at Bellarmine,

he would sometimes ask me for other suggestions, though I'm afraid that sometimes I'd make suggestions even if he didn't ask.

"At the beginning I was a bit terrified about working in a college. It took me about two years to get off my aloofness because of my respect and awe for priests and for college-educated people; then I was more relaxed and worked more closely with Fr. Horrigan and the other administrators and faculty. I got so used to working for him that I even went with him after he left the college and went to the Chancery Office, the Commission on Peace and Justice, and finally as pastor of St. James Church. In fact, I still do occasional work for him. He'll come to my house and I'll give him lunch and then do his work. How do I feel about all those years I served Bellarmine College? I always felt I was doing something worthwhile, something that counted." Her final estimate of her former employer? "I don't think there is any person in Louisville who is better loved than Fr. Horrigan."

Fr. Fred Hendrickson calls him "the idea man" with "the best intellect of any person I've ever known." Furthermore, Hendrickson says, "His vision of the meaning of a Christian liberal arts education and his dedication to human rights" qualfied him perfectly to be Bellarmine's founding father. Hendrickson sums up the pioneer President in these sentences: "He had a great love for young people and a great respect for students' rights. He even stood up for their rights when it meant negative publicity for the college. When *The Concord* ran an abortion ad—though it stood for everything contrary to what he believed—he maintained their right to do so. He and Fr. Treece complemented each other well. They had already proved at *The Record* that they could work together before they came to Bellarmine. Treece was the detail man, the nuts-and-bolts man who translated Horrigan's ideas into reality. I don't believe that Horrigan would have been such a successful President without Treece."

Fr. Horrigan's years of service to Bellarmine, to Catholic higher education and to his home community have been recognized by numerous awards and honors, from honorary degrees to several Man-of-the-Year designations. In January of 1953 he was one of 11 people named to the *Louisville Defender* Honor Role for his contributions to racial advancement. He received the Brotherhood Award of the Louisville Chapter of the National Conference of Christians and Jews in April of 1964. In 1968 he was one of WHAS's Men-of-the-Year. The others were former U.S. Senator Thruston B. Morton and Elvis J. Stahr, Jr., president of the National Audubon Society and former president of Indiana University.

The college that Fr. Alfred Horrigan had shaped as its first President experienced almost consistent growth and prosperity from its founding in 1950 until 1965, when it had become the largest independent college in Kentucky, with more than 1,750 students. It was at this time, however, that the college began to have enrollment and financial problems. The merger with Ursuline College in 1968 not only brought a distinguished academic tradition to Bellarmine and additional students and faculty, but it also exacerbated its own developing weaknesses.

Jack Kampschaefer has been in a strategic position to observe the work of Bellarmine's Presidents: "I've served under all three Presidents, and as data gatherer for the college, I've seen a pattern in each of the first two presidencies, a period of building and a period of decline. During Horrigan's glory period, enrollments went up, fund raising was highly successful and the President's personal popularity, on and off campus peaked." Fr. Hendrickson puts Horrigan's final years as President into a positive perspective. "Fr. Horrigan was perhaps not tough enough on the financial side, but the problems we were having at the end of his presidency were not really his fault. They were largely the results of societal and demographic changes over which he had no control."

At a meeting of the faculty in late April 1972, Horrigan announced his intention to resign. His departure saddened but surprised few people. He had been preparing for his departure for several years. In the fall of 1970 he had helped start the college's 10-year plan called "The Blueprint for the Future," which included ambitious plans for fund raising, construction of new facilities and curriculum changes. At that time he had also moved to an office on the fringe of the campus and turned over most of the President's duties to the executive vice president, Fr. Raymond J. Treece.

At a meeting of the Board of Trustees on May 8, 1972, he submitted his formal resignation, asking that it take effect on May 31, 1972. His reason, he said, was "nothing more spectacular than the conviction that I have held the office of President for an extraordinarily long period and that periodic turnovers in chief executives are as important for colleges as for all other kinds of institutions"—noting that recent college presidents were serving an average of seven years. Fr. Treece would serve as Interim President for the 1972-73 academic year, and board chairman Kenneth A. Barker said that a search committee would be set up with a target date of June 1, 1973 for selecting a new President. (In fact, the deadline was beaten by more than two months when, on March 10, 1973, Eugene V. Petrik was announced as the new President.)

For many people Bellarmine without Horrigan was an oxymoron. On May 4, 1972, under an editorial headed "No Real End to the Horrigan Years," *The Courier-Journal* put it succinctly: "Bellarmine College and the Rt. Rev. Alfred F. Horrigan are so closely linked that it is difficult to imagine one without the other." Horrigan, however, left his old job with optimism for the future of the small, church-related college, as he told a reporter for *The Record,* "I think that not only can we survive but we can survive with distinction."

At the May 1973 commencement at which 327 seniors received degrees, Fr. Horrigan was honored with a standing ovation. A thunderstorm had threatened to disrupt the graduation rites, which were held outside on the Newburg Road side of the

Joe Reibel accepts the Msgr. Alfred F. Horrigan Distinguished Service Award from Msgr. Horrigan and President McGowan at the 1996 Homecoming Awards Dinner.

administration building, but the storm passed over propitiously and the sun shone brightly throughout the ceremony. During his tribute from the faculty Fr. Jeremiah Smith spoke the understatement of the day when he said that Fr. Horrigan had "molded and shaped Bellarmine College."

Indeed, Fr. Horrigan was not completely finished with his work for the college. He would be intimately involved in the transition to a new presidency. As Fr. Treece was moving into the President's office for a year, Fr. Horrigan became chairman of the Board of Trustees and was thus actively involved in selecting his successor. He recalls his role in the search process: "Although I was not on the search committee, I did, however, write the guidelines for the committee and had a vote on the final selection. I was open to anyone and had no preconceived notions about my replacement—whether it be a man or woman, a priest or layman. Even when Dr. Petrik took over, I continued to return to the campus, as a part-time teacher and for special events. I also remained on the board for two more years."

Horrigan was leaving a school he had been instrumental in bringing to life. He had taken Archbishop Floersh's vision and charge and brought it to bricks and mortar, flesh and blood. As he left the presidency, he admitted that Bellarmine had problems and challenges. In an interview in *The Record* in May

1972 he noted the changes, most of which he considered positive, that had taken place on his watch as President. "To my mind the kids are better than they've ever been. There's a greater sense of responsibility, a greater sense of real, true Catholic concern about being their brother's keeper." He also celebrated the post-Vatican II involvement of students and lay people in Catholic life. "These days you don't make unilateral decisions," he said, and pointed to an upcoming vote by the Board of Trustees to make the one student and two faculty representatives full voting members for the first time. Furthermore, he said, "There was not a single full-time lay professor on the faculty in the fall of 1950. Now the faculty is two-thirds lay." Sounding a warning, he said that Bellarmine had never intended to be all things to all people: "It has to do what it can do."

For former President Horrigan there was much life after Bellarmine as he continued to serve his church. He became an executive assistant to Archbishop McDonough. He headed the new Peace and Justice Center on Poplar Level Road and devoted his full time to social justice in such areas as integration, education, employment and prison reform. After 35 years as a priest, he finally got his own parish at the age of 61 when he was appointed pastor of St. James Church. It was a pastorate that completed a cycle in his life. "Like most priests," he says, "there is always the desire to have the opportunity, some time in your life, to be a pastor. St. James is where I started. I grew up in that parish. Now I was back again."

Some 20 years after he resigned the presidency, he was invited to assess his role in the development of Bellarmine College. "Did I make any mistakes? Oh yes, I'm sure I made many. I made some bad personnel decisions, as I'm sure faculty will say. And in my determination to avoid the red brick so familiar on Catholic colleges, I chose the buff-colored brick for our campus buildings. So I won't say I'm pleased with my service to Bellarmine College because that would imply that I did everything right. I will say, however, that I'm happy I had the chance to do what I could do in getting Bellarmine College founded and serving as its President for some 24 years.

"God works in mysterious ways indeed. At one time I wanted to become a Jesuit and asked the Archbishop for permission. He said, 'No, you started as a Diocesan priest and you can't change now.' If I had become a Jesuit I would probably have become an educator. But when the Archbishop chose me to head his new college, I got my heart's desire. It must have been the will of God for me. You see, I am enough of an old-fashioned Catholic to believe that my religious superiors represent the will of God."

When he reluctantly accepted Fr. Horrigan's resignation, board chairman Kenneth A. Barker summed up the outgoing President's achievements: "He has fathered an educational asset in which the entire community can take justifiable pride. He has assisted thousands of young people to reach educational heights they may have thought

HARRY S. TRUMAN
INDEPENDENCE, MISSOURI

June 1, 1959

Dear Monsignor Horrigan:

Thank you very much for your letter of the 20th.

It was kind and thoughtful of you to remember Mrs. Truman with your prayers, and we both are deeply grateful.

She seems to be progressing very well, and I expect to have her home from the hospital within the next week.

Sincerely yours,

Harry Truman

Rt. Rev. Msgr. Alfred F. Horrigan
Bellarmine College
2000 Norris Place
Louisville 5, Kentucky

Letters from Eisenhower, Truman and Robert Kennedy to Fr. Horrigan.

DDE

GETTYSBURG
PENNSYLVANIA

October 17, 1963

Dear Dr. Horrigan:

For some days I have been holding your letter of the twenty-fourth on my desk in the hope that I might be able to send you an affirmative answer to your request that I visit Bellarmine College in early May of 1964. The prospect of a day at your institution is a pleasant one and I wish that I could accept.

My difficulty is merely one of pre-occupation with the many activities that make insistent demands upon my time. It is impracticable for me to send you an acceptance of another engagement, especially when one of its requirements is that I prepare a thoughtful address -- one at least partially worthy of the occasion and the audience.

I am indeed complimented by your invitation and wish circumstances were less pressing upon me as it would be a great privilege to be with you.

With very best wishes,

Sincerely,

Dwight D. Eisenhower

The Right Reverend
Monseigneur Alfred F. Horrigan
President
Bellarmine College
2000 Norris Place
Louisville 5, Kentucky

THE ATTORNEY GENERAL
WASHINGTON

March 29, 1963

Dear Monsignor Horrigan,

I would like to express to you my pleasure at having the opportunity to meet you during the recent Emancipation Proclamation Celebration in Louisville. The benediction which you offered at that time was most appropriate and meaningful and I think added a great deal to the entire program.

I hope we meet again, but in the meantime, my thanks and very best wishes.

Sincerely,

Robert F. Kennedy

Right Reverend Alfred F. Horrigan
President
Bellarmine College
Louisville, Kentucky

Dr. Eugene V. Petrik

unattainable, and has helped, through the college's graduates, to develop the leadership of our community. He has served God, church, college and this community extremely well." Indeed.

Eugene V. Petrik: The Businessman President

During his campus interview, Eugene Petrik was questioned by a board member about his lack of experience in fund raising. "Do you think you are qualified to raise money for this college?" he was asked. He replied, "I can do anything the college needs me to do." It was a quintessential Petrik statement, self-confident yet not cocky.

Indeed, as he settled into the presidency, he was able to fit into any number of shoes and hats, from fund raising to curriculum revision. Although he professed never to like the social circuit, he nonetheless attended cocktail parties, receptions, club meetings and with wife Helen at his side quickly became a major addition to Louisville's social scene.

But first he had to prove to the search committee that he was the man for the job—better, in fact, than any of the other 200 nominees for the position. The people he had to convince were the 17 members of the committee formed in July of 1972 and chaired by James L. Meagher, chairman of the Board of Trustees, and vice-chaired by Kenneth A. Barker, a former chairman of the board. The membership represented a cross section of the Bellarmine community: trustees David L. Chervenak, Dr. Jude Dougherty and Mrs. Rudy S. Vogt; faculty and administrative staff members William J. Stewart, Robert J. Desmond, the Rev. Raymond J. Treece, Dr. Wade Hall, the Rev. John H. Heckman and Dr. G. Daniel Sweeny; alumni Douglas K. Steele and Mrs. William R. Mapother; students Mary

---

DESIRABLE QUALIFICATIONS FOR THE NEXT PRESIDENT OF BELLARMINE COLLEGE

1. An understanding and appreciation of the value of the liberal arts tradition and discipline and an ability to articulate and defend the principles upon which it rests.

2. A conviction that the Catholic liberal arts college can and should succeed at a time of uncertain support and shifting patterns in education.

3. An awareness of the special aspirations and objectives of the various groups which constitute the Bellarmine College community and a willingness to exercise leadership sensitive to each.

4. College or university administrative experience, preferably at a private liberal arts institution.

5. Some college teaching experience.

6. An earned doctorate, preferred.

7. Attractive personality and ability to communicate and project a favorable image to the public.

8. Fund raising ability.

9. Demonstrable ability in financial planning and management.

10. Good physical and emotional health.

11. Preferably in the 35-50 age bracket.

12. A philosophy of education which equips him to exercise when appropriate responsible leadership in the civic and social orders.

13. An openness to inter-institutional planning and development.

14. Appreciation of the value of intercollegiate sports and other extra-curricular activities in furthering the Bellarmine "spirit."

August 2, 1972

Ann Steltenpohl and Merry Ziemnik; and John J. Ford and W. Frank Ryan, Jr., members of the Board of Overseers. These people were independently minded and not easily impressed.

It was a trial by fire that candidates like Eugene Petrik welcomed. Between August 1972 and March 1973 the committee met more than 20 times to consider the mountain of applications and nominations in search of the candidate with the right stuff. After all the sifting and probing and questioning the lot fell on candidate number 60, Dr. Eugene Vincent Petrik, a New Jersey native who was in his fifth year as vice president of Mount St. Mary's College in Los Angeles. In fact, Petrik later said he was not much interested in Bellarmine until he came to Louisville for his campus interview as one of the three finalists. "When I got here," he remembered, "I was very impressed by the toughness of the search committee. I was excited that there was such a group of people associated with the college who were so definite in what they were seeking in a new President." In Petrik the college had found the man to lead the college toward stability and a new period of growth. He was given a three-year contract and assumed duties on August 1, 1973. It must have been a good match because in May of 1976, after close scrutiny and evaluation by faculty, students, administration and trustees, his contract was renewed for five years, with additional renewals until he had served for 17 years. The presidential search budget of $5,600 had been money well spent.

Who was this 40-year-old Catholic layman from New Jersey descended from Bohemian ancestors in what would become Czechoslovakia? Born in Little Ferry, New Jersey, on May 25, 1932, Petrik received his bachelor's degree in physics from Fairleigh Dickinson University in New Jersey and the master's and doctoral degrees in science education from Columbia University. He taught at Fairleigh Dickinson University, at New York University and at Seton Hall University, and served as vice president of Mount St. Mary's College in Los Angeles from 1968 until he became President of Bellarmine College in 1973.

At Fairleigh Dickinson he had met Helen Veliky, who was to become his wife. "It was in an English class," he later recalled, "and we were required to go see the Laurence Olivier film version of *Hamlet*. I asked Helen if she'd like to see the film with me—and she reeled me in from that point." One could add, of

Dr. Eugene V. Petrik and members of his family at his 1974 inauguration as Bellarmine's second president.

course, that the good catch was his. Not only was Helen a bright, attractive companion and picture-perfect college president's wife but she became the mother of their four sons: John, Mark, Thomas and James. According to the father, "We kept trying for a girl, but we finally gave up after somebody gave us a female St. Bernard."

The sons became high achievers as well, and at least one piggybacked unashamedly on his father's reputation. Thomas was elected president of the Bellarmine College student executive committee in the spring of 1979 by capitalizing on his father's popularity among the students. One of his campaign posters read: "What is better than *one* President Petrik? *Two* President Petriks." Apparently the other students agreed. Indeed, at that time there were three presidents named Petrik on campus when Mark was elected president of the men's dormitory. A dramatic testimony of the new President's faith in the college was that three of his four sons attended Bellarmine. Older son John was already in college when the Petriks moved to Louisville. Helen Petrik has said that several of her grandchildren have told her they expect to attend Bellarmine and live in Petrik Hall.

Indeed, the Petrik family quickly settled into the life of Louisville and Kentucky—and Southern Indiana. Helen Petrik confesses that she'd never heard of Bellarmine College until her husband came home one day and asked what she thought of Kentucky. "I said, 'It sounds great' and had visions of bluegrass, horse country and a slower paced life than we were living in Los Angeles and had lived on the East Coast." She remembers her first trip to Louisville: "When I came with Gene to Louisville for his interview, I quickly learned to like the place and the people; but as we boarded the plane to return to Los Angeles, I didn't think we would be coming back. I wasn't sure it was a good fit for Gene or for the college. But I was wrong. The appeal to Gene was the challenge—the need for money, the need for students, the need for buildings, the need for almost everything. He was a man of vision, and he could see what needed to be done and what could be done. Our life at Bellarmine has been truly fulfilling for both of us."

The Petrik family soon bought a 60-acre farm in Southern Indiana, with a 19th century log cabin and barn as a getaway. When they sold their home on Dundee Road in Louisville, the improved farm house became their primary residence. In 1966 they had bought "half a hillside" on Block Island, off the coast of Rhode Island, and built a three-bedroom house for summer use. At both residences and on trips the family enjoyed such avocations as backpacking, white water canoeing, fishing and light farm work. Perhaps the President's favorite pastime, however, was reading, which extended from *Organic Farming* to C.S. Lewis and St. Augustine.

Helen Petrik soon became an indispensable part of her husband's administration. According to his long-time secretary Susie Hubler, "She was his right-hand person. Together they were a model couple for the job." Although neither relished the cocktail circuit, the Petriks quickly became a popular and handsome couple on Louisville's social scene. Although not especially outgoing, he was a good listener and a well-informed talker and performed all his public duties as President with poise and charm.

Petrik was essentially an academician. According to his wife, "He was a teacher and his interest in college administration evolved." But he soon learned that he could be no armchair President. His major tasks, he knew immediately, would be as a fund raiser and image maker. When Fr. Alfred Horrigan, the outgoing President and new chairman of the Board of Trustees, announced that Petrik had been approved unanimously by the trustees, he hailed his replacement in these words: "He has excellent professional qualifications and a solid record of outstanding success in both teaching and administrative work in higher education and he brings the assets of vigor and youthfulness to his new task." Indeed, he would need all the assets he could muster because the task before him was arduous. In a period of declining enrollment and dwindling financial support, his job was to increase income and enrollment. Except for a slight increase in 1971, the enrollment had been dropping each year since its peak of 2,355 in 1967 and was hovering around 1,500 when Petrik arrived.

In August of 1973 he hit the campus running and was soon settled in his new job. After three weeks as President he could tell a reporter for *The Courier-Journal,* "I'm comfortable with it. It feels natural." In one of his first addresses to the college community in the fall of 1973 in which he laid out his vision and his plans for the college, he said, "We are going to have better budgetary controls and more careful use of the resources than we have had in the past." In his inaugural address he further articulated his vision of what he thought the college should become and his plan of implementation: "First, we must recognize and build on the strength of the past. Secondly, we must continue to develop and deliver high-quality services to meet the needs of our community. And thirdly, we need to develop a marketing system by which we can let Louisville know what we are doing." Petrik's third point echoed the view of Bellarmine alumnus Maurice Buchart, '56, vice president and director of sales for *The Courier-Journal & Louisville Times:* "Despite Bellarmine's excellence in faculty and curriculum, the college's 'awareness factor' is very low."

Soon Petrik was proving that he had the tough, businesslike leadership to do the necessary work. He knew that by the early '70s the education picture in Louisville had changed radically, and he knew that in order to survive in the new educational environment, Bellarmine College must change. He faced many new challenges. He had to contend with inexpensive state-supported higher education in Louisville provided by Jefferson Community College and the University of Louisville, which had become state affiliated in 1968. He had to find students to replace the traditional students who were on the decline. He had to fix his eyes firmly on the "bottom line" in the new financial world. He gathered an informal group of local civic leaders and sought their expertise and advice, which he mixed with his own vision and came up with a project with two principal objectives: to strengthen Bellarmine's programs and make them more vital to Louisville and to promote the college's assets.

During his first year as President he began a marketing campaign featuring television advertising that pointed to the success of Bellarmine graduates. These alumni served as models of liberally educated people who were succeeding in a variety of careers— from Dr. Robert O'Connor, a Louisville psychiatrist, to John MacLeod, head coach of the Phoenix Suns professional basketball team. Also included were Dr. Henry Ellert, '54, a vice president of Exxon Chemical Corporation; Al Cassidy, '54, vice president of Anaconda Aluminum Company; Richard Carr, '64, vice president of Chase Manhattan Bank of New York;

and John Habig, '58, executive vice president of Kimball International. He followed that campaign with two more years of television promotion featuring students and faculty who described the assets of the college and campus life. Furthermore, he secured permission to use the popular B.C. comic strip characters in college advertising. In August of 1975 Petrik told *Louisville* magazine that he subscribed to a "Triune God Model" of educational philosophy: God the Father representing high expectations, God the Son representing the meeting of those expectations and God the Holy Spirit representing the continued support of the work.

After three years of raising public awareness of Bellarmine College and building support and bridges to the community, Petrik, with the assistance of Dennis Riggs and the office of development, developed an ambitious ad campaign with the slogan, "Bellarmine Is Vital to Louisville," which was becoming self-evident. The logo with a symbolic heart and stylized artery on a big B led people to ask, "Why is Bellarmine vital to Louisville?" With billboards, bumper stickers, posters and mailing labels, the community was bombarded with the slogan. Finally, the Bellarmine ad managers added a new ingredient to the promotion, "piggyback advertising," which allowed the college to add its logo and other promotions to advertising sponsored by Louisville companies. By 1978 the financial crisis was essentially over and the money problem was stabilized, with funds again available for faculty pay raises, campus improvement programs and an expanding curriculum to serve the community to which the college was proving it was so vital.

From the beginning of his presidential tenure, he built strong ties to the community by assessing the needs of the institutions that form its foundation— business, government, recreation, health services, the arts, religion—and then developed strategies to serve those areas. Results were quick in coming: an MBA in 1975; new programs in cooperation with the Kentucky Baptist Hospital School of Nursing; a new degree, the

B.S. in nursing for registered nurses; and the Center for Community Education was reorganized in 1974 to reach new nontraditional students.

An important component of Petrik's success at Bellarmine College was his involvement in the Louisville community. He had hardly unpacked his business suits before he was busy addressing civic, educational and religious groups all over town, ranging from a neighborhood Kiwanis Club to the Ballard High School commencement ceremonies. Regardless of his topic, he usually found a way to highlight Bellarmine's contributions to Louisville.

He and Helen Petrik courted the community and succeeded in bringing town and college closer together. She said, "Gene made Bellarmine a part of the community." Indeed, in the '70s and '80s he was one of Louisville's busiest citizens, serving as chairman or president of Metro United Way, Leadership Louisville and the Downtown Rotary Club. He also served on numerous boards, including Louisville Central Area, the Inter-Religious Council of Louisville, the St. Charles Montessori School in Louisville's West End, the Cumberland Savings and Loan Association, Commonwealth Life Insurance Company, Louisville Community Foundation and Methodist Evangelical Hospital. "Anytime I'm out there in the public eye," he said, "Bellarmine is out there."

One of his rare failures was his inability to convince a majority of Jefferson County voters to approve a merged city-county metro government. In 1982 as chairman of the Commission on Reorganization of City/County Government, he worked tirelessly for consolidating the two local governments. Out of more than 180,000 votes cast, the merger plan failed by 1,450 votes.

Meanwhile, back on Bellarmine's campus his success was much more pronounced. It was a success based on marketing, the buzzword for the Petrik administration. It was an application of business techniques to the world of education. Business columnist and television host Louis Rukeyser called

Petrik's plan for Bellarmine "a full Madison Avenue-style plan to market itself as aggressively as a new detergent." The first new member of the administrative staff was Dennis Riggs, a thirty-something development director who began to give the college image a face-lift. A public relations and recruitment campaign using B.C. cartoon characters was managed by Fessel, Siegfriedt & Moeller.

In the fall of 1976 as he was entering his fourth year as president, Petrik could point to a much improved enrollment and financial picture. Enrollment was up almost 20 per cent. For the 1975-76 academic year, the school operated in the black, and the $1 million accumulated debt was being eliminated. A lengthy article in the November 28, 1976 *New York Times* praised the college for pulling itself out of a deep hole using Madison Avenue techniques. Included was a photograph of a giant billboard featuring the B.C comic characters who touted Bellarmine as "the affordable alternative." Its popularity led to this conclusion in a January 1977 issue of *Advertising Age:* "Cartoons on outdoor boards, radio spots and newspaper ads have brought Bellarmine College into the community and out of the red." Members of a new marketing test panel included Col. Harland Sanders, founder of Kentucky Fried Chicken, Barry Bingham, Sr., chairman of *The Courier-Journal* and other Bingham-owned companies, and James "Buddy" Thompson, chairman of Glenmore Distillers.

By the fall of 1977 a new advertising campaign with the slogan, "Bellarmine Is Vital to Louisville," was attracting new financial support and students. An article in the April 15, 1980 issue of *The Wall Street Journal* headed "Freshmen Wanted" noted that, faced with inflation and fewer students, colleges and universities were finally learning "the art of the hard sell." Bellarmine had a head start on most schools. Petrik had correctly sensed that the time had ended when a college could simply open its doors and students would automatically come. The college campus was a new playing field, and it was fiercely competitive. Petrik was leading his college into the brave new world where education had to be marketed like soap. In the early '70s some skeptics wondered if Bellarmine had the ability to survive. By 1980 the question was answered affirmatively. Indeed, after six years of progress a new spirit of optimism was sensed all over the campus. According to board chairman Kenneth Barker, Petrik's biggest achievement was not in programs or finance or enrollment or facilities. "Gene Petrik," he said, "has convinced Louisville that Bellarmine can set a standard for excellence."

In September of 1980 Petrik could tell a *Courier-Journal* reporter, without boasting: "We're not only stable, we're developing. We're not really concerned about surviving. We are now concerned with striving for improvement and increasing the quality." Three years later his development director Dennis Riggs said of him, "He took an institution that was essentially moribund and is now so lively that sparks fly off it." But Petrik had not finished his work at Bellarmine—not by a long shot. Much to the relief of the Bellarmine community, in the spring of 1981 he decided against accepting the presidency of Seton Hall University in South Orange, New Jersey, where he had earlier served as professor and chairman of the physics department.

Archbishop Thomas E. Kelly, Maurice D. S. Johnson, Dr. Allan M. Lansing, and Dr. Eugene V. Petrik.

In the fall of 1983 he announced his 10-year plan of fund raising and campus expansion that would bring

Bellarmine to the next level of quality. When he retired seven years later, he could look back on his 17-year stewardship of Bellarmine College with pride and satisfaction.

Although he came to Bellarmine as a stranger and an outsider, he had the background, experience and personal traits for the job of turning around an ailing institution. In May of 1979 he sketched his portrait of a successful college president for *Louisville* magazine: "He must be fairly intelligent. He must be well organized and able to understand complex situations. He must be capable of projecting a positive image for his school. He should have a high energy level, good health and a good sense of humor. He should come up through the faculty ranks. He must be resilient. And he must be a person governed by principle, not political expediency." The people who knew Eugene Petrik during his presidency at Bellarmine College say he fits his presidential profile to a T. He routinely worked 70- and 80-hour weeks to make good on his promise to put the college in the black and back on track. In a memo to the presidential search committee, June 29, 1972, Jack Kampschaefer listed some traits he thought the new president should have, then added: "In searching for the person who will be our President, we should not sell ourselves short. The presidency of Bellarmine College carries with it enough prestige and positive attributes to insure our obtaining an excellent President." Most people thought that is exactly what the college obtained in Petrik.

Here are some of the words used by people to describe him. Board chairman Kenneth A. Barker called him a man with "the ability to manage." Fr. Horrigan said he was "a man who thinks in paragraphs." Faculty and administrators who worked closely with him often described him as "very demanding," a trait which Fr. Crews put into context: "When I was acting dean, I found him to be reserved, somewhat tight, intense, pious and unrelenting when it came to working for the good of Bellarmine College." Jim Stammerman, who served as public relations officer under Petrik, calls him "focused, driven and determined." He quickly earned a reputation for thrift, running "a pretty tight ship," as one colleague said. His conservatism covered a number of areas, as he told a writer for *Louisville* magazine in 1976: "I probably tend to be somewhat conservative in my outlook. As President, I don't want to be out in front, marching down streets or waving banners." A man of deep religious faith, he was probably more of a traditional Roman Catholic and less affected by post-Vatican II changes than most of his faculty.

Sometimes considered stern and strait-laced, Petrik was also noted for his sincerity and sense of humor. As chairman of the Louisville-Jefferson County Charter Commission, he was frequently on the hot seat, especially at public hearings when most of the speakers delivered tirades against the proposed government merger. He often defused a tense situation with humor. Once, when a city resident named Smith attacked at length the proposals, saying that the new government would not be responsive to city residents, Petrik quipped, "I can't imagine any government not being responsive to *you*, Mrs. Smith." In the May 1979 issue of *Louisville* magazine, he spoke of his consistency: "I think Helen and I are the same people whether we're at a cocktail party in Louisville or on our farm in Indiana. I refuse to do anything I judge to be phony simply because it's expedient."

Although sometimes labeled "gruff," his people skills were noted in 1979 by Fr. Clyde Crews, who served as chairman of the theology department: "Dr. Petrik has a talent for turning a crisis into an opportunity. I've seen the way he handles people who are angry with Bellarmine. When they come away, they're usually friends of the college." Georgia Doukas, manager of the college bookstore and, like Petrik, a native of the East Coast, called him "direct and to-the-point," a trait she considered an asset. Alumnus Michael Steinmacher saw a more relaxed side of the President: "He was always highly visible on campus and frequently ate in the cafeteria. Everyone on campus knew him and he seemed to know everyone by name." In the fall of 1982 Petrik even became a part-time student when he took a course in German 101 with Frau Gabriele Bosley.

Susie Hubler, who was secretary to Petrik for more than 17 years, remembers her first impression of him: "All the candidates for President came in to the development office where I was working to talk with the director, Mr. Desmond, and they would walk past the office staff without speaking or looking right or left—everybody except for one, Dr. Petrik. He came in the door, stopped by each desk, introduced himself, learned our names, then went into the director's office. When the door was closed, we all looked at each other and said, almost in unison, 'That's our choice.'"

An honest appraisal of Petrik was given by the late John Daly of the chemistry faculty: "He was strong-willed, goal-oriented, confrontational and determined. When he came we were broke. He got results, though he stayed too long as President and the faculty were in disarray during his last years." A man who served in a number of administrative positions, alumnus Robert Pfaadt has a unique overview and perspective on Petrik's administration: "I joined Gene's Team, as he called it, and worked with it for 12 years. I always felt comfortable working with him. He worked hard and he expected his staff to work hard. He 'lived' Bellarmine. He was honest and methodical. He never pulled surprises on us. I soon learned never to give him a proposal or program or suggestion without putting a number on it." Pfaadt's comments on Petrik's final years as President: "I've always believed that his impatience and shortness with people at the end was caused by his illness, which I think was working on him."

John Oppelt, who served as academic vice president under Petrik, had disagreements with him on institutional philosophy, faculty development and curriculum. Indeed, he said, "We had our differences but we had a mutual respect for each other. Despite some changes that I objected to, the college remained true to its stated mission. Bellarmine has always stood for something. It has never gotten wishy-washy."

Alumnus John J. Ford lauds Petrik for his ability to reach out to the non-Catholic community for support. "At first," he said, "I questioned whether we needed to go so far afield. Surely, I thought, we have enough Catholic people to support the college. But I know now that what he did was not only necessary but it was the right thing to do."

But, as Jack Kampschaefer has noted, Bellarmine's first two Presidencies were characterized by a period of building followed by a period of decline. Many people have felt that both Presidents simply served too long. Marilyn Staples of student services sees the middle part of Petrik's presidency, from the late '70s into the early '80s, as a golden age for Bellarmine. "Petrik was in his prime," she recalls. "He had accomplished many of his goals in fund raising, student enrollment and new programs. There was good communication among faculty and administration and students. People just felt good." Dan Sweeny of the chemistry faculty says, "I don't think that either of our first Presidents harmed the college by staying too long, but I am convinced that both of them did their best work during the first halves of their tenures." Alumna and financial officer Donna Olliges sensed a strain in certain relationships. "I know that near the end of his administration some other administrators and faculty had run-ins with him and meetings were sometimes tense and stressful. But the only time Dr. Petrik ever raised his voice at me was during his last year when he once disagreed with a student payment plan." Jack Kampschaefer observed: "Near the end of his administration Gene was getting burned-out and short-tempered, and he knew it. No one forced him to resign but he did for his own good and the good of the college. He realized that he had accomplished his mission and it was time to move on." Perhaps Fr. Hilary Gottbrath said it best, "He was the one who accomplished the vision."

President Petrik had served the college well. He was a risk taker who moved the college into new directions, strengthening existing programs and inaugurating new ones. He had come to a sick college and left it, if not wealthy, at least healthy. On his watch enrollment had doubled, the number of undergraduate programs had doubled, five graduate programs were added; five major buildings were constructed; endowment had risen from a paltry $134,000 to $7 million; and plans had been made for a $20 million fund-raising campaign, the largest in the college's history. Bellarmine had become Kentucky's largest independent college and one of the best-regarded liberal arts institutions in the region. Most importantly, he had saved the college.

On May 22, 1989 Petrik announced that he would retire. "Joe DiMaggio went out when he was batting .285 and could still play," he said. " I've always wanted to do that, too; not when people are looking at you and wondering when you're going to go." The retirement was effective one year later. At the college's 37th and his final commencement in 1990, he said goodbye to a college that he loved so much he gave most of his life for it. He quoted Elizabeth Barrett Browning's sonnet, "How Do I Love Thee," and promised to love Bellarmine people "always and everywhere." He was made President Emeritus of Bellarmine College. In the fall a new dormitory was christened Petrik Hall. He said he planned to spend more time at his Indiana farm, some 25 miles from Louisville. He also accepted a position as a vice chairman of the Cumberland Federal Savings Bank. He was anticipating a productive and fulfilling retirement with more time for his family.

Sadly, he had but a short time to explore his new job and to enjoy his farm. By February of 1991 he was receiving radiation treatments five days a week for the remains of a cancerous growth which was removed from his thyroid the previous December. On Easter Tuesday, April 2, 1991, he died at Methodist Evangelical Hospital in Louisville. He was 58. He was survived by his wife Helen, his four sons—John, Mark, Thomas and James—a brother Vincent, his mother Anna and six grandchildren.

In his funeral sermon at St. Agnes Church on April 6, Fr. Clyde Crews called him "a man of rectitude and integrity, of earnestness and vision, of faith and fidelity—and a wry sense of humor. A man who went down standing up." He was "the President with that unforgettable Columbia gown that we got to see in all its plumage but once or twice a year. Otherwise we saw him in his academic pinstripes, professionally and personally involved in leading others to lead. A man who was caring yet reserved; innovative but cautious; kind but demanding; trusting but questioning. In baseball terms, Dr. Petrik was a major-leaguer; in equestrian talk, he would be called a Thoroughbred." Finally, he was a man who "gave himself up to death not in despair but in trust," as he said from his deathbed. In a statement he dictated shortly before his death and read by his son Mark, he said, "My family, my friends, my colleagues, my community: please know that just as I have cared for you during my health, so I still care for you in my illness and I will continue to care about you even beyond death. . . . I tried to live my life trusting Him and His providence; I approach death in the same way."

Petrik the philosopher and the man of faith had spoken such words of hope and promise before. In a speech in June of 1977 to the Hodgenville Women's Club, he said that despite the sometimes bleak news of humankind, he believed that it was "a time for rejoicing. . . . To me, the anxiety we feel today is the doorway out of the pride so characteristic of the Modern Age. It is also the doorway into the world for a God who seems to have been silent for so long. I predict that we are on the threshold of a moral and spiritual revolution. I believe that we are being called, as never before, to be 'the salt of the Earth' and to be 'the light of the world.' " In 1978 he told a *Louisville Times* reporter: "For the past 10 or 15 years I've been attracted to the meditative, contemplative life. . . the development of the spiritual dimension. It's a part of my personality that's been hidden by the salesman-community entrepreneur-public side of me."

Presidents Petrik and McGowan at the dedication of Petrik Hall.

Archbishop Thomas Kelly called him "a superb Christian, a faithful Catholic" whose "leadership during his presidency at Bellarmine College was an enormous gift to the Archdiocese of Louisville." More encomiums were delivered at a campus memorial service on April 11, conducted by Fr. Horrigan. Some 18 years before, in a letter to the search committee that would find his replacement, Fr. Horrigan had discussed the qualities he would like to see in his successor, including a sense of direction, a sense of unity, but he emphasized "the President must first of all be the conscience of his college. He must be the chief carrier and interpreter of the ideas and ideals that make it the special kind of institution it is." And so he was, not only in the way he led the college but in the way he faced his death.

In his last report to the trustees, "A Stage on Life's Way," in which he called his administration "Bellarmine's second stage on its way to greatness, the 16 years of its adolescence," Petrik noted that Fathers Horrigan and Treece had "created this place and nurtured it through its birth and childhood." He continued, "I have been privileged, along with many others, to see Bellarmine through its adolescence—a time when the search for identity remained strong, but also a time of growing confidence and control over the future. Bellarmine is about to enter its early adult years—the 'prime time,' the best of years for those who are stimulated by the excitement of creating a grand future. . . . Those of you who carry on will continue to have the privilege of building a grand tradition." After Joseph J. McGowan was announced as Bellarmine's new President, Petrik told a writer for the *Lance* that he felt very secure with the new President, a man, he said, suited to lead Bellarmine College through its next era of progress.

Joseph J. McGowan: A New Leader for a New Century

On February 2, 1990, three finalists for the presidency of Bellarmine College were announced: Thomas R. Feld, president of Mount Mercy College in Cedar Rapids, Iowa; John C. Orr, president of the College of St. Francis in Joliet, Illinois; and Joseph J. McGowan, vice president for student affairs at Fordham University in New York City. Less than two months later, on March 30, Richard D. Thurman, chairman of the Board of Trustees and of the presidential search committee, announced that Bellarmine's third President would be McGowan, a man, he believed, who would "serve

Dr. Joseph J. McGowan, Jr.

as a dynamic leader to advance Bellarmine into the '90s."

In accepting the position, the new President-elect said he had no "very specific agenda." In fact, he confessed, "In the early going I'll be a learner myself." Colleagues at Fordham, where he had spent the previous 21 years of his academic career, described him as "affable and able" and as "an outgoing Irishman who cares about people, does a great Elvis Presley imitation and defuses tense situations with a well-timed sense of humor." These were some of his more obvious talents. As the college quickly learned, the new President possessed a sharp, penetrating mind, a broad and deep understanding of education and persuasive administrative skills.

A native of Louisiana, McGowan held an undergraduate degree in English literature and psychology from Notre Dame and a doctorate in higher education from Columbia University, with additional study at Harvard University's Institute for Educational Management. His experience in higher education included service as assistant director of admissions and financial aid at Notre Dame, assistant and associate academic dean and dean of students and vice president for student affairs—all at Fordham University. He was also the husband of Maureen Barry and the father of twin sons Matthew and Joseph.

McGowan was inaugurated as third President of Bellarmine College in Knights Hall on Friday, October 12, 1990, on the 40th anniversary of the founding of the college. Representatives from some 70 colleges, universities and learned societies were in attendance. Presiding over the ceremony was former board chairman Wilson W. Wyatt, Sr. The investiture was given by board chairman Richard D. Thurman.

In his inaugural address, "Bellarmine College: Hope and Vision," Dr. McGowan echoed a theme of the Petrik administration, "Lighting the Way," which solicited support for the college with brochures that read like this: "Now is the time for Louisville to light the way for Kentucky in higher education. California has its Stanford; Tennessee has its Vanderbilt; North Carolina has its Duke. Each of these private institutions started in the dreams of great men and women. Now is the time for Louisville's leadership to begin casting such a vision for Kentucky."

McGowan immediately saw his mission as articulating and fulfilling what he called a "vision to be the region's premier residential liberal arts college." Indeed, "realizing the vision" could easily be the motto of his presidency. In his inaugural address McGowan announced groundbreaking for the nursing and education building and plans for the library. "My role as President," he said, "is to understand, interpret, and advance this collective vision of the Bellarmine community, a great vision built on a great hope." With the support of the Bellarmine community, he pronounced a benediction that petitioned "our God to bless us all as we now begin together to realize the

rich vision and enormous potential of Bellarmine College *In veritatis amore.*'"

*The Inauguration
of
Joseph J. McGowan, Jr.
as
The Third President
of Bellarmine College*

*Friday, the Twelfth of October
Nineteen Hundred and Ninety*

*in
Knights Hall
(on Campus)
Louisville, Kentucky*

Indeed, McGowan's Inauguration Week paid tribute to both of his predecessors, with the celebration of Mass on the feast day of St. Robert Bellarmine by Fr. Alfred Horrigan and the dedication of a new student residence as Petrik Hall. This is his description and appraisal of the work they had done. "Msgr. Horrigan had started it and evolved it into a solid men's college and had seen it through the merger with Ursuline, but by 1973 the college found itself in serious financial trouble. What was needed was a strong person who could centralize authority, take control of the budget, diversify the college, make it grow and become stable. What the college got was the man they needed, Gene Petrik, for those tasks. By the '70s, however, much of the college family was beginning to feel itself adrift. There was a crisis of identity. By the early '90s, the faculty have told me, the college had had excellent growth and was doing this and that, but they were asking the question, 'Who are we? What is Bellarmine College now? Is it what we want?' The faculty felt—or so they have told me—that they were uninvolved in its mission. It wasn't that the institution had lost its vision. The problem was that the vision wasn't being articulated. From the faculty, then, I learned the vision, and I have been trying to teach it back to them and the entire college community."

Furthermore, McGowan has eulogized his predecessors in these words: "Fr. Horrigan's great contribution was that he was a moral, inspiring, spiritual, effective leader in the grand tradition of college presidents. His undying legacy is that he started the college, set its moral tone and sustained it for more than 20 years. He formed its basic character. Gene Petrik then saved this place. He put it back on its feet and made it stable and strong. He made it better known and respected in the community. Both Horrigan and Petrik prepared the way for me. Neither President could afford to do some of the things I can think about doing. I am building on their good works." Nor has he failed to pay homage to Sr. Angelice Seibert and Ursuline College. "We must never forget the important legacy of Sr. Angelice, her strong leadership as President of Ursuline and the strength that they brought to Bellarmine in 1968."

Although McGowan had not followed Bellarmine's development closely, his awareness of the college went back to the mid-'60s, when he met Fr. Hilary Gottbrath, Bellarmine's dean of students. Fr. Hilary recalled the occasion: "I knew Jay McGowan many years before he became President. I met him in Evanston, Illinois, when he was a student at Notre Dame and was courting Maureen, who became his wife. Maureen was the niece of my good friend, Joe Barry, whose oldest sister had married and lived in Evanston. Joe and I and other friends would go on football weekends to see Notre Dame play. When they played Northwestern in Evanston, we stayed with Joe's sister. That's when I met Jay. I even went up for their wedding.

But I was very surprised years later to get a call from him telling me that he was being considered for the Presidency of Bellarmine."

McGowan recalls that it was Fr. Hilary who first acquainted him with the school. "I've known about Bellarmine since 1966, when I came down to visit my wife-to-be's family—the Barry family, in Louisville and to attend the Kentucky Derby. I saw Fr. Hilary at a party and he brought us out to see the campus. I remember it as small and pretty, with a rather undistinguished building on top of a beautiful hill. At that time it didn't seem like a college that I might want to head. But in the next 20-plus years I grew and changed and Bellarmine College grew and changed." Indeed, that chance meeting of man and institution in 1966 became a serious relationship in 1990, "when I got the opportunity to become President, which I now consider the privilege of a lifetime." He adds, "I loved New York and I'll always love New York, but after some 23 years in Manhattan, I was ready for a small liberal arts college that values good teaching located in a city like Louisville. I was ready for Bellarmine."

And Bellarmine was ready for McGowan. "When I came for the interview," he says, "I felt that the faculty wanted me." What the college got, according to alumni director James Ford was a personable, energetic man with a sense of direction, a vision and a plan. Like his predecessors, he quickly immersed himself in community life, becoming a

Dr. McGowan, 1994 Metro United Way Campaign chair, at the Cerebral Palsy Kids Center.

popular speaker and member of more than a dozen boards, ranging from the Junior League Community Board and the Louisville Metro United Way to the J. B. Speed Art Museum. The students soon learned about his Elvis Presley impersonations. During the Student Presidential Roast on the hillside, the new President took the stage and sang a flawless—well, almost—rendition of "Are You Lonesome Tonight?" His unflappability was demonstrated when he presided over his first graduation in May of 1991 and received, with good form, a marble from each of the graduates as he shook their hands.

By 1992 this laid-back President for the '90s had composed a new "Alma Mater" for Bellarmine, set to a Southern folk tune. His poetic prowess was also being exhibited in memos to the college family, particularly around Derby time. A memo dated 1 May 1996 titled "Schedule for Friday, May 3," read:

> It's been some year, t'will soon be o'er.
> Our five-month winter was a bore.
>
> But May is here and with it, spring!
> And school is out, so dance and sing.
>
> And come next fall when summer's done,
> With Brown Libraire we'll have great fun.
>
> Now, onto Oaks and Derby, too.
> Happy Derby! Y'all leave at noon.

Having scaled the Mount of Parnassus, the following year he tried prose. In a memo dated 1 May 1997, 3:13 P.M., titled "Oaks/Derby Schedule," he wove the names of Derby entrants into the announcement of a half-day holiday:

Hello! This is your *Celtic Warrior* using his *Silver Charm* and his bully *Pulpit* to tell you that at noon on Friday you may all jump on *Jack Flash* in *Concerto* and make yourself a *Phantom on Tour* from your Bellarmine job. After leaving the campus, please go immediately to your not so *Free House* and involve yourself in *Deeds,*

The President's Team at the 1998 President's Classic: Bill Hartman, Jim Lintner, Kathy Lintner, President McGowan, and Tom Musselman.

Not Words to get everything ready for Derby. That goes for everybody from Linda *Shammy* Davis at the Help Desk to *Captain Bodgit* in Security. Enjoy the Run for the Roses which is truly a *Crimson Classic.* As you place your bets, I will wish upon a *Crypto Star* that your horse comes in first; that you know how grateful I am to each of you for your good effort this year on behalf of our students; and that in the next academic year we all work to take our transcendent selves as seriously as we have been taking our historical selves. Peace." Surely, few college presidents can lay claim to such poetic effusions. Little did the trustees realize how he would fulfill their charge to "bring Bellarmine to the next level."

Dubbed "the year of change," the 1990-91 academic year saw numerous developments. Steven Permuth, who had served as vice president of academic affairs since 1985, resigned and was replaced by David B. House. Also resigning was Thomas Greenfield, dean of the College of Arts and Sciences. John Oppelt served as acting dean for two years before being replaced by Theresa Sandok of the philosophy faculty. The residence dormitories were renovated and students were moved from Bonaventure, which was reserved for seminars, group meetings and workshops and the Thomas Merton Studies Center. Believing in the importance of ceremonies to mark important events and changes, Dr. McGowan instituted Convocation and Matriculation for students at the opening of the school year. Furthermore, he hosts an annual dinner for faculty and their guests during the commencement weekend. Other innovations following Thanksgiving included the first annual Light Up Bellarmine celebration, with a large evergreen decorated in front of the newly named administration building, Horrigan Hall. Another first was Professional Image Week in September, sponsored by the Accounting Club, and involving a fashion show and instruction in professional etiquette.

In February of 1991 the new President announced a sort of back-to-the-future move, the dropping of the corporate-looking flame logo and returning to a modified version of the college seal and coat-of-arms, with the motto in Latin, *In Veritatis Amore*. Executive vice president Jack Kampschaefer surveyed the changes in April and labeled it "a year of adjusting and learning." Long-time trustee James Patterson said McGowan had brought "a mood of excitement and exhilaration" to the school.

Dr. McGowan at the 1993 President's Society Dinner.

Merton Center curator Robert Daggy was pleased that the new President wanted the college to "deliver a Renaissance person" and not merely produce students trained in a single vocation. Many faculty and students felt a re-emphasis on the arts and sciences. McGowan had eliminated the two-year Associate of Arts degree in nursing, while breaking ground for the $3 million nursing and education building. In the area of student affairs, he pushed back from 11 p.m. to 2 a.m. the student curfew for having visitors of either sex in dormitory rooms. Closing out his first year as Bellarmine President, McGowan inaugurated the first annual Senior Week in May of 1991, which included a dance, cook-out, day at the races and various events connected with commencement. Appropriately, the theme of the '91 *Lance* was "Changes."

McGowan had taken firm control of an institution that Petrik had left strong and stable but which some people thought had grown in so many directions that its vision was blurred, its direction uncertain and its priorities unclear. Fifteen months after his arrival McGowan seemed to have a firm grasp of his mission and how to achieve it. This is how he stated it in his presidential address at the academic convocation in October of 1991: "My mandate was clear," he said. "Bellarmine is a teaching institution in the best tradition of Catholic higher education. Its center, its soul, is liberal arts and sciences, and, true to its tradition, it is also engaged in professional education, but professional education as informed by the liberal arts and sciences—in business, education and nursing. We want our students to be able, not only to make a living, but to make a life worth living." Furthermore, he said, "service to others" must be "the distinguishing characteristic of student life." Finally, he set the course that would achieve his goals: "Bellarmine must become increasingly residential and diverse in its student body and there must be a vigorous, viable student life, fully integrated with the academic goals of the college."

In 1991 the new President initiated a college-wide strategic planning process, which involved trustees, faculty, alumni, students and other members of the

Bellarmine community. The result was a Five Year Strategic Plan for Bellarmine College linked to the annual budget process. It has been updated and revised annually and now includes the new campus Master Plan.

His plan of implementation has included faculty development, some realignment of academic disciplines, a new library and new academic buildings and a beefed-up student recruitment strategy and scholarship program. Assisting him in this ambitious undertaking were academic vice president David House and vice president for student affairs Fred Rhodes. To enhance student life he announced the creation in Newman Hall of a nonalcohol cafe to be called Hilary's, after Bellarmine's first dean of students, Fr. Hilary Gottbrath, OFM, plus a Nautilus room and aerobics room. There would also be new support for women's sports as well as a new emphasis on spiritual life grounded in the Catholic tradition but with "an interfaith liturgical character and a social action

1994 Guarnaschelli Lecturer Nobel laureate Seamus Heaney with Maureen McGowan, President McGowan, Mr. and Mrs. Wendell Berry.

orientation," under the college chaplain Fr. Callahan. College history would also be honored, and in particular in the naming of buildings and halls for the people "who have given their lives to Bellarmine." Perhaps the best indication of a new sense of direction under the new administration was the reminder, announced earlier, that "we have eliminated the abstract and sterile corporate logo and replaced it with the distinguished traditional seal of Bellarmine with its stirring motto:

In Veritatis Amore—In the Love of Truth." McGowan's relaxed, nonthreatening personal style was demonstrated by the way he chose to conclude his address: "I am fully confident that, working together, there is no question but that this little Bellarmine, we're gonna make it shine. . . make it shine, make it shine, make it shine."

McGowan's second year as President was labeled "Pride in Performance" as academics and extracurricular activities were enriched by speakers like TV documentary filmmaker Ken Burns and a focus on Tibet in preparation for the visit to Louisville of the Dalai Lama. By 1994 Bellarmine academic advancements were recognized by such publications as the *Princeton Review, Barron's, Money Guide* and *U.S. News and World Report,* which named the college one of the top 15 regional universities in the South. Records were being set in admissions, in the number of students living on campus and in international programs. A new program of freshman advising and a tracking system to monitor their performance was begun. The college's Mock Trial Team distinguished itself as national runner-up and an innovative Master of Liberal Studies program was introduced. The African American Leadership Institute was begun, and academic enrichment was provided by a new First Conference Series, with national conferences held on campus that focused on the works of such contemporary authors as Cormac McCarthy and Toni Morrison.

By the mid-'90s McGowan was firmly in the driver's seat. Aided by an impressive board of trustees, including Owsley Brown Frazier, chairman, Michael N. Harreld, vice chairman, and W. Bruce Lunsford, secretary, and including Malcolm B. Chancey, Jr., Dr. Marian Swope, Dr. Morton Kasdan, Dr. Allan M. Lansing, James A. Patterson, Dr. Samuel Robinson and T. William Samuels, Jr., McGowan was well on his way toward positioning the college for a new century and its own second half-century. As the final decade of the 20th century drew toward its close and with the leadership of McGowan in the President's chair and Attorney C. Edward Glasscock in the trustees' chair, Bellarmine could point to improvement on almost every front: a new library, renovated dormitories, improved campus landscaping, broadened diversity, improved technology, more alumni involvement and financial support, endowment increased to over $18 million and new degree programs. The "next burst upward" included a $4.5 million technology plan, a campus Master Plan, construction underway for Our Lady of the Woods Chapel, an Academic Resource Center, new MBA classrooms in the Brown Library and a new administrative team.

How does this President for the *fin de siecle* explain his success? "I decided that what I am and what I have to offer seemed to be some of the things that Bellarmine College wanted and needed in the '90s. The old Mr. Chips model of the professor who becomes dean who becomes president doesn't really work in this new age. Colleges today demand professional administrators who understand the need to run colleges in a new way. I think I'm a contemporary President, a President for the '90s. I don't like the lone-ranger, from-the-top-down management style. I like the team approach, using everyone's expertise. I'm somewhat ambivalent about authority. I respect it and exercise it as a way to get things done; yet I retain a rather adolescent resistance to authority. Yet I feel comfortable in my authority. I don't feel threatened by anyone. I don't have to compete with any other

administrator or with high-achieving faculty. I'm already the President. I have the job I want. I'm therefore delighted when others are recognized for their achievements.

"Anyone who becomes a college president has an ego. One time, after I got to know Gene Petrik well, I joked with him about how we were different. 'Gene,' I said, 'one difference between you and me is that you have a big ego and don't know it, and I have a big ego and know it.' I became an administrator because I like to make things happen. I like to be part of an enterprise where people teach and where people learn. Other than my parents, several of my teachers, and a few other intimate friends and relations, my public role models are people like John Kennedy, Martin Luther King, Fr. Hesburgh of Notre Dame. Why, I even like Elvis—well, perhaps not as a role model exactly. But I do like rock 'n' roll."

McGowan has perhaps not been able to please everyone with his goals and management approach, but the testimonials are not hard to find, ranging from former business manager Donna Olliges, who likes the fact that he can read a financial statement and "remember the figures," to David O'Toole, long-time mathematics professor and now athletic director, who points proudly to his promotion of "gender equity in our athletics program." To Fr. Horrigan he is "an able man with a clear vision for Bellarmine." Although he fears that the primacy of the liberal arts has been reduced, Jack Kampschaefer says that under McGowan, "We're becoming the college that Fr. Horrigan and Dr. Petrik envisioned for us." John Ford, a former member of the Board of Overseers, likes McGowan's "redirection of Bellarmine back to its Christian identity and its Catholic roots." Alumni Affairs head Jimmy Ford likes McGowan's focus in three areas: "excellence in the liberal arts and teaching, increase in residence students and greater diversity in the student body."

Pioneer Class member John O'Regan is "extremely impressed" with "the world-class job" that the search committee did in bringing McGowan to Bellarmine. Alumnus Michael Steinmacher calls McGowan "an interesting contrast to Fr. Horrigan and Dr. Petrik," but maintains that "all the Presidents have had personalities and styles that have been good for Bellarmine." Bud Spalding of the business faculty is cautiously optimistic, when he says, "The instincts and inclinations of Jay McGowan seem to be nudging us along in the right direction." Sue Hockenberger Davis, dean of the Lansing School of Nursing, says simply, "His heart is where the heart of Bellarmine is." And David O'Toole calls him "a new leader for a new time"—the exact description of what the search committee, the Board of Trustees and the college community wanted in the new President.

Finally, this is Dr. Joseph J. McGowan's vision for Bellarmine as it enters the 21st century. "We must emphasize education for living in a multicultural world. A place like Bellarmine that knows what it is, what it stands for, can afford to reach out to other traditions. We can afford to be diversified. To reach this goal we must broaden our student body geographically and include more students from other countries. Like Thomas Merton, the Catholic monk, we need to engage in dialogue with the whole world, much of which is not Christian and not at all like us. Our commitment to Christianity exists in the culture rather than in the classroom. In the classroom we need to be tolerant of and try to understand all positions and beliefs. On the other hand, some schools with Christian foundations have concluded that their Christian roots are incompatible with academic and intellectual life. That's an extreme position. It's not a good position, and it's not ours. You are who you are. We are Christian. Although in the '90s some 60 per cent of our Board of Trustees are not Catholic and some 40 per cent of our students are not Catholic and less than $100,000 of our annual budget of more than $15 million comes from the Archdiocese of Louisville, we are still a Catholic institution. Yet we have obligations to those who are not Catholic, and one of those

obligations is to respect the beliefs and ways they are different.

"Indeed, I celebrate Bellarmine's Catholicity. But a Catholic college today is very different from the old days when we were guardians and preachers of the One and Only Answer. Now we must provide the environment and tools and guidance for one's own process of asking questions and arriving at answers. Most of our students come from families where religion is taken seriously, and one of our primary objectives is to help them work out their own personal faith. For them—and others—Bellarmine can indeed be the 'city on the hill.'"

"By the year 2000 I hope that Bellarmine will have a better sense of its history. I hope we will have the best regional liberal arts and sciences program, the

President McGowan with pop superstar Michael Bolton and SGA president Martha Pfaadt.

best business and MBA program, the best nursing program, the best teacher preparation program, the most imaginative credit and noncredit adult programs. In addition to our new library, I want us to have a new campus center, chapel and dormitory, a lifetime sports and recreation center; and I want us to have about 1,000 more students, while retaining our small college status. In other words, I expect us to have become the premier liberal arts college in Kentucky.

"And where will I be in the year 2000? I don't know. I was 21 years at Fordham. I'll be here at Bellarmine as long as I sense that Bellarmine needs me and as long as the job continues to be fresh and challenging."

Other Administrators and Their Teams

An important mission of college administrators is to help their schools run smoothly like a well-oiled machine headed in a purposeful direction, with a minimum of potholes and detours. The President, the housekeeper, the office assistant, the bookstore manager, the mailroom sorter, the pressman in the duplicating office, the physical plant carpenter, the student affairs specialist, the baseball coach, the development and public relations personnel—all the people who serve the college outside the traditional instructional program—have been an indispensable part of Bellarmine's story. Indeed, the line between the "academic" and "nonacademic" programs of the college is often blurred, when secretaries are also students and administrators are also professors. During the early years almost all of the administrators taught credit or noncredit courses. The resulting academic camaraderie is the kind of family that Bellarmine has always encouraged and nurtured.

Every person associated with Bellarmine is also a public relations representative. A columnist for *The Record* in July of 1959 singled out the switchboard operator for special commendation. When you call

Bellarmine College, he wrote, "You hear this mellifluous, this utterly sweet, sweet voice say in a nice sing-song: 'Bel-lar-mine COL-lege.'" The effect? "Right away you forget who you wanted to talk to because just to talk to the switchboard operator makes you feel good for the rest of the day." Such people work with the attitude that a position at Bellarmine is not merely a job. It's an important responsibility. It has led to a loyal, dedicated corps of Bellarmine workers. And in the words of alumnus and staffer Jim Stammerman, it has given the college exemplary leaders: "Bellarmine has always seemed to have the right people at the right time."

The Rev. Raymond J. Treece

Second in command to Fr. Horrigan was another young priest, the Rev. Raymond Joseph Treece, born in Louisville in 1912, the son of a tailor. He attended Holy Cross School and was graduated as salutatorian from St. Xavier High School, where he was active in debating and school publications and was president of the student council. He later studied at St. Charles College in Catonsville, Maryland., and received his A.B. degree from Catholic University in 1934 and his M.A. in 1935. He took his theological studies at the Sulpician Seminary in Washington and did postgraduate work at Catholic University, after which he was ordained to the priesthood in Louisville in June of 1939. He was appointed assistant at the Cathedral of the Assumption and taught religion at Nazareth College, where, except for two years at St. Xavier High School during World War II, he taught until he was appointed Bellarmine's first vice president.

A columnist for *The Stub,* a Nazareth student publication, suggested that with Fr. Treece's extensive Nazareth connections, the new college might well be called "our little stepbrother." In 1946 he was appointed business manager of *The Record.* Treece served as vice president and chief financial officer until 1968, when he became executive vice president.

As vice president Fr. Treece served a variety of functions, such as supervising accreditation studies and serving as a catalyst for innovative programs, including the merger with Ursuline in 1968 and the development of programs in nursing and a master's degree in business administration. He also, on occasion, headed the campus bookstore, substituted for absent professors and served as athletic director, a position that was at odds with his sedentary lifestyle and chain-smoking habit. In the 1950s he also served as director of Catholic radio programs for the Archdiocese of Louisville. During the 1972-73 academic year he served as Acting President and played a major role in selecting Eugene Petrik as his replacement. The only jobs he ever refused were teaching math and supervising the dormitories.

In 1981 he resigned as vice president but stayed on a final year as special assistant to the President. After 33 years at Bellarmine Treece retired in 1982. The sometimes gruff, plain-speaking founding father was the speaker at commencement that year and used the occasion to criticize the state of higher education, especially the schools that seem to value computers and accounting more than history and philosophy. He lamented the fact that colleges don't lead society as much as they should. "I would have hoped," he said, "that higher education would have demonstrated more creativity, that it would have been out front beating the drums, not tagging at the end of the parade." About his impending retirement, he said, "The concept of a retired priest is only a decade old. A priest used to continue in his parish until he died. In fact, his last official act was his funeral." He joked: "One of the joys of being on Social Security is you can do or say

anything without losing your paycheck." One of his retirement options, he said, was to start a college for senior citizens, where no one under 55 would be admitted.

Noting his retirement editorially, *The Louisville Times* gave him its "butterfly award": "Bellarmine College's success in its 32-year history is not the result of the work of any one person. No one, however, has contributed more to the institution or served it longer than Msgr. Raymond Treece. . . . Msgr. Treece's butterfly symbolizes the community's thanks for helping to create an institution of which all of us, regardless of religion, can be proud."

Upon his retirement the priests who lived with him in the priests' residence recalled his colorful tastes

Fr. Treece at a Bellarmine Foundation reception, December 27, 1959.

and occasionally eccentric behavior. They recalled his love of a peanut butter and anchovies concoction and once suggested a sardine pizza. As director of the priests' residence, early one morning he discovered the presence of termites and fired off a memo to the maintenance staff at 8:02, demanding that the crisis be attended to by 8:20 or he'd blow up the house. His sometimes unpredictable, behavior became a part of campus folklore. Once, when he discovered a new lock on the boiler room door, he demonstrated his intention to have access to every room of the house by taking off the lock and the door. Fr. Crews' version is a bit different. "When the college installed a new door in the priests' living quarters without telling him, he went quietly with an ax and started to chop the door down. It took him about an hour."

In the early days of the college he was nicknamed "Old Steely Eyes" by students because he always seemed to discover truant behavior. For those who got to know him, however, he was warm, understanding and forgiving and served as father-confessor to many students in trouble.

Crews called him "the unofficial counselor to the college."

In his retirement he continued to be active, serving as assistant-in-residence at St. Francis of Assisi Church, executive director of the Archdiocesan Office of Education and head of a committee studying the Archdiocese's financial support of its priests. During the last two years of his life he lived with the Rev. John Eifler.

On March 15, 1985, he died of lung cancer. Of this crusty man with a soft heart, Fr. Horrigan said, "We worked together for 30 years and never had any disagreement. We had a beautiful and happy relationship. He was selfless and affable, a natural-born business manager and a nitty-gritty detail man who would fill in when a cook failed to show up for work." Alma Schuler can testify to his cooking abilities. "Fr. Treece was a very good cook," she says, " and while our offices were still on Princeton Drive, he would make our lunch, unless he was very busy. So he began to instruct me in how to prepare certain dishes like oyster stew. He showed me how to slip the oysters into the stew without causing the milk to curdle."

Fr. George Kilcourse points out two traits that made deep impressions on him, his dedication to social justice and his biblical scholarship. "He also gave personal service to deserving students who needed help to attend Bellarmine by arranging ingenious payment plans for them. He was also an excellent preacher, not only in the pulpit but on radio, where he conducted a Sunday morning Bible class for many years." His cousin, Margaret Maloney, head of Data Courier services on campus, calls him "forthright, honest and kind, with a fantastic sense of humor."

College registrar Robert Pfaadt remembers him as an indefatigable worker. "One time we were discussing a very difficult project and he said, 'Bob, if you think you can outwork me, I want you to try. But you can't. But try. Then I want you to challenge your staff to outwork you and not let them. That way we'll get this work done.' And we did." Indeed, it took such men and women to build Bellarmine College.

Perhaps the most sensitive of all the administrative positions is that of the academic head, variously called academic dean and vice president for academic affairs. Serving in that capacity have been eight men and one woman: Fr. John Loftus, 1950-69; Dr. Robert Preston, 1969-74; Dr. Clyde Crews, 1974-75; Dr. Robert Wittman, 1975-80; Dr. Nancy Howard, 1980-81; Dr. John Oppelt, 1981-85 and 1997-present; Dr. Steve Permuth, 1985-91; Dr. David House, 1991-95; Dr. Neil Thorburn, 1995-97 and Dr. John Oppelt from 1997 on, with a brief tenure as Acting President during Dr. McGowan's 1999 spring semester sabbatical. Dr. Doris Tegart served as acting vice president for academic affairs for the spring of 1999. One faculty wag explained the relative instability of this office: "It's because the dean has to make tough personnel and curriculum decisions and do the academic dirty work."

When the college was founded, Fr. Horrigan served as acting dean as well as President. The first academic dean, however, was Fr. John Loftus, a Barry Fitzgerald look-alike who could have been picked as a priest from central casting. When the college opened he was an English professor, registrar and dean of students. He also served as superior of the Immaculate

Conception Friary on Princeton Drive, the residence of the Franciscan priests on the Bellarmine faculty.

In August of 1953, Fr. Horrigan announced that the 45-year-old priest would officially become academic dean. A native of Ivesdale, Illinois, he had been long associated with Mount St. Francis Pro-Seminary in Floyd County, Indiana. At the seminary he had been a student, high-school principal and editor of the *Companion of St. Francis and St. Anthony,* the Franciscan's national magazine. He spent his novitiate at St. Francis College in Syracuse, New York, and completed his studies for the priesthood at St. Anthony-on-the-Hudson Major Seminary, Rensselaer, New York. He held undergraduate and graduate degrees from Catholic University and was ordained a Franciscan priest in 1932. During World War II he served as chaplain with the Army's Eighth Armored Division in Europe.

Replacing Fr. Loftus as registrar was the Rev. John R. Clancy, a Louisville native with graduate degrees

Fr. John T. Loftus

from Fordham University. Replacing Fr. Loftus as director of student personnel was the Rev. Hilary Gottbrath, who had studied at Catholic University, Notre Dame and Purdue and had an M.S. from De Paul University.

Soon Fr. Loftus became one of Bellarmine's chief spokesmen and a community leader. He was also a favorite with the students, despite what Bill Stewart called a sometimes "frightening demeanor." Fr. Hilary knew all his sides: "He was an excellent teacher and dean, but sometimes a tough man to live with because of his moods. When he was depressed, he would become silent." Most students and staff agreed with Alma Schuler's description: "He had great dark eyebrows that made him look rather intimidating, but I soon found out that he was very kind." David O'Toole remembered him as taking part in the faculty

camaraderie, ususually eating in the college cafeteria surrounded by a dozen or so faculty and students. "He made you proud to be around him," said O'Toole. Jack Kampschaefer recalls his attitude toward students: "He was a man of great charisma, a friend of the students who was always out among us mixing with us more than any other administrator or faculty."

Jim Stammerman remembers his openness in dealing with students. "One summer when I was on the student council, several of us went to Fr. John and said, 'We believe the orientation program in the fall can be improved.' He said, 'Fine. Give me your ideas.' We continued to give him our ideas at several more meetings, and finally he said, 'Why don't you all do it.' So we did. That fall Student Government did orientation using students to introduce freshmen to the college, and it went very well." Al Cassidy, senior class president of the Pioneer Class, assesses his legacy: "He genuinely loved the students. He gently raised our expectations, even our dress and manners as he encouraged socials with Ursuline and Nazareth. We all loved Fr. John's use of language. He could speak and write in poetry." Another Pioneer Class member says simply, "He touched my life in so many important ways."

Fr. Loftus also touched many people beyond the campus, and his interests ranged from civil rights and race relations to the lively arts of literature, painting, sculpture and music. His deep involvements in community life included the Great Decisions Program, the Religion and Labor Council, the United Nations Day, the English-Speaking Union, the Louisville Area Mental Health Center, the Kentucky Opera Association and the Louisville Urban League. In 1965 he took part in the Selma to Montgomery civil rights march.

He once said that the final word in the name of his religious order, the Order of Friars Minor Conventual, was "conventual," not "conventional." Of two divisions of the movement founded by St. Francis of Assisi in the 13th century, he explained, one branch adopted brown habits and lived a life of poverty in rural areas. His own branch adopted an urban, convented life, hence "Conventual." Needless to say, he was not conventional and took many controversial positions. Dr. Margaret Mahoney calls him "a real believer in social justice." In fact, she says, "his civil rights activities led people to call the college and threaten not to make any contributions to the college, but I suspect they weren't going to anyway."

A concrete and permanent record of his closeness to Bellarmine students is his library of personalized memos to them. In a prescient memo dated 21 November 1968, some two months before his death, this awesome, warm, daring, chain-smoking activist and dean of deans, wrote of his "sum of years spent reading, wondering, puzzling, trying, winning, losing, loving, being loved" and of Francis, Christ, Pope John, JFK and RFK, Martin Luther King, Merton "and always Horrigan"—all of them "stars in my nights"— these people who were "Friars, fellow priests, teachers, colleagues" in a "Sacrament of fellowship."

Earlier, in his yearbook memo to "My Friends, the Class of '68," he played class prophet in what would be his last address to a graduating class: "So it ends, I said to myself in the closing ceremonies of your senior year. It simply ends, a decade and a half of being the dean for all the graduates Bellarmine has ever produced. No choke. No quiver. No last hurrah. . . . Yearbooks are for memories, printed today, their value will be found in a year, a decade, a half century from now. You and your children's children will thumb through this volume and with smirk, sigh, or grimace of pain recall the spring of 1968. What will seem important then as the indicia of the times? Vietnam? Peace rallies? Conscience and the draft? The senior prom? Pass-Fail? The Student Senate? Comprehensives? The Children's Crusade? The Tragedies of Memphis and Los Angeles? The first job? You can choose now from a myriad of symbols. Time will serve as a filter. . . . Each year on November 11, I shall light a cigarette on the wrong end. Should you remember that symbol you can assay once more how different have you made

your world. Somehow we shall all know. I am quite confident I shall be pleased. So it ends. And begins." It was dated May 31, 1968. In little more than seven months he would be dead.

On January 7, 1969, he died of a heart attack, stricken at the television studios of WLKY, where he was preparing to tape a panel show called "Pastor's Study." He had just organized a public memorial service for two signal religious leaders of the 20th century, his close friend Thomas Merton and Protestant theologian Karl Barth. The catholicity of his reputation was echoed in the public press. A *Louisville Times* editorial praised him: "He was blessed with a warmth of spirit that kindled response in the young and old, in the proud and bereft, in the meek and militant." *The Western Recorder,* the Kentucky Baptist weekly, said editorially: "There was a warmth and openness about John Loftus that transcended any religious differences or barriers. He was his own man and never spoke the party line unless it was in line with his personal convictions. More non-Catholics in this community probably talked to John Loftus than to any other local Catholic leader." *The Louisville Defender* said of him: "He was 'Mr. Civil Rights' in the white community when that title would have been considered anything but an honor there. That was Father John Loftus, well-known crusader for human decency."

In a tribute to his long-time colleague, Fr. Horrigan wrote in *The Record* of his boldness in the cause of justice: "He supported many an unpopular cause and paid the price without flinching. At one stage of a particularly difficult controversy some years ago, it was necessary for him to change the phone number in his living quarters to escape the incessant flood of vicious crank calls which made sleep impossible night after night." Of his relationship to Bellarmine, Horrigan said that it was "a question of love at first sight."

Eighteen classes of Bellarmine students mourned him like the good father and counselor that he was. Like him, they knew of the good things that the college had opened up for them. Less than a year before his death, Fr. Loftus had tried to express Bellarmine's impact upon his beloved students: "I know its effect upon the students who are dear to me and the delight of my life. They often come to our doors with small vision. They leave with a world view that will equip them to make their own particular kind of contribution to the welfare of mankind." *The Concord* let him say his own eulogy: "There will be an hour—I can hear the minutes throbbing toward it—when the world I love will go on without me. Men will grow and deeds will be done and my role will be outplayed. I am afraid I dread that separation from my friends. . . . So it must be when the final curtain falls. The reviews will be excellent, and I shall know that having been a teacher will not have been a waste of fleeting time." A page one tribute in the same issue concluded: "Let us solemnly proclaim our debt to the man who commanded our highest admiration, our surest trust, our deepest love."

The funeral, held at St. Anthony Church, included a poem by one of those students, poet and professor of English Ron Seitz:

& so take the pen tonight 2 days you're dead now a

    dirty trick leaving us our head hands hearts
    shot thru

why did I wait & now? to write you open letter of love

    sorrowing the page as I go

why not then? breathing words to your face my kiss

    why now this stalling gesture grudged handout affection

      too late to color you my father

    had to wait 10 years your bulk in the doorway before loving

      you

    it took your dying that hospital bed to speak those

words

& you too a hand on my shoulder smiling

10 years I waited that touch

The body was buried at the Franciscan Province cemetery in Mount St. Francis, Indiana.

Succeeding Fr. Loftus as vice president for academic affairs was Dr. Robert A. Preston, a member of the philosophy faculty and a layman with degrees from Belmont Abbey College and Catholic University. His five-year tenure as academic head was a period of

Dr. Robert A. Preston

crisis, of shrinking enrollments and financial emergencies. Lingering problems from the 1968 merger with Ursuline had to be addressed. Programs had to be curtailed and faculty released. "Even tenured faculty were eliminated," remembers Bill Stewart. "It was a hard time for him and for all of us, but it was a matter of survival."

Financial officer Jack Kampschaefer knows the problems the professor-turned-dean faced: "Bob was in the hot seat as academic vice president, but he bit the bullet and helped to save the school by reducing the faculty by almost one-third. It was a bitter pill to swallow, and I think it took a drastic toll on Bob personally, but he knew it was necessary and he knew it was his job to do it. He did it. And he positioned the college for the turn-around that happened on Petrik's watch." Preston resigned from the deanship at the end of the spring 1974 semester and returned to the philosophy faculty until he accepted a position at Loyola University in New Orleans, later becoming president of Belmont Abbey in North Carolina. Despite the bad news that he sometimes represented, he was popular among faculty who respected his academic record and accepted the Draconian measures he had to implement. To librarian Rosalind Parnes he was "the ideal of the scholar-administrator."

Only eight years after he was graduated from Bellarmine College, 29-year-old Fr. Clyde Crews assumed the deanship in May of 1974. A Diocesan priest with a doctorate from Fordham University, this Louisville native served as an activist caretaker dean for one year. Although he and executive vice president Raymond J. Treece were the only Catholic clergymen on the college administrative staff, he told *Courier-Journal* reporter Keith Runyon that the Catholic influence was still strong on campus and in the classroom. Quoting playwright Herb Gardner's *A Thousand Clowns,* he said that a worthy goal of education is "to let human beings know there's a reason that they were born human beings and not a chair." He took the job as dean, he said, "because I believe that Bellarmine has a special

feeling I want to help preserve—an ethos that this is a place where a student can conduct a fearless search into reality."

Following Crews in June of 1975 was Dr. Robert J. Wittman, a 41-year-old professor of classics at Miami University in Ohio. A native of St. Marys, Pennsylvania,

Dr. Robert J. Wittman

Wittman held degrees from St. Vincent College and Tufts University and had also taught at Spring Hill

College in Mobile. He was married to concert soloist Joan Aceto Wittman and the father of two children. Wittman left at the end of the spring 1980 semester for a similar position at Kutztown State College in Pennsylvania. He was replaced by Bellarmine education

Dr. Nancy A. Howard

professor Dr. Nancy A. Howard, who had taught

classes in education and developed the special education program during her previous four years at Bellarmine. When she came to the college, she said she had no ambition to become dean, "But when I was asked, I said, 'That's it—that's what I want.'" A native of Ohio, the new dean held degrees from Wesleyan College in Georgia, the Southern Baptist Theological Seminary and George Peabody College. As a classroom teacher and as an administrator, Dr. Howard has had a long and distinguished career at Bellarmine College. In addition to serving as acting vice president and dean of academic affairs (she was the first woman dean or vice president and first Protestant administrator), she has served as assistant to the President, director of graduate programs in education, director of the MAT Accelerated Program, director of the SACS Reaffirmation Team and director of Special Education. In addition, she developed the MA program using a grant from WHAS and also the

MAT program. She is an indefatigable worker and a creative facilitator with a clear vision of what needs to be done. Then she makes sure it is done.

After one year in the dean's seat Dean Howard returned to teaching and was replaced by Dr. John A.

Dr. John A. Oppelt

Oppelt, who helped to oversee a period of great change during his three years as academic vice president in the early '80s. A native of Baltimore, Oppelt holds degrees in mathematics from Loyola College and the University of Notre Dame. He said he enjoyed being dean because "it makes me break out of my subject field and because of the fun of making things happen." He resigned at the end of the spring semester 1985 and was followed by Dr. Steve Permuth, who served until 1991. David House, with degrees from California State University and the University of Southern California, left an administrative position at Johns

Hopkins University to become vice president for academic affairs in May of 1991. Dr. House described his position at Bellarmine as "guiding, nurturing, connecting, fostering, pioneering."

In August of 1995 Dr. House was followed by Dr. Neil Thorburn. An historian with a doctorate in history from Northwestern University, he had served as president of Wilmington College in Ohio before coming to Bellarmine. He resigned in 1997 and Dr. Oppelt took over limited responsibilities as interim dean and was again made vice president for academic affairs in 1998. His selection followed a national search during which he was selected as the top candidate of over 100 applicants. Dr. Oppelt's permanent appointment as vice president and dean of Bellarmine College was approved by the Board of Trustees in May 1998. During Dr. McGowan's sabbatical in the spring of 1999, Dr. Oppelt was appointed Acting President and dean of education, and his position was filled by Dr. Doris Tegart as acting academic vice president.

Of the many imaginative and hard-working deans of students, the most legendary is Fr. Hilary H. Gottbrath. Although he was appointed to the first faculty of the college, he was sent by the Franciscans to De Paul University in Chicago to obtain a master's degree in mathemathics and actually joined the faculty in September of 1951. Jack Kampschaefer describes his contributions to Bellarmine: "Like most of us, he wore many hats. He taught math, served as dean of students and director of athletics, organized and led the pep band and the dance band called the Bellaires and directed the variety show we put on with Ursuline and Nazareth. He did what four or five people do today. Like all the founders, he was totally dedicated to this college."

After serving the college for 21 years, he resigned in February of 1973. He lists two reasons for leaving the college he helped found. "I didn't really want to leave Bellarmine, but times were changing. Indeed, they had changed drastically throughout the '60s; and I was part of the old guard. It was time for me to

move on. But the more compelling reason was that I had always been in education and had never served in a parish. For a Franciscan like me pastoral work is at the heart of his mission, so I left to become first, administrator of Our Lady of Consolation Church in Valley Station, then pastor of St. Anthony's Church in Clarksville, Indiana. Finally, I worked in the development office at Mount St. Francis. I feel that my vocation was fulfilled."

At Bellarmine he had been one of the campus pillars and remains one of the handful of people who epitomize the college. Marilyn Staples, who worked with him in student services, says, "I fell in love with Fr. Hilary. He was gracious, laid-back and he gave me enough room to be creative. And he knew how to have a good time." He assesses his work modestly: "I had no experience in student services, so I had to learn on the job. I tried to keep in close contact with the students and develop our student programs in consultation with them. Because of our close communication with them, I think we at Bellarmine were able to avoid most of the student unrest of the '60s. While other campuses were torn by riots, our students were mostly peaceful." Indeed, student services under Fr. Hilary and the other directors

John O. Kampschaefer, Jr.

fostered a feeling of camaraderie among students and faculty and administration that has been a hallmark of Bellarmine's history. A small monument to the good works that he did for Bellarmine is Hilary's, the recreation/snack facility for residential students that bears his name.

No one was associated so long and so intimately with Bellarmine College as Jack Kampschaefer—first, as a student, then, as first president of the alumni association and finally, as business manager and chief financial officer. As a faculty member once told him during the tight financial period of the early '70s, "I feel more secure knowing that you are watching and safeguarding the bottom line."

John O. Kampschaefer, Jr., a Louisville native, attended local parochial schools; then in 1950 became a member of the Pioneer Class at Bellarmine College, where he concentrated in accounting and minored in philosophy. Except for two years in the Navy, he worked for the accounting firm of Coopers and Lybrand from 1954 to 1968, when he began his long tenure serving three Presidents as financial officer for his alma mater. His titles have ranged from finance officer to vice president for administration and finance, and his duties have included financial affairs, long-range planning, auxiliary enterprises, construction and operations as well as supervision of the personnel office, the computer center and the physical plant. As a hands-on administrator, he has even climbed up on campus roofs looking for leaks. Whatever his title and whatever his duty, he has kept a vigilant eye on college finances and has helped make Bellarmine College a more secure place to study and work.

His hawk-eyed vigilance, however, has not always made him popular with students—when tuition rates went up—or with faculty, when salary increases declined. Nevertheless, with his help the college has remained open, paychecks were issued on time and bills were paid in timely fashion. As a librarian who has felt the sting of Kampschaefer's thrift, Marquita Breit says honestly, "When it comes to spending money, Jack Kampschaefer can be a stubborn Dutchman." Bernard Thiemann, a professor of business administration noted for his close attention to finances, calls him "a stabilizing influence" in good times and bad, a finance officer who has always told Presidents openly and honestly the cost effectiveness of their programs, whether or not they wanted to hear it.

Kampschaefer's supererogatory service to the college, however, was once pushed to the limit—or so it seemed. In August of 1977 someone stole $36,000

worth of lab and communications equipment from the campus, and the vice president for financial affairs came to the rescue. A fake fencing scheme was set up by local police in what came to be called The Great Southern Sting that netted more than 250 thieves and their accomplices. In order to recover 30 stolen microscopes—which the police had already retrieved—in time for the beginning of the fall term and to help in the recovery of other stolen goods, Kampschaefer agreed to a cover story that he had met with the thieves at 6:30 A.M. in a foggy field and paid a ransom.

Most of the administrators were kept in the dark, including Dennis Riggs, vice president for external affairs, who was completely taken in by the story. When the truth came out and the culprits were nabbed, Riggs said, "I admired Jack for being tough enough, naked enough, so to speak, to go out in a field to confront those thieves. He had me frightened for him. He's a top-notch finance man, but maybe

Jack Kampschaefer

Donna A. Olliges

there's a career for him in acting."

Asked to name at random some of the effective administrators he's worked with, other than Presidents, he listed such people as Robert Preston, academic dean, and Dennis Riggs, head of development and public relations, then adds: "Although I think we have a good team in place with Dr. McGowan, I'm particularly proud of my own people." He gives high praise to such people as these who have reported to him: Ruth Buntley, Robert Zimlich, Roy Stansbury, Tom Fisher, Donna Olliges and Jennifer Williams. Former campus store manager Georgia Doukas says of him: "Jack knows his staff well enough to know what we're capable of doing, even when we think we can't. He not only knows what we can do, but he'll help us when we need it." Indeed, he has appointed and nurtured employees who have made his department one of the strongest branches of the college.

Donna Amshof Olliges, who served him as assistant vice president for business affairs, appraises him in these words: "I think Jack's love of the college spills over to those of us who work for him. He always has the best interests of the college in mind, but he was always tolerant of his staff and let us disagree with him without holding it against us. In fact, I sometimes disagreed with him and even with the President; but I learned from him that once a policy decision was made I should always support it publicly. That's what I expected from my own staff." Like her mentor, she learned to stay up-to-date on new management techniques. "Our management buzzword for 1992," she remembers, "was TQM, for Total Quality Management." She calls her job at Bellarmine "very rewarding, especially during times of budget surpluses."

Although Kampschaefer could have earned greater financial rewards for his wife Sally Parsons and their four children had he stayed in the business world, he has never regretted his decision to make his career at Bellarmine. "I've had a love affair with this institution," he told a *Courier-Journal* reporter in 1975.

C. Dennis Riggs

Leonard J. Moisan

Fr. John Eifler

Msgr. Alfred F. Horrigan

When he retired in 1997, he was still in love. Furthermore, he was pleased to leave his desk and position in the capable hands of Robert Zimlich, a man he had groomed to fill his shoes. "I started growing up when I came to Bellarmine as a student," he says proudly. " I think I'm still growing with Bellarmine almost 50 years later."

The college's main fund raiser and public relations representative has always been its President. All three Presidents have been ably assisted, however, by men and women of character and persuasion, including George W. Dumstorf, Jr., Robert J. Desmond, Fr. John Eifler, Dennis Riggs and Dr. Len Moisan, who served for 10 years under Presidents Petrik and McGowan as vice president for development, resigning at the end of the fall semester of 1996. His replacement was Vince

Archbishop Thomas J. McDonough

Maniaci, who came to Bellarmine from the University of Tulsa after a national search. During his first year of service a record of over $6 million was raised for the college. Publicity and public relations have been adroitly handled through the years by such people as John M. Gatton, Grace O. Wells, Rebecca N. Towles, Gordon C. Layne, Kathleen Scully, Jo Anne Hohman and Edward B. Kanis.

The chancellors have been another vital part of Bellarmine's administrative and support structure. The college was, of course, called into being by its first chancellor, John A. Floersh, Archbishop of the Diocese of Louisville. His vision and early support of Bellarmine College was the firm foundation on which the college was built.

Archbishop Thomas C. Kelly

The first issue of *The Lance* in 1954 included this dedication: "Without his determination and arduous effort Bellarmine would have remained but a distant hope, instead of the promising college it is today." He served the Louisville Archdiocese as Bishop and Archbishop for 44 years and left a legacy of remarkable achievements, of which Bellarmine was the centerpiece. Alma Schuler remembers his sometimes sudden visits: "In the early days the Archbishop was very proud of the college and would bring prominent visitors to the campus, sometimes unexpectedly. In those days we

William J. Stewart

had no air conditioning and on hot days the faculty would sometimes dress informally, but word would quickly spread that he was on campus, and ties and coats would miraculously appear."

Following Archbishop Floersh's retirement in 1967, the Most Rev. Thomas McDonough was named to succeed him and thus become chancellor of Bellarmine College. After a supportive tenure with Bellarmine (his last official act for the college was to deed the campus land to the college corporation), he was succeeded by the new Archbishop Thomas C. Kelly, who has continued to nurture the special, warm relationship between the Archdiocese of Louisville and the college it founded. Archbishop McDonough died at a retirement home in Pennsylvania in August 1998 at the age of 87.

In June of 1996, a Bellarmine tradition was ended with the retirement of William J. Stewart. During his more than 31 years at the college, he served as director

Bill Stewart

of continuing education, director of the counseling center, dean of students, dean of the evening division, director of academic advising and finally as advisor to nontraditional students and coordinator of the Veritas Society. "I could call my years on the administrative staff," he says," 'the adventures of the deans.'" He is a prime example of the loyalty and longevity of many faculty and staff. From 1964, when he became placement director, until his retirement, he was a constant campus presence representing the dedicated people who have given Bellarmine College its special character as a warm, caring place where students feel at home during their college years and when they return as alumni. With his wife Barbara he has been a model of stability and integrity.

Stewart, who attended Bellarmine from 1955 to 1957, received a degree in psychology, then attended the University of Louisville for a master's degree in guidance and counseling. "One of my earlier jobs was room clerk at the Brown Hotel," he says, "where I was paid $9.50 for an eight-hour day. I refused an offer of $10 a day and left to work at a farm implement company. But I think the stress of rooming people and trying to take care of their complaints was a good preparation for my later work at Bellarmine." The stress at Bellarmine accounts for his changed looks, so he believes. "When I came to Bellarmine, I had a lot of brown hair, but I have now lost most of it and what remains has turned gray. I have no scientific

Robert G. Pfaadt

evidence, but I blame it on my 12 years as dean of students."

Stewart says modestly of his contributions to Bellarmine's history: "My claim to fame is that I'm the administrator who has ridden his bicycle to and from campus more than any other." In truth, his contributions are more vital and much greater, being among the handful of people whose name—among students, alumni and faculty—is always associated with Bellarmine College. As a tribute to his years of service to the college, in 1997 the first Bill Stewart Award was given to an outstanding adult student.

Two other members of the administrative staff who have had a long association with the college are Robert George Pfaadt and Marilyn Staples.

Marilyn J. Staples

Pfaadt, who studied one year for the priesthood, was graduated from Bellarmine in 1963 with a degree in history and later earned an M.A. in history from Arizona State. While serving Trinity High School as teacher, assistant principal and athletic director, he also taught classes in Bellarmine's summer schools. In 1976 he left Trinity to become director of admissions and records at Bellarmine. Because he believes that "a teaching administrator understands both the faculty and the students better," he has routinely taught courses in western civilization, American history, Russian history and senior seminar.

Another campus fixture and icon—and a sort of utility infielder—is Marilyn Staples, who came to Bellarmine to work in student services in 1968. Her work with students has ranged from moderating the yearbook to planning frequent socials and spaghetti suppers. During the 1988-89 academic year, she even served as dean of students. About her career at Bellarmine, she says, "For me Bellarmine has been a good fit, and I feel good about what I've been able to do here. I can say without hesitation that I believe in what Bellarmine is."

In this roll call of longtimers, Dr. Fred Rhodes is a relative newcomer, having come to Bellarmine in 1991 as vice president for student affairs and dean of students, a position he describes as "chief advocate of the students." Rhodes, who came from a similar position at the University of Louisville, says he has been "unbelievably satisfied" with his work at Bellarmine, a place that has provided him with "a wonderful opportunity" to go in new directions and grow professionally. As an adminstration leader under President McGowan, he has promoted a number of innovations, including a counseling center, advising for minority and international students, improvements in wellness and health services and a revision of the code of conduct. Under the new pact all parts of the college community—

Dr. Fred Rhodes

faculty, students, administration—have agreed that certain standards of conduct—such as those relating to cheating, lying and stealing—should apply to everyone.

Dr. Rhodes has been extremely successful in realizing President McGowan's vision of increasing student residency and creating a more vital campus life. Students living in residence halls increased from 320 in 1991 to 462 in 1998. In 1998, after a year of discussion by the Student Government Association and in student forums, a no-alcohol policy was instated, under which students are no longer allowed to consume alcohol on campus or at college-sponsored functions. Dr. Rhodes has also enhanced campus residency by bringing faculty and academic programs into the residence halls. Under Rhodes' leadership involvement in student government and in all student activities has increased significantly. Dr. Rhodes and Fr. Hilary Gottbrath both served as presidents of SACSA, the Southern Association of College Student Affairs, a regional professional organization.

Miss Norma Ryan

Finally, let us praise the often unseen and unsung heroes and workhorses of Bellarmine College. These are the people who have prepared the food, swept the halls and cleaned the rest rooms, insured the security, typed the letters, duplicated the memos and class schedules, cut the grass and repaired the leaky roofs. They make it possible to have a safe, convenient and comfortable environment in which to work and learn. In name they range from Anton Latkovsky, an early general factotum for the buildings and grounds department, to Norma Ryan, who came to Bellarmine in 1956 to do publicity and remained for 22 years in various positions, including secretary to Fr. John Loftus and Jack Kampschaefer. Like Ms. Ryan, these people have a unique perspective on the college and its people. She remembers, for example, that "Father John would give us a new word to learn every day." Fr. Horrigan, she says, brought out the poet in her: "I once wrote a poem on the paper clips that he twisted and mutilated while he dictated." She retired in 1978 because, she said, "If Fr. Horrigan can retire after 22 years at Bellarmine, so can I."

The list would include John Mahoney, who managed the cafeteria in the early 1960s. It would include part-time security officer Robert M. Howell, who won the grand prize in the 1980 Kentucky State Poetry Society Contest. It would certainly include the modest and decorous Miss Alma Schuler, Fr. Horrigan's once and only secretary, who was an officer in the National Secretaries Association and was once named Kentucky Secretary of the Year.

Joseph C. O'Toole

The buildings and grounds that make up the Bellarmine campus do not maintain themselves. Since 1950 the college has been fortunate in having a dedicated group of men and women who have been caretakers of the physical campus—from keeping the buildings and grounds clean and neat to rearranging offices as new administrators and faculty join the college family, from making sure that rusty pipes are replaced to guaranteeing that the heating system works on zero mornings in February.

Also named, therefore, should be people like Cecil Mingus, assistant supervisor of maintenance, who came to Bellarmine in 1978, when Dennis Seitz was director of the physical plant. This is his testimony: "Bellarmine was a blessing for me. Before I joined the maintenance staff, I worked at several jobs that had me doing the same thing day in and day out, and I got bored. Bellarmine gave me the opportunity to learn and use different skills. I've been able to be a jack-of-all-trades—carpentry, electricity, plumbing, air conditioning, heating, bricklaying. On my job you never know what to expect: a stopped sewer, a leaky roof or a power outage. Of course, we have men who are especially good in certain areas. Louis Harman, for example, is an excellent carpenter and cabinetmaker. Another is an expert in air conditioning. One is good with locks. And we are all on call 24 hours a day in case of emergencies."

One of his staff calls Tom Fisher "demanding but fair and the best plant manager we've ever had." After four years in the Navy, many more years in industrial management and eight years completing a business degree in Bellarmine's evening school, Fisher became director of physical plant. His good reputation is easy to understand. His responsibilities include maintenance and upkeep of all buildings and grounds, plus security, housekeeping and cleaning. In his words, his mission is "to provide a pleasant, clean, comfortable and safe environment for teaching and learning." Not all education takes place in the classroom, he believes. "I think that particularly in the residence halls we can help students grow and become responsible citizens." He is especially pleased with the frequent compliments he hears about Bellarmine's appearance. "We are proud of our campus," he says. "It is one of our best assets. It makes a good first impression on visitors, whether they are prospective students, faculty or donors. It looks good even as people drive down Newburg Road and see our well-kept golf course and baseball diamond. Contrary to popular opinion and common usage, our jogging track is not a community facility, but we don't plan to put a fence around it. It's another way we serve the larger community. The President wants to make this a model campus, and I think he'll do it."

He has tried to turn his department from a problem department to a help department. "We don't want people to see us as a complaint department. Of course, we can't respond immediately to all requests—in fact, some work doesn't need to be done immediately—but we're not the lonesome Maytag repairman sitting around waiting for a call. We're out working on something all the time. Of course, we have problems. There is occasional vandalism in the dorms. We find trash in classrooms and on the grounds. Sometimes we have a theft. But overall, I am impressed with the way our students and others behave. I'm not surprised when I see the President or a staff member pick up stray bottles or pieces of paper on campus, but I'm delighted when students and faculty do the same. It shows we all feel a part of this

community, and we want it to look good." His final words: "Bellarmine is a great place to work. I love it."

Like other Bellarmine administrators, he tries to put together a hard-working, dedicated and loyal staff and credits them for their good work. He praises Dave Reed, for example, head of security, for keeping the campus safe and secure at all hours of the day and night. "Once we get a good man or woman, they love it and stay."

Indeed, they do. Longevity at Bellarmine is not restricted to faculty and administration. Louis Harman, a carpenter and jack-of-all-trades on the maintenance crew in Physical Plant, came to the college in 1960. "I had been out of high school about a year and was working in construction around town, when I had a chance for a summer job at Bellarmine. Mr. Theodore Frank, who was superintendent of maintenance, started me at $44 a week. I took it and have been here ever since. I stayed on for a lot of reasons. I bugged Mr. Kampschaefer until I got a living wage, especially after I got married. I've liked the good working conditions, the steady work, the interesting, varied jobs I've done, and the fringe benefits, such as a good retirement plan and free tuition for my children. Bellarmine's been a great place to work. I now report to Tom Fisher, who is as good a maintenance and grounds manager as we've ever had. I've even gotten used to coming in every morning to a work schedule of 20 jobs that have to be done first!"

Tom Thornton

And how could the college function without a postal system—one that operates intramurally and extramurally? Despite ready access to telephones and e-mail-equipped computers, a college could not survive without old-fashioned paper and print. So hail to men like Tom Thornton, Tom Allen and John Kissel—men who have filled our boxes with memos from deans and letters from publishers and an occasional lure of a better job. Thornton joined the Bellarmine staff in the housekeeping department in 1959 and five years later transferred to the mailroom, where he remained until his retirement almost thirty years later. He quickly became a favorite with faculty and students, and they with him. As he once said, "It's hard to have friends for four years and then have to say good-bye to them at graduation time." It was just as hard to say good-bye to him at his retirement.

Tom Allen worked under Thornton as a work-study student and then replaced him. Allen said that he felt he was doing an important job in the mailroom. As a faculty member once told him, "We don't miss the President or a dean very much when they are absent from campus, but if you don't show up, we all know it quickly."

Jennifer Williams, director of the print shop and mailroom, has found Bellarmine not only a comfortable place to work but a convenient place to study. The daughter of a professor at the Southern Baptist Theological Seminary, she has found Bellarmine to be "a wonderful and supportive place. Here I've been able not only to do meaningful, creative work, but I've been able to finish up my college degree and become the mother of my daughter Brittany. I also feel that I'm an important part of the college community. In the print shop we touch on virtually all the work of the college, from class schedules and college catalogues to admission brochures and scholarly journals and books. With the help of hard-working and supportive staff members like Gwen Kirchner, I've been able to learn computerized design and printing and be creative in putting together the finished product."

Finally, we shall let Cheryl R. Love, secretary to Jack Kampschaefer and to his successor, Robert Zimlich as the college chief financial officer, represent all those dedicated and sometimes long-suffering administrative assistants who have made academic life pleasant for the rest of us. Mrs. Love not only received her degree from Bellarmine College but she also found her future husband in an English class. "I have been very pleased with both," she says.

All parts of the college ideally work together toward a common goal of education. A vital link in that chain of education is the college bookstore, managed by a succession of patient, long-suffering men

Susie Hublar   *Patricia Allen*

and women—like James Stammerman and Georgia Doukas. She came to the college as director of development, then switched to manager of the bookstore, which she described as "an income-producing arm of the college, selling books, educational materials and miscellaneous items like college memorabilia and soft goods that get Bellarmine's name out into the community. Every time a student wears a T-shirt or a jacket with the Bellarmine name on it, it promotes the college." She also calls the college store a listening post on campus. "I get to know the students and faculty and administration very, very well. I know that students,

Tina Milan

even when they're complaining about course work and the cost of books, have a lot of respect for the faculty. I work closely with faculty and I know and respect them, though I also know who will always be late with book orders and who will make last-minute changes." Like a lot of outlanders, Doukas soon became acclimated to Louisville and Bellarmine. "As a native New Englander—I'm from Wellesley, Massachusetts—I miss the ocean very much, but I have learned to love this community, the city and the college. It's home now." She left the college in 1998 and the bookstore is now operated by Follett College Stores.

Indeed, care has always been taken to make all Bellarmine people, regardless of their educational level or rank or position, feel vital in implementing the mission of the college. And so they were. And are. Norma Ryan was hardly exaggerating for herself or others when she concluded: "Bellarmine was my life."

The Faculty

Although the process of education has been greatly complicated since ancient Greece, when a school was formed once a teacher and a learner met, its essence can still be reduced to teachers and students. At Bellarmine this relationship is still at the core of the college mission.

Dean of Students Fred Rhodes puts the centrality of faculty this way: "I've asked students at different schools, 'What is the heart of the campus for you? What do you think you will remember most about this school after you leave?' At many schools students have answered the dorm life or the library or the student center. At Bellarmine College most of the students have talked about faculty. Ask a Bellarmine alumnus about his college days, and chances are he'll mention a favorite professor." Alumnus Michael Steinmacher verifies Rhodes: "What I like best about Bellarmine is the faculty."

Indeed, Bellarmine has always preached and practiced the belief that the college is only as good as its faculty. Buildings and grounds and equipment and good programs and high-powered administrators are all important, but the faculty remain central. Alumna Kaelin Rybak suggests why Bellarmine students think so highly of the faculty: "I was overwhelmed by the academic acumen of most of my professors."

Most faculty who have come to Bellarmine have found a congenial, professor-friendly college. Indeed, the loyalty and longevity of

Bellarmine faculty and staff are such that few schools can equal. For example, retiring at the end of the 1995-96 academic year were nine people who collectively represented 243 years of service to the college. The retirees included Rosalie Baker, assistant to the library director, 45 years; Thomas E. Kargl of the chemistry faculty, 37 years; Sr. Pat Lowman of the history faculty, 31 years; William J. Stewart of student services, 31 years; and Wade Hall of the English faculty, 27 years. At that time many members of the active faculty had already served the college for more than 30 years.

Other characteristics of the faculty are worthy of noting. A very high percentage of Bellarmine's faculty have held Ph.D.s or other terminal degrees in their fields—84 per cent in the mid-'90s, compared with 60 per cent nationally. Despite Bellarmine's Catholic origins and continued emphasis, the college has always had a diverse faculty with an open-door policy for non-Catholics. Faculty have had three major responsibilities as members of the Bellarmine community— teaching, scholarship and service— with the primary emphasis on

Sr. Pat Lowman and Trudie McManus

Dr. Thomas Kargl

teaching. Indeed, for a college focused primarily on teaching, the faculty have been remarkably productive as scholars and artists and have contributed heavily to the improvement of the campus and local community.

The early faculty members set a high standard. Dr. Jack Ford, who joined the philosophy faculty in 1952, profiles their uniqueness: "Most of the early faculty were first generation M.A.s and Ph.D.s who were teaching first-generation college students. We were all hungry people who were highly motivated. We developed a contagious spirit. There was a lot of pride in self and pride in our disciplines, but we also were proud of the work being done in all the departments. We talked to each other and had not only personal but interdisciplinary dialogue. It was my great privilege to serve with exceptional faculty and exceptional students. I'm not sure what we had could happen again—unless we could duplicate the same chemistry in another place."

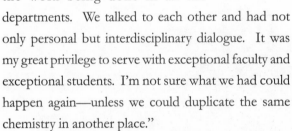

Dr. Dan Sweeny

During this pioneer period faculty, administration and students were keenly aware of the enterprise they were undertaking and the risks involved; and they worked together for the common good. Faculty taught overloads. Administrators were classroom teachers. There were no binding "job descriptions" or clear-cut delineations between faculty and administration.

Dr. Jack Daly

Everyone worked to enhance student activities. Alma Schuler, secretary to Fr. Horrigan, remembers that everyone worked hard without complaining: "Those first years were exciting, interesting, fun days when we all worked

until the work was completed. No one watched the clock."

Dan Sweeny remembers that during his first years at Bellarmine in the late '50s, the faculty had to set up and take down the chairs for the graduation ceremony in front of the administration building. "We had to move them from the second floor of the administration building. Not everyone liked it, but we did it." He also had four separate course preparations during his first semester in the fall of 1957. Jack Daly said that when he came to Bellarmine he was a chemistry department of one, "so departmental decisions were always unanimous." He also taught all the chemistry courses offered, "but I didn't feel burdened because I was young and energetic."

In trying to create an immediate academic reputation, the faculty sometimes set Ivy League standards—or so the students thought. Fr. Killian Speckner of the English faculty admitted his guilt: "The students thought we worked them too hard. I suppose we were tough on them. They complained about all the papers I had them write and the poetry I had them memorize. In some of my classes the students were required to learn 500 lines of poetry. They sometimes grumbled about the requirement, but I think they liked it after they had done it. I still meet my old students who can recite at least some of those lines." Fr. Killian, who stayed with the college for more than 15 years, was known for his sometimes strange habits: "I had a reputation for being a bit eccentric, and maybe I was. I do remember my habit of sometimes bouncing a rubber ball against the wall during class."

The pride felt by the perhaps overworked students is evident in this testimonial by a member of the Pioneer Class. "We didn't have the buildings, the facilities or the programs of older schools, but I never once felt shortchanged because I had come to Bellarmine. We respected the faculty and they respected us. I felt we could learn as much as they could teach. It was a great learning atmosphere."

Who were these faculty so highly praised by their students? Late in August of 1950 Archbishop Floersh announced 18 members of Bellarmine's first faculty. Ten of them were Archdiocesan priests, two were Franciscan Conventual priests and six were laymen. The five full-time priests of the Archdiocese were the President and vice president, Fr. Horrigan and Fr. Treece; the Rev. John T. Lyons, who taught French and logic; the Rev. Chester Bowling, who taught mathematics and philosophy; and the Rev. John D. Davis, who taught economics.

Bob Fitzpatrick

Part-time professors lent by the Archdiocese were Msgr. Felix N. Pitt, secretary of the local Catholic School Board, who taught philosophy; the Rev. Richard J. O'Hare, who taught psychology and speech; the Rev. Raffo Bowling, who taught biology; the Rev. Stanley A. Schmidt, who taught German; and the Rev. John W. Dickman, who taught Latin. The two Franciscans were the Rev. John Loftus, college registrar and instructor in English, and the Rev. Killian Speckner, who taught English.

The six lay faculty were Messrs. Edward J. Kimmel, who taught chemistry; Edward S. Schroering, who taught accounting; Robert J. Fitzpatrick, who also taught accounting; Robert T. Burke, Jr., who taught business law; Irvin Hopkins, who taught "art crafts"; and Miss Betty Delius, college librarian, who established the precedent—practiced until recently—that all Bellarmine librarians would have faculty status. Delius, with degrees from Nazareth College and Catholic University, technically became the first member of the Bellarmine faculty.

In addition, a number of priests began graduate studies at various Catholic universities to prepare for teaching at Bellarmine. The Rev. John Clancy studied education at Fordham. The Rev. Lawrence Kieffer began work in psychology at Catholic University. The Rev. Carl Biven enrolled in economics at St. Louis University. Fr. Eugene Scherzer was selected by the Archbishop to attend Fordham to prepare for teaching English and communications arts. Finally, two Franciscan fathers started studies at Notre Dame, the Rev. Urban Wagner in religious education and the Rev. Edwin Borntraeger in political science. By 1954 the faculty had grown to 34, with 14 priests full-time and

Fr. Fred Hendrickson

2 priests part-time, plus 6 laymen full-time and 12 laymen part-time. Despite attempts to prepare additional priests for teaching, the percentage of priests on the faculty would continue to diminish as time passed.

Throughout the college's history and down to the present, however, clerical members of the faculty have been an ever-ready and ever-vital presence. In the beginning this church connection was emphasized in college publicity. In an article in the August 11, 1951, *Record,* Fr. John Loftus, then college registrar, stressed the fact that the core faculty consisted of Archdiocesan priests and Franciscan fathers, who were assisted by laymen. A student from the '50s remembered one of the priests this way: "Fr. Jeremiah was an Irishman who told us some of the wildest stories we'd ever heard, but we assumed they were true. After all, he was a priest, and back then you believed anything a priest told you."

Many of the early clerical faculty also served as assistant pastors in local parishes. In the fall of 1957, for instance, Fr. Charles K. Rusterholtz was appointed an instructor in mathematics but continued to serve at St. Francis of Assisi Church; and Fr. Howard French served both the theology department and St. Paul Church. Indeed, it is hard to imagine Bellarmine without its roll call of priests, from Fr. Horrigan to Fr. Kilcourse. Fr. Eugene Zoeller helped to make theology

Sr. M. Bernadette Trance

a professional discipline at Bellarmine and forged strong ecumenical ties to the community as well as to Catholic institutions like the Abbey of Gethsemani. Another prominent priest was Fr. Vernon Robertson, who was an Episcopal priest until his conversion to Catholicism in 1961. In 1967 he was ordained in

Rome by Pope Paul VI and in the mid and late '60s taught and headed the John XXIII Institute at Bellarmine.

A priestly fixture on campus has been Fr. Fred Hendrickson since he became a part-time instructor in philosophy in 1961 and assumed full-time status in 1963. He is a native Kentuckian. "I would like to say that I'm from Chicken Gizzard Ridge in Casey County, but I'm actually from the more prosaic-sounding Dry Creek, near a small Catholic enclave called Clementsville surrounded by Protestants. As a professor, I'm not much of a metaphysician. I'm more interested in the practical application of philosophy, especially in areas like medical ethics." Indeed, it is in the field of medical ethics that he is a recognized authority. He believes his priesthood at Bellarmine has been well spent. "I think that I have fulfilled my vocation by being a philosophy professor at Bellarmine College. I have not wasted my priesthood by serving in a college classroom."

The first nun to teach at Bellarmine was Sr. M. Bernadette Trance, an Ursuline who joined the education faculty in the fall of 1963. One previously skeptical student said after a semester in her class, "Sisters make very capable college teachers. I'd like to

see Bellarmine have more of them." His wish was prophecy. In the following years nuns on the faculty have included Sr. Patricia Lowman, OSU; Sr. Clarita Felhoelter, OSU; Sr. Rose Howard, SCN; Sr. Theresa Sandok, OSM; and Sr. M. Serra Goethals, SCN—all of whom have served the college long, productively and with distinction. Other nuns served on the faculty during the transition period of the merger of Ursuline and Bellarmine in the late '60s and early '70s. Among those who served for shorter periods were Sr. M. Raymond Carter, Sr. Vera Del Grande, Sr. Paula Hunt, Sr. M. Alphonsine Lesousky, Sr. M. Madeline Andriot, Sr. M. Consuelo Price and Sr. M. Concetta Waller.

Joan Riehm, an Ursuline alumna, journalist and former deputy mayor of Louisville, remembers fondly many of her professors, including Sr. Clarita, who, she says, "not only taught me a fabulous appreciation of English literature but helped me learn how to write and edit—something I've never forgotten." Another alumna, Evelyn Williams Poppeil says this of her: "I had Sr. Clarita before and after the merger of Ursuline and Bellarmine. She was a wonderful teacher but very demanding. We thought she must have worked weekends to think up work for us to do. One important lesson she taught me was to use my imagination."

Sr. Pat Lowman also has many devoted former students. "I've been an Ursuline for well over 50 years, and I cherish that title above all others. It outranks my Ph.D. I have, indeed, loved being a nun, but I guess I'm one of the wild nuns. After Vatican II made it possible for us to wear modified habit, I began to wear one in 1968 with a veil, which I soon discarded. I decided I wanted people to determine who I am without the habit or the veil. I love the changes that have occurred in the Church since Vatican II. It is more human now."

Several priests have left the faculty because of their resignations from the priesthood. The first to leave was Fr. John D. Davis of the theology faculty, who left the priesthood in August of 1969 because of his opposition to mandatory celibacy for priests. He was denied permission to remain on the faculty by Archbishop McDonough because of a Vatican order that forbade ex-priests from serving in their old positions. Also resigning over the celibacy requirement was Fr. John Heckman, a 39-year-old philosophy professor, who left the school and the priesthood in 1973. Despite resolutions sent to the college administration by the Student Assembly and the Committee of the Faculty, Acting President Treece said it violated Archdiocesan policy to retain an ex-priest in his same ministry.

James Leahy

Heckman had been a Franciscan priest for 13 years and had taught at Bellarmine for six years. The Board of Trustees formalized the exclusion of ex-priests from the Bellarmine faculty in May of 1973.

Indeed, the new lay faculty added during the decade of the '50s contributed greatly to the building of the college. Joining the faculty in the fall of 1953, for example, was John Daly, a chemist at Du Pont Company of Charlestown, Indiana. In the fall of 1954, part-time instructors Fr. William Hogan in sociology and Fr. Raffo Bowling in philosophy became full-time. New faculty that year included Fr. Neil Callahan in English and language instructor George White. Also the fall of 1954 marked the first time that a woman joined the active teaching faculty, when Ellen Mochel became a part-time instructor in the chemistry department. By the fall of 1954 women had also begun teaching noncredit courses in the community education program. Margaret Dagen, for example, offered an evening course entitled "Human Problems in Industrial Relations."

Of the five new instructors added for the fall 1955 semester, three were priests: Fr. Joseph H. Voor,

psychology; Fr. Howard French, theology; and Fr. Edwin J. Scherzer, English. The laymen were Henry S. Wilson, chemistry, and James Patrick Leahy, math. Dr. Wilson, who had been a member of the faculty at Louisville Municipal College, the black branch of the University of Louisville, had lost his job when the all-black college was closed in 1951. He had worked as an executive with Mammoth Life & Accident Insurance Company and as a research chemist before joining the Bellarmine faculty. His great-great-great grandfather came to Louisville in 1783 in an oxcart as a slave from Virginia.

The three new faculty appointed for the fall 1956 semester were all laymen: Benson S. Alleman, pronouncer for the National Spelling Bee in Washington, in speech and forensics; Robert J. Raitt, French; and Richard W. Sames, biology. Ed Hamilton, a recent Bellarmine graduate, was appointed to direct alumni affairs, student recruitment and job placement.

By the fall of 1957 the faculty had grown to 60, including a number of new faculty, the Rev. Arnold G. Dearing in theology; the Rev Charles K. Rusterholtz in math; Helen Lyford in biology; Thomas M. Sheehan in English; and G. Daniel Sweeny in chemistry. James Spalding, a 1955 alumnus, was appointed assistant coach and instructor in biology. Dr. Lyford, who had

Gus Coin

taught part-time since 1955, became Bellarmine's first full-time female member of the teaching faculty.

The 1958-59 academic year marked the addition of 10 more full-time faculty, including two who were to be among Bellarmine's most prominent professors: Jude P. Dougherty, with degrees from Catholic University, in philosophy; and Margaret H. Mahoney, with degrees from the College of Great Falls in her native Montana and from the University of Minnesota, in history. Likewise, illustrious additions were made in the fall of 1959, with the addition of Stanley Zemelka, a German native with a doctorate in economics and international finance from the University of Innsbruck in Austria, as an instructor in business administration; Alex Groza, a native of Martins Ferry, Ohio, who was named head basketball and baseball coach as well as instructor in education; and David P. O'Toole, a Louisville native with degrees from the University of Louisville, as an instructor in mathematics. The new part-time faculty included Robert F. Munson, a psychologist trainee at Veterans Hospital, with degrees from the universities of Louisville and Kentucky, as a lecturer in psychology.

The decade of the '60s would see many more laymen, women and alumni joining the Bellarmine faculty and staff. In the fall of 1960 W. Windell Bowles, a 1957 graduate, became an instructor in accounting. John Moll, '55, was appointed assistant registrar, and Eugene J. Hunckler, '59, was named assistant director of college relations. At the beginning of the new decade the faculty count was 84, with 59 full-time. Joining the faculty in September of 1961 were the Rev. Bonaventure Crowley, in history and philosophy; Italian native Dante Vena, a respected painter who became director of art; and Gus Coin, who moved from part-time to full-time director of music.

Anna Jackey

Dr. Kathleen V. Lyons

Joining the faculty in 1961 as a visiting professor of philosophy was Daniel C. Walsh, who had taught Thomas Merton at Columbia University and who had pointed him toward the priesthood and the Abbey of Gethsemani. He had come to the abbey the previous year to do a research project with Merton, studying manuscripts and texts of little-known medieval authors. As a close friend of the Kennedy family, Thomas Merton and Fr. John Loftus, he was devastated by the deaths of many of his friends in the '60s. At the age of 60 in April of 1967 he was invited by Archbishop Floersh to join the priesthood. Because he had never studied in a seminary, he joked, "I suppose you could say I'll not be a clerical but a lay priest." Walsh, who had never married, was in semi-retirement at Gethsemani when he was ordained a few years before his death.

When Kathleen V. Lyons was appointed to the English faculty in the fall of 1963, she was the third woman to serve Bellarmine in that capacity. With degrees from Nazareth College and Fordham University, she was beginning an illustrious career at Bellarmine that would include a stint as assistant dean. Also beginning a lengthy tenure that year was N. Robert Sullivan, a Bellarmine graduate with a master's degree in business management from the University of Kentucky. Sullivan became an instructor in business and director of student financial aid, a position he would hold for more than three decades. A refugee from Cuba, Dr. Ofelia Perez-Daple, also joined the faculty as a teacher of Spanish; and Fr. Frederick Hendrickson, who had been teaching philosophy part-time and was assistant editor of *The Record*, became a full-time philosophy professor.

In the fall of 1964 Thomas E. Kargl, a professor of chemistry, brought the entire science program from Ursuline College to Bellarmine as a part of the

Dr. Thomas J. Kemme

coordination program which would lead to the 1968 merger of the two colleges. The father of eight children, Dr. Kargl and his family lived on a small farm near Jeffersontown, where they raised chickens, rabbits and calves for food and also grew bushels of fruits and vegetables for their table. "Gardening is pretty much a necessity with eight kids," he once told a writer for *The Concord*. Other new faculty added that semester included John J. Finnegan in accounting, Thomas J. Kemme in English, Sara-Jean McDowell in English and Scott W. Cole, a state labor leader who joined the business administration and political science faculty. Robert F. Munson moved from part-time to full-time in psychology. In the spring of 1965 James W. Douglas, a scholar and expert on Vatican II, became the first lay professor of theology.

Dr. Maureen Norris   *Dr. Barbara Hulsmeyer*

Joining the philosophy faculty in the fall of 1966 was Robert A. Preston, and Bernard F. Thiemann was added in business administration. The following year Anna M. Jackey was appointed to the accounting faculty and Joan Tucker Brittain to English. In 1969 Wade Hall became the new chairman of the English department. He would be the subject of great notoriety in December of 1974, when he purchased an original etching by James McNeill Whistler at a local flea market for $2.50 which was worth more than $5,000. The resulting story in *The Courier-Journal* was syndicated and circulated around the world.

Dr. Serra Goethals

Professors added to the faculty in the '70s included Sr. M. Serra Goethals, who became head of the department of education in June of 1975. With degrees

Jerry L. Rodgers

from Brescia College, Spalding University and Peabody College of Vanderbilt, she also brought a wealth of teaching experience that included seven years at Indian mission schools in New Mexico. Frank Slesnick became a professor in business administration and economics in the fall of 1975. Among new faculty one year later were Nancy A. Howard in education and Fr. Theodore Vitali of the Passionist Order in philosophy. In the mid-'70s the program in nursing was begun by Lucy Erwin, who came to Bellarmine from Western Kentucky University. By the fall of 1978, 18 of the 53 full-time faculty members were women, and *Concord* editor Ruth Lancaster commented that "Overall, Bellarmine has an admirable record in hiring and promoting women faculty." One of the college's most popular faculty members of the late '70s was Jerry Lee Rodgers, who was called in a *Concord* profile "Bellarmine's Own Renaissance Man"

Dr. Margaret Miller

because of his teaching (in English), writing (plays and poems), singing (with the Kentucky Opera Association chorus) and plumbing expertise (on his old Victorian house in the Highlands).

Dr. Rose Howard

Notable among the new faculty added in Bellarmine's fourth decade was David Brown, a former president of Transylvania University, who was named to the first Brown & Williamson Chair in Economics in the fall of 1983. As Bellarmine's pioneer faculty began to age and retire, younger members were appointed in the '80s and '90s, including Allison Brennan in education, William E. Fenton in math, William Tietjan in biology, Graham Ellis in chemistry, Ann Jirkovsky in psychology, Joanne Dobbins in biology, Joshua Golding in philosophy, Gail Henson in communications, Tim Swenson in business administration and Carole Pfeffer, John Gatton, Charles Hatten, Bert Hornback, M. Celeste Nichols and Anthony O'Keeffe—all in English. Dr. Hornback, a native of Bowling Green, Kentucky., came to Bellarmine in 1992 from the University of Michigan, where he had taught and authored scholarly books for almost 30 years. Susan Hockenberger Davis joined the nursing faculty in 1983. Other new members of the nursing faculty included Margaret Miller, Barbara

Harrison, Sherill Cronin, Barbara S. Hulsmeyer, Chris Algren, Joan Masters, P. Sue Biasiolli and Mary E. Pike. As one faculty wag stated it, "Despite all the grayheads on campus, Bellarmine's faculty is not getting older; it's getting better, especially with the infusion of all that young blood."

With advanced degrees from dozens of respected universities all around the country—and world— Bellarmine's faculty had reason to take pride in itself. But impressive academic degrees are not the only criteria of a good faculty. A track record in business or industry, teaching experience and dedication, scholarly productivity and the achievements of alumni are also measures of a good faculty. Many of Bellarmine's faculty in commerce and the sciences, in particular, have brought invaluable on-the-job experience to their classrooms. Jack Daly, the youthful, jovial, laid-back member of the chemistry faculty for more than 40 years, is a prime example of a faculty member with a rich background of industrial experience. "I think it's very important for professors to have business and professional experience and consulting experience," he says, "because the contacts are good for your students who need summer and permanent jobs and admission to good graduate schools."

Dr. Anthony O'Keeffe

Dr. William E. Fenton

Dr. Charles Hatton

Dr. Ann Jirkovsky

Dr. Bill Tietjen

J. B. Searles

G. Daniel Sweeny also worked for Du Pont before moving to Bellarmine to teach chemistry for more than 35 years. "I worked at Du Pont for two years," he says, "just long enough to tell my students of the pitfalls of an industrial career."

J. B. Searles' knowledge of marketing and business administration was based on a lengthy career in business before he joined Bellarmine's marketing faculty in the '80s. "I knew Gene Petrik through the local Chamber of Commerce. He knew about my jobs in marketing and advertising with a number of large national corporations and my work with General

Electric in Louisville. When I retired Gene asked me to apply for a position at Bellarmine. I came and talked with Stan Zemelka and Bernie Thiemann and other faculty members and was impressed enough to spend a very enjoyable and fulfilling decade at the college. I think my main contribution to our program in commerce was my ability to bring the real world of business into the classroom, especially in the MBA program, where I used real-life case histories. I could say, 'This is what we did in a similar situation. This is what happened. This is what went wrong and what went right.' You see, I wasn't talking merely about theory because I had been on the business firing line for most of my life. I think it's crucial for business professors especially to keep in touch with life off campus through consulting—even if they've had prior business experience. It keeps them up-to-date."

Bellarmine has, indeed, been fortunate to have such men and women on its faculty. It has also been fortunate to have a productive and colorful faculty—people of strong and passionate personalities. No one can say that Bellarmine's faculty has been cookie-cut out of the same dough. Take librarian Marquita Breit. The daughter of a man nicknamed "Snakebite," she once considered becoming a brain surgeon but was stopped not by gross anatomy, she says, but by chemistry. She is now an avid reader of mysteries, especially ones "filled with dead bodies." Or consider Thomas Devasia, a native of India, who joined the history faculty in the fall of 1972. His wit and exotic charm added a special dimension to the campus for almost two decades. Or regard the two Nancy Howards on the faculty at the same time. Nancy S. Howard was an admissions counselor, and Nancy A. Howard was a professor of education and sometime dean. Said Dean Howard of the frequent confusion between the two: "It's understandable. After all, we're both witty, charming and intelligent." Enough said.

Or take the personable Robert Frank Munson, who taught and practiced psychology for more than 30 years. Like many of the Bellarmine faculty, he grew

Dr. Robert F. Munson

Dr. John Voor

up in very modest surroundings in Louisville's West End. His mother died soon after he was born, and he was placed briefly in an orphanage, then was taken in by relatives living in one of Louisville's poorest neighborhoods. "I grew up in a house on an alley," he recalled, "with an outdoor privy. We were so poor I was sent each summer to live with other relatives on a farm in Hardin County to work and get enough to eat. I think my background is one reason I liked my Bellarmine students so much. In the early years almost all our students were from blue-collar families. They were the first generation in their families to go to college and were work-oriented, hungry and highly motivated. They knew then that a college degree was a guarantee of a good job and a better life."

Few faculty members have had a background as dramatic as Stanley Zemelka of

Dr. Stanley Zemelka

the school of business. Born on the German-Polish border, he was drafted into the German army during World War II and served as a combat infantryman in the invasion of Russia. On Christmas Eve 1943 he was severely wounded in both arms during the winter retreat from the Ukraine and spent the rest of the war in army hospitals.

After the war he managed to go to Austria to resume his studies and in 1951 came to the United States with his wife Magda to do postgraduate work at the University of Illinois. For five years previous to joining the Bellarmine faculty, he worked as a payroll auditor for General Motors. After he felt that he was proficient enough in English, at the age of 39 he resumed his first love of teaching and soon became one of the mainstays of the business faculty. Ironically, he discovered after coming to Bellarmine that one of

Ladtodkis, the original spelling of his name, arrived in the United States with his wife and six children—Victoria, Aurelia, Generosa, Anastasis, Emerita and Leonard Jr.—from Latvia. (There would be three more children born in Louisville.) The Greek and Latin names of his children reflected his devotion to the classics. The family was accompanied by Latkovski's elder brother Anton, who was given a job on the college maintenance staff.

Professor Leonard Latkovski leads a language class in 1951.

his new colleagues, Leonard Latkovski, had been in Riga, the capital of Latkovski's native country of Latvia, when Zemelka's unit helped to capture it during their drive on Leningrad.

In Bellarmine's gallery of colorful faculty, none has stood out more than Leonard Latkovski and his large family. Less than a week before Christmas 1950,

Latkovski, who spoke 12 languages and had taught Greek and Latin at a Catholic boys school before the war in Latvia, said his "arrival in a free country is our Christmas present." With the help of a long-time friend, Dr. Stanislaus Jaudzems, a physician at the Hazelwood Sanatorium, the family had been sponsored by the National Catholic Welfare Conference and resettled in America. At a World Refugee luncheon at the Kentucky Hotel in March 1960, Latkovski received a certificate of appreciation from actress Celeste Holm designating him and his family models of the refugee settlement program.

He reported that the Communists had confiscated all their money and property when they took over in 1941; then, he said, the Nazis had come and occupied the country until they retreated in 1944, taking his family with them to Germany, where they were set to work digging antitank ditches near the Rhine River. Years later he said, "I personally destroyed a fine turnip crop." He was liberated by the American army. Because of the Communist regime in Latvia, the Latkovski family had remained in Germany following the war, and he taught technical languages in a Displaced Persons camp. Teaching at Bellarmine he soon became known to everyone simply as "the professor" and a campus legend. As a professor-of-all-languages, he frequently taught small classes for students interested in exotic languages which no one else could teach.

The professor and his family were immediately welcomed by the city, and stories about his cultural *faux pas* began to circulate. Soon after he arrived he was interviewed by *The Louisville Times*. Later, as he was walking down the street with an American friend, he saw a large brick wall with only the words "Early Times" written on it. He asked, "Do you subscribe to *The Early Times?*" His friend laughed and said, "No, I don't because Early Times costs more than a nickel."

Gradually, however, he and his family settled into the American lifestyle; and although he retained a fondness for European breads, he even learned to like strange new American dishes like chili. John Ford remembered him fondly but questioned his conversion to American ways: "What I remember most about him was his guilelessness and his kindness and his honesty. But he was always a man of the Old World. He could have lived here a million years and never really been Americanized, though he tried very diligently. My wife and I tried to convert him to American baseball and took him and his family to games, but we didn't succeed very well. One of his sons became a good athlete, but the Professor said, 'I want him to study more and play ball less.'"

At his retirement from Bellarmine in 1976 at the age of 70, the college awarded him the degree of Doctor of Letters. It was a degee that he had earned with his dignity, his breadth and depth of knowledge and his dedication to learning. His boyhood dream, he once said, was to become a professor. "Professor for me," he said, "meant a man who knows, one who can answer your questions and who will sit with you to discuss." One of his colleagues, Jack Daly, said of him: "He loved scholarship for its own sake, in the Old World sense. Indeed, he never got over his Old World respect for the position of professor. It even affected his relations with a member of his family. Because his brother Anton worked on the Bellarmine grounds crew, the two men could not associate socially in public. Leonard was the professor and Anton was the grass cutter."

Jack Daly gave many gifts to this college that he loved and served for almost 40 years. A native of Lexington, Kentucky, he left his job as an industrial chemist with the Du Pont Corporation, took a large pay cut, and joined the Bellarmine faculty in the fall of 1953. Msgr. Horrigan remembers Daly's first contact with Bellarmine. "The day before classes started Jack came into my office, introduced himself and said, 'I work at Du Pont, but I don't want to spend my life in corporate chemistry. I want to get into academic life.' I didn't have an opening—at least I didn't think I did— but that night our chemistry professor called and said he wasn't coming back. So I quickly called Jack and offered him the job." In Jack's words: "I had just returned from my summer honeymoon to Florida when Fr. Horrigan called to offer me the job. I took a leave of absence from Du Pont, started teaching, loved it and stayed. That first year my salary was $3,600 and a free lunch. In those days faculty could eat free in the cafeteria." After his retirement he could say, "For almost 40 years I got up every morning and came to a job that I dearly love." Not many people can make that statement.

Many of Bellarmine's faculty have once been Bellarmine students. Because they are alumni they know the kind of liberal arts, value-centured, spiritual-dimensioned education that Bellarmine stands for. They often make excellent members of the faculty they learned under. The list is a roll call of familiar names: Windell Bowles, Bernard Thiemann, Clyde Crews, George Kilcourse, Jim Spalding, Ruth Richardson Wagoner, Pat Holland, Mary E. Pike, James Sullivan, Barbara S. Hulsmeyer, Ron Seitz, Gregory Coin, Steve Kirn, Carole Pfeffer—to name but a few. Thiemann, a graduate in accounting, earned his M.B.A at Indiana University and a law degree from the University of Louisville. After practicing law for a while and working in marketing for Ford Motor Company, he finally settled into a lifetime career as a professor of business

Fr. Clyde F. Crews

administration. It is a position he thoroughly enjoyed because of the "fun and fulfillment" he's had, despite what he calls the "ridiculous salaries" that college professors receive.

Another prime example of the success of this student-to-faculty tradition is Fr. Clyde Crews, who enrolled in the fall of 1962 on a full scholarship, having chosen Bellarmine over Xavier University in Cincinnati. He returned in 1973 as a member of the faculty, serving as a professor of theology, chairman of the department and acting dean of the college for one year. "It's good to have some students who return to teach. Such faculty have a sense of the college mission from two perspectives, that of the student and of the faculty." Crews considers himself fortunate to be a kind of all-Bellarmine product. "From the beginning, the college has been like a family to me. It was here that I decided to become a Diocesan priest. Many of Bellarmine's

faculty were role models for me, people like Jack Ford, Jude Dougherty, Kathy Lyons. I am especially pleased with the bonding with students, past and present."

At Bellarmine he has also been able to fulfill himself as a theologian, a priest and a local historian. "I have a strong sense of place and consider it a privilege to be able to teach in my hometown. My roots go deep in Louisville. Both my mother and grandmother were involved in local politics, and I learned from them the value of local involvement. Of the eight books I've written [by 1992], four are about the Louisville area. With my brother Steve Crews and my friend Allan Steinberg of Jefferson Community College, I founded the Louisville Historical League, as we say, 'to bring history from the books into the streets.' Moreover, at Bellarmine I've been able to teach courses in Louisville and Kentucky history." He has also been able to search for such historical items as paintings, manuscripts, photographs and religious artifacts for a museum at the Cathedral of the Assumption.

Other alumni have returned to fill staff and administrative positions, including John O. Kampschaefer and Robert G. Pfaadt. Herman R. Silverstein returned to become physical plant director. Peyton Badgett became campus minister. The positive image of Bellarmine sports in the '70s was partly the work of Nanette Schuhmann, who, while working full-time as a secretary in the admissions office, also served as coordinator of sports information, writing press releases, designing brochures and keeping statistics for the athletic programs. Kaelin Kallay Rybak served two years as coordinator of alumni affairs beginning in 1983. She also went into business with another alumnus, Lou Conkling, and with Helen Petrik, and built a successful travel agency, Knights Travel, named after the Bellarmine sports teams.

What are the pluses and minuses when alumni become faculty or staff? Timothy Swenson, who

Tim Swenson

Dr. Bernard F. Thiemann

earned both his bachelor's and his M.B.A. from Bellarmine, addresses the question: "There are advantages and disadvantages to returning to your alma mater to teach. Too much inbreeding is obviously not good—you need people with varied backgrounds from different schools for academic dialogue—but you do get a kind of continuity with alumni and you get people who know the school from both sides of the desk. In 1992 I think we had a good mix in the accounting department. At that time of the six full-time faculty members, two of us—Windell Bowles and I—were Bellarmine graduates. I was fortunate to have a non-Bellarmine exposure when I worked for several years in the private sector, as an internal auditor and later in the office of human resources at Capitol Holding Corporation. I was invited to teach part-time in the evening school, and I soon realized that I liked it and in fact had found my 'calling' as a teacher. When a full-time position opened up, I applied. Since I've been here, I've felt right at home. I don't feel closed off from people in other departments, and I chaired the Ohio Valley Antiquarian Book Fair for several years. One year we had 40 dealers from 11 states. Where else would an accounting instructor have had the opportunity to do that?" The book fair, co-sponsored by the Friends of the Louisville Free Public Library and Bellarmine College, had been moved from the public library downtown in 1985 to Frazier Hall.

It is already apparent why many of Bellarmine's faculty chose to come here and then chose to stay. There are other reasons. Particularly among the early faculty and staff, there were close and intricate connections of Bellarmine people with each other and with nearby institutions. Librarian Joan Wettig holds a degree from Nazareth. Fr. George Kilcourse was a cousin of Fr. Treece, one of the founding fathers, and theology professor, Fr. Zoeller, had taught him Latin

at Trinity High School. Bernie Thiemann has been close to the college since before it opened. He grew up two blocks from the campus and played on the wooded grounds as a boy before the first student enrolled. As a 13-year-old in 1954, he

Dr. Margaret H. Mahoney

remembers the Pioneer Class marching down Alfresco Place in front of his house on the way to St. Francis of Assisi Church for bacculaureate services.

Margaret Maloney, who joined the Data Courier staff in 1978, can also trace her association with the college back before it opened and can point to a number of college connections. "As a girl I can remember the Corpus Christi services on the grounds that would become Bellarmine College, when thousands of people from all the parishes of the Archdiocese would gather for the annual celebration of the Body of Christ. In addition, Fr. Treece and I were double first cousins. Fr. Kilcourse and I are also cousins. His great-grandfather and my father were brothers. My husband and I took our marriage instructions from Fr. Horrigan. We even bought his old Hudson car and took it on our honeymoon! My daughter has a Bellarmine degree, which she values highly. All these ties to the college through the years have made Bellarmine seem like a family affair."

But many of Bellarmine's faculty and staff have no local connections. Margaret Mahoney, Mike Krukones and Bob Lockhart are but three pillars of the faculty who came from afar. Theresa Sandok found out about Bellarmine during a philosophy conference in Texas and accepted a one-year appointment to the philosophy faculty in 1982. After ten years she was still here and serving as dean of the College of Arts and Sciences and in other positions. "I was the first woman on the philosophy faculty," she says, "and I suppose I became a role model for the women in the student body who were philosophically inclined. Soon after I arrived from Minnesota, I fell in love with the people and with Kentucky. And after I got to know the philosophy faculty—professors Hendrickson, Vitali, Den Uyl, Valone and Mathews—I considered myself the luckiest person in the world. I found them not only to be a productive faculty but also a cohesive, supportive and friendly faculty." She is also a productive scholar and is a nationally recognized translator of Polish

philosophers and theologians, including works by Pope John Paul II.

Margaret Mahoney is a campus icon. A *Concord* profile in 1983 called her "a stabilizing force." She also soon became the college's unofficial historian, who could recall and cite chapter and verse for college events, policies and procedures. In the fall of 1958 she became Bellarmine's "first lady of the faculty." She was such a standout, she remembers, that "everybody thought I was a secretary." Indeed, for many years she was elected secretary of every committee to which she was appointed.

For a woman who doesn't drive, Mahoney has covered a lot of ground and come a long way from her hometown of Great Falls, Montana, a town she says is "about a thousand miles from any place." Although she had an almost idyllic girlhood in Great Falls, she used to muse, "There are three billion people in the world and none of them are here." She soon went out to meet some of those people. First, like a female Thoreau, she traveled a great deal in Great Falls, from the library to the Missouri River, where she played with her siblings. Then as a teen-ager she began expanding via trains to cities north, east and west— even down into Mexico. Finally, after meeting Fr. John Loftus at a meeting in Minneapolis, she came south. "Fr. John told me that Bellarmine was located in 'the Athens of the South,'" she says. "He also told me that Bellarmine had no woman on the full-time teaching faculty, that it was time for one and that I should be it. On September 3, 1958, I arrived at Union Station with everything I owned in a big steamer trunk. I got off the train into a city with no skyline, a 94-degree heat and high, high humidity and a sign reading 'Colored Only.' I was about ready to jump back on the train and return to Minneapolis when a little red convertible arrived from the college to take me to my apartment. Immediately, the picture began to brighten, and I stayed.

"When I visited the campus, I saw two buildings, Old Pasteur and the administration building, which housed the chapel with its fake stained-glass windows on the second floor. There were only two buildings but trees everywhere. And then there were the students and the faculty. I was the third member of the history faculty, which consisted also of Fr. Jeremiah and Fr. Roger Bartman, two Franciscans. I was always impressed with the Franciscans because they were interested in so many things and could do so many things. Fr. Hilary, for example, not only taught and administered but he organized and led 'that damn band.'

"My first year I taught 15 hours or 5 classes and about 240 students each semester, with classes ranging in size from 72 to 130. My teaching load included American history, for which I had not been prepared in graduate school. When I resisted, Fr. John said, 'Miss Mahoney, you have a Ph.D. from the University of Minnesota, and it qualifies you to teach anything you need to.' And so I did, though I remember my first year as a sort of blur. All that I can remember clearly is going to class, rushing home to prepare for the next one and on weekends grading tests. I also remember that there was no rest room in Pasteur for women."

Oh yes, Mahoney has continued to travel, spending more than 30 summers visiting all the countries of Europe and North Africa and enriching her teaching of ancient and European history in the process. For many years she could be seen on campus early in the morning before faculty or staff arrived walking her dog Pumpkin, a pointer actually belonging to Bellarmine alumna Shelle David. After more than 40 years on the Bellarmine faculty, she is considered by most of her former students as one of the college's eternal verities. Bellarmine College without Margaret Mahoney? Why, there's no way. . . .

Michael Krukones of the political science faculty is a Chicago native of Lithuanian descent. He came to Bellarmine, he said, not intending to stay the rest of his career but has done so. Teaching at a small college like Bellarmine, he says, is "a trade-off." On the negative side, as the only full-time political science professor, he has lived in a kind of "professional isolation" with limited sabbaticals and a small library. On the plus side, he has taught small classes, with consequent fewer papers to read, had good personal contact with his students, less pressure to publish or perish and the opportunity to know faculty in other disciplines.

Lee Bash was appointed to the faculty to develop the jazz program. He was immediately confronted with the realities of talent limitation and meager financial resources and, therefore realized that he could not develop a program that he had envisioned. Instead, he focused on the development of small performing groups, such as the jazz trio, which provided talented students with opportunities for professional development and gave Bellarmine a positive showcase to the community. Indeed, the program has produced many outstanding performing students, such as jazz trio members Philip Burkhead and Todd Hildreth.

John Oppelt, who has not only served as academic vice president but also as dean of arts and sciences and professor of mathematics, came to Bellarmine in 1981 from George Mason University in Virginia. Why did he move hundreds of miles to work at a small college? "All of my teaching had been in large public institutions," he says, "and I came to Bellarmine to get back to a private, independent college. The reason is this: In public institutions you don't usually work with a clear goal or mission in mind. Whatever identity the institution has is constantly changing, and there is no sense of a well-defined whole. In fact, the nature of public institutions is such that you probably can't have a whole concept. But a private school such as Bellarmine can have a soul, a permanent identity that doesn't have to change with politics or fads or even finances.

"Another reason I came here is that at a public institution most faculty are committed first to their professions and secondarily to their institutions, but at a private school it's the reverse. When I first came to Bellarmine, I was impressed by the avid commitment of its senior faculty, those who had been with the institution for many years and knew its mission. In those years, especially under Frs. Horrigan and Treece and Loftus, there was a great sense of common purpose. By and large, we still have it, but I think that kind of commitment needs to be fostered in the newer faculty."

Dr. Robert W. Korn

Robert Korn, a professor of biology since 1968, had also studied and taught at much larger institutions but decided he wanted to teach and do research at "a good small school." This is how he came to Bellarmine: "A professor friend of mine at Indiana University suggested that I get in touch with Bellarmine. I talked by telephone with Jim Dyar, who had one of the friendliest voices I've ever heard, and came for a campus visit. I was awestruck by the quality of students and the supportive faculty and administration. Here I have found good students, a friendly environment and no great pressures. That's the kind of school I wanted." As one of the most productive scholars on campus—his specialty is computer-based plant cell research—he has been able to achieve what he calls "a careful balance" between research and teaching. "I've done a fair amount of research here and am able to keep up with developments in my field by reading the scholarly journals and attending professional meetings."

Dr. James J. Valone

James J. Valone, a native of Rochester, New York, came to Bellarmine in the fall of 1973 from Boston College, where he was completing his Ph.D. in philosophy and doing a social action program. "My plan," he says, "was to come to Bellarmine for two or three years, finish my dissertation, then go to a larger university. But I am still here after more than 20 years, and there are several reasons for that—the tight job market, my growing attraction to Bellarmine and to the city of Louisville. Like everyone else, I have to teach a heavy load of four courses, but once I've done that, Bellarmine has allowed me to do whatever I'm interested in, whether it's social action projects or work in the theater. Bellarmine has also allowed me to learn to teach, and I think I've developed into a good teacher." In 1997 he was made chairman of the philosophy department.

Even while being critical, Bellarmine faculty tend to be upbeat and enthusiastic about the college and their relationship to it. Although he was sometimes known as the faculty gadfly, Bob Munson also echoes Valone's praise for the growing space that Bellarmine gave him. "I loved teaching and Bellarmine gave me the freedom to be a damn good teacher," he said shortly after his retirement. "I loved my students and they loved me. We have had many outstanding graduates in psychology. Out of 14 psychology graduates in the class of 1968, for example, 12 of them went on to get Ph.D.s. One of our best students was Steve Kirn, who went on to become director of training and development for Sears."

The college also gave Munson the freedom to practice his profession. "The college allowed me to continue my practice as a clinical psychologist," he said, "and that enriched my teaching because I could use real life case histories. I was also allowed to start a program of internships and sent students to companies like Ford, GE, Kentucky Fried Chicken, UPS and Our Lady of Peace, where they could learn to participate in real situations with professionals."

He mutes his criticism of some administrative policies with an understanding of the necessity for them. "I disliked Petrik's business model that he imposed on the college. I think it and certain other politics and personnel decisions tended to reduce the

Dr. James "Bud" Spalding

sense of community that we had at Bellarmine, but I know he had to do some things in order to keep the college from going under. All in all, Bellarmine has been a good place to be. For every bad thing I can say about my experience at this college, I can name 25 good things."

James "Bud" Spalding has many good reasons for coming and staying at Bellarmine. Spalding, who is approximately a fifth cousin to coach Jim Spalding, joined the business faculty in 1982. He came, he says, "because I had taught for 20 years in large factory-like universities, and I was weary of large impersonal classes. I was burned out. I wanted a school like my own small undergraduate college, Maryville College, in Tennessee. Bellarmine seemed to fill my needs. So

Dr. Michael G. Krukones

did Louisville. My wife Ann and I love the arts scene here as well as the temperate climate and fine restaurants. Louisville is a fine blend of Midwestern and Southern. It's also a good location for us to be fairly close to our families and it's an easy place to travel from."

Most of Bellarmine's faculty—priest, nun and lay—have seen teaching as a calling, a vocation, as one faculty member put it, "that moves society onward and upward." In addition to the numerous priests and nuns who have served as faculty, particularly in the early years, many of the lay faculty have had some seminary training or have at

Dr. Carole C. Pfeffer

one time seriously considered a religious vocation. Michael Krukones remembers that many Catholic boys of his generation, especially those who attended parochial schools, were influenced to consider the priesthood. But, he said, his leaning in that direction took a sharp turn backward when he got his first taste of seminary food. Other men changed their professional directions for more profound reasons.

Carole Pfeffer of the English faculty speaks the mind of many Bellarmine faculty when she says that her teaching is not only "a good life for me" but "a way to do the will of God."

Ursuline nuns like Sr. Pat Lowman and Sr. Clarita

Sr. Clarita Felhoelter

Felhoelter say they have fulfilled their vocation as women and nuns when they became teachers. Sr. Clarita, a first-rate poet, says she always knew that her primary calling was teaching. "As a girl and young woman I agonized over whether I should become a nun because I knew that I'd have to give up having children—and I love children—but God played a gracious trick on me because as a teacher I've had hundreds of children, though their legs were a little longer than I expected. I can say honestly that I've never had a day when I regretted my decision. God has blessed me as a nun and as a teacher." Fr. Eugene Zoeller of the theology faculty echoes Sr. Clarita's words: "My days of teaching at Bellarmine have been a gift, a grace. Furthermore, the college has given me

Dr. Susan H. Davis

a platform and a presence in this community that I could not have had anywhere else."

Sue Hockenberger Davis is an ebullient, affirmative, articulate native of Ohio, who was a practicing surgical nurse when she accepted a part-time position at Bellarmine in 1975 and rose to become dean of the Lansing School of Nursing. She says plainly, "The faculty are why I'm here." She has a strong sense of vocation. "When I came along, as a woman I could become a nun, a teacher or a nurse. First, I chose nursing. Then I got into teaching. Now I have two of the three vocations, and I love them both. As a professor I can have my finger on the pulse of the radically changing health care field. I believe the challenge of the future is to balance high tech and high touch in health care."

One tradition that most faculty prize at Bellarmine is the policy of academic freedom, and faculty voices have been raised all along the opinion spectrum on many issues, ranging from religion to politics to such college matters as curriculum and personnel. Most of the faculty would agree with James B. "Bud" Spalding's attitude toward authority. "I believe a person should always have a healthy disrespect," he says, "for his commanding officer in the army and for his dean in academia." It was a tradition of free expression started by the first President of the college, Fr. Horrigan, who often took moral but controversial positions on civil rights and peace. A key to Horrigan's defense of freedom of expression for faculty can be discovered in his remarks about Archbishop Floersh's defense of him: "He was always supportive of me, even when there was pressure on him about my activities. During a period when I was active in a local United Nations group, he had one regular correspondent who was convinced that I was

a communist sympathizer and should be removed from the presidency of Bellarmine College. Each time he received a letter, he'd call me to say that he was sending it to me for a response. But he never asked me to stop doing what I was doing."

The letters-to-the-editor columns of local papers have featured many declarations from Bellarmine faculty, from the right to the left. Marie Mathews in sociology and Raymond Bailey of communication arts wrote occasional letters to the editor. During his time on the Bellarmine theology faculty in the early '70s, for example, Fr. Patrick H. Reardon published letters on subjects ranging from conditions in local jails and proper attire for nuns to pacifism and abortion. In a letter to *The Record* in August 1974, Fr. Reardon disputed another priest's defense of the church's position regarding the use of grape juice in the Eucharist and on divorce. In a December 1972 letter also to *The Record* he commented on conversions to Catholicism from other Christian groups, suggesting that such people should "brush up on their theology" because "there is no evidence that the Lord Jesus, in bidding us be fishers of men, intended thereby our robbing the aquariums of others."

Bob Munson was also a faithful critic of his church. In an interview with *The Louisville Times* in November of 1969, he said, "Rome is wasting its ammunition on trivial things," and named birth control and clerical celibacy as examples. Earlier, in the summer of 1966, two priests on the faculty debated the celibacy of priests, with Fr. Davis, chairman of the theology department, arguing against the policy and Fr. Jeremiah, chairman of the history department, in favor. Bob Lockhart could also be outspoken. In 1977 he protested the selection of a Japanese-born New York sculptor who had been chosen over several local artists to create a sculpture for the Hall of Justice.

For a man of strong opinions like Professor Leonard Latkovski, expressing them was as necessary as breathing. In many different forums he held forth on politics and religion as well as many lesser matters.

In a letter to *The Courier-Journal* in October of 1974, he even came to the defense of the recently resigned U. S. President. "Nixon has been pushed out of office by his own party," he wrote, "by men who want to save their necks in November elections. The Watergate Committee has been threshing empty straw for more than a year while inflation continues and the prices are skyrocketing." On the other end of the political spectrum was another political activist, Caroline Krebs of the political science faculty and a die-hard George McGovern supporter in 1972. In June of 1974, she became chairperson of the Louisville Archdiocesan Peace and Justice Commission.

Dr. James J. Dyar

Priests on the faculty often went public with their politics. In an October 1972 letter to *The Courier-Journal,* Fr. Arnold G. Dearing concluded his remarks in which he lambasted President Nixon on just about all points, with his preferences in the impending election. "My conscience tells me I must vote Democratic," he wrote. "It is just one vote, but it will be cast for George McGovern, Dee Huddleston and Romano Mazzoli." At least, he was on the winning side for two out of three races. In 1998 Dr. Karen Cassidy, associate professor of nursing, ran for a seat on the Louisville Board of Aldermen. Alas, she lost, though she ran a good race.

In such an atmosphere of free expression, there are bound to be some embarrassments. Sometimes they are caused by college personnel and sometimes by supporters who use their connection to the college for political clout. During the Congressional campaign of November 1962, for example, Louis A. Arru, who was serving as chairman of the Board of Overseers, sent out a letter stating that although he was not writing officially as chairman of the group, he was urging a vote against "creeping socialism" and for Republican candidate Eugene Snyder, who was running against the incumbent Democrat, Frank W. Burke.

Of course, what one says and does today that is acceptable and even politically correct may turn out, in time, to be just the opposite. Take the matter of research. Bob Korn, who grew up in the Lutheran church in Milwaukee, considers a Catholic college like Bellarmine "a friendly environment" for scientific inquiry and a place where he can teach with fewer restrictions than on many state campuses. "The intellectual tradition of Catholic higher education," he says, "is compatible with scientific research. Catholics have been in the vanguard of modern scientific research," naming Louis Pasteur, after whom the college named its first building. On the other hand, scientific knowledge is always tentative and partial, as James Dyar of the biology faculty discovered over time. In the mid-'60s non-smoker Dyar, holder of a tobacco research grant, published an article in *The Concord* in which he said that despite a new report from the U.S. Public Health Service linking smoking and lung cancer, "the case against tobacco has not been satisfactorily proved."

In the name of fairness, both sides of a controversial issue are often represented. One of the most divisive issues of the '60s and '70s was the Vietnam War, which most Bellarmine faculty and students apparently opposed. In the fall of 1971, however, the U.S. Marines set up a recruitment stand on campus. Then in January of 1973, 15 priests and one nun on the Bellarmine faculty signed a full-page call for peace in *The Record,* with more faculty and students signing a full-page ad in *The Courier-Journal* endorsing a peace march.

The freedom of expression generally extended to all members of the Bellarmine community. Even the annual reports of various college offices and departments are interesting to read for their sharp honesty. In his 1984-85 annual report, Bill Stewart, who was then director of student services, gave his assessment of the move into the new Brown Building: "The cafeteria, campus store and student services offices did not require moving by the start of classes in August, but were done so without consultation and without concern for the users, students and staff alike. When I was much younger, I thought only the U.S. Army could bungle a move on such a massive scale. But I was mistaken." About Frazier Hall, he wrote with subtle sarcasm: "Even though the platform was not built to my recommendation (it's 4 feet too shallow), it was ample for many users."

Ruth Wagoner, who has frequently voiced her opinions in faculty counsels, says, "The administration and faculty have a tradition of support for a diversity of opinion, as anyone knows who has ever served on a faculty committee." Needless to say, Bellarmine professors have often voiced opposition to what they perceive as arbitrary administrative policies. Regarding merit raises based on teaching, scholarship and service, faculty have often expressed frustration at what they perceive to be a new emphasis on scholarship and having to be productive in all three areas. Fr. Kilcourse expresses the view of many heavily laden faculty: "We have too large a spectrum of courses to teach and too many classroom hours to be good teachers and good scholars." Thomas Kemme of the English faculty, who came to Bellarmine in 1964, "found a niche for myself and tried to fill it," argues that the college "needs to articulate a clearer vision of what is expected of the faculty now, with our limited resources and limited support for scholarship." And so the dialogue and debate have continued on campus about academic problems and world problems.

Indeed, academic freedom is a Bellarmine trademark that all three Presidents have honored and supported, even when they may have personally opposed a position or activity. One of the most publicized controversies in Bellarmine's history had to do with the visit of Swiss Roman Catholic theologian Hans Kung in the fall of 1981, when it was stated in the local secular press that the liberal Kung was being sponsored and honored by Bellarmine College.

In a letter to *The Courier-Journal* President Petrik, a religious conservative, disassociated the college from Kung's visit. "Bellarmine is neither sponsoring Hans Kung's visit nor bestowing honors on him," he wrote. He added, however, a commitment to academic freedom: "I have in the past and will continue to defend Bellarmine's right to encourage free and fair discussion of ideas. Such defense is never pleasurable, and it is rarely without some jeopardy to the institution; but it is my obligation to protect the college as a forum for exchange of thought, regardless of my personal convictions." Kung, who had visited Bellarmine in 1968 without controversy, spoke at the Louisville Presbyterian Theological Seminary and was guest at a luncheon on Bellarmine's campus, though without official college sanction.

It is obvious, then, that as part of the dialogue of a growing, searching, youthful institution, there has been much agreement and some argument. Faculty and administrators have not always agreed on college direction or plans or means of implementation. There have been turf battles. As the curriculum has changed, there have been additions and deletions. Personnel dedicated to the college have often and honestly disagreed with each other on policy decisions. In a climate of free inquiry and debate, however, there have been few Bellarmine people who were hesitant or afraid to voice their contrary views. Let an unnamed administrator in student affairs speak in his year-end report for all those who have sometimes served the useful and necessary role of the loyal opposition, as he writes in righteous indignation of what he perceives as "the overall contempt and complete disregard with which the student affairs area has been systematically dismantled this year by the other top administrators at the college."

There are many other dimensions to the college faculty. Bellarmine professors are known for going to great lengths to make the college a comfortable, hospitable, as well as challenging, place for students to spend four years. Gail Henson tells her students: "I'm your mom away from home. Feel free to come and see me anytime." Students remember the refreshments and sweets brought to class by John Gatton and Peggy Baker and the countless meals prepared by faculty and served in their homes to hordes of hungry young people. They hear Good Samaritan stories like the time the Veep for Student Affairs Fred Rhodes drove to Murfreesboro, Tennessee, to rescue six theater students who were involved in a van accident on their way to a conference in Florida.

The faculty-student-staff-parent camaraderie is facilitated by the many meeting places they have—in the cafeteria, on social occasions, at ballgames—as well as in classrooms and labs and the

Dr. John S. Gatton

Dr. Gail Henson

library. In the late '60s when there was discussion of a separate "Faculty Dining Room," many students and faculty disapproved of the idea, fearing that it would lead to fractionalization on campus. Sometimes they perform together in musical and theatrical productions. Sometimes they contribute to the same campus publications, such as *Ariel,* the literary magazine. In the spring 1996 issue, for example, in addition to student writers there were faculty members John J. Bethune, M. Celeste Nichols and staffers Jennifer Williams and Gwen Kirchner. Sometimes they even trade places. In April 1989, as a charity fund raiser, students were given the chance to bid for the chance to take the position of an administrator for a day. For $50 student Rusty Hooper won David Goldenberg's position as assistant vice president for academic affairs. It was money well spent, she said. "Next time I'll take the President's place."

Most students realize how fortunate they are to be able to study with faculty who put them first. Ruth Wagoner says, "I think the faculty always knew that the most important thing they did occurred in the classroom, and I appreciate how incredibly patient they were with people like me who were wandering through." As a student in the early '70s Carole Pfeffer remembers "a caring and spiritual community, a scholarly, nurturing, fun community. I was awe-struck by my professors. My classes were a joy—all of them, even the disciplines that were new to me, like science and psychology."

Probably no faculty member loved his students more or did more for them than

Mrs. Gabriele Bosley entertaining international students in her home.

chemistry professor Jack Daly. They loved him in return. He was an informed, inspiring teacher who produced some of Bellarmine's most successful alumni. In his words: "We've had a legion of outstanding graduates, including Hank Ellert, a member of the Pioneer Class and the first Bellarmine graduate to earn a Ph.D., Jim Hartlage, a Chicago business executive, and Jim Heck, now a Harvard Ph.D., and dozens more I could name." Daly's mission to his students did not end at the classroom door or on the graduation stage. He was their adviser, their friend, their confidant and he kept in close contact with them, nurturing them as they continued their graduate education and went out to claim their places in the business and professional world. By the day of his retirement he had received more than 100 college mugs given him by former students who had gone on to graduate school. "I've had a close relationship with my students," he said modestly. "I know where every graduate is." In many ways Jack Daly was a model of the men and women that Bellarmine has sought to produce through the years, a man of science and business and arts and faith—the Christian Knight and scholar.

Despite their full teaching loads and primary mission as teachers, the faculty at Bellarmine have been unusually active and productive scholars, creative writers and artists, consultants and performers, sharing their time and talents with colleagues and laymen alike. Sometimes they have spoken to local groups. Indeed, there is hardly a faculty member who has not addressed a civic, professional or church group on subjects ranging from reviews of current books to a history of Theresa of Avila, which history professor Margaret Mahoney delivered to the Carmelite nuns in April of 1962. Each spring a host of faculty and administrators make the rounds as commencement speakers. In 1962 a speakers bureau was established on campus by the public relations office to connect more than 30 faculty volunteer speakers to area clubs and organizations. Soon thereafter a student group, Operation Pride,

announced its own student speakers bureau, with subjects like "Youth Today—Try and Understand Us."

Bellarmine faculty have been frequent guests on local radio and television. In July of 1963, English professor Thomas M. Sheehan produced and hosted a cultural series called "The Spectator" on WLKY-TV. On the first program he discussed Shakespeare's *Romeo and Juliet* with a group of fifth and sixth graders. During the same period Bellarmine was co-producing with Ursuline and Nazareth a weekly current events program, "Campus Viewpoints." For some 15 years in the '80s and '90s Wade Hall of the English faculty produced and hosted an interview series on WKPC-TV called "Kentucky Desk."

Bellarmine faculty have often been subjects of articles in the local press and consulted as authorities in media features. In a *Courier-Journal* article in January 1958, the Rev. J. H. Voor was profiled as an authority on the new advertising fad using subliminal perception. Increasingly, faculty have become a source of expert advice for the community. In an inteview with *Courier-Journal* writer Keith Runyon in November of 1974, a

Fr. Jeremiah J. Smith

period of rampant inflation, Stanley Zemelka offered a number of tips to cope with higher prices. Walk more and drive less was one of his suggestions. Fr. Fred Hendrickson and Fr. Eugene Zoeller were often quoted on current issues relating to ethics and theology. In November of 1978, Wade Hall was featured on WAVE-TV's noon news for a weeklong series celebrating Louisville's 200th anniversary. Fr. John Loftus, Fr. Jeremiah Smith and others served as panelists for many years on WHAS-TV's "Moral Side of the News." Priests have served as chaplains to local groups, and in the early '70s Edward Rosenbluh of the psychology faculty was adviser to the Louisville Police Department.

Faculty and staff have been deeply and broadly involved in the community, serving as advisers and leaders of many organizations. They have served on boards, from Hospice of Louisville to the Kentucky Humanities Council to St. Meinrad Seminary. A number of faculty have worked with the Highland Community Ministries, and in the '70s Thomas Kemme served as president. Robert Munson was deeply involved in community activities, leading group therapy sessions at Maryhurst School and consulting with Catholic charity groups, religious organizations and seminaries. Kathleen Lyons served for several years on the St. Meinrad Seminary Board of Overseers, and in 1980 was appointed chairperson of the Louisville-Jefferson County Human Relations Commission. In the '70s Marie Mathews, professor of sociology, chaired the Louisville Archdiocesan Social Action Commission and the Family Relations Center and worked in programs to rehabilitate former prison inmates.

The nursing outreach has gone as far as China and the Philippines. With her husband, a pediatric surgeon, Chris Algren, former director of the Master of Science in Nursing program, participated in a mission of mercy called Operation Rainbow, which performs surgery on indigent children. Ann Kleine-Kracht Weeks and Mary Pike have extended the Bellarmine nursing program boundaries from Pippa Passes to Paducah, from Alaska to Ireland.

Professors in the arts and humanities have been especially active showing their talents and their college to the community. In the mid-'70s academic dean Robert Wittman even performed occasionally with the Louisville Ballet, and his wife Joan, a concert soloist, gave many recitals locally. In the early '90s English professor Bert Hornback quickly established a tradition with his portrayal of Charles Dickens reading "A Christmas Carol" on campus and around town. But it has been the music and art faculties that have penetrated the community most consistently, beginning in the '50s with Robert Fischer, who directed the College Glee Club in many campus and community

Dr. Bert Hornback

concerts and featuring through the years the talents of Gus Coin as the broadcast voice of the Louisville Orchestra, vocal soloist Sharon E. Schuster, jazz pianist Don Murray and Steve Crews, leader of the jazz quartet called Soundchaser. And one must not forget Fr. Eugene Zoeller, who has appeared in several local operas as a bishop or cardinal!

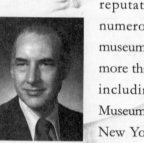
Don Murray

Dante Vena may have begun Bellarmine's reputation as a productive art center, but Bob Lockhart, from the '70s through the '90s, proved himself to be one of the most productive and widely known and respected members of the entire faculty. As a sculptor, painter and printmaker, Lockhart has earned a national reputation and has works in numerous collections and art museums. His work is found in more than 60 private collections, including the local Speed Museum, the Whitney Museum in New York and the Art Institute Museum in Chicago. A show of his works at the Byck Gallery in May of 1976 became a hit with many of his Bellarmine colleagues. The exhibit spoofed several administrators and colleagues in sculpture caricatures named "The Great Pea-Tricker," "The Darting Hallwader" and "The Bulgarian Bob-Witt." Needless to say, the works demonstrated great daring, insight and truth.

Bob Lockhart

Lockhart has been called by one critic "a

wizard with a funky sense of humor who makes gentle statements about the human condition and encourages us to laugh at ourselves." He has shown himself to be a kind of serious absurdist with an admiration for surrealism and a talent for irreverence. Indeed, his "Holy Family" pieces installed at the Cathedral of the Assumption in 1974 caused a tempest at the Cathedral because of his realistic rendering of Christ crucified and a very old and weary-looking Mary and Joseph. Mary is a middle-aged mother mourning the loss of her son and Joseph is a grief-stricken father, anxious and confused. When critics called the figures "too Jewish," he said, "As a Catholic, I think we're used to seeing Mary as a 16-year-old Swedish virgin."

Another controversial work by Lockhart was his "Salvador del Mundo," an altar carving commissioned in 1994 by the Metropolitan Cathedral of San Salvador in El Salvador. The three-ton mahogany Christ figure, carved by Lockhart and four Salvadorian apprentices, was modeled with features of the local people. It became a victim of the country's violent politics and now lies in broken pieces in the cathedral yard. Another of his local installations is a bronze chameleon for the Louisville Zoo in 1989. He is particulary attracted to animal forms, he says, because they are warm, pleasurable and nonthreatening. In fact, his human forms often feature animal parts.

His major project at the end of the '90s has been a 14-foot, two-and-one-half-ton armored and bearded knight astride a war horse. Dubbed "The Bellarmine Knight," it is modeled after its donor, former Bellarmine Board of Trustees chairman Owsley Brown Frazier, Jr., and was installed and dedicated on September 12, 1998 on the campus quadrangle between Horrigan Hall and the Brown Library. It is a friendly knight, Lockhart says, a contemporary version of the medieval knight, noted for his chivalry, his courtesy and his religious devotion.

In more recent years from the biology faculty, Dr. Dave Robinson has served on the

board of the Friends of the Louisville Free Public Library, and Dr. Joanne Dobbins has served on the environmental affairs committee of Greater Louisville, Inc. Members of the chemistry faculty conduct Saturday morning seminars for the Whitney M. Young Scholars Program. The education faculty has been especially active, with Dr. Maureen Norris serving as chair of the Seven Counties Services Board, on which Dr. Nancy Howard has long served. Other professors of education include Dr. Serra Goethals, who serves

Dr. Joanne J. Dobbins

on the AACTE Board and Professor Marie Sanders, who is on the statewide committee for middle school education. From the art department Ms. Caren Cunningham serves on the LVAA Board and the Kentucky Foundation for Women Board. Among the many professional and community activities of Dr. A. T. Simpson are workshops he conducts with the West End Boys Choir and free concerts for Black History Month. Dr. Gail Henson of the communications faculty is a former member of the Jefferson County (Ky.) School Board and heads the High School Press Day on the Bellarmine campus.

Members of the administration are also active in many community projects and organizations. Dr. McGowan, for example, is on the board of the J. B.

Dr. A. T. Simpson

Speed Art Museum, has chaired Metroversity and headed the 1994 Metro United Way Campaign. Bob Zimlich is on the Trinity High School board, and Dr. Oppelt is a member of the board at St. Xavier High School. Holly Gathright, executive assistant to the President, is on the boards of the Louisville Science Center and the Louisville Waterfront Development Corporation.

Many Bellarmine faculty have regularly reviewed books and provided articles for local papers as well as for professional publications. From Jude Doughtery's articles for the *New Catholic Encyclopedia* in the mid-'60s to Gail Henson's and Margaret Mahoney's essays in *The Louisville Encyclopedia* at the turn of the 21st century, Bellarmine people have been contributors to standard reference works. In the '70s and '80s Windell Bowles of the accounting department wrote a column for the *Kentuckiana Purchasor.* Fr. Clyde Crews wrote a lead article in the new *Encyclopedia of American Catholic History,* published in 1997, which also featured an entry on Bellarmine College by Fr. George Kilcourse. Fr. Kilcourse also wrote essays for the 1998 edition of *The Merton Annual* as well as essays for the *Encyclopedia of Religious Controversies in the United States,* published in 1997.

Fr. George A. Kilcourse

Faculty reviews in *The Courier-Journal* and *The Louisville Times* were appearing in the '50s signed by Fr. Joseph M. Miller and Richard W. Sames, a tradition that has continued down to the present, with the Rubel School of Business faculty providing weekly reviews of business-related books in the '90s, such as those by David T. Collins of the accounting faculty and Frank Slesnick and Michelle Trawick of the economics faculty. Indeed, in a single year, 1986, Bellarmine was the home of the Society of Educators and Scholars and the Thomas Merton Studies Center and was hosting several professional journals as well as other campus publications—*The Kentucky Poetry Review, The Merton Seasonal, The Ark, The Lansing Journal, The Bellarmine Magazine, Scholar and Educator,* and *The Kentucky Journal of Economics and Business.* Other journals with national circulations have been published at other times.

The Bellarmine College Press has published a number of books and monographs related to the

college and its programs. *Roots of a Catholic College,* edited by Fr. Horrigan in 1955, is a collection of addresses connected with Bellarmine's first

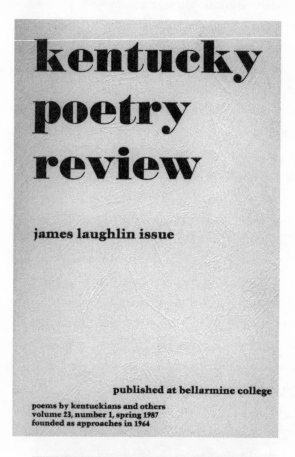

commencement exercises in 1954. *Patrons in Profile* is a 1961 collection of biographies of the "patron saints" with whom Bellarmine has associated itself: St. Robert Bellarmine, St. Bonaventure, John Henry Cardinal Newman, Louis Pasteur, as well as an essay on the Christian Knight. A 1977 publication was *The Role of Ethics in American Life,* edited by Robert A. Preston, and developed from a three-day seminar in January of 1974 in connection with the inauguration of Eugene Petrik as President. Other publications by the Press include a literary study of author Cormac McCarthy and a biography of Wilson W. Wyatt, Sr., a chairman of the Board of Trustees.

Bellarmine has often been host to scholarly and professional meetings that have attracted participants from all over the United States. The first of the First Conference Series was convened in October of 1993 and focused on the writings of Cormac McCarthy. Other First Conferences have been devoted to novelist Toni Morrison, chaired by Dr. M. Celeste Nichols, and poet Jane Kenyon, chaired by Dr. Bert Hornback.

A bibliography of faculty publications would be lengthy, and it would range from Fr. Clyde Crews in theology and Thomas Kemme in English to Bob Korn in biology and Michael Krukones in political science. In 1984, for example, Krukones published *Promises and Performance: Presidential Campaigns as Policy Predictors,* a study of how well candidates keep their promises once they are elected President. His conclusion that Democrats tend to have a better record than Republicans was explained, he said, probably by the fact that "most Republican Presidents have had to cope with a Democratic-controlled Congress." Productive creative writers include English professor Ron Seitz, with numerous books and magazine articles to his credit, and Wade Hall, who has published some 15 books and monographs and numerous articles, essays, reviews and creative works.

History professor Eric Roorda's book, *The Dictator Next Door: The Good Neighbor Policy and the Trujillo Regime in the Dominican Republic, 1930-1945,* won

two prestigious awards: the Steuart L. Bernath Book Prize given by the Society for Historians of American Foreign Relations for the best book in 1998 and the Herbert Hoover Book Award for 1998.

The science professors have been especially fortunate in winning and using research grants. The first such grant was received by Richard Sames, an assistant professor of biology, in April of 1957, when he won a $2,200 grant from the U.S. Public Health Service to study viruses that cause gangrene. Like many Bellarmine faculty, Dr. Sames was a frequent contributor to *The Record,* where in February 1958 he published an essay discussing the impact of Sputnik on the American education system. Jack Daly was one of the most active science researchers, publishing a career total of more than 40 articles in professional chemical journals.

College faculty have attended hundreds of state, national and international meetings of their professional organizations; and they have taken dozens of short courses to sharpen their professional skills. Sister M. Vera Del Grande, who chaired the education department at Ursuline College before the merger and also chaired the department at Bellarmine-Ursuline for several years, took one of the longest professional trips. In the early '70s she spent 35 days on a world tour to study education systems in other countries, including Switzerland, Russia, Lebanon, Turkey, Hong Kong and Japan. She was impressed, she said, with the nursery schools in Moscow. In Tokyo she met Professor Shinichi Suzuki, who developed a special method of teaching violin to young children.

Bellarmine professors have led numerous tours to points around the world. In 1964 and 1965 Fr. William E. Hogan of the psychology faculty led tour groups to Europe and elsewhere. For a number of years Fr. Hilary Gottbrath was tour director for Franciscan Tours to Europe and Hawaii, which included visits to Franciscan shrines, museums and historical sites and audiences with the Pope. In more recent years, student tours have been led by Caren

Cunningham of the art faculty and Dr. Tim Welliver of the history faculty, including a 1998 trip to Egypt. Honors students have been led on tours by Dr. Hornback (to Ireland) and by Dr. Henson (to England). Dr. Fred Rhodes and Dr. Sue Davis have also led student trips for service projects.

The talents of Bellarmine's full-time faculty have been augmented by choosing part-time faculty from a large community pool of professionals, ranging from the performing arts to law to business to the ministry. This use of community resources was already underway by 1952, when Judge Raymond Bossmeyer of the Jefferson Circuit Court taught a course in business law. Other early adjunct faculty included speech instructors Fred Karem and Ed Kallay, who was sports director of WAVE radio and television. An amusing incident from Kallay's class was reported in *The Courier-Journal* of February 27, 1953. Kallay made a speech assignment on such topics as "How I Wash Dishes," "How to Take a Photograph" and "How to Make a Bed." Unfortunately, speech teacher Kallay's enunciation was apparently not very clear and student Ray Fehribach presented an impressive speech on "How to Make a Bet."

Most of the class agreed that "Bet" is the way they heard the teacher say it. "I guess," said teacher Kallay, "the teacher should enunciate better." Years later Kallay's daughter Kaelin became a graduate of the college. She said that such people as her father "bring the ivory tower to the real world." Of the many talented journalists who have taught writing courses, one of the most notable was *Courier-Journal* writer and novelist Bryan Wooley. Alfred P. Tadajewski, who was director of the Guidance Clinic of the Catholic School Board, not only taught courses part-time but led college-sponsored forums and seminars on mental health. Adjunct professors from the political world

Dr. Thomas Devasia

have included Louisville Mayor Jerry Abramson and Kentucky Senator Mitch McConnell.

Bellarmine professors have often held temporary appointments at other colleges and universities, a tradition that was begun in the early days of the college. In the summer of 1958, for example, both Fr. Quintin P. Roohr of physics and Fr. Jeremiah Smith of history taught their respective disciplines at Catholic University in Washington. In 1962 Fr. Jeremiah was teaching his eighth consecutive summer schedule at Catholic University. Also in the summer of 1962, Richard Sames of the biology faculty was a visiting professor in bacteriology at Indiana University, and in 1965-66 he took a year's leave of absence to head the National Science Foundation's Undergraduate Research Program in Washington. That same year art director Dante Vena served as a Fulbright lecturer at the Blackpool School of Art in England.

Sometimes a Bellarmine faculty member's leave of absence became permanent. In 1983 Thomas A. Devasia, who joined the history and political science faculty in 1966, agreed to return to his home country to head the new Ghandi University in his hometown of Kottayam in southern India. He later returned permanently to India. After serving as Bellarmine's art director for six years, Dante Vena accepted a position on the art faculty at Ohio University in 1967. In 1968, after 12 years as a professor of philosophy, John Herbert "Jack" Ford became president of Mount St. Agnes College in Baltimore. That same year Bellarmine lost one of her best-known faculty when Jude P. Dougherty, who had been at the college for nine years, became the first layman appointed dean of the School of Philosophy at Catholic University of America.

Bellarmine's distinguished permanent faculty have been frequently enriched by visiting professors, such as the Rev. Pierre H. Conway, a Dominican priest and author, who served as a visiting professor of philosophy in 1957-58. Before coming to Bellarmine he taught for two years at the Pontificum Athenaem Angelicum in Rome. Art professor Dante Vena's replacement for the 1965-66 academic year was English artist Trevor Hodgson, who held a number of exhibitions on and off campus during his year at Bellarmine. His farewell show at Merida Gallery was called by *Courier-Journal* art critic Sarah Lansdell "serene and tasteful." She also said that his presence in Louisville had been "a stabilizing and stimulating influence." Just before he returned to England he found out that he had won the $250 first prize for best painting at the Kentucky State Fair. Another popular visiting professor was John Batstone of Liss, Hampshire, England, who was visiting professor of English during the spring semester of 1976. His appointment was arranged by the Kentucky Branch of the English-Speaking Union. He taught a course in English drama and took two courses in American literature, which he said was insufficiently known in England. Mr. Lee Thomas, former CEO of Vermont American Corporation, recently served as executive-in-residence in the Rubel School of Business.

Bellarmine faculty have always been involved with college governance and policy making, more or less. In the beginning, it was likely to be less. Fr. Treece remembers that when the college was young, he and Fr. Horrigan made most of the school decisions after checking with the Archbishop. But that would change as the faculty increased and especially after laymen and women became a significant percentage of the total.

Indeed, at least from the mid-'50s, faculty have had a voice in policy decisions through such channels as policy committees, the Bellarmine Faculty Association, a short-lived chapter of the American Association of University Professors, the Committee of the Faculty, the Faculty Welfare Committee and the Faculty Assembly. There has seldom been a feeling of a we-they or labor-management relationship with the administration. A writer for the *Louisville* magazine

in June 1978 referred to the accessible, warm, open-door campus as "a truly democratic community." Donna Olliges of the business office says, "To my knowledge there has never been a staff association or union at Bellarmine. For two reasons: first, all of us—faculty, staff, administration—are underpaid about equally. And people come to this college for reasons other than money."

Soon after David House became academic vice president in 1991, he began a dialogue with the faculty that led to a new system of governance designed to improve communication between faculty and administration. "When I came to Bellarmine," he said, "I felt that many of the faculty felt disfranchised and held a kind of them vs. us mentality. I have tried to move toward a collaborative administration. I think faculty should be involved in the decision-making processes of the college."

There have, of course, always been faculty meetings at which professors voiced many consonant and dissonant opinions. Margaret Mahoney describes an early meeting: "Our faculty meetings were always held on Friday nights in the periodicals room of the library. Roll was taken by Fr. Clancy, a man so organized and methodical I always thought he should have had a German name. Faculty were not allowed to miss meetings except for two reasons—you were being married or buried the next day. Indeed, we rather envied Dan Sweeny his absence when he was about to get married. There was a reward at the end of each meeting, however, when we would move to another room for a social hour. There we had our choice of drinks—bourbon and water, bourbon and soda or bourbon and ginger ale." Sweeny remembers that one time both Fr. Horrigan and Fr. John Loftus were out of town and Fr. Clancy ran the meeting and reversed the usual order with the drinks first. "It was one of our livelier meetings," he said.

There have been a number of informal, mostly social and academic groups for faculty and staff—faculty forums, faculty wives clubs and the like. Jude

The First Faculty Meeting, 1950.

Dougherty founded an interdisciplinary Faculty Forum in 1960 to bring together the two cultures of science and humanities. It met twice a month with a faculty member from Bellarmine or a sister institution delivering a paper, usually based on a faculty research project, followed by discussion.

In addition to curriculum changes, the main point of conflict between faculty and administration is frequently salary—or too little of it. Salaries were not a big budget item in the beginning because most of the faculty were priests who contributed their services to the college and were paid a modest pocket-change amount each month—sometimes in the neighborhood of $50. As the lay membership of the faculty increased

and included professors with spouses and children, salaries became a crucial item in the budget. By 1961 the faculty was composed of 23 priests and 36 laymen, all full-time, and 25 laymen part-time. Indeed, the main justification for tuition raises through the years has been to raise faculty salaries.

On the eve of the fall semester 1956, the salary scale ranged from $3,000-$4,000 for instructors to $5,500-$7,000 for full professors. In the fall of 1958, salaries were increased by 15 per cent, with a minimum of $3,800 for instructors and $6,500 for full professors. It was a salary scale, as Fr. Horrigan pointed out, that compared favorably with other independent colleges. The contributed services of the 24 priests on the faculty that year amounted to about $125,000. A survey of college salaries in Kentucky in the spring of 1970 showed that the average salary at the University of Kentucky, the highest in the state, was $15,190, while Bellarmine's average, which ranked somewhere in the middle, was $11,240.

Beginning in the '70s and throughout the '80s much of the salary discussion centered on "merit pay," a term which meant that faculty would henceforth be held responsible for their performances in teaching, scholarship, and college and community service, which would be used to justify salary raises. No longer would raises be across-the-board and automatic. Not even cost of living raises would be routine. It was fairly easy to evaluate a person's achievements in scholarship and service, but the big question was how to judge a professor's effectiveness in the classroom. The new buzzword became "course evaluations." Various personal and standard evaluation forms came into use. In the fall of 1971, the decision to use a standard form was opposed by some of the faculty, including English professor Thomas Kemme, who wrote a letter to *The Concord,* in which he distinguished between "a serious student" and a mere "enrollee" and recommended "that only students who have compiled a 3.0 grade point average and who are approved by the academic dean be permitted to participate in the analysis, evaluation and publication of sensitive information." The controversy has continued down into the '90s over acceptable ways of evaluating faculty and their courses. By the '90s, however, most faculty had gotten used to the concept of faculty accountability.

While faculty were being held to rising standards, the college struggled to begin new ways of supporting the new expectations with leaves, summer stipends, sabbaticals and clerical assistance. From the first decade of the college it was common to grant leaves of absence, sometimes subsidized, for faculty to complete graduate studies. In the fall of 1959, for example, Thomas Sheehan of the English department, began work on his doctorate; and in 1962 Fr. John Davis of theology took a year's leave to study and teach in Israel.

Summer study grants were in place by the summer of 1964, when Frank J. O'Rourke of the business administration faculty and Robert J. Fitzpatrick of accounting received grants to study at Indiana University. Summer stipends made it possible for faculty also to do short research and writing projects. Theresa Sandok of philosophy, for example, spent several weeks during the summer of 1984 in Poland in connection with work on her translation of a religious work by an Ursuline sister. Finally, a system of sabbaticals was added during the decade of the '80s, with the college providing the grantee one-half salary for one or two semesters.

During the last two decades other forms of support for faculty teaching and research have included secretarial help and the availability of computers and computer instruction for faculty and staff, thanks to a generous grant from the Lilly Foundation. More recent support has come from the Knight Foundation and the C.E.S. Foundation and through technology grants from the James Graham Brown Foundation and others. Dan Sweeny remembers that when he came to Bellarmine in the late '50s there was little or no secretarial support for faculty. "We either typed our work ourselves," he says, "or took it to one of the administrative secretaries, who typed it when she had

nothing else to do. I remember vividly seeing Jack Daly pounding away on the old Remington manual we had in the chemistry office. Jack never unlearned that hard-touch technique, and even when we got electric typewriters and later computer keyboards, he continued to pound it as if he were back attacking the old Remington."

With modest support from the college's strained budgets, Bellarmine faculty have won considerable professional and scholarly recognition, publishing seminal papers and books and winning grants, awards and other forms of recognition. A bibliography of books, monographs and articles written, papers read, music composed and art objects created would itself make a book. It would extend back to a biography by a young Fr. Jeremiah Smith almost 50 years ago of a Polish priest, Fr. Maximilian Kolbe, who died in 1941 at age 47 in a Nazi concentration camp. And it would extend forward to Bob Lockhart's monumental sculpture, "The Bellarmine Knight," installed on the quadrangle as a reminder of the ageless principles and precepts upon which the college was founded.

Praise and recognition should be given, however, to at least some of those who have labored in this academic vineyard and brought forth wondrous

Bellarmine College
is riding high

harvests. Numerous awards from the National Science Foundation have been won by faculty in the social and natural sciences for research and equipment. One of the college's most successful grants writers, Jack Daly was instrumental in raising an estimated $800,000 over his almost four decades as a chemistry professor, with awards from the National Science Foundation, the Atomic Energy Commission, the American Chemical Society and other groups. Also winning awards in the sciences were G. Daniel Sweeny, Robert Korn, James J. Dyar and Richard W. Sames. Dr. Korn, for example, won a $17,500 grant from the NSF in 1981 for the study of cell shape through the use of geometric analysis. In 1998 Dr. Graham Ellis received a NSF grant funded by Ameritech as part of a four-college collaborative project to use the Internet to teach chemistry. To facilitate another kind of communication, Professor Gabriele Bosley received a 10-year grant totaling $500,000 to support and strengthen the foreign language program.

Other departments and disciplines have also been successful. In 1964 Margaret Mahoney of the history faculty won a Danforth Foundation Teachers Grant for one year of graduate study. She spent one semester at the University of Minnesota to complete her doctorate. Stanley Zemelka of the economics faculty was named a Ford Foundation Fellow for 1968-69 and studied international economics at Duke University and the University of North Carolina. In 1972-73 Joan T. Brittain received a National Endowment for the Humanities Fellowship to do research for a book on Laurence Stallings. Others receiving significant awards include Sr. Pat Lowman, who won a Fulbright Travel Fellowship to India, and Richard Sames of biology, who was awarded several research grants from the U.S. Public Health Service in the '50s and '60s.

The hard work for which the Bellarmine faculty is noted has paid off not only in "merit raises" during annual salary reviews but also in various kinds of campus awards, many of which carry a welcome cash stipend. One of the most coveted is the William T.

Miles Memorial Award, established by Bellarmine overseer Harry E. Miles in 1961 in memory of his son. The award is made each year to the faculty member "who in the judgment of his or her colleagues, made the greatest contribution to the fulfillment of the purposes of the college." Winners have ranged from Margaret Mahoney to John H. Ford. The award is especially meaningful since it is given by vote of the faculty. Another significant honor is the Teilhard de Chardin Award given by the campus Biology Club to a faculty member or administrator for service to the college and the community. Winners have included Richard Sames and Don Murray.

Another signal honor is the Teacher of the Year Award, inaugurated by the Student Government Executive Council in the spring of 1965, and given to a faculty member by vote of the student body. Winners have included John H. Ford, the first recipient, Sr. Pat Lowman, Robert A. Preston, Fr. Fred Hendrickson, Bernie Thiemann, Margaret Mahoney, Thomas Kemme and John J. Bethune.

Now, as Bellarmine College approaches its 50th year, veteran faculty and staff have begun to retire in large numbers. Their careers at Bellarmine sum up a large chunk of the college's history. They are people whose legacies cast long shadows:

Dr. John J. Bethune   *Dr. Paul Mathews*   *Dr. Marie Mathews*

Sr. Clarita Felhoelter, Tom Devasia, Jack Daly, Bob Fitzpatrick, Mary Ann Fueglein, Wade Hall, Anna Jackey, Kathleen Lyons, Paul Mathews, Henry Schoo, Fr. Jeremiah Smith, Dan Sweeny, John Voor, Stanley Zemelka, Betty Delius, Fr. Hilary Gottbrath, Ann Kleine-Kracht Weeks, Jim Spalding, Joy M. Brands, Bob

Miss Mary Ann Fueglein

Sullivan, Joan Wettig. These men and women and more join Bellarmine's first retiree, Dr. Henry S. Wilson, the college's first full professor, who retired in May of 1967.

Sadly, some of these retirees have already been lost to death. Others were struck down while still serving the college. Fr. John Loftus. George Albert White. Marie Mathews. Vicki Owsley. Msgr. Raymond Treece. Windell Bowles. Gus Coin. Bob Munson. Jack Daly. John Voor. Daniel C. Walsh. Claude Moore. Charlie Stark. William Haney. Anna Jackey. Richard O'Hare. Fr. Hilary. Eugene Petrik. . . .

Perhaps at no time does the Bellarmine faculty and family come together more as a community than they do when celebrating the life of a deceased colleague. Gus Coin, who died May 2, 1992, was celebrated at an ecumenical memorial service at St. Robert's Chapel on May 8. The homily was given by Fr. Clyde Crews, with participation by members of the Bellarmine family. The Prayer of the Faithful, written by Dr. Kathleen Lyons, concluded: "In thanksgiving for Gus, the lovable Greek, who was both Socrates and Zorba; the musician and teacher, who responded with feeling to Mozart, Wagner and Benny Goodman. Gus loved life and he knew how to live."

Some died young. Fr. Joseph Raffo Bowling died of cancer on February 14, 1963, at the age of 48. A native of New Haven in Nelson County, Kentucky, he was a graduate of St. Xavier High School, St. Mary's College and St. Meinrad Seminary. His will left an estate of $55,000 in common stocks and a $5,000 fund which students, aided by college officials, were directed to invest with profits going into a Bowling Student Fund to assist needy students. Art professor and painter William Haney died in April of 1992 at 52.

Richard A. Dolin, formerly of the business administration faculty, died in 1999 at the age of 54.

The unexpected death of M. Celeste Nichols in April of 1996 at the age of 45 shocked the entire college. A member of the English faculty, Dr. Nichols was a native of Tulsa and the first African American to receive a doctoral degree in English from the University of Louisville. At Bellarmine she taught courses in black authors and classes in the college's African American Leadership Institute, which teaches management, leadership and communication skills and prepares black students for the MBA program. In addition to her many community and church-related activities, she also served as the Bellarmine coordinator of the National African American Read-In Chain and chaired the First National Toni Morrison Conference at Bellarmine in April of 1995. In the spring of 1996 the college established the Dr. M. Celeste Nichols African American Collection, focusing on African American literature and history, to be housed in the new W. L. Lyons Brown Library.

Each faculty member has made his or her mark on the history of Bellarmine College. It is a rich legacy. Yet there is work to be done by the present faculty and teachers yet to come. A knowledge of what has been accomplished by Bellarmine's faculty when resources were much more meager than they are today should serve as an inspiration for the present and future faculty. An encouraging sign is that many of the talented, younger faculty expect to spend their careers at Bellarmine. In Fr. Kilcourse's words: "As a boy I walked this place when it was mud. Raymond [Fr. Raymond J. Treece] carried my sister across a campus puddle to protect her patent leather shoes. I go back to the beginning and hope to be a part of the college for a long time to come."

An early faculty meeting in the reference room in the Horrigan Hall Library.

Students and their activities

Students are, of course, the reason for Bellarmine College. The faculty, the administration, the curriculum, the buildings and campus—all the parts that go to make up Bellarmine College exist for the purpose of educating students. Who are Bellarmine's students? Where did they come from? Why did they choose Bellarmine? What did they do on campus? What did they do after graduation? What do they think of their alma mater after they leave? These questions—and more—are posed when we consider the place of students in Bellarmine's history.

In the June 24, 1960 issue of *The Record* recent honor graduate Walter Emge attempted to profile Catholic college students of his generation. Describing them as "mildly confused and frustrated," he maintained that they were torn between a society that they must live in and an educational system that has led them in sometimes alternative directions. "It is a society," he wrote,"that can become more excited over the tailfins of the latest model car than over the gross injustices of our treatment of the Negro. It is a society that could produce corruption in labor unions, unethical practices in big business and the big professions, payola and a thousand other excesses."

On the other hand, the Catholic educational system and its leaders, he said, "have tried to introduce students into a world of ideas, values, truths, a world of beauty and dignity. They have tried to make our young people the responsible, intelligent, productive individuals that the world and the Church need. They have tried to replace a material world with a spiritual world." Students are thus torn, he maintained, between "the practical, down-to-earth, business-like world of our modern society" and "the intellectual, idealistic, principle-conscious world of our liberal arts colleges." With the optimism of youth, he concluded that out of such conflicts young people were becoming fighters and rebels as they worked to reform society. Surely Emge's essay—from its lean and eloquent style to its moral and spiritual tone— provided ample proof that Bellarmine College had been about the business that its founders envisioned.

In 1960 Bellarmine had been in business for ten years. Its decade-long history recorded much success and pointed to a wide-open future. Enrollments were increasing. Programs were expanding to meet the needs of the ever-larger student body. Community support was building. A well-educated, dedicated faculty was in place. Modern buildings were beginning to punctuate the beautiful rolling campus. And students were proud to be Bellarmine College students. On March 2, 1960, Fr. John Loftus sent a memo to Fr. Horrigan describing a meeting with several students, led by Charles Kincaid, who wanted to begin an organization of students that would cultivate pride on campus and in the community about the college. They wanted, he said, to become

Bellarmine College
Operation Pride

presents

BELLARMINE'S BEST

"part of a program to 'sell' Bellarmine, especially to students." He said they planned to enlist students who would be part of a program they had dubbed "Operation Pride." They would begin with visits to local high schools to talk with prospective students about coming to Bellarmine.

Led by Alan Adelberg and Perry Carney and advised by faculty member Eugene Hunckler, the first year membership rose to more than 40. Work committees were formed. A brochure headed "Facts on Bellarmine College" was published. Visits were made to high schools, and campus tours were conducted for prospective students and their parents. A high-school newspaper contest was sponsored.

By the second year membership was over 60. A spin-off called Pride Ambassadors was formed to visit such local leaders as school heads, directors of museums and libraries, bankers and businessmen and women and religious leaders to tell them about the college and how it was serving the community. They visited such prominent leaders as Dean Allen W. Graves of the Southern Baptist Theological Seminary and Wathen R. Knebelkamp, president of Churchill Downs. At the same time, members of the service organization were learning about how the community was organized and how they could serve it. Renamed the Pride Corps in 1962, the organization quickly became an important link between the college and the larger community. Soon the group began to present an annual "Alumnus of Whom We Are Most Proud Award," with the first honor going to John Kampschaefer of the Pioneer Class. This grassroots student initiative was dramatic evidence of student pride in their school.

But how can a new school quickly accumulate a tradition in which students can take pride? Obviously,

members of the Pioneer Class entered the college on faith and promises and the richness of the Catholic college tradition. Fortunately, students responded. Early in January 1950, Fr. Horrigan and Fr. Treece began recruiting students, speaking to senior classes at both St. Xavier and Flaget high schools to explain the admission requirements, the courses and curriculum of the new school to open that fall. In November of 1949, Fr. Horrigan said he hoped to have 100 students in the first freshman class. He did 15 better than that.

As a tuition-dependent college, Bellarmine's student recruitment has always been vital to its survival and success. Innovative and imaginative techniques have been employed by all three administrations to attract qualified students. In the 1950s the college began to recruit students aggressively, with an annual High School Day held to acquaint high-school seniors and their parents with Bellarmine's programs, costs and financial aid. The April 1954 event attracted more than 300 students from nine local high schools, public and Catholic. In September of that year Bellarmine also cooperated with Nazareth and Ursuline in sponsoring a college booth at the Kentucky State Fair.

By the 1960s Bellarmine was hosting College Fair Day in Knights Hall, where high-school students and their parents could obtain information from several dozen private and public colleges. In the fall of 1984 more than 60 colleges and universities showcased their programs, student activities and student aid. In the early '60s Bellarmine was also giving advanced placement exams for high-school seniors who could receive college credit for high scores when they entered college in the fall.

Initiatives in student recruitment by academic departments included Bellarmine's annual math competitions, begun in 1961. Prizes were cash awards, books and a plaque for the school of the winning team. In February of 1972, the Bellarmine Math Club sponsored its 12th annual math contest, the Mathematics Invitational Competition, with some 500 students from high schools in Kentucky and Southern Indiana participating.

Many talented students have been brought to Bellarmine because of the influence of individual faculty members. Ruth Wagoner transferred to Bellarmine in 1969 because of the presence of debate coach Raymond Bailey. "Bellarmine's debate program," she says, "was so superior to the University of Louisville's. Its superiority was due to Bailey, with whom I had a mentoring relationship. He helped me raise my sights that led me to earn a master's degree at Western and finally a Ph.D. at the University of Kentucky." Michael Steinmacher, '93, had several influences that caused him to choose Bellarmine. "Two of my uncles," he says, "helped plant trees on campus. Doug Starr of the music faculty helped me to start a leadership program at Holy Cross when I was in high school. I had also taken almost a full year of courses through Bellarmine's Advanced Placement Program. It just seemed natural for me to come to Bellarmine." Meanwhile, the public relations office began working with the student recruitment staff in developing informative publications as well as making Bellarmine more visible in its primary market area through local and regional media outlets. It seemed that no stone was left unturned to interest students in and prepare them for Bellarmine College. In the summer of 1960, for example, under the direction of Fr. Joseph H. Voor, director of guidance, Bellarmine offered a College Skills Program, an intensive six-week class to prepare high-school students for college work.

As competition for good students has intensified in the '90s, new approaches have been invented and tested. In November of 1993, Ed Wilkes was appointed vice president for enrollment management and began an aggressive and innovative recruitment program, including new strategies in financial aid and a large number of new printed brochures on such subjects as financial aid and the honors program. One of the most imaginative and successful initiatives is the Bellarmine Junior Fellows Program, begun in the spring of 1995. Regional high schools are invited to nominate their top achieving juniors. From that list fellows are selected and invited to attend periodic seminars and events on campus.

The more recent work of Tim Sturgeon, dean of admissions, combines efforts of admissions, financial aid, continuing studies—indeed, the offices and resources of the entire campus—in a concerted effort to identify, attract and make possible the enrollment of qualified students from diverse backgrounds. A recently constructed website with extensive information about the college has spread Bellarmine's recruiting outreach into cyberspace. The results of these various programs have been larger freshman classes with greater geographic and ethnic diversity and better academic preparation.

In the beginning, however, Archbishop Floersh envisioned a college that would produce Catholic lay leaders for the Archdiocese. The young men who came to Bellarmine would be educated for leadership in business and the professions and then remain in the Archdiocese. For that reason, most of the recruitment focus in the early years was on the Louisville area. As late as 1975, 80 per cent of Bellarmine's full-time students were Louisville residents.

From the start, it was, therefore, apparent that most of the first students would come from the Archdiocesan boys high schools. The first person to apply for admission to the new college was 17-year-old David Baird, a senior at St. Xavier High School, a varsity basketball player, cartoonist for the school paper, and vice president of the Religious Activity Club. He said he planned to major in commerce. In addition to St. X, Flaget, De Sales and St. Joseph School in

Bardstown were important "feeder schools" for the first classes. After its opening in September of 1953 with a freshman class of more than 100, Holy Trinity High School became an important source of students. Following the merger with Ursuline in 1968, such Archdiocesan girls schools as Assumption, Sacred Heart and Presentation would become major student sources.

Because of its proximity to Bellarmine and its long academic tradition, St. X provided a large percentage of the college's first students and leaders. In the fall of 1961, for example, all four freshman class officers were St. X alumni: Quentin P. Seadler, president; James Lally, vice president; Paul Ray, secretary; and Martin Schnurr, treasurer. By the fall of 1963, however, class honors were being shared with other high schools. President of that year's freshman class was Joseph A. Haydon, a graduate of St. Joseph School in Bardstown; vice president was A. G. Hilbert, Jr. of Flaget; secretary was Thomas E. Lynch of De Sales; and treasurer was John T. Hickey of St. X. Of the 1,860 students enrolled in 1960, 650 were from St. X, Flaget, Trinity and De Sales high schools.

As one of Bellarmine's main feeder schools, St. X has always had strong and friendly ties to the college. One reason for the close relationship was that many St. X alumni have filled important positions at Bellarmine. An early example was Fr. John R. Clancy, who, as professor and registrar, kept in close touch with St. X students. A significant and continuing influence on Bellarmine's growth was signaled in May of 1957, when Trinity High School graduated its first class of 83. According to a poll of the senior class, of the 76 per cent who planned to attend college, 40 per cent said they would choose Bellarmine. In fact, two seniors won

Bellarmine scholarships, J. Donald Herp and Fred Fuchs; and a popular member of the Trinity faculty, Thomas Sheehan, announced that he would join the Bellarmine English faculty in the fall.

By the end of its second decade Bellarmine was drawing students from dozens of states and foreign countries, including refugees from Cuba in 1964. Perhaps none had come from as exotic a location, however, as Fr. Agapitus Sasa, who arrived at Bellarmine from the slopes of Mt. Elgon in Uganda. In January of 1970, he became a math major at Bellarmine and associate pastor of St. Augustine Church in downtown Louisville. A number of exchange students from Britain have been sponsored by the Kentucky Branch of the English-Speaking Union. In January of 1976, the four British students who were studying at Bellarmine reported that they liked their American experiences very much, like more flavors of ice cream, basketball, the politeness of most people. One of them, however, missed "real tea." John Birdwood said to a *Concord* reporter: "You have it in teabags, as opposed to making it properly." In the fall of 1996, 21 international students were on campus from such faraway places as Tibet and Nepal as well as France, Northern Ireland and Colombia. Out of a

Bellarmine's Global Outreach.

total enrollment of 2,236 in the fall of 1997, 1,536 were from Jefferson County, with only 320 from out of state. Bellarmine was still serving a predominantly regional market. When he spoke of the need to increase diversity on campus, President McGowan also meant geographical.

Despite the handicaps of a new and unknown school, Bellarmine's enrollment increased almost sixfold in the first seven years, even with the negative influence of the Korean War. Indeed, before the beginning of the second semester in February of 1951, 12 of the original 115 students had been drafted by the armed forces, and only 65 returned for that second semester. Nevertheless, "Enrollment Agains Hits a New High" was a *Concord* headline that was repeated like a refrain throughout the '50s and most of the '60s. By 1955 enrollment had risen to some 700 students. In addition to first-time students, many upperclassmen were transferring from the University of Louisville, the University of Kentucky and other state schools. The sixth year enrollment totaled 716. At a November 1956 Diocesan fund-raising dinner, Fr. Horrigan announced the impressive growth, from 115 full-time day students in the fall of 1950 to 639 in the fall of 1956. He predicted that, with evening and part-time students, total enrollment would reach 4,000 by 1970— an overly optimistic projection, as it turned out. Nevertheless, student enrollment would show a healthy and consistent increase for eight years.

But there was trouble on the horizon. At the end of the fall 1958 semester, academic tightening led to the largest number of students ever in academic trouble. More than a third of the student body, including most of the basketball players, were either dismissed or placed on probation. Fr. John Loftus was not overly concerned. Academic standards, he said, needed raising and the crisis was not as serious as it looked. A Bellarmine student could be placed on probation if he was making passing grades but not doing his best.

Then in the fall of 1959 enrollment dropped 11 per cent. Day school enrollment was down over 14 per cent. Fr. John Clancy, the registrar, gave several reasons for the drop: tighter academic requirements, fewer transfer students, fewer students from feeder schools like Flaget and fewer veterans enrolled because of the expiration of the GI Bill of Rights for many of them. Increases resumed in 1960 and 1961, when enrollment rose from 1,276 to 1,382. During the Korean and Vietnam war periods, enrollment was affected by concern over the draft and deferments— and sometimes the luck of a low draft lottery number. On December 1, 1969, a student who drew a "three" said: "I think I'll go and find some one's and two's and then go out and get drunk."

As the decade of the '60s concluded, several factors were impacting Bellarmine's growth—the transfer of Passionist seminary students to Bellarmine and the merger of Bellarmine and Ursuline. A disappointed President, however, announced at the first annual Founders Day Convocation in September of 1968 that enrollment was only 2,021, or about 330 fewer than the combined enrollments of both Bellarmine and Ursuline the year before. Not only was it a disappointment to the President but it was also, he said, "a problem." The school would operate at a deficit. But Bellarmine was not alone. All of Kentucky's independent schools were hard hit by steep declines. The percentage of college students attending private colleges in Kentucky had dropped from 34 per cent in 1961 to 18 per cent in 1971.

At Bellarmine the enrollment slide continued until 1974. By the fall of 1979 Bellarmine again had a record enrollment of 2,085, the highest since the merger with Ursuline in 1968. By 1981 campus enrollment reached 2,585. Classrooms were jammed and many instructors were teaching overloads. Most students were from Jefferson County, some 79 per cent of them. The majority of them came from Catholic high schools. St. X led the way, with 46 in the freshman class alone. Among public schools,

Atherton was first with 13 freshmen. Thirteen states were represented in the freshman class, and 34 international students were in the total student body. Between 1973 and 1983, when enrollment topped at 2,809, the increase was more than 144 per cent. Females had outnumbered males since 1977. A decline in enrollment followed until 1995, when the college had its largest full-time student body in 11 years. Total enrollment for the fall 1997 semester was 2,236. The grand total, undergraduate and graduate students, for the fall of 1998 was 2,301.

Students choose Bellarmine for many reasons, including its liberal arts and sciences core curriculum; its small size and individual attention; its location and accessibility; its choice of quality professional undergraduate programs in business, accounting, nursing and education; its dedicated, teaching-oriented faculty and, perhaps most consistently, its religious and value-centered education. Accounting graduate Tim Swenson speaks for thousands of Bellarmine students: "I was a product of Louisville Catholic schools, from grade school through high school—I went to Trinity— and I knew I would be comfortable at Bellarmine. I knew I would get an education based on moral and ethical foundations. That was important to me and to my parents. My choice of Bellarmine turned out to be a good one. As an accounting major in a liberal arts college, I was able to become editor of *The Concord,* something I don't think would have happened if I had gone to a large state university."

The cost of tuition, however, has not been a reason to choose Bellarmine, especially after the University of Louisville joined the state system in 1970 and began to lower its tuition. Competition from the state-sponsored Jefferson Community College since the late '60s has also been a problem. Despite statistics that show that Bellarmine's tuition has been consistently lower than comparable colleges nationally, the fact is that for many prospective students Bellarmine is not only a quality alternative but an expensive alternative to nearby state schools. The

college has, however, succeeded in remaining competitive through an extensive financial aid program, from scholarships and grants to loan programs.

When the school opened in 1950, there was no cost differential with area schools. In fact, tuition was intentionally set to be the same as that paid by University of Louisville students. Tuition was $10 a semester hour or $150 per semester, with books and fees adding perhaps another $50. Despite the low tuition, college officials soon realized that in order to attract top students, they had to offer scholarships. By April of 1955 the college was giving competitive scholarship exams, with full-tuition scholarships to be awarded to the highest scorers at each of three local Catholic boys high schools—St. X, Flaget and Catholic High. (Opened in 1921 as Catholic Colored High School, Catholic High School was Louisville's only Catholic high school for African Americans until it was closed in 1958. It was located on Cedar Street.) Competitive scholarships were also made available to students in the Archdiocese living outside Louisville.

Catholic High School on Cedar Street.

Soon competitive scholarships were being awarded in four academic areas—forensics, creative writing, accounting and science. Before long, scholarships worth $1,200 each were being awarded each year to such top students as Hugh R. Coomes of St. Joseph Preparatory School in Bardstown, Theodore J. Bach of St. X and Clarence M. Buechler of Flaget. By 1960 the scholarship program had expanded to include more areas in Kentucky as well as towns in Indiana, Tennessee, Ohio and Missouri. One of the most unusual scholarships was presented to Mr. and Mrs. Edward L. Mackey in November of 1952 by Fr. Treece. It was for the use of their one-month-old son when he came of college age. How did young Mackey earn the one-year scholarship? His parents named him Robert Bellarmine Mackey.

N. Robert Sullivan, Director, Student Finances with A. Richard Tillmar.

Tuition at $10 an hour was maintained until the fall of 1958, when it was increased to $14. To cushion the shock of the increase, the college announced that the $10 lab fee would be dropped, that student aid would be increased and easy credit terms would be available to deserving students. The college already had in place a short-term loan program with a $100 limit for students unable to pay tuition at registration. A new loan program allowed students to borrow up to $1,000 from the college over four years. Fr. Horrigan explained to students that the increase was necessary to offset a projected operating deficit of about $25,000 caused by an increase in lay faculty members.

In 1961, when tuition rose from $14 to $19 an hour, the increase was offset in part by the reduction in degree requirements from 136 hours to 128. Thirty-three freshmen scholarships were awarded, double the number of the previous year. In May of 1962, the college announced the award of 33 scholarships for the upcoming academic year, including five Chancellor's Scholarships, the highest scholarship awarded. One of the recipients was Clyde F. Crews, a senior at St. X, later to become a Diocesan priest, a member of Bellarmine's theology faculty and a respected and prolific author of books on local and church history. In the summer of 1964 scholarship aid for the first time was available to students in the evening division. In the fall of 1964 the college awarded 62 scholarships worth about $25,000.

Tuition was up to $30 an hour by June of 1967, with some of the increased revenue going toward improved faculty salaries. Full professors saw their salaries increase from an average of $9,000 a year to $12,000. An example of innovative marketing occurred during the spring semester of 1967, when the parents of Bellarmine students could take evening division courses at a 50 per cent discount. It was also the last year that tuition at the University of Louisville was higher than Bellarmine's. In 1967 U of L's resident tuition was $1,200 a year while Bellarmine's was $900. After the university entered the state system in 1970, its tuition was gradually reduced and the cost differential between it and Bellarmine began to widen. Tuition for state residents at U of L was down to $850 by the fall of 1974, while Bellarmine-Ursuline's was up to $1,200. Nonresidents, however, paid more at the University of Louisville—$1,950 as opposed to $1,200 at

Bellarmine. Indeed, costs at state schools remained fairly stable during the inflation-ridden '70s, while independent schools like Bellarmine had to keep afloat financially by raising tuition almost every year. A headline in *The Concord* of February 16, 1979 tells the story: "A Tuition Increase As Usual Next Semester."

In addition to scholarships and loans, the college also helped students find part-time jobs while they were in school. The office of placement services in the dean of students office assisted students in finding jobs. A May 1973 report said that some 75 per cent of Bellarmine's students worked part-time in order to stay in school.

Because of inflation and the costs of campus development and instruction, Bellarmine's tuition rose during the first 30 years from $10 to $75 per hour. Fortunately, additional sources of financial aid became available, including government funds. Beginning in the fall of 1959 the college participated in the new college aid program under the National Defense Education Act, which provided long-term loans to qualified students at 3 per cent interest. In May of 1975 Gov. Julian M. Carroll announced the allocation of $500,000 for a tuition grant program earmarked for private school students that had been provided by a 1972 law; and soon many Bellarmine students were receiving state grants from the Kentucky Higher Education Assistance Authority. In the fall of 1977, 331 Bellarmine students were receiving state grants that averaged $633 per person. In the spring of 1975 one-half of all Bellarmine students received some form of federal aid, whether grants, loans or work-study.

By the 1983-84 academic year, Bellarmine students were paying a yearly tuition of $3,600, while the cost at U of L was $934 and at Jefferson Community College, only $414. Yet with a combination of scholarships, grants, loans and work study—plus its special mission as a church-related liberal arts college—Bellarmine was able to survive and thrive. In 1995 tuition reached $9,450 a year, which, as President McGowan noted, was about 25 per cent

below the average of other private institutions nationally. Some 90 per cent of full-time freshmen, he said, were receiving some form of financial aid, worth an average of about $7,300 a year. Students in the college Honors Program had four-year, full-tuition scholarships. The President's Scholars Program has now been supplanted by the Bellarmine Scholars Program, which provides full tuition and an opportunity to travel abroad. By 1996 Bellarmine's annual tuition had grown to $10,320. In 1998 tuition was $11,600—still 20 per cent below the national average for independent colleges. And students were still coming. Indeed, the college is open and operating and building new facilities and starting new programs as the 21st century approaches. After four years of lectures, seminars and tests—and tuition paying—most students are ready to become alumni. The graduation rite of passage is an important landmark in their lives. It is the commencement of their professions and a symbol of their maturity, the door to the world that they have been preparing to enter. At Bellarmine graduation activities have included not only the traditional baccalaureate services—usually at St. Agnes Church—but such various activities as awards dinners, sports banquets and senior celebrations. Until the '80s the degree-awarding ceremony usually took place in late May or early June outside on the west or Preston Park Lawn, on a portable stage with a castle-like backdrop suggesting the knightly days of chivalry. When inclement weather threatened, the ceremony was moved to Knights Hall.

An impressive processional signaled the start of the ceremonies, with the President, various other administrators, the Archbishop, the faculty and the degree candidates all decked out in the colors and cuts of gowns signifying their universities, their degrees and their disciplines. For family and friends of the seniors, it was a colorful spectacle to be recorded on film for picture albums and scrapbooks. Jim Stammerman remembers graduation ceremonies in the '50s when even small classes produced huge crowds. "Graduation was always a big occasion," he says, "because in most cases it was the first time anyone in the family had graduated from college." On May 29, 1955, the second graduating class had 38 members. The honor graduates were chemistry major John Gilbert Esterle, math major Robert Charles Gipperich and psychology major John Valentine Kiesler. The baccalaureate speaker was Maj. Gen. Patrick J. Ryan, Army Chief of Chaplains; and commencement speaker was Fr. Philip Hughes, a distinguished English historian teaching at Notre Dame. The oldest member of the class was former journalist James Sullivan, 47. Another member was James R. Spalding, 22, a graduate in biology who won the Silver Knight Award for athletics. Spalding would later become Bellarmine's basketball coach and long-time director of athletics. The speaker for the third graduation was Senator Eugene McCarthy of Minnesota, who told the graduates: "Our calling is to save the world rather than to judge it." Of the 48 graduates that year, five planned to marry soon, 14 were veterans, 17 were about to enlist in the service and nine planned to go to graduate or professional schools.

At a huge outdoor ceremony on June 5, 1957, Bellarmine graduated a class of 86 students. James F. Morris received the Faculty Merit Award for outstanding academic achievement by an athlete. An English priest, the Rev. Joseph V. Christie, S.J., told the graduates: "Christian educators should never allow themselves to be regarded as a luxury tolerated by the state, but should make it clear that it is they and they alone who can maintain the foundation of the democratic way of life." The Class of '58 had 96 graduates, with honor students David L. Chervenak, Michael A. Greenwell and Donald J. Kiesler. Chervenak, 25, was an accountant, father of three and dabbler in amateur theatricals, gardening, softball and badminton.

In 1961, 121 seniors received their degrees, and John Guarnaschelli won the Freshman of the Year Award. Honorary degrees were given to Robert M.

Watt, chairman of Kentucky Utilities, Dr. Roy J. Deferrari, retired secretary-general of the Catholic University of America, and the late Thomas E. Murray, a diplomat and consultant on atomic energy. There were 356 students in the graduating class in May of 1969. Commencement speaker was Senator Marlow W. Cook, who criticized unruly student protests against the Vietnam War. He received cheers when he said that the nation's military forces must be reduced because "as long as we keep an army that big, it will find something to do." Receiving honorary Doctor of Laws degrees were Archibald P. Cochran, a retired Louisville businessman, and Barry Bingham, Sr., editor and publisher of *The Courier-Journal* and *The Louisville Times*.

The following year 357 students were graduated and addressed by County Judge Todd Hollenbach. Honorary degrees were conferred on John Howard Griffin, author of *Black Like Me*, and W. L. Lyons Brown, chairman of the board of Brown-Forman Distillers Corporation. For the first time, in December of 1977 the college held a midyear graduation ceremony for 56 seniors and graduate students. By the '80s graduation ceremonies were being held exclusively in air-conditioned Knights Hall. Such prestigious faculty honors as the Miles Award and the Wyatt Fellowships have also been given at graduation.

Freshman of the year, Bobby Todd, with Fr. Hilary Gottbrath.

Perhaps the most coveted award is the Archbishop's Award for Academic Excellence, which has been won by Bellarmine's top graduates, including Robert K. Brimm, David L. Chervenak, Robert J. Caster, Michael Joseph Mudd, Edward J. Burke, Joseph

R. Reinhart and Walter G. Emge. Latin honors are the result of four years of hard work and have been won by such outstanding graduates as Robert K. Brimm, James F. Morris and John E. Kleber. Several dozen Bellarmine students have been awarded summer scholarships by the Kentucky Branch of the English-Speaking Union to study at British universities. Winners include Chuck Bronson, Tom Petrik, Elise Hart, Melanie Votaw, Dina Abby, Steve Knadler, Anne Koester, George Schenetzke, Douglas K. Steele, Lawrence E. Minogue, Hayward D. Poling, Russell Cashon and Larry Blume.

The In Veritatis Amore Awards are given annually to juniors and seniors for scholastic achievement and participation in campus activities. Winners have included such well-rounded students as Anne Miller, Paul Kleine-Kracht, Joe Cassidy, Cele Clements, Tom Schurfranz and Regina Hennessy. Biology and chemistry graduates have routinely won National Science Foundation Fellowships for study at such outstanding graduate schools as Purdue and the University of Michigan. In the spring of 1962, four seniors in accounting were given awards for graduate study at Indiana University: Bernard F. Thiemann, Edward J. Burke, Richard E. Steinmetz and Joseph R. Reinhart.

A number of Bellarmine students have won Fulbright Scholarships and Woodrow Wilson Fellowships. In the spring of 1962, William C. Schrader III, a senior history major, won a Fulbright Scholarship to study at the University of Erlanger in Germany as well as a Woodrow Wilson Fellowship for graduate work leading to college teaching. He was the second Bellarmine winner of the Wilson award, the first one being Walter Emge in 1960. Other Wilson Fellows from Bellarmine include Anthony G. Covatta, Clyde F. Crews, Frank L. Schmidt, C. Donald Hall, Michael L. Murray and Sr. Lucille Marie Fiandaca. In the spring of 1963, Owen J. Lustig, a senior in political science, won a Lilly Endowment Fellowship to the University of Virginia as well as a Fulbright Scholarship for study

in Santiago, Chile. Clyde F. Crews was graduated *summa cum laude* in May of 1966 and was awarded a Danforth Fellowship to attend the graduate school of his choice. The first Bellarmine student to win a Danforth was Walter Emge in 1960.

In the summer of 1965, Gary J. Dill and Dennis C. Zvinakis won two of the 200 scholarships given by the East-West Center at the University of Hawaii. In 1996 chemistry major John A. Hoerter was named a Barry M. Goldwater Scholar for graduate study worth $7,000 for the academic year. In addition to these awards, several hundred Bellarmine students have been elected to Who's Who in American Colleges and Universities. Among the winners of the Lenihan Memorial Awards for student and community leadership have been Robert G. Pfaadt and Bernard F. Thiemann. In 1965 Bellarmine produced the nation's Outstanding Young Adult Catholic. He was John A. "Tony" Peake, a 21-year-old history major from Louisville who had worked in Eastern Kentucky in the mission of the Rev. Ralph Beiting.

The Silver Knight Award given by the Alumni Association for exceptional athletic achievement and sportsmanship has been given to such superior athelete-scholars as Joseph C. Reibel. Other honors won by Bellarmine students have ranged from Kentucky Derby Festival Princess to Mountain Laurel Queen. In December of 1975, freshman art student Gloria Wollmann won a local art contest for her Bicentennial logo sponsored by the Louisville Bicentennial Commission. Her design, which was displayed on city buses and elsewhere, featured the fleur de lis and a series of strips within a circle placed at the center of a five-pointed star. In January of 1977, Danny Lawless, a senior English major, won a five-states poetry contest with his poem, "Young Man As I Am."

For many graduates the most meaningful honors are grants to attend prestigious graduate schools, and Bellarmine seniors have won their share. Indeed, in 1961 one-eighth of the graduating seniors received awards for graduate study. Bellarmine alumni have thus attended as scholarship recipients such major graduate schools as Northwestern, St. Louis University, Georgetown University, Florida State, Arizona State, California Institute of Technology, Georgia Tech, Catholic University, Johns Hopkins, Chicago, Loyola University of Chicago, Toronto, Yale, Iowa State, as well as the state universities of Illinois, Kentucky, Wisconsin, Tennessee, Indiana, New Mexico, Florida and others. Indeed, Bellarmine's professional schools in business, education and nursing are producing students who earn advanced degrees from top-ranked schools. Mike Huggins, for example, received his B.S.N. from Bellarmine and his M.S.N. from Vanderbilt.

A distinguishing characteristic of a Bellarmine education has been the camaraderie of faculty and administration and students, a sense of joint participation in the educational process. Such a feeling of community did not happen by accident. In the fall of 1961, for example, Fr. Horrigan was conducting a presidential chat series called The President's Notebook, during which he presided over informal get-togethers with students to discuss various topics. In his first chat with some 60 students, he admitted that his duties as President, especially fund raising, didn't allow him as much contact with students as he wanted. Unfortunately, he said, when he talked to them it was about "tuition increases and dismal subjects like that." His first chat focused on books and their importance in shaping thought and attitudes. Presidents Petrik and McGowan also provided occasions for dialogue with students.

Numerous other administrators and faculty have gone out of their way to develop good communication with students inside and outside the classroom. Fr. John Loftus set a high standard for camaraderie in his personal contacts with students and in his legendary memos. On November 21, 1968, in one of his last memos, just two months before his death, he called the students "my life/my meaning/my reward/my hope/my promise." Sue Hockenberger Davis's description of her classroom experiences is typical: "The comfort level I have had in the classroom with students is remarkable." Another testimonial comes from Fr. Fred Hendrickson: "Students have been a constant surprise and joy to me. They have kept me young and on my toes. One semester on the first day of classes, when I was feeling old and worn-down, I went into my logic class and I saw a hippie-looking young lady with dyed blonde hair and a black streak running down the middle. I took one look at her and said to myself, 'I can't take this much longer. There's no way this young woman will learn logic.' Was I mistaken! She turned out to be the best logic student I've ever had, making perfect scores on almost all my exams. She is now a Ph.D. student in psychology at Purdue, and, I am gratified to report, has a head full of dark hair with no streaks."

Students and faculty were, of course, frequently running into each other on campus—in the cafeteria, the library, the mailroom, at sporting events and campus socials and at meetings of all major decision-making committees, on which they became voting members in the late '60s.

The good feeling between faculty and students has contributed to the passionate loyalty of alumni and their common habit of making Bellarmine students out of their own children. Students have always had a high and favorable attitude toward their alma mater. A national poll in April of 1983 found that Bellarmine's students gave their college a 4.29 out of a possible 5 points, with parking and food ranking lowest. Campus improvements and informal surveys suggest that in the last 15 or so years the college has made progress on both counts. Indeed, a recent survey conducted by student affairs revealed that over 90 per cent of Bellarmine's students would recommend the college highly to their friends and peers.

Students will even come to the aid of their college when they feel it has been unfairly criticized.

Witness a letter by Bellarmine senior Robert F. Teaff to *The Louisville Times* on January 26, 1965, in response to a letter from several students to the "Lemme Doit" column. The students cited possible fire hazards in the library and then signed themselves anonymously "lest we suffer the wrath of college administrators." Said Teaff: "Bellarmine administrators have never wreaked vengeance on students in retaliation for their exercise of free speech." In fact, he said, "the college motto is 'In the Love of Truth.'"

Student loyalty extends over the decades as Bellarmine has aged and as parents, then their children, their grandchildren and succeeding generations become Bellarmine students. In May of 1981 the fifth member of the family of Mr. and Mrs. Fred B. Tewell received her degree in business administration. Others who had already graduated were Fred, Cathy, Patricia and Dennis. All three of Kaelin Kallay Rybak's brothers attended Bellarmine. Seven of Jim Spalding's family are Bellarmine graduates, including his youngest daughter Christa, who served as Student Government Association president. Few families, however, can rival the record of Mary "Mame" Garner, who earned her degree in psychology in 1977. By the spring of 1996 seven of her nine children were Bellarmine graduates— William III, Mary Jo, John, Kathryn, Paul, James and Thomas.

Sometimes the camaraderie among students lasts beyond college as they remain good friends or marry. Two 1997 honor graduates, Monnica VanDyke and Courtney McMillen, were roommates during their college years; and both served as vice president of Student Government. After graduation both accepted jobs in Louisville and continue to share an apartment. Through class reunions and homecoming activities Bellarmine alumni continue to see and socialize with each other.

Of course, Bellarmine students are not saints and sometimes have behaved like rowdy boys and girls— at least a few of them. A Derby Eve ruckus at Fourth and Broadway in 1965 resulted in the arrest of some 75 students from five colleges on charges of disorderly conduct. According to *The Louisville Times,* only one college had responded with plans to curtail the perennial rowdyism during Derby. That college was Bellarmine, which had only one student arrested. Two Bellarmine students apparently misbehaved and did minor damage to property in the fall of 1997 at a college party held at the Kentucky Derby Museum. But these are the exceptions. For the most part, Bellarmine students have conducted themselves properly whether partying on or off campus.

A few students have been the victims of accidents and unexpected illnesses. Tragedy struck on January 29, 1965, when John Robert Wirth, an 18-year-old freshman died of tetanus following a sledding accident on campus. After the accident in which one of his legs was punctured by a sled runner, he was given a tetanus shot at St. Joseph Infirmary but died several days later because of a rare immunity to the shots and an extreme susceptibility to the disease. In early January of 1966 Donald Joseph Zitter, 21, was killed in a car accident when he apparently dozed off as he was returning from a date late at night and hit a tree on Eastern Parkway. Sixteen-year-old Anatolis Latkovski was killed while on a student tour to Europe in August of 1971, when he fell from a rooftop in Nice, France. In October of 1982, Elise Hart Amshoff, '80, a history graduate who had returned to Bellarmine to prepare herself for medical school, died unexpectedly of a stroke. After an outstanding cross-country runner, Chris Jones, died as a result of an automobile accident, the college named the Chris Jones Invitational Cross-Country Meet in his honor.

And so students have come to Bellarmine for 50 years. Most of them have stayed for four years and have been forever changed by the experiences they had. Here they have learned how to make a living—and more importantly, how to make a life—or, in the words of President McGowan, "to make a life worth living." Here is a testimonial from an anonymous alumnus that could serve as a generic endorsement of a Bellarmine education: "I had opportunities at Bellarmine that I wouldn't have had at another school. Bellarmine taught me the importance of spiritual and moral values and as a child of God not to settle for second best. I learned that if I really want something, I should go after it. Bellarmine empowered me to go after whatever I wanted."

Student Life. . .

College life is not all books and papers and examinations. Occasionally, students must take time out for sports, social gatherings, club meetings and all the other activities that go on outside the classroom and library. It is where they can learn more about themselves, about others and about community life. It was a side of college life that Bellarmine's founding fathers recognized and encouraged from the beginning. An ad in *The Courier-Journal* of May 7, 1950 signed by Fr. Horrigan and Fr. Treece announced: "A balanced program of the usual extra-curricular activities— cultural, social and athletic—will be offered at Bellarmine College. These activities will be devised to support the main academic purposes of the school."

In listing the Bellarmine advantages in an August 1951 issue of *The Record,* Fr. John Loftus gave a status report: "Bellarmine, with its common sense view of man as a whole, sanctions and encourages all activities conducive to a well-rounded Catholic personality. A sensible, balanced program of athletics and social affairs with societies and teams which serve the entire student body as well as a select group of individuals has been planned and put into operation. Basketball and baseball teams have already carried the scarlet and silver of Bellarmine to victory in intercollegiate competition; an intramural athletic program has been established with enthusiastic success; social affairs have brought memorable moments to students in Bellarmine's first year. As years go on, these and similar activities will be increased and expanded."

Indeed, the founders could hardly have envisioned the scope that student activities would assume over the next 50 years. Reflecting the *zeitgeist* of the times, they range from organizations like Delta Sigma Pi, a national business fraternity; a 1977 Bellarmine version of "The Gong Show," a popular television show featuring bad taste and bad talent; to five jazz ensembles and the Wilson Wyatt Debate Forum of the '90s. The routine of academic life was even punctuated from time to time by special events, sometimes produced by Mother Nature. On January 16, 1966, an inch of snow and subfreezing temperatures combined to produce a massive traffic jam near the campus. Bellarmine students endeared themselves to stalled motorists on Newburg Road by filling several large containers with coffee and taking them down to stationary motorists and bus passengers. The '74 tornado disrupted campus routine with downed trees and leaky roofs and students and faculty who couldn't make it to class.

A more recent disruptive event produced by Mother Nature was the record snowfall of January 16, 1994. The college was closed for a full week. Everyone was snowed in. Dr. Ruth Garvey, director of residence life, and Michael Jackson, assistant director, were faced with feeding and caring for more than 400 resident students without the usual college help. The resident students, however, were not about to go hungry—not with plenty of food in nearby Koster Commons. The ingenious students found a canoe in storage, pulled it over to the Commons, loaded it with anything ready-to-eat, and pulled it through 21 inches of snow back to their dorms—and feasted. Necessity is, indeed, still the mother of invention.

College publications reflected student life and taste. A campus survey in the '90 *Lance* contained this list of "Campus Favorites" for 1990: Favorite Movie: "Dead Poets Society"; Favorite TV show: "Cosby"; Favorite Actor: Sean Connery; Favorite Actress: Kim

Basinger; Favorite Vacation Spot: Daytona Beach; Favorite Fad: no socks; Favorite Saying: "Ho!"; Favorite Food: pizza; Favorite Musical Group: Paula Abdul.

Service and Social Activities...

Hank Schmidt

Most of the organized student activities came under the umbrella of the dean of students or dean of student affairs, depending upon whatever the nonacademic office was called at a particular time. Directing that office have been some of the hardest working and most imaginative and patient men and women ever to work at the college: Fr. Hilary Gottbrath, Hank Schmidt, Bill Stewart, Terry Hohman, Dr. Fred Rhodes. But to many Bellarmine students and alumni, perhaps no one epitomizes student activities more than Marilyn Staples, former director of student activities and first recipient of the Sr. Pat Lowman Student Advocate Award. She has served under all three Presidents and has seen interest in student activities ebb and flow.

"All three administrations have been fairly supportive of our work," she says, "but I think President McGowan has been especially generous." Dr. Rhodes agrees. "Dr. McGowan," he says, "with his over 20 years of student affairs experience, has been most supportive." Indeed, the McGowan administration supported a $50 student activity fee in the fall of 1991 ($85 in 1999), which made possible an expanded range of activities, including movies on campus, guest comedians, intramurals, volunteerism, pie-throwing contests at faculty and administrators, ThinkFast celebrations, ski trips, a Fall Fiesta, visiting dramas like "Mark Twain on Tour," hillside concerts, and the first "Bellarmine Olympics" with competitions in basketball, sand volleyball, tug-of-war and a balloon bust.

Once, when asked to describe a good student activities director, Staples used these words: outgoing, flexible, versatile, likes to work with people, interested in guidance and counseling, loves sports. It was almost a self-description. The mission of student activities, she says, has changed dramatically since she arrived at Bellarmine in December of 1968. At that time, the emphasis was on social activities. Now there is much more emphasis on developing leadership skills, counseling and promoting diversity and service. She has also seen a great change in why students come to her for guidance. At the beginning of her career, it was usually superficial boyfriend or girlfriend problems, friction with roommates or minor money shortfalls. In the '80s and '90s problems became more basic and serious—pregnancies, serious depression, sexual abuse by family members and neighbors. "I have often felt like a mother confessor," she says.

Bellarmine social history is also dotted with student managed projects like the 1992 Fine Arts Performance Dinner, which brought students, led by Michael Steinmacher, from music, theater and art together in a spoof of TV's "Star Trek" to raise money for fine arts scholarships. Started by Bob Lockhart of the art faculty, ThinkFast is a series of campus-wide efforts to raise money (some $30,000 so far) by students, faculty and staff to promote such projects as feeding the hungry, promoting peace and social and political justice.

Not all of the activities of the students occurred on campus. Before the college had adequate facilities for dances or banquets or even sporting events, those activities had to be held off campus in rented quarters. Moreover, Bellarmine students have participated in numerous performing arts groups in the Louisville area, ranging from amateur theater groups to the Kentucky Opera Association. Don Petersen, a 19-year-old singing laboratory technician and night student in chemistry, was crowned king of the 1957 Crusade for Children. In the late '70s Chuck Bronson became a dancer with the Louisville Ballet while still a student.

In the fall of 1979, when Mikhail Baryshnikov danced with the Louisville Ballet, two Bellarmine people were on stage with him—Bronson and academic dean Robert Wittman. Several Kentucky Derby Queens have come from Bellarmine, including Kristen Zapata in 1986, Heather Peet in 1990, Michelle Mays in 1992, Leslie Ann Corbett in 1997, and Michelle Ackerman in 1999.

Of course, on the periphery of student social life each year has been the Kentucky Derby, as the '69 *Lance* aptly said, "well-inserted into the exam schedule." Large numbers of Bellarmine students, however, usually managed to find their way to Churchill Downs and to the infield, where they usually lost their bets. But after all, as a perspecacious *Lance* editor wrote, "The Kentucky Derby isn't the sort of thing you win or lose; it's something you're there for." That almost throw-away line may be the best description yet of what happens in Louisville annually on the first Saturday in May.

In addition, students frequently do religious and charity work off campus. Sometimes it is across town. The freshman class in 1972, for example, collected more than 4,000 books and boxes of magazines for the Jefferson County Jail library. Sometimes it was at a greater distance. For several years in the mid-'60s, for example, students worked as volunteer carpenters, teachers, recreation leaders and laborers during weekends, summers and vacation periods for Fr. Ralph Beiting's Christian Appalachian Project (CAP) in the Kentucky mountains. During the 1965 Easter vacation some 100 students from throughout the country converged on Jackson County, Kentucky, to assist in building dorms, dining and bathing facilities for Camp Andrew Jackson, a youth facility sponsored by the CAP. Coordinated by the Bellarmine chapter of the National Federation of Catholic College Students, the facilities were built with materials solicited by Bellarmine students and donated by Louisville-area businesses. During spring break of 1998, 11 Bellarmine students and alumni and campus minister Fr. Nelson Belizario

joined more than 230 students from throughout the United States to help residents of Clay and Magoffin counties repair and winterize their homes. It was the seventh year the Christian Appalachian Project had held its Work Fest. Campus groups have also raised money for clothing and food distributed locally and in the mountains. In addition, in the mid-'80s groups of students worked with Mother Teresa's Missionaries of Charity in Jenkins, Kentucky, and in the Bronx of New York City.

Numerous Bellarmine students and graduates have served in the Peace Corps as volunteers in underdeveloped countries around the world. As of 1997 Bellarmine had produced 34 Peace Corps volunteers. Creighton Mershon, general counsel for BellSouth-Kentucky, has said that Bellarmine's liberal arts and service traditions influenced him to join the corps after graduation. During his two years in Venezuela, he taught high-school courses in health and worked in a health clinic as the country was going through its difficult transition to democracy. It was, he told a reporter for *The Courier-Journal,* "an enlightening and maturing experience." Closer to home, in 1995 under a program called Alternative Spring Break students gave up their vacations to help renovate a building for the Louisville Housing Authority. Indeed, service to others has always been a part of the Bellarmine experience. In 1974 the college formed a Volunteer Council to coordinate community service, and the Student Government Association created a vice presidency to coordinate student volunteer activity. In the summer of 1995, freshman orientation included for the first time a community service project.

Dr. Fred Rhodes has taken the lead in securing a four-year grant to develop service learning and improve volunteerism in the community. He has also taken several groups of students to countries in Central and South America to see firsthand the needs of Third-World countries. During the 1997-98 academic year,

Bellarmine College offered over 25 classes that included a service component.

These service and social activities are merely a sampling of what Bellarmine students have done to take their minds off academics—at least temporarily. It was a feast of opportunities available to all students. Carole Pfeffer, a popular English professor and two-time recipient of the Sr. Pat Lowman Student Advocate Award, has said, "I didn't live on campus, but I did live on campus—because I was able to participate in so many activities and get to know the faculty and other students outside the classroom." She could have added, outside the city, the state and the USA.

Orientation. . .

First, students have learned about campus life during a series of programs for newcomers called orientation. The 1958 student handbook defined the college prelude as a time "to help a student get acquainted with himself and his college." Sometimes it was called "Welcome Week," described in the '81 *Lance* as "a time for thinking, playing, resting, laughing and becoming a part of the Bellarmine Connection." By the '70s it was a smorgasbord of activities including, in addition to tests and talks, an outdoor ecumenical service, a reception, Mass, a coffeehouse, a swim party, a mixer and a hayride to La Grange. During the 1974 orientation students were entertained by the rock group Ginger.

At orientation—at least in the early years—freshmen were told what was required of them in terms of behavior and dress. In the fall of 1954, for example, they learned that they must wear an ID tag at all times, that they could not attend social functions or use the main entrance or the game room of the administration building and that they must wear a red and white beanie for two weeks. They also had to be able to sing the school fight song and "Alma Mater" when required by a senior. They learned that at no time during their years at Bellarmine could they step on the college seal

in the lobby of the administration building without penalty. Freshmen who failed to observe certain rules—like addressing all upperclassmen as "Sir"—had

STUDENT ORIENTATION, ADVISEMENT AND REGISTRATION
APRIL 25, JUNE 15 AND JULY 17, 1998

BELLARMINE COLLEGE

to pay the price, which in 1955 involved a tug-of-war over a watered mud pit. In the early days there was a room check each evening at 11:30 and no visiting was allowed afterwards. Also in place was a detailed system of demerits which could lead to expulsion. Some of the restrictions for freshmen were lifted at a dance in their honor in early October each year. Gradually, most rules were liberalized or eliminated.

Dress Code. . .

And then there was the dress code that new students were expected to observe. From the opening day of the college in 1950 students were expected to dress in a dignified manner. Early editions of *The Student Handbook* set fairly stringent codes of dress, including the wearing of dress slacks, dress shirt and tie for chapel, for class, for the dining room and for all school gatherings. The 1955-56 *Handbook* was more liberal: "The College has no wish to dictate the details of student dress, but it is certainly in place to suggest that in neatness and general propriety the student's dress should be in harmony with his vocation." After reminding students that "in the great Catholic universities of the Middle Ages students were marked as a special class in society by a distinctive and particularly dignified manner of dress," there was a caveat: "Calculated sloppiness in dress is a by-product of sloppy thinking." The 1958-59 *Knights Handbook* spelled out the requirement: "As a minimum standard of dignified dress, Bellarmine College expects its students ordinarily to wear a coat or jacket and a necktie." Three years later, after the college had tightened the dress standard, *The Concord* editorialized that such regulations suggested "the distinctive dress of the medieval student," while "times have changed." One student complained that it was hard to concentrate in class "with what feels like a noose around your neck." A student who identified himself as a "non-Catholic" wrote the student paper: "I do not understand why or how a person's personal appearance can affect his learning."

Many observers noted, however, that the regulations had improved the overall appearance of the campus. Fr. Clyde Crews recalled that as a freshman in 1962, "We wore ties and coats to class because if we didn't, we were counted as absent." A student could, however, rent a tie from the registrar's office for a quarter. He said when he objected to the policy, he was told that such clothes were "part of the code of the Christian gentleman."

In 1968 new philosophy professor Robert A. Preston wrote a somewhat tongue-in-cheek letter to the editor of *The Concord* in which he feigned shock to learn that the college had a dress code because, he said, "my observations had led me to assume that the student body was composed largely of a group who conformed to some strange tribal customs that demanded sloppiness of dress." Now, he said, he realizes that students were "required by college regulations to dress in such barbaric fashion." Then, pretending to support the students who opposed such bizarre regulations, he wrote: "I think Bellarmine students should be allowed to wear decent attire on campus and not be required to wear Levis, dungarees, sport shirts, sweaters, lumber jackets or what other regalia that is proper only to high schoolers." He concluded mock-seriously, "Strike a blow for freedom and sartorial splendor and wear a coat and tie one day each week until the regulations are changed." The following year, after the death of Fr. John Loftus, Preston became dean of the college. Needless to say, the dress code faded until it became nonexistent, and newcomers no longer had to be "oriented" to proper attire.

Clubs and Other Extracurricular Activities. . .

What used to be called extracurricular activities have taken many forms at Bellarmine, from building an award-winning college float for the 1958 Pegasus Parade to celebrating Halloween in the late 1990s with the annual Ball on the Belle Halloween Dance, when some 350 students party and dance down the Ohio River on the Belle of Louisville. Halloween of 1950 was a relatively quiet one in Louisville, except for a few leaf fires, some soaped-up cars and store windows, a few toilet-papered dwellings and one case of destroying public property, which produced the only arrest during the holiday. Bellarmine student 18-year-old Robert S. Taylor was fined $25 in police court for shooting out street lights in the Camp Taylor area just because he "got the urge," he said.

A little known campus project was a 7-watt, closed-circuit AM radio station, WHUT-AM, which featured campus news and various kinds of music, from jazz to classical. Founded by David Kirwin and John Lindstrom in February 1968 and using a volunteer staff of 31, it broadcast from Newman Hall to dorm radios from 4 p.m. to 1 a.m. In the early '70s another station, WBUC, lasted for several years.

One of the most sensational extracurricular events—one which was covered by radio, television and the print media, including *The New York Times*—was the discovery in October of 1982 of a brown paper bag containing $35,000 in cash in an abandoned college locker. The bag was removed from an unused locker by dean of students Bill Stewart and physical plant director Herman Silverstein and taken to Stewart's office, where it was opened by senior history student David Kellerman. City police said that Bellarmine could claim the money if the owner did not claim it within 90 days. Suddenly, everyone was discussing how to spend the windfall. Then in late November Kellerman brought suit against the college and the city of Louisville and requested that the court award him the money. Kellerman claimed that the college had thrown away the bag containing the money and that he had retrieved it from a trash can. A circuit court judge ruled in Kellerman's favor but the college appealed. An out-of-court settlement was finally reached.

More conventional and routine activities included clubs, parties and dances, drama and debate, art exhibits and concerts. First, the clubs. People with similar interests tend to form clubs, and Bellarmine has been the home of many diverse groups with common causes. Many of the early organizations were church-related. The Bellarmine chapter of the Militia of Mary Immaculate, founded in 1951, required daily prayers to the Blessed Virgin and the wearing of the Miraculous

Medal. Other religious groups included the III Order of St. Francis and the Catholic Students Missionary Crusade.

By the mid-'90s the campus had more than 50 recognized student organizations in academic, social, athletic and personal development areas. Here is a partial roll call of some of the campus clubs over the last 50 years: the Boogie Knights, the Weightlifting Club, the Vets Club, the Latin Club, the Monogram Club for letter winners in sports, the Pep Club, the Glee Club, the Canoe Club, the Debate Club, Black Student Union, the International Relations Club, the SAE or Student Association for Equality. The Bellarmine International Club and the UMOJA Black student organization are but two of the organizations that support and celebrate diversity projects.

Clubs were often tied to majors or career interests: Computer Science Club, Nursing Club, Philosophy Club, Art Club, Accounting Club, Biology Club, Sociology Club, Mathematics Club, Student National Education Association, Psychology Club. Each club sponsored a variety of activities and projects. The Marketing Club, for example, invited local businessmen and women to speak to its membership and took field trips to other cities. In April of 1965 the club sponsored a trip to Chicago, which included a behind-the-scenes tour of Marshall Fields department store and its management offices and a Notre Dame dance in the Chicago Sheraton Hotel. Faculty advisers were chosen for their expertise and willingness to work with students after hours. The moderator for the Investment Club was Bernard F. Thiemann—who else?

One of the first groups active at Bellarmine was the National Federation of Catholic College Students. In fact, along with Ursuline and Nazareth, Bellarmine hosted the annual meeting of the organization in August of 1960. More than 600 students were present representing 191 Catholic colleges from across the country. The meeting was chaired by Bellarmine senior George Dumstorf, Jr. and moderated by Fr. Hilary Gottbrath. Among topics discussed were the "Catholic intellectual lag" and the lack of intellectual leadership among Catholics.

Other clubs and organizations were also formed early. The Gamma Mu chapter of Delta Epsilon Sigma was organized at Bellarmine in 1959. Established in 1939 to recognize academic achievements at Catholic colleges, for many years it sponsored the semi-annual Dean's Dinner honoring dean's list students. The local chapter of Alpha Delta Gamma, a national Catholic social and service fraternity, was formed at Bellarmine in February of 1961, with Guy Eugene Gunn as president. In the early '90s it was moderated by Bob Lockhart and sponsored blood drives, socials for children at St. Joseph's Children's Home and various orientation activities. The International Relations Club, moderated by Stanley Zemelka, sponsored United Nations Day activities on campus and collected books for Catholic mission schools in Africa. Among its other activities, the Black Student Union has sponsored Black Awareness Week, with a basketball game, fashion show, a jazz concert and a banquet.

Delta Epsilon Sigma

NATIONAL SCHOLASTIC
HONOR SOCIETY

HANDBOOK FOR MEMBERS

Circle K, a service club and junior division of the Kiwanis clubs, was begun at Bellarmine in the spring of 1976. Moderated for several years by James Valone, its activities included tutoring, visiting the elderly in nursing homes, aiding in blood drives and assisting with Handicapped Awareness Week and Dare to Care. Sometimes the blood drive for the Red Cross would net half the student body. In the fall of 1981, Circle K became VISION, or Volunteers In Service In Our Neighborhood. In the early '90s Ariel was organized with John Gatton as moderator. In addition to publishing a literary magazine, the club sponsored

public readings during Black History Month and Women's History Month.

Political clubs included the Young Republicans and the Young Democrats. Spin-off groups included Youth for Nixon in 1968 and Young Kentuckians for Wyatt in 1958. Headed by Richard Eckert and David Thompson at Bellarmine, the Wyatt organization issued a statement applauding Wyatt for being "a good honest man with the ideal of good government at heart"—a man who could raise the reputation of Kentucky politicians. Wyatt never became governor (he became lieutenant governor), but he did become chairman of Bellarmine's Board of Trustees almost 30 years later. Many other politicians have visited Bellarmine, including John Kennedy and George McGovern and most Kentucky candidates for office since 1950. Although the student body has generally been predominantly Democratic, a straw ballot in May of 1956 showed overwhelming support for Eisenhower, who received 203 votes to 96 for Adlai Stevenson. In the mid-'90s the Bellarmine Young Republicans sponsored a community debate with Republican and Democratic candidates for Congress Anne M. Northup and Mike Ward.

Student Government. . .

From the beginning student government, under various names, has occupied a central role in student life. The 1955-56 college catalogue described its functions: "The Student Council, made up of elected representatives from the various classes and approved College organizations, serves as a medium of contact between the faculty and the student body, and exercises a general supervisory role in regard to student extracurricular activities." Many organizational changes have been made through the years. An early student handbook stated that the student body and its activities were governed by the Student Government Association, which activated two bodies: the student council, which was elected, and formed the executive branch; and the student senate, comprised of delegates from classes and organizations, the legislative branch. The committees of the senate acted in conjunction with the dean of students, who represented the faculty, in the implementation of the activities program.

At the close of the 1956 spring semester, Jim Elliott, a staff writer for *The Concord,* surveyed the previous year and pronounced it a grand success, in large part, he said, because of the responsible leadership of the student council members Ed Hamilton, John Maloney, Fred Hamilton and Windell Bowles. "We feel that the students of Bellarmine College," he wrote, "have exemplified in the past year a spirit and determination which has surpassed any attempts in the past years. There is a sort of unity at Bellarmine which cannot be described in words. We would not like to say that Bellarmine is some type of Utopian community with perfect harmony on all matters, but it is a unified body of men who have the same ideals and goal." Perhaps the good work done in the day school was reason enough for the launching of a student government for the evening school in June of 1957. By the early '80s there was a student government for the residence halls.

The student government components have changed with the times. In the fall of 1966, for example, a five-member student academic council was formed to provide a regular channel of student opinion in educational affairs. According to the campus paper, "Ideas and criticisms which were previously confined to the cafeteria can now be presented to the dean." In addition to the Student Government Association, by the mid-'90s student government branches included the residence hall council, the inter-club council, resident assistants, orientation advisors and college committees. A residence hall council was formed in the early '90s as the residents grew from 300 to almost 500. A small activity fee was introduced to support the program events of the resident assistants and residence hall council officers.

In addition to providing routine channels of communication between students and faculty and administration, the mission of student government has also grown. In the fall of 1962 the student executive council tried to promote a "cleanliness campaign" by imposing fines on mess-making students who defiled the college environment. The directive read: "This means that if you prop your feet on chairs, tables, or on the wall you are liable for a fine. Likewise, making a mess with someone else's discarded garbage gives you sole ownership." Despite the warning, not everyone cooperated. A few weeks later a *Concord* reporter noted: "At one o'clock every day the 'mess' hall still looks like the beaches of Dunkirk." Other projects were more successful. In December of 1970, for example, the student executive committee presented Dr. Ivo Poglayen, the director of the Louisville Zoological Gardens, with two snowy owls named Yukon and Aurora.

In the waning years of the 20th century, the student government association was composed of two main bodies, the student assembly and the student executive committee, both elected by the student body. They represent student interests in all phases of academic and social life. Activities have included a textbook exchange begun in 1980, fund-raising phone-a-thons, charitable drives and alcohol and drug awareness weeks. Leadership training has become a vital part of student government work. In the early '90s the student affairs staff worked with the elected student leadership to create annual leadership retreats and workshops for resident advisors, orientation leaders and student government leaders to develop a sense of community and to learn about the college's faculty, administration, curriculum, rules, clubs, social events and campus ministry as well as college history and philosophy.

By and large, students at Bellarmine have been fortunate in selecting their leaders. Hardworking, dependable officers have included Steve Kirn, Ben Freville, Mike Brennan, Tom Petrik, Tom McCormick,

Carl A. Nett, Robert G. Pfaadt, Martha Pfaadt, Christa Spalding, Rob Shilts and JoAnne "JoJo" Burch. In April of 1972, Mary Ann Steltenpohl, a junior in psychology, became the first woman to head the student executive committee. In 1997 the SGA body voted to develop the Bellarmine activity council to separate and improve the quality and participation of the student body. The new group has committees devoted to such areas as lectures, entertainment and special events. But all has not been sweetness and light. In March of 1997, *The Concord* blamed a botched student election on "the severe lack of intelligent leadership in the Student Government Association." It was a reminder that campus political life is like politics elsewhere: there are good times and there are bad times.

Bellarmine College
Student Handbook
1998 – 1999

Division of Student Affairs
2001 Newburg Road
Louisville, KY 40205
(502) 452-8150

Forensics. . .

Perhaps in no other student activity has Bellarmine won more distinction than in debating. The college began its first year of full-scale intercollegiate debating in the fall of 1956, when two debate teams were fielded in novice tournaments at Bowling Green, Kentucky, and Indianapolis. Team members were Paul Schuler, Jack McGrath, Viss Vissman and Bill Barnett at Indianapolis and Tom Russell, Jim Marquart, Bill Dolan and Don Nugent at Bowling Green. In December of 1957, Bellarmine hosted the first of a long series of tournaments, the annual Kentucky

Intercollegiate Debate Tournament, with participants from seven schools. Winning trophies and championships soon became routine for Bellarmine debaters and teams. By March of 1957, Bellarmine was debating teams from Vanderbilt University, Indiana University and the University of Kentucky. In March of 1959, Bellarmine met a team from Harvard University to debate the development of nuclear weapons. By the end of that year Bellarmine debaters had taken part in 19 tournaments, under the expert coaching of Benson S. Alleman, chairman of the arts department and official pronouncer for the National Spelling Bee.

Bellarmine's sponsorship (with the Louisville Junior Chamber of Commerce) of the Interstate Novice Debate Tournament was soon attracting participants from more than two dozen colleges and universities in the Eastern United States. In January of 1960, Bellarmine hosted the annual Invitational Debate Tourney for high schools, with 17 Kentucky and one Tennessee school participating. In December of that year a novice team from Bellarmine, which included John Guarnaschelli, won the Western Kentucky State College Invitational Tournament.

In February of 1961, Benson Alleman died of a heart attack at the age of 56. In five years he had created one of the most respected forensics programs in the nation, and Bellarmine debate teams had gained distinction against national powerhouses. Before joining the faculty in 1956, he had been in journalism, public relations, advertising and quail farming. For 14 years this self-professed "lousy speller" had been the official pronouncer for the National Spelling Bee. He died shortly after returning with his debate team from a tournament at Northwestern University.

Bellarmine's novice debate tournament was named the Benson S. Alleman Debate Tournament for the meet on April 7-8, 1961, when debaters from 23 colleges and universities and 13 states came to Bellarmine to debate compulsory health insurance.

Succeeding Alleman as debate coach was Fr. Joseph M. Miller, who took the Bellarmine debate program to the next level. An undated memo from Fr. Miller to Fr. Horrigan headed "Report on Debate Trip to Rochester," stated: "It gives me a great deal of pride to report on the success of Bellarmine's recent invasion of New York State. I think you will agree that invasion was the word, for we went through New York like Sherman through Georgia." Indeed. At the St. John Fisher Debate Tournament, Bellarmine competed with 25 other schools, including Fordham, New York University, University of Vermont, Columbia and Colgate, and of seven trophies awarded, Bellarmine walked away with four. Another sign of Bellarmine's reputation as a debate center was the meeting of Tau Kappa Alpha, the national forensics honor society, at the college in May of 1961, with Senator Thruston B. Morton and Barry Bingham, Sr. as speakers.

For the first time, in February of 1963, Fr. Miller took his team to one of the top forensic events in the country, the Harvard University Invitational Debate Tournament. In April the Seventh Annual Alleman Tournament took place in the Louisville Armory, with 34 teams from 15 states. The topic was whether the non-Communist countries of the world should form an economic community. The championship, televised on WAVE-TV, was won by debaters from Northwestern University, followed by the University of Alabama, the University of Kentucky and Wabash College. The following year participating schools

Dr. Raymond Bailey

included West Point, the U. S. Naval Academy, Northwestern and the University of Wisconsin. In April of 1965, the University of Alabama novice team flew to Louisville in football coach Paul "Bear" Bryant's private plane to participate with 83 other colleges in the ninth annual Alleman Tournament. With funds in short supply, the debate team was told in March of 1967 that the school could not afford to send it to a Pasadena, California, tournament. An anonymous donor stepped up and paid the expenses.

Throughout the late '60s and the '70s Bellarmine continued to enhance its debating reputation with students like Sr. Ann Margaret, Michael Jacobs, Stephanie Dumstorf, Nora McCormick and Jim Wagoner. The program thrived under the direction

Dr. Ruth and husband James R. Wagoner

The Concord

Volume 49, Number 21　　*The editorially independent student newspaper of Bellarmine College*　　*Louisville, Kentucky*

Mock Trial brings home national title

of Professor Raymond Bailey, who also originated the "Reason and Controversy" series for high schools in 1970. In 1975, with Ruth Wagoner as director of forensics, the varsity team of Vanessa Washington and Dotty Elder won 25 rounds and lost 17.

In the '90s Bellarmine's forensic activities have moved from debate to mock-trial teams which have won numerous trophies. In the fall of 1995, the team won two major victories, top honors at the Miami (Ohio) University Invitational Tournament and the University of Dayton Invitational. An article in *The Courier-Journal* in April of 1996 paid tribute to the mock-trial team, comparing it to the basketball program at a sister institution. Bellarmine's team was one that shared "some important traits with the University of Kentucky's men's basketball team: hard work, fierce pride and a record littered with trounced opponents." By then it had been coached for some 11 years by communications professor Ruth Wagoner, assisted by her attorney husband Jim Wagoner. It had achieved national recognition by finishing in national tournaments near the top, far ahead of such institutions as Brown, Cornell, Notre Dame, Georgetown and Northwestern.

In April of 1998, Bellarmine's mock-trial team placed second to the University of Maryland in the finals of the national mock-trial competition in Des Moines, Iowa. Coached again by Dr. Ruth Wagoner and her husband Jim, it was the fourth time in 11 years that Bellarmine's team had been national runner-up.

Team members included Vanessa Cox, Heather Jackson, William Armstrong, Jason Butler, Nathaniel Cadle, Ryane Conroy and Sean Fox. In 1999 the team brought home the national title.

Bellarmine's forensics program was not the only place on campus where serious—often controversial—topics were addressed in an environment of reason and understanding. The first catalogue in 1950, in fact, stated what seemed to be a call to social action: "The college does not accept the notion that a school's responsibility is to teach students simply to fit into the society in which they live. It submits that students must be taught to evaluate this society and to exercise their trained human powers to change it whenever necessary." Freedom of discussion and debate at Bellarmine did not stop with academic freedom for faculty. Students were encouraged to take stands—even if they were unpopular or misguided. As Fr. Horrigan's long-time secretary, Alma Schuler, said, "Both Fr. Horrigan and Fr. Treece believed that students have to learn from their mistakes, so they gave them freedom to do certain things." Bob Yeargin, editor of *The Concord,* reminded his readers that the college paper had two main missions: "to keep the college community informed of important events" and "to stimulate thought on important issues."

Good Causes and Controversies...

Of course, many humanitarian projects by students have been universally applauded—support for muscular dystrophy, blood donations, homeless shelters, Earth Day, Ecology Awareness Week, world hunger, drug and alcohol awareness, food and clothing drives for the poor, toy and food collections at Christmas, recycling projects and campus clean-up days. In March of 1952, more than 100 students and faculty, from a student enrollment of 150, donated to the Red Cross Blood Drive. During the Christmas season of 1960, students at Bellarmine and the University of Louisville collected and distributed 50 baskets of food to needy families in Louisville. During the Earth Day environmental teach-in in April of 1970, two students spilled a can of garbage on the floor of the New Science Theatre to dramatize the problem of pollution. The theater was then the site of a panel discussion on pollution—surrounded by tin cans, paper bags, wadded paper and cigarette butts scattered on the floor. One of the speakers was state senator Romano Mazzoli, soon to be elected congressman from Kentucky.

But others have not been popular. One of the first controversies on campus focused on the Vietnam War. Although many Bellarmine alumni and students acceped the draft or volunteered for service during the war, other were adamantly opposed. In early March of 1968, some 60 members of the Bellarmine community, including four faculty, four seminarians and three women, marched a five-mile route from the campus to the Federal Building at Sixth and Broadway to protest the war. One student carried a sign with a quotation from Dante: "The hottest places in hell are reserved for those who in times of great moral crisis maintain their neutrality." Fr. Horrigan defended their right to protest. "I have no illusion," he said, "that my stand is a popular one. In fact, it may even cost us financial contributions and community support." Both Fr. John Loftus and Fr. Horrigan were active in Negotiation Now, a national group dedicated to ending

the war by negotiations. Later that month a former Bellarmine student, John Phillip Matlock, was reported killed in action. Others, like William S. Ross, survived and won service medals.

Bellarmine-Ursuline College participated in Moratorium Day, a national day of prayer and protest on October 15, 1969, with a movie, a panel discussion and a memorial service for the American war dead. Some 400 students and faculty, including 75 students from the Louisville Presbyterian Theological Seminary, heard Fr. Horrigan say that as an individual he approved of the demonstration against the war. Coordinator of the day's events was David Thurmond, chairman of the student assembly, whose mother drove from their hometown of Hopkinsville to support him and his brother Robert in their opposition to the war. The '70 *Lance* showed a photograph of five Bellarmine-Ursuline students cavorting on a tank near Fort Knox, each one showing the V-Sign. In the early '70s a draft counseling service was set up on campus. The Persian Gulf War of January 1991, though short-lived, was also controversial and brought out pro and con positions. A candlelight vigil to pray for peace and safety of the troops was held.

Controversies over drug use were also causing unrest on many campuses. In the spring of 1968, Bellarmine had approved a national Joint Statement on Student Rights, which set guidelines for student dissent. The following year the college issued a policy statement that clarified some points on potential campus unrest. While recognizing "the right of orderly, responsible student protest," it stated that the serious disruption of college activities would result in suspension and/or prosecution of the offender under civil law. The dean of students, Fr. Hilary Gottbrath, also said that the few isolated cases of illegal drug users would be provided counseling, but serious cases of selling and abuse could lead to suspension and prosecution by the civil authorities. A Drug Abuse Information Center, designed to marshal community resources against drug abuse, was located in the

Community Chest Building on Market Street and headed by John R. Hollon, a senior at Bellarmine-Ursuline.

President Petrik's administration was less pro-active than Horrigan's and attempted to maintain a neutral position on some controversial issues. A memo dated 26 August 1975 to members of the President's staff set forth the policy on the use of campus facilities: "Bellarmine College tries to maintain an apolitical stance and will not rent its facilities to strong advocacy groups dealing with highly volatile issues particularly on the evening before major disruption in the community may occur." Except for abortion and perhaps for gay and AIDS-related issues, there have been relatively few issues in the last 15 or so years to cause major controversy on campus. The Psychology Club sponsored a panel discussion on gay sexuality by members of the Louisville Gay Liberation Front in

ThinkFast feast, spring of 1995.

January of 1972, before an audience of some 200 students.

In the '90s programs sponsored by ThinkFast, moderated by Bob Lockhart, have encouraged four days of fasting and reflection on various societal problems, from drug abuse and hunger to abortion

and AIDS. In February of 1997, ThinkFast sponsored a weeklong series on AIDS that featured Msgr. Robert J. Vitillo, who has worked internationally to develop church-based programs in response to the disease. In the spring of the same year an HIV-positive man and his friend presented a program on "Friendship in the Age of AIDS." In January of 1998, nursing student Monica Owen published an essay in *The Courier-Journal* urging fair play and respect for people with AIDS.

Other "causes" have gradually met with general public approval or acceptance. In March of 1996, Taste of Health, a series of workshops and speeches sponsored by EarthSave Louisville, was held on campus to promote vegetarianism and healthy food choices. In the Brown Center more than 4,000 eager tasters sampled meatless dishes prepared by Louisville restaurants. Tobacco-free buildings are now commonplace on Bellarmine's campus. Furthermore, the Bellarmine community has studied and adopted a new smoking policy beginning in June 1999. Smoking is now permitted outside all buildings only, with the exception of a smoker's own residence hall room. Such a crusade would have been met with derision and protest in 1961, when the Philip Morris Company held a campus contest for the largest collections of used cigarette packages—their brands, of course—with the first prize a stereophonic console record player and the second prize an FM radio. The first prize winner was Jerry Hubbuch, who collected over 11,000 packages. In many ways, Bellarmine in 1999 is not the same campus it was in 1950. Most students and faculty would say that it is more open and healthier—intellectually and morally. In 1997 the Education Club coordinated "Make a Difference Day," which drew over 400 people from the college interested in improving the quality of life in the Louisville community. It was a good sign.

The Bellarmine Belle-aires under the direction of Fr. Hilary Gottbrath.

Dances...

Much of campus social life has centered on regular dances and mixers held throughout the college year. The doors had hardly opened, however, when the pioneer students cleared enough weeds and bushes for a hot dog roasting pit; and the first social was underway, complete with chiggers and mosquitoes. Indeed, when the Pioneer Class was on campus, social life centered around five main events: the Freshman Mixer, the Pioneer Dance, the Mid-Year Ball, the Dance of the Roses and the Junior-Senior Prom. The school's first major dance took place on Thanksgiving Eve of 1950 at the Knights of Columbus Hall. Covered wagon and campfire decorations graced the entrance to the hall. The second Pioneer Dance was held in the Rainbow Room of the Henry Clay Hotel. The Dance of the Roses each May soon became the most important social event of the year. In 1954 more than 175 couples attended the semi-formal affair at the Seelbach Hotel.

The dances were usually sponsored by clubs and classes and held several times a month. There were the Student Senate Dinner Dance, the Veterans Club

Dance, the Spanish Club Dinner Dance, the Junior-Senior Prom, the Sadie Hawkins Dance, the Homecoming Dance, even the Hemophilia Dance, sponsored by Delta Sigma Pi. Music was provided by such groups as the Sammy Kaye Band and Art Glaser and His Orchestra or, more likely, by the Belle-Aires, an eight-piece dance band organized by Fr. Hilary Gottbrath and student Larry Kaelin in November of 1951. One of the most popular

---

BELLARMINE COLLEGE

Pioneer Dance

K. of C. HALL—525 South Fifth Street

Wednesday, November 22, 1950

Admission $1.50 Per Couple   Nine Till Twelve

---

has been the annual Halloween Masquerade Dance, whether held on campus or on the Belle of Louisville.

In the early '60s there was an annual Closer-Ties Dance, designed to promote closer ties between students and their parents and the college. Formerly known as the Father-Son Dance, it was an informal dance held in the school cafeteria. In the words of the '69 *Lance,* "The leaves were sparce, the air cooler, and the time for witches and goblins had come"—and so had the colorful costumes of the annual Halloween Dance. The Dance of the Roses, the big formal, began the first year of the college at the Henry Clay Hotel. A columnist for *The Louisville Times* reported on May 26, 1953, that Bellarmine student Albert Breckinridge Clem delivered newspapers the morning after the dance in his tuxedo accompanied by his date in a full-length evening dress. It seems that after dancing ended at 1 a.m., the students had moved on to private homes for breakfast; and Clem decided it was too late to go to bed, so he and his date stayed up and delivered his papers in the Wellington subdivision.

Before there were large numbers of women on campus, Bellarmine men were often paired with women from sister institutions at Nazareth and Ursuline, with sock hops at one of the three campuses and more formal dances held at downtown hotels like the Brown or the Seelbach or at places like the Wildwood Country Club and local American Legion posts. In the mid-'50s Bellarmine students were bused to Nazareth's downstate campus near Bardstown to be paired with their "dates" from Nazareth College for an evening of dining and dancing. The dinners and dances were free and men from Bellarmine flocked to sign up. In the fall of 1957, 48 men were requested and 75 showed up.

Interest in dances has waxed and waned. In the mid-'70s dancing became more popular, as students gathered in dormitory lobbies for impromptu "lobbyland dances," including "the Bump," which involved bumping hips and backsides to upbeat rock music. In the '80s and early '90s interest in dances, especially the "record hops," had declined as other activities became more popular—ski trips, canoeing, ice skating and trips to amusement parks. By the end of the decade, however, dances were again gaining in popularity, with more than 500 attending the formal Pioneer Dance in 1998.

Other social activities with women from Ursuline and Nazareth were also popular, ranging from mixed doubles bowling tournaments in the mid-'50s to dramatic productions. Men from Bellarmine were much in demand for plays at Ursuline and Nazareth. "A couple of deep-voiced Bellarmine boys" rounded out the cast of Ursuline's 1958 production of *The King and I*. By 1965 Nazareth was called Catherine Spalding when their Roswitha Players got two for the price of one as Bellarmine twins Don and Ron Weis appeared in the fall production of *See How They Run*.

NUB Variety Shows. . .

Perhaps the best example of social cooperation among the three colleges were the annual benefits called the NUB (Nazareth-Ursuline-Bellarmine) Variety Shows. With the first show premiering on February 1, 1953, and running into the '60s, the series raised thousands of dollars for Catholic students in the United States and abroad. The 1953 show was performed in the Ursuline College auditorium to raise funds for the Overseas Service Program of the National Federation of Catholic College Students. Titled "Life on Basin Street" and including musical and dramatic skits, the show featured the Bellarmine Belle-Aires who formed themselves into the Dixieland Quartet, with Fred Hamilton, Frank Knoop, Larry Kaelin and Kenny Erwin—plus Ursuline songstress Maria Meek. The jazzy streets of New Orleans had moved to Louisville! With casts ranging up to more than 100, the variety shows included a satire called "A Day in Television"; "For Heaven's Sake," a Broadway-type show with ballet numbers, vocals, tap dancers and comedy acts; "Wilhouettes of '58," which featured Bellarmine "crooner" Tom DeMuth; and "The Chase," the 1961 show that included a spoof of T.S. Eliot's *Murder in the Cathedral.* Aided by directors Fr. Hilary Gottbrath and David Chervenak, the shows were written, produced and performed by students from the three colleges. Sometimes the shows led to more than a brief period upon the stage. In the case of Fran Witt and Maurice Buchart, who met during work on the 1954 production and performed again in the 1955 show, they led to marriage in September of 1956.

The eighth annual variety show in 1960 may be used as representative. It had a cast of 60 students—plus a support crew of some 40 stagehands, make-up artists and lighting technicians—from the three colleges and was performed twice for the benefit of needy South American students through the National Federation of Catholic College Students. The show was loosely centered around two characters, a beatnik and "Joe College." The music was provided by the Bellarmine Belle-Aires, a 12-piece ensemble under the direction of Fr. Hilary and Gus Coin. A review in *The Record* of February 10, 1960, described the show: "After a modern jazz overture, the first act of the show opened on a nightclub scene, followed by a visit, in the company of a Beatnik and a Joe College (Dick and Dave Bizot, respectively) to a coffee house, a bar, and a theater. A semibeatnik quartet (Dick Bizot, Jim O'Leary, Dave Dattilo, and Charles Kincaid) who rendered 'Teen Angel,' a dance by 12 phosphorescent leg puppet couples, and two songs in the modern style by Judy Carrico were enjoyed by all present, especially the audience."

The summary by critic Betty Jean Timmel could well have applied to all the NUB Variety Shows: "There was no message, no overpowering theme evident, but if its intent was to provide entertainment and to be a showcase for the talents of the three colleges, the NUB Variety Show fulfilled its purpose." Not all the reviews were so favorable. Another of the shows was reviewed by *The Concord's* critic, who wrote, "Never have so many spent so much time to accomplish so little." The campus critic in 1967, Mike Moran, was more generous: "Well, the cast sure had fun and for a change the audience did, too." Regardless of the critics' words, the shows were always popular and usually drew more than a thousand paying customers each year, with profits approaching $1,500.

In February 1964, the show had to change its name to the Tri-College Variety Show when Nazareth became Catherine Spalding College. The show that year was performed in the Brown Theater and was directed for the fifth time by Bellarmine alumnus David Chervenak. The show was named "Max Bath, or Shakespeare in the Raw" and according to its director was "a loose *West Side Story* treatment of *Macbeth*."

Characters in the updated satire included Max Bath's accomplice Lady Bird Bath and their victim Dunkin Hines. The script was written by four Bellarmine students—Joseph Peacock, Daniel Ridge, Robert Schuler and Robert Sullivan. A reviewer for *The Record* commented that after seeing the colleges perform "we thought the Ed Sullivan Show was truly a drag Sunday night." One of the last shows was a 1967 revue called "American Hysteria," a pun-filled review of American history from Columbus to the speak-easies of the 1920s.

Alcohol . . .

As a long-time member of the student activities staff, Marilyn Staples has been a close observer of student variety shows and other forms of student social life. Not all of it was commendable. Most student misbehavior was related to underage or excessive drinking. "Alcohol has always been a problem, although the college has loosened up a bit and become more realistic. Until the opening of Petrik Hall, alcohol was forbidden in all campus residences. For several years students over 21 were allowed to drink responsibly in their rooms in Petrik Hall." Then in the fall of 1998, according to dean of students Fred Rhodes, drinking was once again prohibited in the residence halls and at all college-sponsored events. It was a return to early college policy which prohibited the use of alcoholic beverages at all college-sponsored social events, whether on or off campus.

Despite the prohibition, there were sporadic problems at social events. In the late '60s, however, an experiment in on-campus drinking was attempted. It started when several students approached dean of students Henry A. Schmidt about the possibility of getting a campus beer license. After extensive

State Refuses Beer License For Bellarmine

The state Alcoholic Beverage Control (ABC) Board today denied an application for a retail beer license on the campus of Bellarmine-Ursuline College, 2000 Norris Place.

The ABC board gave no specific reason for denying the application, saying only that "there was sufficient evidence presented . . . to sustain the refusal" of Walter M. Kimbell, acting malt-beverage administrator, to grant the license.

The board did note, however, that the license was sought for premises on the college campus and that the college would hold an interest in the business to be conducted.

The license application failed to list Bellarmine-Ursuline as a party interested in the application, as required by ABC regulations, the board said.

Corporation Makes Application

The application for the license had been submitted by Servomation Mathias, Inc., which listed its address as the Bellarmine-Ursuline campus.

After Kimbell turned down the application, his action was appealed to the ABC Board.

ABC officials had said that, had the application been granted, Bellarmine-Ursuline would be the first college in the state to serve beer on campus.

discussions, campus authorities agreed and machinery was set in motion to obtain a beer license through Servomation Mathias, Inc., which operated the college food service. The beer license plan immediately generated negative publicity for the college. Many campus neighbors objected. Some church groups attacked the proposal. A local radio station ran a satirical skit ridiculing the plan. The Lexington *Herald-Leader* conducted a public opinion poll, which showed that 81 per cent objected to the sale of beer in campus snack bars. Only 17 per cent approved. Finally, in February of 1970, after much talk and controversy the college dropped its efforts to sell beer on campus.

Another effort at controlled drinking on campus was tried in the spring of 1975, when the college announced that students over 21 would be allowed to keep alcoholic beverages in their dormitory rooms. Fr. Treece said the experiment was based on the belief that adult students should be treated as adults. He cautioned, however, that the policy could be lifted at any time if it was abused. Despite the relaxing of the absolute prohibitions against alcohol on campus, there have been periodic public abuses. One of the most serious occurred in September of 1991 following a hillside concert attended by more than 3,000 people. Two students were assaulted and injured in the parking lot by several non-Bellarmine students as the crowd was dispersing. As a result, several restrictions were added for future hillside concerts, including a ban on alcohol, controlled admission and additional security. The reforms reduced attendance but eliminated the violence.

There have also been a few instances of property destruction on campus and some obscene phone calls to co-eds. A male intruder with a white painted face was discovered in the women's dormitory in October of 1982. Residence life is somewhat like military life. A lot of people living in close quarters are constantly bumping into each other, violating each other's space and coming into conflict. It is little short of miraculous, in fact, that so many people can live so

close together for so long in relative harmony. There are a few documented cases of student vandalism. In a letter written in March of 1980, William Stewart notified a student that he was being dismissed from the college for his part in doing some $440 worth of damage to the Newman Hall recreation room. He was asked to remit a check for his share of the damage, $145, before he left the campus. In a memo from Peyton Badgett, director of dorms, to Bill Stewart in September of 1984, Badgett reported positive conditions except for certain Friday and Saturday nights, when there were excessive noise, occasional vandalism and alcohol use in the dorms.

Jim Stammerman was dorm director for Kennedy Hall when it opened in 1964. "Most of the kids were well behaved," he remembers, "but some of them had to be disciplined. We expelled a couple for drinking in the dorms. I knew that Derby Eve was going to try my patience. So I told the fellows that I was going to check their rooms throughout the night. About 1 a.m., I was in my office when a student rushed in to say there was a horse standing at the top of the steps between Kennedy and Newman Hall. I ran out and sure enough, there was a bridled horse standing there with his tail end toward me. None of the students knew, of course, where he came from. I went to the telephone and called the police. "Officer," I said, "has anyone reported a missing horse?" He said, "No." I said, "Well, we have an extra one over here at Bellarmine College." I went back to the horse and told the students, "Guys, get him out of here." When I came back a few minutes later, he was gone. No one ever told me where he came from or where he went. The director of residential life in the fall of 1990 was Harold "Buzz" Hall, who, according to the '91 *Lance*, was qualified to handle such a problem. "Buzz comes with a background in dealing with juvenile delinquents, so he was prepared for anything that Bellarmine students had to throw at him."

The '80s and '90s have seen a large increase in alcohol-related incidents across the country, and

Bellarmine has not been immune to the epidemic. The new policy eliminating alcohol from college events was based on concerns about liability and safety. But, by and large, Bellarmine students have been remarkably well behaved and orderly. Marilyn Staples agrees that the college has been very lucky in not having had chronic problems on campus. Despite her sensitive work in student activities, she says, "Unlike many of my colleagues at other institutions, I've never received an obscene letter or been threatened in any way."

Social Facilities. . .

Social facilities—or their lack—on campus have been a constraining influence on student activities. By the beginning of the '90s, however, the college at last had decent accommodations for most campus events outside the classroom, from sports to concerts. When he was a student in the '60s, as Bernie Thiemann remembers, there were such informal social clubs as the Key Club, the Squires Club and the Page Club, several of which rented nearby houses for their social activities of card playing, light drinking and TV watching.

In October of 1967, the social activities committee set up a temporary "coffeehouse" on the stage of Knights Hall, where, according to a notice in *The Concord,* just about anything will be in order— "poetry reading, dramatic recitation, songs, kissing, drawing, kissing, loving." A critic called it "a wild success" and it was repeated several times. Finally, in 1969 Bellarmine had a permanent coffeehouse in the new Student Activities Building, complete with snacks, folk singers and poetry readings. The '69 *Lance* described it this way: "Poems, candles, a crazy piano, Snoopy specials, and a hell of a lot of peanuts decorated the scene for the first Coffee House."

In the early '90s Hilary's (named for the first dean of students, Fr. Hilary Gottbrath) in Newman Hall became a convenient social gathering place, with a pool table, darts, meeting areas, chat spaces and occasional concession stands. Snacks offered by students Jim

Wade and Leigh Anne Rudzinski in 1993 got rave reviews.

Food. . .

Of course, students have voracious appetites, which have to be fed. From the first semester in 1950, there have been snack areas and cafeterias catering to students and faculty. Also from the first semester— and every succeeding semester—students have complained about the cost and quality of cafeteria food. It is the fate of institutional food everywhere. Students were complaining about cost in 1957, when the average meal cost 78 cents, according to manager John Mahoney.

"Same old....same old...." is a constant refrain heard by cafeteria servers; and during the 1965-66 school year manager Owen F. Morris of the food service firm of A.R.A. Slater, began periodic "monotony breakers" to relieve the boredom of the same old food served the same old way. A Syrian Night featured shishkabob, Syrian bread and Syrian salad. Italian Night featured all the spaghetti a student could eat. At another time it was all-you-can-eat hamburgers and milk shakes. One of the most popular nights was the make-your-own sundae, which featured a base of ice cream with help-yourself bowls of nuts, cherries, whipped cream, as well as chocolate, butterscotch, pineapple and strawberry syrups. Indeed, 1966 was a banner year for food innovations. In the fall of that year, when the church's prohibition of meat on Friday was lifted, Bellarmine students were offered meat as well as fish. Another highlight of the fall food season that year was a feast made possible by a college neighbor, George W. Dumstorf, Sr., who donated to the college a 110-pound watermelon a friend brought him from Hope, Arkansas. After cooling for a couple of weeks in the college's walk-in freezer, the watermelon was cut and shared with eager and ever-hungry dorm students.

Many efforts have been made by college officials to appease students' appetites and their anger at being captive customers. In the spring of 1976, students could pay only for those meals they wanted with a new coupon system, whereby they bought coupons from the business office and exchanged them for food. In 1979, chef Bud Foster cooked up ethnic dinners several times a month, with dishes from Iran to Belize. He would dress up his 250 pounds or so, wearing a grass skirt for a Hawaiian dinner and for Hillbilly Night blacking out a few teeth and donning overalls to serve fried chicken, grits and turnip greens. His motto, said Chef Bud, was KISS—Keep It Simple, Stupid.

One attempt at variety backfired in March of 1982, when the Annual Pizza Eating Contest during homecoming festivities was depicted by some faculty and students as an obscene exercise in gluttony. Kathleen Lyons of the English faculty went so far as to express her aversion to the event with a letter and petition sent to dean of students William Stewart. Such an event, she said, implied callousness and a lack of compassion for the starving people of the world. Responding seriously and graciously to her protest, Stewart replied by memo, explaining that when it was first suggested to him it seemed like a good idea, though he admitted that it might be improper as a homecoming activity. "I thank you for your concern," he concluded, "and for your willingness to take what may seem to others to be an unpopular stand." The petition, which was signed by a "minority" of the students and faculty, noted that it was especially inappropriate in the year in which Mother Theresa of Calcutta had received the Bellarmine Medal. "Let us at Bellarmine College," it read, "not, through 'eating' contests, appear to place ourselves in solidarity with the greedy of the world who seem to be responsible in one way or another for the needy of the world." The episode showed that not only was one of the Seven Deadly Sins alive and well at Bellarmine College but so was conscience and compassion.

In the present decade, food service operation has changed from college operation in 1990 to contract service with the Marriott Corporation in 1991 and Aladdin Food Services in 1997. To monitor standards and provide "feedback," the SGA Food Committee meets regularly as a forum for student opinion and to evaluate cafeteria operations and catering services.

The ever-changing management of the cafeteria has meant an ever-changing menu, as described by *The Lance* at the beginning of school in the fall of 1987: "The cafeteria once again became crowded, and new items were being offered. Now there was frozen yogurt, a deli, bagels, and, of course, the usual salad bar, grill, hot food, soups and stuffed potatoes." And so, as the college positions itself for the 21st century, food service vendors still have the challenge of serving the same old foods in new combinations and guises.

Student Residences. . .

Although Bellarmine opened in 1950 without a dormitory and although most of the student body have always been day students, it has always been the aim of the college to foster a resident atmosphere and to increase the number of resident students. A revolutionary dorm program was tried in the fall of 1972. Dubbed Resident Life Grant Program, it was designed not only to fill empty rooms but to make dorm life an important part of the educational program. That fall 50 students lived in the college's two dormitories free, paying only $580 for a year of meals. Under the auspices of Henry Schmidt, dean of students, classes were held in the dormitories and faculty members were encouraged to visit and perhaps spend a weekend in a dorm. Residence Hall Awareness Weeks were held during the '80s.

The term "dorm" was changed to "residence halls" when the college designed a management system of student governance, paraprofessional student staff or resident assistants (RAs), provided a series of academic programs and recruited master's and doctoral level educators to coordinate learning in and out of the classroom. The six-year effort by the President and student affairs to improve the residential environment has led to increased requests for housing and a higher retention rate.

BELLARMINE COLLEGE Residence Hall Review 1988 - 89

Since the opening of the first residence hall, there have been perennial "improvements in residential life," including in 1991 the addition of Hilary's, a commons area, new Nautilus equipment and new cardiovascular workout stations. In the summer of that year, while most students were off campus, the dorms were gutted and completely refinished with new lighting, new ceilings, new carpeting, new paint and new furniture. The dorm government began to take a more active part in campus-wide activities, including the sponsorship of the fall and spring hillside concerts.

The Fine Arts. . .

Bellarmine's student life has been greatly enhanced by the fine arts of music, drama and art. While the fine arts are degree-granting disciplines with classroom and studio instruction, they also present a showcase to the college and the larger community. Bellarmine's highly rated art curriculum and faculty have provided cultural enrichment for the entire campus not only in the classrooms and studios but in frequent faculty and student exhibits and traveling exhibitions. From Dante Vena to Bob Lockhart, Bellarmine's art program has been the envy of much older and larger colleges. It has encouraged and developed such talented students as Rex Lagerstrom, M.D., and Kathy McQuade while providing a basic knowledge of art history and appreciation of art aesthetics for the entire student body. It has reached out to many parts of the local arts community, including in the fall of 1960 an exhibit of work by two young black artists, John Daniel and Sam Gilliam, Jr.

At first art was displayed on library walls, classroom corridors and lobby areas. In the fall of 1958, Fr. Loftus designated the large lobby on the ground floor of the administration building as an informal art gallery. In the '60s a broad corridor on the second floor of the administration building beame the Art Lounge. Finally, a proper gallery, the McGrath Art Gallery, was built as a part of Wyatt Hall and opened in 1984. Regardless of the space, however, Bellarmine has hosted dozens of exhibits, ranging from a Louisville China Painter's Guild display to paintings by artist and printer Victor C. Hammer of Lexington in 1959. In the '60s exhibits included pop art, op art, work by Upward Bound students, African sculpture, photographs from the Civil War period, and an IBM collection called "22 Painters of the Western Hemisphere." In the summer of 1965, youngsters taking an art course taught by Dante Vena painted a 65-foot long mural depicting the history of Kentucky on a basement wall of the administration building. Exhibits included prints by Picasso, Matisse and Degas and faculty shows from the University of Kentucky and Murray State. The art department sponsored an Edible Art Exhibition in March of 1978, with an invitation to the public to bring fresh art that would be judged and then eaten. The controversial winning entry consisted of three tin cans, without labels, entitled "Untitled."

Bellarmine's musical showcase, ranging from classical to jazz concerts, was well in place in the early '50s, when the College Choral Club, directed by Fr. Angelus La Fleur, with Clara Schnurr as accompanist, performed on campus as well as on radio and television. In the fall of 1958, the Glee Club provided a 20-man chorus for Kentucky Opera Association's production of Verdi's "Rigoletto," and the Choral Club performed for the WHAS-TV Crusade for Children in the fall of 1957. In the fall of 1959, Fr. John Loftus decided to pipe classical music over the public address system from his office in the afternoons. He said it was for the "development of the whole man." The students dubbed it "sound conditioning."

Jeff Sherman providing musical instruction.

By 1959 the Bellarmine Glee Club was a 40-member group under the direction of Robert M. Fischer, with Fr. Edwin J. Scherzer as accompanist. In the early '60s the Glee Club was being directed by music professor Gus Coin, who also formed an octet to

Dr. Doug Starr

perform at weddings, civic meetings and conventions. Concerts of religious music from Advent to Easter were performed on campus and in churches. In September of 1971, the Louisville Orchestra played a free concert in Knights Hall, with conductor Jorge Mester and pianist Lee Luvisi. By the mid-'70s performances by student and faculty jazz ensembles were common in the New Science Theatre and elsewhere. Recitals and concerts by students and faculty—Patti Long, Pete Loehle,

Sharon Schuster, Tom Lee, Don Murray, Doug Starr and others—enriched the cultural life of campus and community. Frequent concerts were performed by Soundchaser, a jazz ensemble led by Steve Crews. As a part of the 10th Town and Gown Week in March 1973, Gus Coin directed "A Night with the Blues," a concert in honor of the 100th anniversary of the birth of W. C. Handy. In 1974 the college started a degree program in jazz, at that time the only school in the area offering one, and in the summer of 1975 the first annual Mason-Dixon Jazz Clinic was held on campus, directed by James Aebersold. By the mid-'70s the College Singers had begun their popular spaghetti dinners to raise money

Bellarmine College Singers
& Drama Club
present

Kiss
Me
Kate

Sharon E. Schuster-Director
Gus Coin-Conductor

Performance Dates:
April 11 & 12, 1980 - 8:00 P.M.
April 13 - 3:00 P.M.
Large Theater Bellarmine College Campus

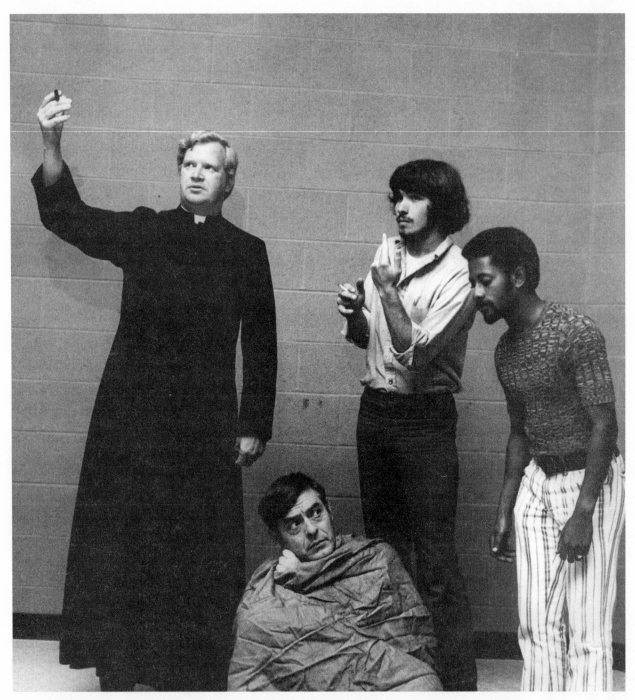

Fr. Eugene Zoeller, Jack Landis, Marty Robertson and Thyron Cyrus rehearsing the stage production J.B.

for such activities as their seasonal tours and campus productions like "Charlie Brown."

In the late '70s, Gus Coin directed the annual River City Ramble Jazz Festival at the Iroquois Amphitheatre, which developed out of the 1978 summer jazz clinic at Bellarmine. In the summer of 1976 music students and faculty performed as the Jazzmobile, a series of 48 free concerts around the city as part of Mayor Harvey Sloane's Summerscene program. Performers included Ed Lyons, Jim Abrams, Jimmy Williamson and Mike Tracy—under the direction of music professor Gregory Coin.

New musical groups were constantly being formed, as talent and demand dictated. In June of

1979, for example, these musical groups were performing: the Bellarmine College Singers, directed by Sharon Schuster; the Pep Band, directed by Ed Lyons, which performed at sports activities on and off campus; and the Jazz Performance Labs, student improvisational groups that entertained audiences from all over the city. In the mid-'80s the musical groups included the Bellarmine Jazz Trio, the College Singers, the Chamber Singers and the Show Choir. During the directorship of Doug Starr in the '80s the College Singers were especially active, making several regional tours each semester. Also during the '70s and '80s the College Singers, sometimes in collaboration with the Drama Club, produced a number of first-rate musicals, including "Godspell," "You're a Good Man, Charlie Brown," and "Kiss Me Kate."

Musical groups with national followings have been frequent visitors to Bellarmine. They include the Dave Brubeck Quartet, the Chad Mitchell Trio, Dr. Billy Taylor, the Lettermen and Sha-na-na in the '60s and '70s and Lionel Hampton in 1986, when he received an honorary degree from the college. Folk singer Judy Collins was in concert in Knights Hall in March of 1969. Jorge Mester conducted the Louisville Orchestra in several campus concerts in the '70s. In the fall of 1974 a Broadway cast production of "Stop the World—I Want to Get Off" played in Knights Hall.

In the early '90s Alexander T. Simpson became director of choral activities and led Bellarmine's musical groups to new heights of achievement. As chairman of the department of fine and performing arts, Dr. Simpson has been instrumental in developing a full complement of musical ensembles, including the Bellarmine Brass Ensemble, the Bellarmine Chamber Ensemble, the Bellarmine Choral Touring Ensemble, the Bellarmine Handbell Ensemble, the Bellarmine Music Technology Ensemble and the Bellarmine Music Theatre Society.

Dramatic activity at Bellarmine has waxed and waned, but there have always been dramatic opportunities and exposures for students. Drama began at Bellarmine in January of 1952 when student Paul Davin performed in *A Phoenix Too Frequent* with the Roswitha Players of Nazareth College and other Bellarmine students did technical work on the production. Nazareth student Kathleen Lyons, later to become a Bellarmine professor of English, was also involved in the production. It was the beginning of a tradition in which Bellarmine students played male roles in plays at Nazareth as well as Ursuline College. Indeed, Bellarmine students, including Paul Davin, played major roles in a 1953 production of *The Heiress* at Ursuline. They were also cast in T.S. Eliot's *Murder in the Cathedral* at Nazareth in the same year. In May of 1953, Bellarmine lent another kind of support when the college orchestra provided music for the Catholic Theater Guild's production of *Meet Me in St. Louis,* directed by Mary Ann Fueglein, later to be a member of Bellarmine's education faculty. The college also provided males for plays in local Catholic high schools for girls, such as Presentation Academy's February 1957 production of *Murder in a Nunnery.*

The first full Bellarmine play production on campus occurred on April 15 and 17, 1955, when the junior class sponsored Samuel Spewack's *Two Blind Mice,* a political satire. Directed by Pat Hohman, who was assisted by Toddy Darst, the play featured Ray Barry as a free-lance reporter and was presented using theater-in-the-round techniques. By December the college had an acting group called the Paduan Players, who presented *Twelve Angry Men,* which was followed in succeeding years by such plays as Herman Wouk's *The Caine Mutiny Court-Martial,* under the direction of Robert M. Fischer, and *Murder in the Cathedral,* with James E. Shollenberger as Thomas a Becket. A group called the Round-Table Players in the spring of 1962 performed Bridget Boland's *The Prisoner,* a play about the conflict between a Communist interrogator and a Roman Catholic cardinal.

A golden age of Bellarmine drama was reached in the early '70s, with Raymond Bailey's productions of numerous plays, including *The Rainmaker, J.B., Spoon River Anthology* and *Bell, Book and Candle.* A feature of the 1970 Town and Gown Week was a community production of Lorraine Hansberry's *A Raisin in the Sun,* directed by Bailey, and featuring such celebrity players from the community as Faith Lyles and Cara Lewis as well as faculty and students. After Bailey, a Baptist minister, left the faculty to pastor a church in Newport, Kentucky, several plays were produced by guest directors Bekki Jo Schneider and Paul Lenzi. For several years music professor Sharon Schuster directed plays for the Drama Club.

Another high point of drama at Bellarmine was reached during the tenure of Andrew Vorder Bruegge in the early '90s. The Bellarmine Players became a student-faculty cooperative group that put on five shows in 1991-92, directed by Vorder Bruegge and students Rebecca Sturgeon, Jon Lancaster and Michael Steinmacher. In 1993 Steinmacher directed *Rosencrantz & Guildenstern Are Dead,* featuring a cast of faculty and students, including chemistry professor Graham Ellis and philosophy professor Jim Valone in the title roles. After the theater program was curtailed in the mid-'90s, productions have continued. In the spring of 1996, for example, the Bellarmine Music Theatre Society produced *Snow White and the Seven Dwarfs;* and in the spring of 1997 the Bellarmine Players performed Jane Martin's *Talking With....* More recently the dramatic tradition at Bellarmine has been carried forward by English professors John Gatton and Bert Hornback and by Mark Sawyer-Dailey, an assistant professor of theater and head of the theater program.

Supplementing Bellarmine's live play productions is a campus tradition in films. Long before big-screen television sets and the availability of quality films on television and in local film theaters, Bellarmine had an art film series. A series in the fall of 1958, for example, under the Community Education Program, tried to integrate academic and extracurricular activities. John Ford taught a course, "The Motion Picture as a Commentary on American Life," which included the

viewing of such films as *All the King's Men, Blackboard Jungle* and *Death of a Salesman.* A film course the following spring included *Sitting Pretty,* based on a novel by Louisville writer Gwen Davenport; *Pinky, On the Waterfront, Saturday's Hero* and *Citizen Kane.* In the '60s and '70s such film classics as *Rashomon, The Heart Is a Lonely Hunter, The Man in the White Suit, Wild Strawberries* and *La Strada* were shown on campus.

The Future. . .

As Bellarmine faces the dawning of a new century, student activities relevant to a new age are being developed. There are still many purely social activities—dances, dinners, banquets, sports—but more emphasis is being placed on career counseling, internships and volunteerism. Volunteer opportunities are growing—Alternative Spring Break with the Housing Partnership, service at the Society of St. Vincent de Paul and St. John's Day Center, tutoring Whitney M. Young Scholars and Iroquois Middle School students. The Student Government Association still tries to keep its fingers on the pulse of the student body and develop programs meaningful to a new era. Record numbers of students now live in the residence halls. Student activities personnel are working hard to maintain and strengthen their partnership with the academics in the development of such programs as NEXUS, a co-curricular transcript program developed in 1996 by student affairs and a faculty committee of the faculty assembly.

College and Student Publications. . .

Colleges have traditionally run on paper. Printed matter is necessary for communication and for records. From admission letters to yearbooks, various kinds of publications keep the wheels rolling. Some formal publications—like catalogues and promotional materials and student handbooks—are essential. Others—the college newspaper, literary magazines and

"Make Love, Not War" or "Love a Student Nurse" or "ThinkFast." In the '80s new words like AIDS began appearing in campus publications.

The '71 *Lance* reflects the campus and the times. It is mostly pictures and peace symbols, and jagged poetry evocative of the year: "Remember: Feeling goofy...A Pet Puppy...Solemnity at Opening Mass...Police Sub-Station on Campus...Sleep...Kent State Benefit...Halloween's Haunted House...Football and its fans, strategy, power, speed, coaches, pain, victory...." Perhaps the most nontraditional and most controversial yearbook was the issue for 1975-76, edited by Philip Bisig and Brooke Beyerle, who, eschewing "objective, photographic documentation," used old movie stills "to heighten moods" in an attempt "to express some of the emotions that this year has produced." After a heated debate between the SGA, which funds the yearbook, and the *Lance* staff, the recommendation was made to provide financial support. The student body then approved an increase in the student activity fee by $10 to provide a copy to each student. Despite editorial eccentricities and controversies and with the guidance of Dr. Gail Henson, the collected volumes of *The Lance* continue to provide a valuable pictorial and emotional history of the college.

yearbook—make life easier and provide an important writing outlet for student talents. Most student publications have had their ups and downs—including occasional hiatuses, when they did not even appear—but overall the history of campus publications at Bellarmine is a good one. Except for occasional independent publications—like *The Yolk,* a periodical of student humor and satire—the major publications have been *The Lance, The Concord* and several literary magazines with different names.

The first yearbook, dubbed *The Lance,* edited by Robert O'Connor and Edward Seitz and moderated by Fr. Angelus, covered the year of planning and the first four years of the college, from 1949 until the June 1954 graduation. Since then it has been a graphic chronicle of Bellarmine's progress through the decades. Surfing through its pages, one can follow the years by the length of hair, the dress length, office equipment—from typewriters to primitive Kaypro computers to slick MacIntoshes, the representative images, even the style of writing. Peace symbols indicate the early '70s. If no one is shown smoking a cigarette, it must be after 1990. The messages on T-shirts reveal a lot too:

The campus literary magazines have had the most uneven history. With the pioneering work of Ben Erskine and Tom Shannon, the first issue of *The Flagon* featuring short stories, poetry and articles appeared in 1954. The road ahead was rocky. The 1963-64 issue became embroiled in controversy over its "pornographic" content. Editor Jim Breen announced in advance of the 1965 issue that the new edition would be "a literary magazine and not a 'passion pulp.'" It had appeared irregularly for several years and then died, to be resurrected under a variety of names. Steve Griffin revived it as *approaches* in 1966, editing it on the premise that "the subject is not as significant as the approach." Controversy surrounded the issue of the following year over the cover, which showed a young man and woman kissing as they lie in front of a fireplace. Publication was delayed for a while, but the Student Senate allowed its distribution provided each copy be marked "solely a student publication" and provided that legal releases be obtained from the two people in the picture.

In the fall of 1969, a newly formatted magazine named *The Blue Lick Review,* edited by Mike Robinson, was introduced. This expensive experiment into periodical literature was followed in 1971 by a much scaled-down **Footnotes,* which emphasized content over appearance. Then in 1973 the literary magazine, edited by Mary Stuber, was merged with *The Lance* and became a section of the yearbook. Finally, in the '80s with the appointment of John Gatton to the English faculty, the literary society he moderated, Ariel, began publication of a journal by the same name.

The best record, however, of student life—as well as serving as an overall college chronicle—is the college newspaper, *The Concord.* The first issue was published December 11, 1950, under its one and only name, though not without opposition from those who preferred a runner-up, "The Scarlet Quill." The name chosen was taken from the dictionary. The editor was Paul Davin, with Hank Ellert as features editor, Al Cassidy and Bob Cooper as news editors and John

O'Regan as sports editor. Ads in the first issue included Boland-Maloney Lumber Company, Du Laney Cleaners, Girdler Motors, Fulton Fish Market, Bisig's Dairy Products, Hubbuch in Kentucky, Office Equipment, featuring "The New Royal, The Easiest-Writing Portable Ever Built!," and Kaelin's, "the home of those delicious cheeseburgers."

In addition to serving as a gadfly to a sometimes lethargic student body and student government, drumming up support for campus activities, from speakers to sports, stinging the administration and faculty from time to time and lamenting the condition of campus buildings, the newspaper has provided reviews of books, movies, plays and concerts—all by a mostly talented cadre of student critics. It has also been the home of an independent editorial page, a lively letters-to-the-editors column and occasional essays by faculty members—such as one by Robert A. Preston in February of 1967, entitled "Philosophical Skepticism." As an ever-vigilant observer of the campus scene, *The Concord* took notice in February of 1967 of the fact that several of the top administrators were frequently absent from campus, Fr. Horrigan having just returned from a trip through Latin America and Fr. John Loftus, just returned from Rome and the Holy Land. "Have you ever wondered what would happen to a small, liberal arts college if the entire administration was suddenly wiped out?" the paper asked editorially. Absolutely nothing, was the reply. Not one student had even noticed that the administrators were gone.

It soon became a vigorous, spunky newspaper that took strong positions on campus and national issues, from library hours, school spirit and blood drives to race relations, political candidates and social issues. In two December 1962 issues the paper attacked the college's reputedly low admission standards, while praising the high quality of the faculty. Indeed, as the newspaper aged into the '60s it became more of an autonomous voice on the campus. In the fall of 1963, with a modified name, *The Bellarmine Concord,* it announced "a new editor, staff, masthead, and a new philosophy." It was a time of national and local turmoil over the war in Vietnam, explosive race relations and the John Birch Society. Editor Thomas A. McAdam, III and faculty "expostulator" Margaret Mahoney guided its mostly liberal directions. It also featured a new column, "Rumblings on the Right," by conservative student writer Robert Caummisar.

There was some immediate opposition to the reinvented paper and "the free and vigorous press" it espoused. Editor McAdam responded editorially in his second issue: "A chance remark made by a Bellarmine student seems important to this discussion: 'I think you put too much emphasis on the Negro trouble in your last issue. I mean, you can't pick up a paper anymore without reading about the bad times Negroes are having. I'm getting tired of reading all that stuff.'" McAdam comments: "So are we; and so, we imagine, are the Negroes." In the same issue columnist Lawrence Rapp even criticized the selection for the Book-A-Semester program, Giorgio Diaz de Santillana's *Origins of Scientific Thought.* During this period William Bradford, II authorized a snappy "Arts in Louisville" column. In November of 1963, the paper published a special supplement on the Peace Corps prepared for national distribution. Before long, the paper was running color on some pages—long before *The Courier-Journal.* In November of 1982, the first 16-page issue was published, and by the early '90s, when Gail Henson became faculty advisor, students could earn academic credit for working on the paper

Editor Joe Hoerter outlined his plans for the paper in his first editorial on September 6, 1968: "It is

the intention of this editor that *The Concord* should function as an independent organ within the community to serve the community as a vehicle for campus viewpoints and for items of general campus interest." One viewpoint was soon sounded in the paper, when David Thurmond shared his impressions of the Democratic National Convention held in Chicago in August of 1968. He had attended as an alternate delegate.

Indeed, in the '60s and '70s the paper became a convenient outlet for student and faculty opinion, not only in the letters column but in special articles and essays. An essay by Episcopalian Ken Vinsel in the fall of 1976 opposing priesthood for women was quickly answered by staff writer Courtney Fleenor, who supported their ordination. In the fall of 1977 Jim Valone wrote a series of articles headed "Philosophy Is a Blast," in which he defended the significance and excitement of his teaching area. Throughout the period students and columnists like Paul Wadell voiced their opinions on subjects ranging from the war in Vietnam to parking problems on campus. During the mid-'70s student and faculty poets like Ron Seitz, Daniel Lawless and Melanie Votaw began contributing their poetry to the paper.

The editorial page writers and columnists of *The Concord* have always had the freedom to express their opinion without fear of retribution. During the build-up of U.S. support for the Diem Government of South Vietnam, a headline in the September 27, 1963 issue read: "U.S. Finances Viet-Nam's Oppressive Government." In March of the same year *The Concord* apologized for the boorish behavior of some students when the Democratic nominee for governor, Ned Breathitt, spoke on campus. A mock ballot just prior to the election, however, showed Breathitt beating his Republican opponent by 239 to 34. *The Concord* also endorsed local and national candidates, usually Democrats, and worked for their election. In the November 1966 elections, for instance, the paper endorsed Democrat Norbert L. Blume over Republican

William O. Cowger in the 3rd Congressional District race, saying that Cowger as Louisville mayor had "accomplished little," whereas state legislator Blume had shown leadership in education, taxes, civil rights and labor. In March of 1976, editor Vickie Schneider condemned President Ford's pardon of ex-President Nixon, calling it "a dangerous precedent."

On the one hand, editorials were written criticizing the pop hits available on the cafeteria juke box and suggesting perhaps "a few not-too-far-out jazz selections" be added. They were also written to make eloquent appeals for brotherhood, racial justice, peace, blood donations to the Red Cross, money donations for the new gym-auditorium and silence for the library. Indeed, Timothy Swenson did a piece of investigative reporting on the library in the fall of 1982. Then when things had quieted down in the late '70s, staff writer Ray Pruitt in an essay entitled "Where Have All the Rebels Gone?" saluted the "strange and nervous" and exciting sixties and lamented "the shameful mediocrity" of student voices of his own time. "The student of the sixties resisted, even challenged, authority *vis-a-vis*," he wrote. "The student of the seventies discreetly avoids protest and trouble, very much like a criminal on the lam."

The Concord nonetheless seemed to relish being in the midst of controversy, whether it was the merits of Black Power or gun control or the mandatory wearing of beanies by freshmen. But it was birth control and abortion that perhaps caused the biggest stir on campus and in the community. In October of 1958, the paper editorially opposed the dissemination of birth control information as being contrary to Catholic belief. Then, some 13 years later, on September 10, 1971, a small ad ran in *The Concord* headed, "Pregnant? Need Help?" and read: "We will help any woman regardless of race, religion, age or financial status. We do not moralize, but merely help women obtain qualified doctors for abortion, if that is what they desire. Please do not delay. An early abortion is more simple and less costly, and can be performed on an out-patient basis." At the end of the ad was a number to call for "Woman's Medical Assistance," a nonprofit organization.

Responding to the immediate furor caused by the ad, editor Chris Covatta maintained the right of the paper to publish the ad because "abortion does exist" and because "a woman has the right to her own body and the right to dictate how she wishes to handle her body," though, he wrote, such a position "does not mean that we condone abortion." Furthermore, he wrote, "the paper remains neutral in moral issues, leaving the decision to the reader." He added: "As far as what the college believes, we do not hold that *The Concord* must be of the image and likeness of Bellarmine. The newspaper is solely a student endeavor, a paper that allows all groups to express their views."

The newspaper's position on the ad was attacked and supported. "Once again the misfits are in charge of the paper," wrote one student. Support came in the form of a letter from Ursuline alumna Joan Riehm, who, while stating her own opposition to abortion, supported the right of the paper to publish the ad. "If the Catholic Church would liberalize its teaching on birth control," she wrote, "and actively support various forms of family planning before a child is conceived, then we certainly wouldn't have to worry so much about abortions." Dean of students Henry A. Schmidt noted that the principles on which the college was founded "are in direct conflict with the abortion ad," but nevertheless said he would allow the ads to continue. "The college's position," he wrote, "is we don't in any manner or fashion support the abortion ads. The ads are there because the student newspaper has the freedom of press." A number of people pointed to Fr. John Loftus' statement, published in *The Courier-Journal* following Pope Paul's 1968 encyclical on birth control which reaffirmed the ban on artificial means of contraception. Fr. Loftus had said that he believed birth control should be an individual decision.

Other controversial ads were published in the early '70s. In June of 1970, the state Alcoholic Beverage Board gave the Anheuser-Busch Company the option of a three-day suspension of its beer business in Kentucky or a $3,000 fine. The offense? The company had sponsored a beer ad in *The Concord*. In the fall of 1972, the paper carried ads for a Pennsylvania company that sold term papers, with 30,000 on file "typed in finished form with bibliography and footnotes."

Despite the controversies into which they were sometimes mired, the editors of *The Concord* have been, by and large, a competent, responsible, gifted group of men and women. They have been some of Bellarmine's finest: Ray Tillman, Ellen Baker, Skip Hardesty, Timothy Swenson, Michael Steinmacher—ably assisted by features editor Tracy Sullivan, David Polston, Denise Essenpreis, Ruth Lancaster—to name a few. In the fall of 1973, Kaelin Kallay, a junior in languages, became the first female editor. Some readers immediately saw a feminine slant when in one of her first editorials she announced that she would highlight "An Eyesore of the Issue," which she defined as "a picture of some location on campus which for some reason detracts from the overall appearance of the college." The first eyesore was P-260, with its leaky roof, ruined ceiling tiles and carpeting. Her crusade continued with other eyesores to be remedied. She also editorialized for a constitutional amendment banning abortions and for better dorm security. Her husband-to-be was ex-Passionist seminarian Bill Rybak, who had served as sports editor. "I was his first—and I hope—his last girlfriend," she says. About her position as editor of *The Concord,* she says, "I felt we had as much independence as we wanted. Sometimes I opposed a campus project or policy, but generally we got along very well. One time I editorially condemned a decision to move *The Concord* office to an out-of-the-way location, and Petrik never let me forget it—in a good-naturedly way. But there was never any censorship."

Assisting the editors were generally hard-working, able staffers—in particular, the students who served as critics and had the awesome responsibility of reviewing not only campus exhibits and productions but professional groups like Actors Theatre of Louisville, the Kentucky Opera Association, the Louisville Orchestra and the Louisville Ballet. In the mid-'50s David Chervenak wrote "Critics Corner," a mature look at the local arts scene that included movies, books, drama and music. When Chervenak was criticized for reviewing films shown at the Crescent Theater, an art theater in Crescent Hill that sometimes showed condemned films, editor Tony Banet suggested that Catholics could influence the availability of good films by patronizing the good ones and ignoring the bad ones. In his column called "Front Row Center," Jack Humphrey reviewed plays, movies, operas and concerts in the late '50s.

A tradition of honest reviewing was soon established, and *Concord* critics felt free to call art exhibits, even a local one, "mediocre, non-enlightening, and uninspired"—as Edwin Ford did in October of 1967. In the mid-'80s Beverley Ballantine continued the tradition with her gutsy, pointed and trenchant reviews of movies. Vince Aprile reviewed Actors Theatre of Louisville's first productions, two plays by Chekhov directed by Ewell Cornett, in November of 1964. In his review of ATL's *Arms and the Man* in March 1965, critic Jim Breen said, somewhat presciently: "There are many who feel that the ATL is the best thing that has happened to Louisville in some time." Billy Bradford reviewed the opening play of the fall 1966 season at ATL, Arthur Miller's *All My Sons,* with a cast headed by film-star-in-the-making Ned Beatty, and acclaimed it "a promising season." *Concord* critics were not hesitant to pan a play they did not like. Mike Hardin called a January 1967 production of *In White America* "disappointing in virtually every area." In 1970 Mike Robinson panned ATL's production of *Cat on a Hot Tin Roof,* especially a "weak performance" by Jon Jory as Brick, who "came out sounding like a

Hell's Angel from South Oakland trying to be cute after a few beers." The critic's pen was still sharp in the fall of 1997, when critic Stephie Mues reported on ATL's production of several short Thornton Wilder plays. Weak scripts and weak casts, she said, probably had Wilder "turning in his grave."

Recordings and television shows—even restaurants—were being reviewed by the mid-'70s. Two fictitious food critics, "Ima and Ura Hogg," reviewed the cuisine at the college cafeteria with unsavory conclusions. In October of 1981, however, Joe Cassidy penned a tribute to the sometimes maligned Twig and Leaf Restaurant at the corner of Douglass and Bardstown Road, calling it "an alternative to dried out hamburgers in waxpaper," as well as chili in styrofoam cups and slow-moving lines. "Whenever you want the standard hamburger (cooked to perfection)," he wrote, "or something more exotic like breaded veal, the Twig and Leaf is ready and waiting to serve."

Talented writers have also covered sports for *The Concord*. Some of the best writing in the newspaper has been on the sports pages under the by-line of Bill Rybak, Ed Cahill and Ron Cregier. Three other sports writers also stand out for their inventiveness. In the mid-'60s Jim Fitzpatrick was not only writing straight sports reportage but columns headed "Losing with Dignity," about a lesson he learned during a boyhood game of hide-and-seek, and one called "That Sporty Feeling," about an embarrassing adolescent episode when he became a voyeur to a couple next door in order to learn the art of kissing. Even, however, in his main-line sports columns, he could hardly resist dramatic flourishes, such as noticing during the final basketball game of the 1966-67 season against Kentucky Wesleyan "that Wesleyan coach Guy Strong's purple vest surpassed in elegance Jim Spalding's crimson socks."

Two of the most consistently readable sports columnists were Andy Eggers and Randy Rorrer, who, under the by-line of Andy 'n' Randy, not only kept

their *Concord* readers informed about Bellarmine sports but kept them in stitches as well. One column began: "We dedicate this column to all the mistreated people in the world and hope it reaches them. The people we include in this category are the boat people, Cambodians, NFL middle linebackers, Twig and Leaf customers, and Little House on the Prairie viewers." In the April Fools' issue for 1980 they voted themselves the first annual "Absolutely Greatest Couple of College Newspaper Sports Columnists in the Country Award." The columns usually featured grotesquely distorted photos of the authors. In the fall of 1980, after Eggers transferred to another school, Rorrer continued the column and called it "Randy Minus Andy."

Humor was not confined to the sports page. The long-running series called AKOH was begun in 1961 by staff writer Joe Hammer, who wanted to write a column of humor and satire. Benson Alleman, the faculty debate moderator, was responsible for the name of the new column. He said that he was convinced that audiences didn't listen to the words sung by members of the band he played with in the Rathskeller of the Seelbach Hotel. The tenor saxophonist tested his theory by having the band stand up and sing "Aye, aye, aye, aye and all kinds of horseshit." Sure enough, no one noticed. As a sort-of tribute to the debate coach, who died in 1961, Hammer named his column AKOH after the final four words of Alleman's lyric. Hammer took as his pen name the two characters from Samuel Becket's *Waiting for Godot* and began signing his sometimes outrageous column Vladimir and Estragon.

The first column, which appeared on March 5, 1961, begins: "There is a garden, a wonderful garden of sunshine and romance and flowers. . . ay-ay-ay-ay, AKOH." Within a month another columnist who signed himself Jared II took it upon himself "to bring some light into the darkness created by those two advocates of AKOH." In the fall of 1962, Thomas McAdam joined Hammer as cowriter of the column, and AKOH called itself "that last bastion of humor and level-headed thinking." The column ran until the early '70s, then resumed in the fall of 1982. The horse cartoon that symbolizes the column was drawn by Jim Wills and first appeared on September 27, 1963. In addition to Estragon and Vladimir (sometimes spelled Vladmir), other characters from Becket's plays were used such as Nells and Nagg and later such names as Amnion and Chorion, Cecil and Clyde and Cecilia. In the spring of 1999, the column was authored by Cecil D. Mule, who was still raising Cain, attacking the food service, praising far-out movies, raking campus muck and stinging a few pompous asses.

Although many members of the faculty, staff and student body have been targets of the column, the favorite lovable target is Margaret Mahoney. On September 27, 1963, the first of a long series of "Messages to Maggie" appeared. A sample message from the fall of 1969: "Money cannot buy love—but it sure makes shopping for it a lot of fun." Hardly anything was off-limits to AKOH, including film reviews. This is an AKOH parody: "A Schoolbus Named Desire. Screen play based on the Amy Loveman prize-winning novel of the Tennessee Valley. Story deals with corruption, small-town scandal, seduction, immorality and Sabbath-breaking. It's the story of a boy and his dog."

Humor and satire has also been evident in other pages of *The Concord*. In the fall of 1958, when it was revealed that Pope John XXIII was the first Supreme Pontiff to smoke cigarettes, *Concord* columnist Tony Banet imagined a scenario in which Madison Avenue copywriters were planning to capitalize on it. One suggestion for a line exploiting papal infallibility: "Where there's a Supreme Pontiff, there's a Marlboro." At one time the paper created a fictional student named Osgood Gostolovitch, who roamed the campus in search of a good time. The annual April Fools' Day issue called *The Discord* has routinely ridiculed everyone and everything within reach and occasionally teetered on the brink of poor taste.

The college paper has also been fortunate to have had the talents of many good cartoonists, including Bruce Tinsley and Graham Pullen. After graduation, Tinsley, who drew cartoons for *The Concord* in the late '70s, became the author of a nationally syndicated political cartoon series. In the early '80s Pullen drew cartoons that were comparable to those in the country's best dailies.

With so much talent, hard work and freedom, predictably *The Concord* has won frequent honors and awards, including first-class ratings, from the National Associated Collegiate Press and the Kentucky Intercollegiate Press Association. Under the leadership of editor Jason Cissell and faculty advisor Gail Henson, the paper won more than 20 awards from the KIPA in 1997 for such areas as investigative reporting, feature writing, editorials and photography. With Erin Keane as editor for 1997-98, *The Concord* has continued to serve the college community with a readable and lively reflection of campus events and issues. At the 1998 Kentucky Intercollegiate Press Association conference in Lexington, *The Concord* won 33 individual and staff awards, including Journalist of the Year for 1997, Jason Cissell.

College Athletics...

On December 28, 1950, with only two weeks notice, Coach Norb Raque assembled an undersized but scrappy basketball team against St. Mary's College. *The Louisville Times* announced the team's debut with this lead: "Another name is added to the sports calendar of our town tonight when Bellarmine College opens its athletic program." It was already two weeks overdue. Ice and snow had forced cancellation of an earlier game with Villa Madonna. The starters for the Bellarmine Pioneers, as they were called then, were Ed Seitz and Chuck Long, forwards, Bob O'Connor, center, and Jack Sinkhorn and Bill Crush, guards. Also on the team were Ted Wade, Ben Erskine, John Ford, Tom Weber, Ted Henle, Bart Brown, Ed Coots and Terry Gerhardt.

Unfortunately, the delay didn't seem to help coach Norb Raque prepare his team to win against the new opponents, the St. Mary Seminarians, who downed them 79-66 at Holy Trinity Gym. Only Long and Crush had played on their high-school varsity teams. A Bellarmine partisan, however, must have written the headline for *The Times* the next day: "Bellarmine Off to Good Start Despite Loss to St. Mary's." The best—and tallest—player on the team was golfer Bart Brown at 6 feet, 1 inch. It was a valiant fight, however, with Bellarmine tieing the score with seven and one half-minutes to play. The coach put his own spin on the results. "At this stage," he said, "winning is not as important as getting an athletic program established." With that objective, he succeeded. But winning was still not in the cards when they played their next game with Villa Madonna in Covington. Villa Madonna ended a seven-game losing streak by whipping Bellarmine 87-36. Bellarmine boosters knew the outlook would brighten. Then Bellarmine fell to Club Cuero.

The fourth time was the charm as the yearling Knights trounced the Bantams of Louisville Municipal College 67-36. Unfortunately, there were eleven more games in the season but only one more win, when Louisville Bible College crumbled 64-51. With a starting record of 2-14, the next year looked better. It had to be. At the school's first athletic banquet on April 4, 1951 in the school cafeteria, Fr. Horrigan said hopefully, "With each event, whether scholastic or athletic, we are setting a tradition here at Bellarmine College." Fr. Killian, athletic director, said that plans were being made for seasons in baseball and track. Letters were awarded to Bob O'Connor, team captain, and to Crush, Sinkhorn, Wade, Brown, Seitz, Erskine, Ford, Henle, Long and Weber. Letters were also given to team managers John O'Regan and Bob Russell. Although the Knights, as they had been renamed, hadn't set the world on fire, Coach Raque admitted, they had made a foundation on which to build. In fact, before the end of the spring semester in 1951,

Bellarmine had a winning team, the baseball club, whipping Union Local 89 twice in a double-header at Shawnee Park on May 27.

At the beginning of the second school year, Fr. Horrigan announced that "basketball will certainly be the major sport at Bellarmine, and we shall make every effort to develop our program as quickly as possible." To put into practice what he preached, he announced that Fr. John Davis would be serving as athletic director and that Norb Raque was returning as head basketball coach. Most of the freshman team was back. Prospects looked promising. The first game was with Campbellsville Junior College at their gym. Bellarmine lost but the record improved. Indeed, the record for 1951-52 showed marked improvement, with a 22-game season and 5 wins—against Lindsey Wilson Junior College, Georgetown "B," St. Mary's College (ah, sweet revenge!), Transylvania and Centre.

In May of 1952, Bellarmine announced that Eddie Weber, director of athletics at Kentucky Military Institute for 20 years, would assume a similar job at Bellarmine in the fall semester, replacing Fr. Davis as athletic director and Raque as basketball coach. Although best known for his prowess in tennis, Weber also starred in football, baseball and basketball at St. X. At the University of Louisville he played varsity basketball for four years, baseball for three years and helped the school win three straight tennis championships. After graduation he coached at St. X and at U of L before going to KMI. In accepting the position at Bellarmine, he said, "All I can promise is honesty, perseverance and hard work toward getting a winning program started." He also announced that he wanted eventually to expand the athletic program to include tennis, golf and possibly swimming and track. In addition to coaching, he taught chemistry.

At the end of the 1953-54 basketball season, Bellarmine was second in the KIAC, with 12 wins and two defeats. In January of 1954, Coach Weber was so encouraged, he said, "I guess it is about time for a school to have a school song when it has won 10 games in a row. But we still have the same problem. We can't find a word to rhyme with silver." Bellarmine cagers were stepping tall—right up to the top of the KIAC. Weber suggested reasons for their success: "Hard work and enthusiasm, I guess, are the answers. The team has great spirit and never quits scrapping. We haven't any boys who were great high-school stars, but the boys like to play."

1964-65 Basketball Team

Handicapped by losses to the military, a small student body from which to draw, the lack of a big-time sports tradition and the lack of facilities, the Bellarmine Knights had its ups and downs from year to year. The 1954-55 team was injury-plagued and dropped to a record of 7-20. The next year, under new coach Paul Miller, the record was 6-13. In 1956-57 it was 13-11, followed by a record the following year of 17-9—then a reversal of 6-18.

An athletics picture with basketball as the star was just the kind of scenario that Fr. Horrigan had in mind as he began to plan the entire college program from scratch in the fall of 1949. At that time he wasn't sure whether the athletics program would be "amateur" or "professional" or "big-time." He did say that the program would probably start with

When Bellarmine played Louisville.

a freshman basketball team. "We are inclined to feel it would be wise at first to concentrate on basketball. Football presents a big problem." And so it would be basketball on which Bellarmine would pin its hopes for athletic success. Fr. Horrigan, who had been a scholar-athlete and won two letters in basketball at St. Joseph's College in Collegeville, Indiana, could take heart that his new college was succeeding in sports as well as academics. For nine years the road to basketball glory had been a rocky one, but, then, no one really expected the teams to win big or consistently.

Expectations, however, jumped in the summer of 1959, when the college announced that Alex Groza, the former University of Kentucky basketball star, had been appointed head basketball and baseball coach. He won fame as one of the Fabulous Five at the University of Kentucky in the 1947-48 season. That year the starters included Ralph Beard, Kenny Rollins, Cliff Barker, Wah Wah Jones and Groza, who had been the scoring champion of the 1948 Olympics. In the early '50s, the 6-foot, 7-inch center and two of his Kentucky teammates were given suspended sentences by a New York judge for conspiring to fix games. The three time All-American returned to his hometown of Martins Ferry, Ohio, and for a while operated the family tavern, then worked for an industrial firm and as a television sportscaster.

Finally, he was able to get back into sports when Bellarmine's coach was killed in a car accident and the college offered him the position. Said Groza upon accepting the job at Bellarmine: "At first, I felt like crawling on a shelf and hiding. Finally, I decided I couldn't hide anymore. People knew me. They had to begin taking me for what I am and not what I had been. I've done 10 years of penance. People are really forgiving." Letters poured in from all over the country praising the college for giving him a second chance. Not a single critical letter was received.

Under Groza the basketball record began to improve immediately, despite an uphill battle. In January of 1965, he told a *Courier-Journal* reporter of his difficulties on the road recruiting good players: "I was in Danville, Illinois, a few days ago to look at some prospects when I ran into a recruiter from Georgia Tech. We went into the high-school gym together during practice. He got the red-carpet treatment. I got, 'Bellarmine, where's that?'" During his seven years as Bellarmine coach, however, his players, dubbed "Grozamen," won 91 and lost 78 games.

Even the losses could have an aura of victory. After Bellarmine had been defeated at South Bend by Notre Dame 71-52 in December of 1961, *Concord* sports columnist Bob Pfaadt commented: "In losing to Notre Dame at South Bend, Bellarmine has nothing to be ashamed of because only once in the last six years has Notre Dame been beaten on their home floor." Twice in his last three years Groza's teams gained berths in the NCAA College Division tournaments. His best record was 21-6 in 1963, when the Knights won the tournament and season championships in the Kentucky Intercollegiate Athletic Conference, and he was selected as KIAC Coach of the Year. The team that year included Estil L. Alvey, Judge Mosley, Ben Monhollen, Tom Hugenburg, George Hill, Richard Schulten, Dick Carr, Mel Blaylock,

Tony Hildenbrand, Don Kalmey and Denny Zvinakis. In March of 1963 Bellarmine was the host team for the South Central NCAA College Division Tournament and won third place. Groza's final season was a winning season at 13-8.

In Groza's letter of resignation to Fr. Horrigan in February of 1966, he said that he had discussed the decision with his wife and they decided it was best for his career. "If I am to make a move, this is the time to do it," he wrote. After serving as business manager for the Louisville Colonels, he joined the San Diego Conquistadors as vice president, general manager and coach. In his later years he would say of his Bellarmine tenure: "Bellarmine was the beginning of a new life for me. I'll always be grateful to those people." Bellarmine was also grateful to Groza for the good work he had done, not only on the scoreboard but in forming young men of character. At the finals of the Quincy, Illinois Holiday Invitational in 1962, when

Jim Morris '55 - '57

Western Illinois lost to Bellarmine, the Illinois coach wrote Groza: "I want to congratulate you on the well-coached Bellarmine team in the tournament. If I were to give a trophy for sportsmanship, it would go to your team." When Groza died in San Diego in 1995, he was national sales manager for Reynolds International.

Selected from 30 applicants to succeed Groza was 33-year-old assistant coach Jim Spalding, who commented, "Following Alex is going to be a big job." Louisville native Spalding was graduated from Bellarmine in biology in 1955 and had taught and coached at Trinity High School for one year before joining the college faculty. In his years at Bellarmine he has been a standout basketball player, a teacher, basketball coach and finally, director of dthletics. As head basketball coach for five years, Spalding amassed an overall record of 71-60. His teams participated in NCAA tournaments in 1969 and 1970. His teams played respectable—even brilliant—ball against the big-time teams. In the fall of 1966, the Knights played No. 2 ranked University of Louisville and lost by a landslide, but in January of 1967, Coach Spalding's roundballers almost beat a major team, DePaul University in Chicago, losing by 64-63. A writer for the *Chicago Daily News* described the losing coach this way: "Spalding is the skinny, sandy-haired 34-year-old coach

Dave Kelly '52-'55

of Bellarmine College's basketball team in Louisville. He wears colorless horn-rimmed glasses. He speaks softly . . . and he coaches extremely well." Coach Spalding said of the almost-win: "For our kids, it's something they'll tell their children about some day—how they almost beat DePaul. . . the big-time team."

In December of 1969, Bellarmine was defeated by a prayerful Oral Roberts University team 84-76 in Knights Hall. Afterwards, Roberts himself suggested their hidden weapon, "We said a few prayers before this game, and without embarrassment, I might add." Coach Spalding later recalled an after-game meeting with Oral Roberts. "The team and I had returned to the locker room feeling depressed. All of a sudden,

Coach Jim Spalding

the door opened and in came Oral Roberts himself. He walked up to me, put his hand on my shoulder, looked me straight in the eye and said very knowingly, 'Jim, your team is just about to turn the corner. You'll start winning and you'll have a successful season.'" Indeed, the team went on to have a winning 17-10 season.

A profile of Spalding in *The Louisville Times* in January of 1968 showed a man obsessed with his work. After a game or practice session, he said, "I can't go home and go to bed. If I left everything back at school, I'd be able to relax. But I take coaching home with me. I stay up late—sometimes until 3 a.m.—until I'm too tired to think about it anymore." One of his favorite wisecracks was, "During basketball season, I go from ghastly to ghostly," referring to his usually slim figure which thinned out even more during the season.

In March of 1971, Fr. Horrigan announced that Spalding would replace acting director of athletics Fr. Hilary Gottbrath, who had, in turn, replaced Jim Connor. In his new job Spalding would oversee an athletics program that would grow from four sports in 1971 to some 15 in the early '90s. Indeed, no one has contributed more to Bellarmine athletics than Jim Spalding. One of his fans, Pioneer Class member John O'Regan, has suggested that in order to honor his work Knights Hall should be renamed Spalding Hall.

Spalding's replacement as basketball coach was Joe Reibel, a former Bellarmine basketball star who had been his assistant for less than a year. Before returning to Bellarmine, Reibel had coached nine years at St. Xavier, where his teams won 168 games and lost only 65. In fact, during his first year as head coach at St. X in 1962, he led his cagers to the Kentucky high-school basketball championship. In 1966, after he had coached the Kentucky High School All Stars to a win over Indiana, a *Sports Illustrated* writer said that Reibel could just about have his choice of college coaching jobs in the entire country. It was, therefore, a surprise to many fans and observers of college athletics when he chose to come to Bellarmine in 1970, especially since he had spurned overtures from two major colleges. To Reibel his decision made a lot of sense. He wanted to complete his master's degree at the University of Louisville, and he wanted to get some college experience as assistant coach. Where else but Bellarmine could he conveniently do both?

During his quarter century as basketball coach he proved the wisdom of his decision.

During his first season at Bellarmine as head coach Reibel won five of the first six games, then lost six straight. When asked by a *Louisville Times* reporter at midseason what was wrong, he said, "That's a superb question." Once, after losing to an upstart Northern Kentucky team 103-92, Reibel said to a reporter: "I almost decided not to answer any post-game questions. I didn't think I'd be able to talk intelligently about the kind of performance we put on tonight. It defies description." His first three years were all losers: 9-17, 12-14, 12-13. But even in lean times Bellarmine's basketball program had respect. Coach Ron Fifer of Indiana University Southeast in New Albany said of his opponent: "Getting on Bellarmine's schedule was a big step for us. You have to be respectable in order to play a school like Bellarmine."

Sometimes even the promising seasons turned up disappointing. The 1974-75 season, for example, had superb players like guards Floyd Smith and Bobby Todd and forward Jim Hall, but could manage only 15 wins against 10 losses. Near the

end of the season and on the eve of a big game with Kentucky State University, Coach Reibel told a sportswriter for *The Louisville Times* that he was thinking about making two requests in his next year's budget, a couch for his team's locker room and a psychiatrist to serve as an assistant coach to use the new couch to figure out what was wrong with his players. The team went on to lose to KSU 96-87. But even in this season there were highlights. The Knights trounced archrival Kentucky Wesleyan 100-79, and on December 17 they upset Austin Peay University, which was scheduled to play the University of Alabama a few days later. Even after improving to an 18-7 season in 1975-76, the college lost its bid for a spot in the NCAA Division II Basketball Tournament.

Indeed, in January of 1976, Jim Spalding recalled the earlier dreams of Fr. Schuhmann of big-time basketball for Bellarmine. In the summer of 1964, Fr. Horrigan signaled the growth of the athletic program by appointing Fr. Henry B. Schuhmann as the first athletic director. It was a time of great prospects for the program, and the new director was enthusiastic. "We're going to go just as far as we can as fast as we

1966-67 Bellarmine Knights

can," he said. "Matter of fact, we'd like to play in Madison Square Garden—and be No. 1 team—this year." Indeed, perhaps realizing the limitations of Bellarmine's program, Jim Connor resigned in the summer of 1970 after four seasons as athletic director and basketball and baseball coach and took a job as coach at Boone County High School in Florence, Kentucky.

Bellarmine's earlier dreams would never become reality, as Coach Spalding also acknowledged. "At the time," he said, "I'm sure it wasn't unrealistic for those people making the decisions to strive for it. But in hindsight, it had to be unrealistic for Bellarmine. It had to be unrealistic because our resources weren't those of, say, Oral Roberts...." And so by 1976 Bellarmine was no longer playing Creighton or DePaul, Miami of Ohio or Louisville. The college had set its sights lower, and its schedule was filled out with Georgetown College, Transylvania and Thomas More.

Nevertheless, Bellarmine could still have good teams and compete with other good teams. The 1976-77 season was one of its most successful, and it was the first time in seven years that the college was invited to the NCAA II tournament. The good times continued, and in December of 1978, Dick Fenlon, sports editor of *The Louisville Times,* called Bellarmine basketball "the best-kept secret around." The 1979-80 season was 17-9, a year that Coach Reibel said made him "pleased but not satisfied." He was pleased because he was concluding Bellarmine's sixth consecutive winning season. He was not satisfied because he was not invited to the NCAA II play-offs. In 1982 Bellarmine won the first Richard Scharf Trophy for the finest all-sports program in the Great Lakes Valley Conference, and in the same year the Knights were again in the NCAA Division II tournament.

Winning seasons became a habit, and in March of 1984, the Knights went to the NCAA II tournament for the second time in three years. It was the seventh appearance of the Knights in the national tourney and

the seventh time the Knights lost in the opening game. In 1990-91, with a 24-6 record, Bellarmine shared the GLVC title, and in January of 1991, Reibel had his 300th college basketball victory, with a decision over Northern Kentucky. Despite the leadership of GLVC Player of the Year, Tom Schurfranz, the Knights had a disappointing season the following year. While the Knights were making lackluster records in the mid-'90s, the Lady Knights were gaining in prestige as they played in the NCAA Regionals almost every year. In addition, GLVC championships were being won in men's tennis and golf and in women's basketball.

With the spotlight on basketball, however, other sports were not ignored. Indeed, by 1954 Bellarmine was in varsity competition in golf, tennis, baseball and track as well as basketball, plus many intramural sports. That year the tennis team went undefeated. The rolling hills of the campus are a natural setting for golf, and in the spring of 1955, Bellarmine opened its own nine-hole course. Track was firmly established early, with decathlon athletes like Charles "Butch" Kincaid, a star of track and field events in the early '60s. At the time Coach Jim Spalding said of him: "He's the greatest athlete this school has ever had." In its first issue of the new academic year in the fall of 1956, *The Concord* stated that "Bellarmine at present offers to its students the fullest opportunity of an extracurricular life" and named a number of intercollegiate and intramural sports. Bellarmine also had its own cricket club by 1961 and in the spring of 1963 a fencing team, led by Phil O'Daniel. For several years in the mid-'60s the college varsity bowling team was regional champion in the Southeastern College Bowling Tournament.

By 1974 there was a soccer team, coached by a native of Ghana, Matt Afful, an engineer for General Electric, and a local teacher, Doug Foland. During the 1976-77 season the soccer team won its first Kentucky State Soccer Championship under Coach Bill Beattie, and in 1978 even beat the University of Kentucky team. The first Campus Tennis Center Invitational was held in August of 1974 and featured

1998-99 Men & Women's Cross Country Team

Women's Soccer

1993 Men's Golf Team

Men's Baseball Coach Al Burke

Men's Track Coach Larry Quisenberry

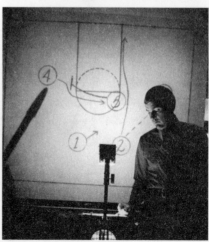

*Men's Basketball
Coach Joe Reibel*

Men's Basketball Coach Joe Reibel

center director Mickey Schad and Jackie Cooper, pro at the Louisville Tennis Club. In 1981 the tennis team was 23-5 and won the GLVC Championship. In October of 1975, the first annual Cross Country Classic was held on campus. In the fall of 1995, the golf team was ranked 14th in the nation among NCAA Division II schools, with a record of 74-21-0. Although outside the college-sponsored athletic program, Bellarmine did produce the local light-heavyweight boxing champion in the mid-'50s, Ramsey Jackson, of the maintenance department.

Al Burke coached the Baseball Knights for five years, from 1976 to 1981, with a record of 151-106-3, and led his teams to be runners-up in the NCAA II Regional in 1979 and 1980 and to the Great Lakes Conference Baseball Championship in 1980. Al Burke was one of an army of part-time coaches, community and faculty volunteers and others whose hard work made the total athletics program possible. Windell Bowles of the accounting faculty is a fine example of the volunteer coach who led numerous Bellarmine bowling and tennis teams. Sociology professor Larry Quisenberry resurrected the college's track and cross-country programs in the mid-'70s. Fr. John Deatrick was not only college chaplain

Bob Pfaadt, Kaelin Rybak and Sr. Pat Lowman

David O'Toole

but baseball coach. He said he often enticed baseball players to Bellarmine with this offer: "Come and play your baseball at Bellarmine, and when you find the right girl, the coach will toss in a free wedding for you." By May of 1971, he had married off three of his players.

Others who deserve mention for their work in such sports as tennis, bowling, cross-country, cricket

and track include Gene Weis, Bob Cooper and David O'Toole. Along with Sr. Pat Lowman, O'Toole has been a long-time faculty champion of a balanced academic-athletic program at Bellarmine. For more than a quarter of a century, from the 1968 merger with Ursuline to her retirement in the mid-90s, history professor Sr. Pat Lowman has served Bellarmine athletics untiringly as women's official scorekeeper,

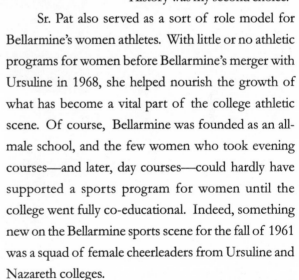

women's athletic coordinator and faculty liaison to the athletics program—and as the faculty's No. 1 sports fan. Says Sr. Pat: "I come from a sports-minded family in South Carolina. My father was a semiprofessional athlete, and in high school I played basketball, softball and tennis. For a while I was a playground director and planned to be a physical education teacher and coach. History was my second choice."

Sr. Pat also served as a sort of role model for Bellarmine's women athletes. With little or no athletic programs for women before Bellarmine's merger with Ursuline in 1968, she helped nourish the growth of what has become a vital part of the college athletic scene. Of course, Bellarmine was founded as an all-male school, and the few women who took evening courses—and later, day courses—could hardly have supported a sports program for women until the college went fully co-educational. Indeed, something new on the Bellarmine sports scene for the fall of 1961 was a squad of female cheerleaders from Ursuline and Nazareth colleges.

With the increasing numbers of women on campus in the late '60s, their presence became known in such sports as basketball, tennis and volleyball. Soon they began to produce winning teams against such schools as Kentucky, Louisville, Indiana University Southeast, Kentucky State, Belmont College and

Morehead State. Ursuline graduate Kay Whelan was appointed coach of the Bellarmine Belles in the fall of 1973 and soon became an effective activist for competitive basketball for women. During the Petrik administration full-tuition grants in basketball were made for both men and women. Partial grants were made in other sports.

In the spring of 1974, under Coach Whelan, the Bellarmine Belles beat Kentucky State University to become the first winner of the Kentucky Women's Small College Tournment in basketball. With assists from such regulars as forwards Anne Mueller, Mary Ann Hoben and Martha McGrath and guards Ruth Potts and Ursula Stegall, the Belles repeated their performance the following year also against Kentucky State. As he handed out the awards in Knights Hall, County Judge Todd Hollenbach said, "This is the first girls' game I've seen, and I'm impressed." Their 1976-77 record of 12-8 was also impressive.

Although they were usually in the shadow of the male team, the Belles often posted a better record. By late 1977 Coach Whelan had put together five consecutive winning seasons, with the aid of players like Cathy Gravatte, Lisa Siegwald, Mary Jane Hoben and Mary Beth Thieneman. The Belles finished the 1982-83 season with a 22-5 record and the Great Lakes Valley Conference Championship, while the Knights had a losing season of

Women's Coach Charlie Just cutting down the net.

13-14. The same year the Belles softball team finished 24-1 and were Kentucky State Champions in the KWIC tournament.

In June of 1984, Charlie Just left Mercy Academy and became coach of Bellarmine's women's basketball team. In the spring of 1986, the Belles were cochampions of the GLVC and appeared for the first time in NCAA tournament play. While the Knights struggled to get a 16-27 season in 1989-90 and finished fourth in the GLVC, the Belles compiled an impressive season of 25-6 and finished second in the league. Their record in 1991-92 was 23-5. By February of 1996, Just had earned his 250th career win at Bellarmine. During his 12 years at Bellarmine, he had a .741 winning percentage. In 1997 the Lady Knights finished second in the GLVC and received an NCAA tournament bid. During the '70s, '80s and '90s Bellarmine women were also playing and competing in other sports, from football and volleyball to field hockey. Women athletes have not been given nearly the attention that men have commanded, but they have made an important contribution to Bellarmine's athletic tradition. In basketball they include Lois Taurman, Mary Wagner and Stephanie Tracy. In the fall of 1975, Angela Merici track star Ann Zoeller became a member of Bellarmine's track squad along with the male members. The Great Lakes Valley Conference voted to include women's basketball in 1983 and eventually a full slate of women's sports. Bellarmine's women were already ahead of the game. In the early '90s the names of the women's teams were changed from Belles to Knights.

Since 1995 Bellarmine has fielded 16 intercollegiate sports— nine women and seven men. The 225 student-athletes that compete in these sports are 115 women and 110 men, with the distribution of expenditures for grants and operating budgets reflecting this proportion. The college measures quite well in gender equity evaluations for its intercollegiate programs.

One program the college has never fielded is football. In the '50s there were frequent mentions in

The 1973 Women's Basketball Team.

Martha McGrath Todd jumps to victory!

the sports pages of the local papers of long-range plans for football at Bellarmine, including a stadium. Perhaps the testimony of the Rev. Vernon F. Gallagher, president of Duquesne University, helped to dissuade the founding fathers from football. Speaking at the opening Mass at the Cathedral of the Assumption in the early '50s, Fr. Gallagher said that Duquesne had just eliminated their winning football program because it was costing them $50,000 a year. There was only one objection, he said. Athletic director Jim Spalding told a *Concord* reporter in October of 1979 that "it always comes back to the cost factor." He said that "football programs at 90 to 95 per cent of schools lose money." The question of football was raised as late as the '80s by *Concord* sports editor Ed Cahill, but each time the cost was deemed prohibitive. The only exception has been touch football in the intramural sports program and its annual Pioneer Bowl.

Bellarmine has affiliated with regional and national athletic associations, beginning with both the National Association of Intercollegiate Athletics and the Kentucky Intercollegiate Athletic Conference in 1953. The college, however, dropped out of the KIAC at the end of the 1964-65 academic year. According to Fr. Horrigan, this move would allow the college to pursue "athletic relations with colleges in other sections of the country." Bellarmine was instrumental in founding the Great Lakes Valley Conference in July of 1978 and became one of its original members. Member schools have included the University of Indianapolis, Kentucky State University, Kentucky Wesleyan College, Northern Kentucky University, Southern Indiana University, Saint Joseph's College and Ashland University.

President McGowan and Professor O'Toole have been significantly involved with the work of the NCAA. Dr. McGowan served a four-year term (1993-1996) on the NCAA's President's Commission. It was during this time that the organization was going through a significant period of change as a result of serious questions about the integrity of intercollegiate sports and the lack of institutional control over the operations of their sports programs. The President's Commission called for a reorganization of the structure of the NCAA. Dr. McGowan played a leading role in this restructuring process. In fact, it was his model of formal inclusion of presidential authority in the structure that was adopted and is presently in place for the NCAA. He was also responsible for establishing a similar structure for the Great Lakes Valley Conference.

Professor O'Toole was also significantly involved with the management of the NCAA when he was elected to a five-year term on the management council of the organization. This term from 1994 to 1998 spans the time of the reorganization of the NCAA. He was particularly involved with issues of "initial eligibility" for incoming freshmen and the area of legislation that required students to maintain progress towards their degrees to remain eligible for intercollegiate athletics. Indeed, it is unusual for two representatives from the same institution to serve on

these management groups at the same time. They both have made very positive impressions on officials in intercollegiate sports at the national level and continue to be respected leaders in this area.

A roll call of Bellarmine's outstanding athletes would be prohibitively long. There are, however, some names that can stand for this roll of honor. The athletic department sent out a mail questionnaire in the fall of

Baseball Coach '70 - '73 Nick Weber

1968 asking long-time Bellarmine basketball fans to name the best five players as of that date. The results: Phil Popp, Al Stevenson, Jim Schurfranz, Rudy Montgomery and Tom Hugenberg. Others picked at random—all in basketball: Buddy Cox, Don Kalmey, Mike Clark, Bobby Todd (who earned the title "the Bellarmine Flash" because of his whirling dervish style of dribbling, passing and shooting), Floyd Smith, Dewey Minton, Chris Renfroe, Dwight Moore, Bruce Olliges, Tom Schurfranz, Steve Mercer. A Bellarmine All-Star was John MacLeod, who earned a total of ten letters—four in basketball, three in baseball and three

Tom Schurfranz

in track. He would become head basketball coach of the Oklahoma Sooners, the NBA's Phoenix Suns and Notre Dame.

Tennis stars include John Hurley, Andy Latkovski, Al Feige and Jimmy Miller. Golf standouts include Jerry Baker and Vance Kennedy. Track and cross-country stars include Larry Block, Michael Cowherd, Chris Clark, Larry Rechtin and Rick Miller. Dominique Latkovski was a standout in soccer. Bellarmine baseball greats include Jack Haury, Dewey Minton and Johnny Herbert. In August of 1956, Herbert was signed by the Washington Senators. He had pitched Bellarmine to two cochampionships in the KIAC, with a two-season record of 19-2.

One of the most important aspects of Bellarmine's athletic program is its solid tradition of student-athletes, young men and women who excel in the classroom as well as on the playing field. From the beginning of the college, athletics has been subordinated to academics. A letter writer to *The Record* in July of 1956, Raymond F. Hart, complimented the college for keeping academics foremost: "Some of our Catholic colleges are showing a high sense of leadership and responsibility in combatting the athletic overemphasis evil. Our own Bellarmine has turned down outstanding athletes who have applied but could not make the grade scholastically, but who have been welcomed at 'athletic colleges' as valuable additions to their teams."

During the 1954-55 academic year, with some 14 varsity players on full athletic scholarships, the school was poised for what some fans hoped was basketball glory. Despite the prospects, however, Fr. Henry B. Schuhmann, college athletic director, told a reporter for *The Courier-Journal* that the college would not compromise its academic standards to build its sports program. "You know, there's a lot of chicanery in collegiate sports," he said, "but we'll have none of it. We could go out and buy a team right now, but we haven't chiseled yet and we never will. The education of the athlete must come first." And so it has. Indeed,

as Jack Kampschaefer has pointed out, "Our student athletes' grade point averages are similar to non-athletes, and their graduation rate is better."

In 1982 Jim Spalding wrote an "athletic profile" of Bellarmine, which stated that the sports program was in line with the college philosophy of developing the whole person. "Bellarmine College has attempted through the years to develop a program of athletics which will complement the academic program of the college, equating quality athletics with quality academics," he wrote, "while also providing opportunities for the development of student qualities of leadership, cooperation and fair play."

The student-athlete has, indeed, been the ideal of the athletic program; and Bellarmine has an enviable record of graduating its athletes. A report compiled in 1978 showed that from 1950 through 1977, 92 per cent of Bellarmine's athletes had completed their degrees. "Bellarmine Shows the Non-Seamy Side of Athletics" read a headline in *The Louisville Times* in May of 1980 for a profile of Coach Joe Reibel. According to the article, for the coach "the ultimate pay-off comes off the floor," citing the fact that in 30 years 93 per cent of Bellarmine's players who completed their eligibility had graduated. The headline for a January 1983 column in *The Courier-Journal* by Billy Reed boasted that "Bellarmine could Teach NCAA a Lesson in Academics." In 1983 the college made the policy plain and simple: "While the College feels that athletics are an important facet in the development of a total education program, no concession of any kind in regard to academic standards will be made in favor of a student participating in athletics or any other extracurricular activity."

Good examples of the scholar-athlete are easy to find. Dewey Minton, an accounting student, attended Bellarmine on a basketball and an academic scholarship. Minton and Floyd Smith are also good examples of the "little man" who could play at Bellarmine and make an athletic reputation. In January of 1977 *Courier-Journal* sports editor Dave Kindred wrote: "All those who believe basketball ought to be a little man's game should adopt Bellarmine College of Louisville as their surrogate hero. More precisely, they should pay attention to what Floyd Smith and Dewey Minton do." Minton at 5 feet, 10 inches and Smith at 6 feet were a marvel to watch, he said, "so quick they catch their own passes." Both men said attending Bellarmine was one of the best decisions they ever made, despite the fact that on campus they were both minorities. Smith was black and Minton was a Baptist. In the spring of 1977, just before his graduation, Minton told a *Concord* reporter, "I've enjoyed every minute of the time I've spent at Bellarmine."

Of course, there were modest downsides to Bellarmine's athletic profile. In the mid-'50s athletic director Eddie Weber noted that many prospective athletic recruits overestimated their ability to play for Bellarmine. "Every substitute on his school's baseball team," he said, "gets ideas after he is sent in to bat in the ninth inning with the bases loaded and strikes out. He considers this showing qualifies him for an athletic scholarship." Another downside—at least to the athletic program—was the inability of some athletes to maintain Bellarmine's academic standards. Take art major Ron Belton, the New York native who averaged almost 20 points and more than 12 rebounds per game during the 1968-69 season. He was a serious student and did well until his senior year, when he became academically ineligible. He said matter-of-factly: "A school like Bellarmine expects you to give 100 per cent on the court and then be a good student and give 100 per cent in class." And sometimes a fellow simply ran out of energy. More typically, however, was a student like freshman guard Mike Purdy who said, "I wanted a good education while playing ball." That's what Bellarmine always tried to offer its athletes.

The Bellarmine athletic program has been remarkably free of accidents and injuries. Two notable tragic events—both occurring off campus—are nonetheless a part of its history. Tragedy struck Bellarmine alumnus Rudy Montgomery, '60, in

September 1962, when he died of injuries suffered in a car accident while in military training at Ft. Ord,

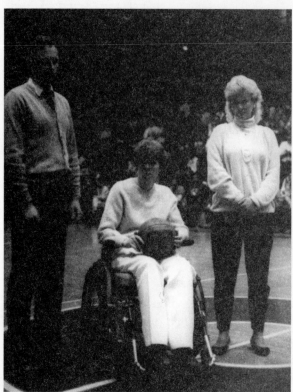

Charlie Just, Lois Taurman and Roxanne Cox.

California. Montgomery had been a player at Louisville Central and as a star athlete at Bellarmine had held almost every record in the book—most total points, most rebounds, more free throws and most field goals over his four-year career.

Another of Bellarmine's sports heroes, Lois Taurman, was severely injured on October 12, 1984, when an accident paralyzed her permanently. While she was cleaning gutters at the home of the Eugene Petriks on Dundee Road, her ladder slipped and she fell backwards, cracking the base of her neck against a railing, then tumbling down a stairwell, where she almost drowned before she was discovered by Helen Petrik some 90 minutes later. She was earning money to pay her expenses as a nursing student at Bellarmine. A year and a half earlier, she had graduated from Bellarmine as a biology major with honors and with the distinction of being the college's best all-around woman's athlete. She was a standout in three sports—softball, volleyball and especially basketball, scoring in four seasons a college record of 1,414 points. The good news is that she has responded well to physical therapy and in 1988 attended the '88 Olympics in Seoul, Korea, and competed in the wheelchair races.

In the October 13, 1953 *Courier-Journal,* sports editor Earl Ruby wrote that Bellarmine "has the makings of the most complete and commodious athletic plant in the South." Two natural bowls on campus, he said, would make a baseball diamond and a football field cost "a fraction of similar accommodations requiring steel underpinnings." Perhaps Ruby's vision was somewhat grandiose, but the college was already attending to some of its athletic needs. Under construction was a regulation A.A.U. cinder track patterned after Southern California's Olympic track. A football practice field would be placed within the track. At the other end of the grounds bordering Newburg Road, a baseball diamond was being built—plus all-weather tennis courts and an outdoor basketball court. These modest beginnings in athletic facilities were being supported principally by the Bellarmine Athletic Association and its some 300 members. The feast day of St. Robert Bellarmine, May 13, 1954, was marked by the dedication of the new athletic fields, featuring a baseball game and track meet with the University of Louisville and a tennis match with Georgetown College. Throwing out the first baseball was Edward J. Doherty, president of the American Association. It was a proud day for Bellarmine's fledgling athletic program and facilities. Bellarmine beat Louisville in baseball 11-4 and won the tennis match with Georgetown, while losing in track by one point.

For a decade, however, the big deficiency in the athletics program was the lack of a gym. Basketball games were routinely and inconveniently played at such local high-school gyms as Male. That was remedied on December 6, 1960, with the dedication of the new fieldhouse, later to be named Knights Hall, when the Knights under Alex Groza played the Louisville Cardinals under Peck Hickman. Since then, other athletic spaces and facilities have been added and improved, from the campus golf course to the indoor tennis center. In the final years of the 20th century, Bellarmine students can find facilities on campus adequate for most sports.

Bellarmine's athletic progam has been handicapped by limited funds available from the college. On the other hand, the program has been wonderfully supported by a legion of fans, volunteers and financial backers. A new college with no alumni has to start from scratch to build fan support and financial support for all its programs, including athletics. In mid-November of 1949, Fr. Horrigan told a *Courier-Journal* reporter that he hoped for immediate support from "synthetic alumni," that is, boosters who would support an athletic program for a new college without official alumni.

The boosters began to imagine incredible scenarios. "All they have to do is hire Paulie Miller from Flaget as coach," said one. "Let him bring all the seniors on his Flaget High team this year into Bellarmine's freshman class next fall. He'll have the nucleus of a good freshman football team right away. By the time the boys are seniors, Bellarmine would be ready to play the top competition in intercollegiate football." Another booster suggested hiring former St. Xavier coach Bob Schuhmann. "In a couple of years," he said, "you'd be seeing Notre Dame playing Bellarmine at the Jefferson County Armory in basketball." *The Courier-Journal* commented, "The development of Bellarmine athletically should be interesting to follow." As, indeed, it was. In early January 1950, more than eight months before the first classes were held, Fr. Horrigan announced that the school had received its first contribution, a check for $500 from Maloney-Davidson for the athletic fund.

Despite the generous support of many individuals and businesses, however, the athletic program has survived on a meager budget. The program lost money almost every year, beginning with $3,700 in 1954 and rising to $33,000 by 1972. In the early '70s, during a severe budget and enrollment crunch, there was debate over dropping intercollegiate athletics altogether. A report prepared by the faculty athletic committee in January of 1973, however, noted that "if intercollegiate sports were to be dropped, the savings would be negligible in comparison with losses that would be associated with our programs, publicity, a rallying point for students, spirit, public image, recruitment, etc. It is very difficult to measure these things as to dollars and cents." And so, with the help of various fund-raising groups and activities, the program has managed to survive.

Chronic low attendance at sporting events has further clouded the financial picture. Beginning in the early '50s *The Concord* has complained about a lack of school spirit as evidenced by empty seats at sporting contests. Coaches Spalding and Reibel had trouble filling the 3,000 seats in Knights Hall for basketball games, even in championship years. During the 1977 season, with a record of 12-3, the gym was seldom more than half-full. Reibel said he was at a loss to explain the lack of fans. Nonetheless, he said, he liked his program and his players. "They're good students, they're likable, they're good athletes and they're fun to be around."

Fortunately, the college has always had a hard-core following of faithful fans. In the fall of 1952, the Bellarmine College Athletic Association was organized, with Fred J. Karem as president, John E. Plamp, Jr. as secretary-treasurer and Edward L. Mackey as vice president. Some 200 people quickly joined the group, which held its organizational meeting on December 10, with addresses by Fr. Raymond J. Treece, vice president; Fr. John D. Davis, faculty athletic director; and Edward H. Weber, athletic director. Membership in the association was open to men and women for $10 a year. The membership fees were used to help pay expenses of running the varsity and intramural

sports program and to help build sports facilities. Members received a season pass to the home basketball games. The first Father-Son Banquet was held at St. Francis of Assisi in November of 1953, with Tom Blackburn, coach of the University of Dayton Fliers, as speaker to more than 300 Bellarmine boosters.

Numerous fund-raising activities have been held from the '50s down to the present. By the mid-'70s fund raisers included raffles, weightlifting tournaments, the leasing of Knights Hall and playing fields, benefit concerts and benefit nights. At Knights Fun Night at Louisville Downs, which began in 1970, owner Bill King donated a percentage of money wagered, which during the 1977 event made $9,000 for the program. One of the most successful Fun Nights featured a special celebrity sulky race with Mayor Harvey Sloane, Jefferson County Judge Todd Hollenbach, President Petrik and Coach Reibel. The race was easily won by Hollenbach. Petrik came in fourth.

The Bellarmine Athletic Boosters cosponsored several concerts on campus, including the popular singer and songwriter Jimmy Buffett, "The Amazing Kreskin" magic show and the Lettermen. They also sponsored an annual "Beat the Bishop Golf Tournament," in which golfers tried to beat Bishop Thomas J. McDonough, who took up golfing at 50. The success of these fund raisers finally meant that athletes wouldn't have to raise funds to support their own programs. For years, for example, baseball players had to raise money to pay for their road trips.

Perhaps the most stable source of outside support has come from Friday Night Bingo, which started in February of 1976 and was soon averaging 600 people a week and has netted over $3 million to the college in its first 22 years. Unfortunately, some of that money was lost in August of 1984, when thieves broke into the safe in Knights Hall and stole more than $10,000, most of it money from the weekly bingo receipts. The Bellarmine Booster Bingo was still going strong in October of 1997, when a flyer advertised the "Octoberfest Special," with a coverall minimum of $600 and dinners at 5 p.m. in the lobby of Knights Hall. The Boosters also ran an October auction and raffle. Auction items included tickets to the Kentucky Oaks, a Florida vacation and an Oxmoor gift certificate.

Other fund raisers included sports camps and clinics held on campus. In the summer of 1971, the Adolph Rupp and Dan Issel Basketball Camp for boys 8 to 16 was held in Knights Hall. Consisting of seven one-week sessions, the camp featured an exhibition game with Issel, Bud Olsen and Rick Bolus. In August of that year and succeeding ones Joe Reibel's weeklong Bellarmine Pro Basketball Clinic was held on campus. In the summer of 1974, the Kentucky Colonels-Bellarmine College Basketball Camp for boys 8 to 18 was led by Jim Spalding and Joe Reibel, assisted by Colonels stars like Artis Gilmore and Louis Dampier. Summer clinics were also held in basketball and soccer for girls. In June of 1975, following his first year as

Basketball Clinic in Knights Hall.

coach of the baseball team, Lou Snipp began a series of summer clinics. In January of 1985, Pete Rose, who was then player-manager for the Cincinnati Reds, conducted a baseball clinic in Knights Hall.

Whether Bellarmine's teams at home or on the road were winning or losing, they usually got good press coverage, with headlines like "Bellarmine Shows Its Class on Road," "Bellarmine Was a Winner While Losing" or "Bellarmine Lands NCAA Tourney Berth." When the baseball club lost to the Louisville Redbirds

in an exhibition game, a headline read, "Bellarmine Makes Redbirds Take Note Before Losing 3-1." People who never attended a Bellarmine game were made aware of the college through television and press reports. Even in defeat the teams were often applauded for their sportsmanship. When Bellarmine lost in the Great Lakes Regional of the NCAA Division II basketball tournament in March of 1982, sportswriter Bill Doolittle wrote: "They fought down to the last second. And if the Great Scorekeeper in the Sky really does take note of how you play the game, then Bellarmine walked away from this a winner."

Indeed, Bellarmine's athletic program has done well with its resources. There are still, however, people who need instructing. The April 1977 issue of *Louisville Today* suggested in an April Fool's article that if the University of Kentucky should drop out of the SEC, it could always drop down and schedule independent Kentucky colleges like Bellarmine. Upon reading the implied put-down, Nanette Schuhmann, director of sports information at Bellarmine, shot off a letter reminding the magazine that Bellarmine College receives no tax money for its sports program and, in fact, has competed rather well with UK—on several fronts—defeating Kentucky in soccer and splitting a double-header in baseball.

In the beginning of the last decade of the 20th century the athletic program continued to thrive under Jim Spalding and Joe Reibel, then more recently under Jay Gardiner as athletic director and Bob Valvano as men's basketball coach. To ensure academic success among student athletes, academic guidelines and regulations are published in the *Student Athlete Handbook*. Furthermore, academic and athletic schedules are better coordinated, and coaches continue to keep tabs on an athlete's class attendance and performance. Women's sports have been especially successful. In 1993-94, for example, the women's basketball team compiled a 25-6 record and finished in the NCAA Division II Final Four. The women roundballers under Coach Charlie Just completed a

24-4 season in 1995, playing a schedule on a level with the men's team.

In January of 1998, the college announced that Just would replace Valvano, who planned to resign after his fourth season at Bellarmine. Valvano, a popular speaker and media personality in Louisville, left a 45-50 record. Just, a graduate of St. Xavier High School and Ohio Northern, had coached the Bellarmine women to a 292-100 record in 14 seasons. Just's move from a 21-year career of coaching women's teams to the men's is almost unprecedented, but athletic director David O'Toole said it was not a matter of Just moving up the ladder. Just agreed. "I don't consider this a promotion," he said. "I consider it a job change." After a lengthy career as a professor of mathematics at Bellarmine, O'Toole retired in December of 1997, then accepted the position of acting athletic director for the spring of 1998 and was later appointed to the position full time.

In the solid tradition of responsible reporting and commentary, *Concord* sports editor Matt Rich kept students informed of the sports scene in 1997-98. At the end of the basketball season, the best one since 1991-92, Rich predicted that the cagers would "continue to surge to the top of the GLVC standings." It was a year in which the intercollegiate sports program included competitive teams in field hockey, men and women's soccer, volleyball, men and women's cross-country, men and women's golf and women's tennis. Moreover, women were finally achieving parity with the men.

Meanwhile, with little more than a year to go, Bellarmine's coaches, players and fans awaited the coming of the new century and its opportunities. The college could look back on an honorable athletic history. Bellarmine's academic standards, good sportsmanship and commitment to developing a fully educated student have made the athletic program a model for other colleges. Despite ups and downs for almost 50 years, the sports program, both intercollegiate and intramural, has provided Bellarmine College with a showcase to the community, a rallying point for school pride and a chance for players and fans alike to learn the hard lessons of sportsmanship, winning and losing.

Bellarmine's Championship Par 3 Course.

Bellarmine's Learning Tree:
Courses, Concentrations and Curricula—Inside and Outside the Changing Classroom

In ancient Greece about all a novice scholar needed for learning was a willing teacher, a place to meet and a convenient roof in case of rain. Bellarmine has provided a bit more structure for its students. A complex society also requires that educational institutions have written rules and standards that must be observed and certifications that must be obtained. The modern educational mix includes a campus with approriately furnished buildings, a faculty to instruct, an administration to supervise and a program to implement. Bellarmine's program of instruction has always been based on a broad core of liberal arts and sciences, with concentrations that allow preparation in a number of professional or graduate school areas. The instructional program has been flexible in curriculum as well as in location. While observing broad accreditation standards, the college has been able to shape a program that is uniquely Bellarmine's.

By the fall of 1955, the college was in the middle of its first accreditation process. To be accredited by the Southern Association of Colleges and Secondary Schools, the college had to graduate two classes, conduct a self-study, submit a written report, its administrators had to be interviewed and an

> The President and the Faculty
> of
> Bellarmine College
> Louisville, Kentucky
> announce the
> accreditation of the College
> by the
> Southern Association of
> Colleges and Secondary Schools
> December, 1956

accreditation committee had to visit the campus. Indeed, Bellarmine was admitted into the society of reputable educational institutions in minimum time and received the seal of approval on December 1, 1956. Bellarmine's faculty, facilities and curriculum had passed all the standards of the Southern Association with flying colors. At that time Bellarmine began to enjoy the privileges of other fully accredited colleges and universities, including the easy transfer of credits and eligibility of grants from many private foundations.

Soon college units were being recognized for their superior programs and given special certification by professional organizations. In the fall of 1963, the chemistry department received the seal of approval of the American Chemical Society, becoming the only Kentucky college without a graduate school to win such recognition. As the years passed other programs were added and received accreditation. One of the most recently approved programs was nursing, which was accredited by the National League of Nursing. In 1995 the teacher education program received national accreditation for its undergraduate and graduate programs from the National Council for the Accreditation of Teachers of Education (NCATE).

Rev. Quinton Roohr, Asst. Professor of Physics and Mathematics.

Periodic self-studies, usually at ten-year intervals, have continued to affirm Bellarmine's quality programs, facilities and faculty. But while exulting with the rest of the college community in its newly earned status, *The Concord* added an editorial caveat in December of 1956: "Accreditation is not an end. It is, in a very real way, only a beginning." And so it is, as a look at Bellarmine's academic programs will show.

Before a college can become anything, it has to be based on explicit aims and missions.

In a series of articles published in *The Record* in May and June of 1950, Fr. Horrigan stated clearly many of the aims and purposes of new colleges such as Bellarmine College. He discussed "the new

responsibilities of American colleges," that is, the extended scope of the contemporary college that goes beyond its traditional mission. More colleges, he noted, are being located in urban centers and are serving additional, nontraditional groups of people and thus do not "limit their interests to young men and women of conventional college age." He added, "It has become very evident that people do not lose their capacity for, nor need of, systematic education just because they have passed their early twenties." Because such people desire continued intellectual development, he said, they want a college degree or are "simply seeking cultural and vocational advantages."

Furthermore, he continued, noncredit courses will need to be developed for people with no interest in obtaining degrees. Another aim for Bellarmine would be to establish "a labor school," with the purpose of offering "guidance and training in the principles of sound economics viewed in the light of Catholic social philosophy." Finally, acclaiming Bellarmine's church ties, he pledged that the college will "offer valuable assistance to the various parishes in carrying out plans for marriage and pre-marriage courses, and inquiry classes in the teachings of the Church."

A large ad in the April 8, 1950 *Record* announced day and evening classes in the following areas of instruction: English, languages, psychology, history, social sciences, philosophy, biology, chemistry, mathematics, journalism, teacher training, speech and drama, accounting, economics and business administration as well as pre-legal, pre-dental and pre-medical courses. It was a class list that asserted the primacy of the liberal arts and sciences and the availability of professional and vocational courses. It was a pattern of classes that would hold true for almost 50 years and through many years of educational fads and curricular experimentation. It was a curriculum with a core requirement that has usually been 60 hours or more. In 1997, adjusting to new educational and market realities, the faculty, President and the Board of Trustees adopted a revised core curriculum, providing for a core of 49 hours.

With the opening of the fourth year of classes on September 20, 1954, the outlook was bright. Enrollment was up some 30 per cent. Campus facilities had doubled since the previous year with the opening of the new administration building. The new programs included a pre-engineering curriculum in connection with the University of Detroit. The arrangement allowed a student to receive an A.B. degree from Bellarmine after four years and a B.S. degree from Detroit at the end of the fifth year. A new three-year program led to certificates in business administration and accounting in the evening school, which was open

to both men and women in the business world. For the first time women could earn a degree from Bellarmine. Indeed, the contours of Bellarmine's academic program have changed through the years. Majors (or concentrations) have been added, dropped and sometimes added again, as student demographics and economic trends dictated.

The college has taken measures to meet the special needs of its students. For example, because most of Bellarmine's early students came from families whose members were not college-educated, the college decided in the fall of 1961 to require all new students to take an orientation program which would help explain to these first-generation college students what they should get out of college and a liberal arts education. Thus business students would understand better why they should take art and music, and English majors would lower their complaints about studying chemistry and biology.

The college has also attempted to stay up-to-date with Church policies and directives. In April of 1967, in a supplement to the college's 10-year report to the Southern Association of Colleges and Schools, Fr. Horrigan anticipated the impact of Vatican II on Catholic schools of higher education: "The Catholic college and university of tomorrow must reflect fully the spirit of Vatican II in respect to the many things the Council had to say about openness, freedom, ecumenism, renewal, catholicity of charity and responsibility, the nature of the Church, the role of the laity, and dialogue between the Church and the modern world." The recommendations of Vatican II have truly influenced the direction of Bellarmine's programs, from curriculum to seminars to special speakers.

Other academic changes in programs and policies have been practical and sometimes even mundane. A Pass-Fail policy was begun in the summer of 1969 to encourage students to take courses outside their concentrations. The policy allowed juniors and seniors to take any nonrequired course without a letter grade.

BELLARMINE COLLEGE

LOUISVILLE, KENTUCKY

Catalogue for 1950 - 1951

A COLLEGE OF LIBERAL ARTS AND SCIENCES

For some two decades physical education was a two-year noncredit requirement but was dropped in the early '70s. In the fall of 1967, St. Thomas Seminary became a division of Bellarmine. By the fall of 1967 Bellarmine was beginning to offer a bachelor's degree in theology and appointed the first two non-Catholics to the theology faculty, Dr. Herbert S. Waller, rabbi of Temple Adath Israel, and Dr. Victor L. Priebe, pastor of Buechel Park Baptist Church. During the 1968 merger with Ursuline the free period was eliminated, then restored in the spring of 1971. In the fall of 1972, the faculty began giving out C+ grades, which designated a point halfway between a B and a C.

The cut system has undergone a number of changes. In the beginning only three cuts (or unexcused absences) were allowed. Then the number was increased to three weeks of cuts. Finally, in the spring of 1972 the institutional policy on a cut system was done away with completely, leaving it up to faculty members to determine their own.

The foreign languages program has gone through a number of ups and downs. The initial two-year requirement in foreign languages was dropped in the early '70s, and by the fall of 1973, only Professor Leonard Latkovski remained as a part-time professor in languages. Finally recognizing the critical need for bilingual professionals in the global village, the college re-established a department in foreign languages in 1995 with Professor Gabriele Bosley as director.

Other programs have also been added and dropped. Headed by Lucy A. Erwin, a curriculum in nursing leading to a bachelor's degree was begun in the fall of 1977. It allowed registered nurses to earn degrees while working full-time. The program was housed in the division of science and mathematics until spring 1982, when the Allan and Donna Lansing School of Nursing and Health Sciences was formed. Trustee and former chairman of the Board of Trustees, Dr. Allan Lansing is a noted heart surgeon who, with his wife Donna, has been a generous supporter of Bellarmine's nursing program. The nursing curriculum has undergone many changes, including the addition of a master's program. Sue Hockenberger Davis, dean of the Lansing School of Nursing, describes the Bellarmine program as dynamic, with a constantly changing structure and curriculum. The Nursing Outreach Program, designed to offer higher degree education to underserved areas of the state, she says, was begun in response to the changing needs. Program sites were opened and closed all over Kentucky, from Hazard to Paducah. A related program was medical technology, which ended its short-lived stay on campus in 1983 because of the shrinking job market for graduates.

Degrees in history, mathematics, English, chemistry and other such traditional subject fields have been offered throughout Bellarmine history. But many less main-line disciplines have had their ups and downs. The music program, for example, has seen good times and lean times. With a faculty that included such jazz master professors and performers as Gus Coin and Don Murray, Bellarmine became one of the first colleges in 1976 to offer a degree in jazz. In the fall of 1977, a new program in education, Learning and Behavior Disorders, was begun under the direction of Dr. Nancy Howard. During President Petrik's tenure programs were opened in health services administration and computer engineering as well as pre-professional studies in law, pharmacy and veterinary medicine. A short-lived theater program

begun in the fall of 1989 under the direction of Andrew Vorder Bruegge was phased out in the '90s because of cost and limited facilities. It was recently redesigned under the leadership of Mark Sawyer-Dailey and is again a vibrant part of the college scene.

For the first 25 years Bellarmine College had no graduate programs. Robert Preston, academic dean under Fr. Horrigan, was adamantly opposed to any and all graduate work. He believed that graduate courses would dilute the liberal arts character of the college and siphon off funds. Fortunately, his fears have proved largely unfounded, as the college has been able to retain its primary liberal arts identity while adding graduate programs.

The first graduate degree offered by Bellarmine was the Master of Business Administration, begun in 1975, during the silver anniversary of the college, and directed by Tom Wilkerson as a two-year program with evening and Saturday classes. In 1981 the Master of Education was added with an emphasis in special education. In 1984 the Master of Science in Nursing was begun with 40 students as part of a restructuring of the nursing curriculum that included the phasing out of

Dr. Ann Kleine-Kracht Weeks

the two-year Associate Degree in nursing. According to Dr. Ann Kleine-Kracht, former dean of the Lansing School of Nursing, it was hoped that new state licensing standards would require that all new nurses hold at least a bachelor's degree. Dr. Susan Hockenberger Davis, however, reports that the change in state law never occurred. At the same time Bellarmine announced a cooperative nursing program with St. Catharine College in Springfield. In 1986 a Master of Social

Administration was begun. A Master of Arts in Liberal Studies was added in the fall of 1992 and closed some seven years later.

With four schools in metro Louisville—University of Louisville, Indiana University Southeast, Webster University and Bellarmine—offering MBA programs by 1996, in July of that year Ed Popper, dean of the W. Fielding Rubel School of Business, announced that his faculty had redesigned the degee at Bellarmine. The new degree, he said, would be more diverse, high-tech, international, convenient and attractive to a new kind of MBA student. Under the new set-up, the course tuition would include a laptop computer and business travel abroad. In the summer of 1996 a class traveled to Perm, Russia. An earlier MBA program targeting African Americans had attracted 25 new students and increased minority participation from 3 per cent to 15 per cent.

Bellarmine's curriculum has usually been flexible enough to respond quickly to current needs and opportunities. Special midyear freshman classes were formed for returning Korean War veterans in late January of 1953. One-time courses designed to exploit an historical anniversary or a current event have frequently been taught. An obvious example is "Literature of the American Revolution," which was offered by the English department in the spring of 1976. Permanent flexible content courses have also been taught in many departments under such designations as "Special Studies" or "Independent Studies." Noncredit courses sometimes reflected such current fads as yoga and speed reading in the early 1970s.

In the late '60s and early '70s Bellarmine began offering courses in black history, African art and civil rights. In January of 1970, the college offered a new

BELLARMINE
COLLEGE

OFFICES OF ADULT SERVICES

ANNOUNCES

The
Bellarmine
FLEX PLAN
FLEXIBLE
LEARNING,
EDUCATIONAL
EXCELLENCE

13-week course called "Black Experience: History and Culture," using funds from a $13,000 federal grant for minority studies development. Courses in ecology were added in the '70s.

Flexibility in the college curriculum is also evident in a new program begun in the fall of 1988 called FLEX, Flexible Learning Educational Excellence, in which full-credit, accelerated courses could be completed in seven weeks, or about half the traditional time.

There has also been a tradition of curriculum and teaching experimentation from the beginning. Bellarmine was a pioneer in 1958 with the use of foreign language labs to supplement the traditional lectures. Using wire recorders and headsets, students could hear and speak the language they were learning. The new aural-oral approach was the technique used in an eight-week language institute at Bellarmine in the summer of 1959.

Bellarmine's size and decision-making speed have allowed the college to participate in many significant experiments in educational innovations. In the fall of 1959, for example, Bellarmine was among the first of some 200 colleges to participate in a new testing program for college-bound high school seniors. Developed at the University of Iowa, the new American College Testing Program (ACT) offered a number of advantages—such as lower cost and expanded areas—over the older College Entrance Examination Board, usually called "College Boards."

Curriculum Flexibility...

The academic program has also been much affected by technology and new delivery systems. In the fall of 1959, students at Bellarmine, Ursuline and Nazareth could earn chemistry credits for participating in a national television program called "Continental Classroom," which was broadcast locally at 6:30 each weekday morning over WAVE-TV. By January of 1981, students could earn college credit for television courses through Metroversity in such areas as writing, business, astronomy and humanities.

Bellarmine's response to Sputnik and to the computer revolution is worthy of praise. Following the launching of the first earth satellite by Soviet Russia in 1957, which signaled the Age of Sputnik, Fr. Horrigan issued a "Special Report of the President," a 21-page monograph which updated and enlarged the college's founding principles. He wrote: "The thing we call our way of life has its roots in profound scientific, cultural, philosophical and religious truths. To preserve and communicate these truths is the highest task of a college such as Bellarmine." One Bellarmine response to Sputnik was the opening of a full program of physics in the fall of 1958.

Bellarmine was one of the first colleges in the area to welcome computers and computer instruction. An early course in computers was offered as an adult education class in the fall of 1963. It was called "Electronic Computers" and taught by Don Erwin, a sales engineer in the computer department of the General Electric Company. By the fall of 1964, Bellarmine was offering series of courses on the use of computers in the evening division. It was the first college program in Kentucky leading to a certificate in data processing. The following year the four-year curriculum of the accounting department was modified to include a similar certificate for day school students. Computer courses continued to be added throughout the '70s, and in the fall of 1975 the Center for Community Education was holding workshops on "The Computer Revolution." In the fall of 1981, a new bachelor's degree in computer science was created, and the math department became the department of mathematics and computer science, headed by David O'Toole. The new degree allowed an emphasis in either data processing or in mathematics. During the decade of the '80s the campus became computerized, and by 1997 faculty members had their own office computers

and e-mail addresses. In 1974 the fully staffed Data Center, headed by Sam Rosenberg and, later, Roy A. Stansbury became a campus fixture.

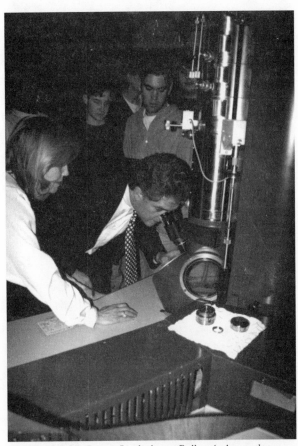

Dr. Joseph J. McGowan, Jr. checks out Bellarmine's new electron microscope.

Advanced information technology was an integral part of the design for the W. L. Lyons Brown Library when it opened in January of 1997. The library included over 70 personal computers for student use throughout the library, over 400 data drops connected to the campus network for laptop users, a laboratory for technology instruction and two multimedia classrooms that allow professors to access CD ROMs, satellite transmissions, video tapes and the Internet in the classroom. They have proved so popular that eight new multimedia classrooms have been added in Horrigan, Pasteur and Miles halls.

During all the additions and subtractions and changes brought by scientific and cultural progress, Bellarmine's core requirements—at least until recently—have remained fairly constant. The academic philosophy underpinning general education requirements were spelled out in the first catalogue: "No course of study at Bellarmine College will be merely vocational in the narrow sense of that term. Every student, regardless of his choice of a field for concentration, will receive a complete course in Scholastic philosophy and a solid grounding in the humanities and social sciences."

In 1957 Fr. Horrigan was obviously satisfied with how the Bellarmine plan was working. In a speech he made at an education workshop conducted by the Archdiocese of St. Louis in September, he elaborated on Bellarmine's philosophy of higher education: "Democracy is incompatible with an aristocratic system of hereditary political privilege. It is not incompatible with an aristocracy of intelligence and virtue. The requirements of true democracy are satisfied by providing each individual with the opportunity of the fullest development of his native powers and aspiration. It requires equal but not identical opportunities." Furthermore, he said: "One of the wildest superstitions fostered by certain philosophers of education during recent generations has been that uncontrolled electivism is a necessary application of democratic principles. Democracy does not require that a talented adolescent must be left free to neglect those subjects of studies without which the achievement of intellectual excellence becomes a practical impossibility." Thus, in the Bellarmine core requirements as well as the parameters set for the courses of concentration may be seen a kind of "controlled electivism"—that is, student choices within limits set by more experienced faculty. Call it paternalism, if you will, but it has worked for most of Bellarmine's history.

Almost from the beginning there were occasional student and faculty voices complaining about a "tilting"

of instruction toward the humanities and the arts. A *Concord* editorial in November of 1962 expressed the views of some students in business, accounting and the sciences. "The program of concentration offers the student an opportunity to train in a field of his choice while integrating these courses with those designed to round out his entire intellect. However, several of the integrating courses require more specialization than the actual concentration field. Our curriculum stresses more of the arts than would seem necessary, and in so doing, renders it difficult to gain full knowledge in a student's chosen field." The writer concludes that "Bellarmine, then, is a liberal arts college, specializing in the arts." One of the ironies of this perceived imbalance, as campus wags pointed out, was that the science building, Pasteur Hall, was the first building on campus.

Students protest the curriculum changes at the W. L. Lyons Brown Library dedication.

Although perhaps overstated, *The Concord* had made a valid point. Take the sacrosanct fields of philosophy and theology. In the beginning all students were required to take a total of 18 hours in philosophy, and all Catholics—which was almost every student— were required to take a two-hour religion course each semester they were enrolled. Members of the Pioneer Class, for example, were required to take, in addition to courses for their concentrations, eight courses in theology, seven in philosophy and psychology, four in

English, four in a foreign language, four in history, including two in American history, and two courses in either mathematics or natural science.

Bellarmine educators were not, however, completely deaf to criticism or to changing academic standards. But during the campus crisis years of the late '60s and early '70s, when many schools were watering down their curricula, Bellarmine held fast to its large core curriculum of arts and sciences for all students. Modifications of the original design have been made through the years. In his 1961 President's report Fr. Horrigan affirmed the original intentions of the school as it opened in 1950, maintaining heavy requirements in theology, philosophy, literature, history, natural sciences and social sciences. He did, however, admit the need to adjust to the realities of the marketplace and announced that the foreign language requirement for students in education and engineering was being dropped, though retained for all other programs.

The college's first large concession to the prevailing *zeitgeist* was to loosen up the core requirements a bit more in September of 1970. Under the leadership of Dean Robert Preston, and after considerable study, discussion and debate by the curriculum review committee, the college dropped the foreign language requirement, reducing the number of required core hours from 72 to 60, and allowed students to concentrate in broad areas like the humanities or natural sciences instead of specific disciplines like biology or English. A Bachelor of Science degree for the evening division was also established, and theology and philosophy requirements were reduced to nine hours each. As late as the '80s, however, alumnus and college administrator Robert

Dr. Doris A. Tegart

Pfaadt could say that the core curriculum had changed little since he was a student in the late 50s and early '60s.

In the fall of 1972, the curriculum review committee's recommendation for reorganizing the academic disciplines took effect. The departmental organization of 17 academic areas was replaced by the divisions of humanities, social sciences and natural sciences. (This reorganization was actually a return to the early '50s, when departments had been grouped into five divisions: the divisions of commerce, humanities, mathematics and natural sciences, philosophy and social sciences.) By the fall of 1984, the college curriculum was taught through three major

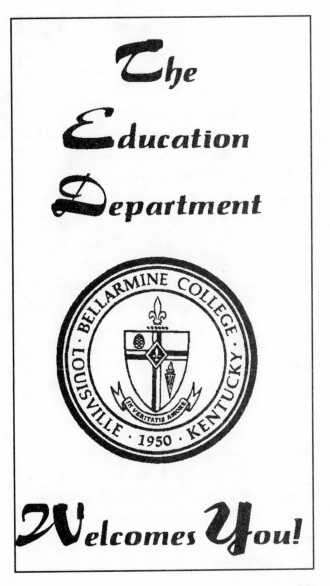

academic subdivisions: the College of Arts and Sciences, the W. Fielding Rubel School of Business and the Allan and Donna Lansing School of Nursing and Health Sciences. In 1998 the education department was made a separate academic unit headed by a dean, Dr. Doris Tegart.

Moreover, in efforts to adjust to changing educational theories and student expectations, the college has made many innovations in teaching techniques and academic organization. During Dr. David House's tenure as academic dean in the early '90s, he led the faculty in a new program called Collegium, funded by a $500,000 grant from the Knight Foundation, which developed interdisciplinary faculty seminars and team-taught courses. Lee Bash, a former member of the music faculty, reckons that one advantage to teaching at Bellarmine was that music is integrated with all the other disciplines. "It is something that I couldn't have done so well," he says, "at a larger university."

The college has made a number of efforts to assess its success in meeting its goals. In an effort to determine how well Bellarmine was meeting needs of the local community, in October of 1966 the college mailed 1,500 questionnaires to leaders of "opinion-making bodies" in the Louisville area—college officials, news media, business executives, religious and professional leaders. Numerous task forces and study groups have made reports recommending changes in the academic programs. One such paper was "The Colorado Report," which was composed by Bellarmine representatives at the 1975 Danforth Foundation Workshop. It contained a college statement of purpose and suggestions for revising the curriculum. In the fall of 1982, the college appointed Dr. William F. Eckstrom,

Dr. Joseph Horton

a former administrator at the University of Louisville, as a consultant for academic planning.

Which concentrations have been the most popular at Bellarmine? Predictably, as might be expected from a student body from families with few college graduates, the first students were overwhelmingly attracted to such practical, "money-making" fields as commerce and accounting. On October 1, 1950, two days before the college officially opened for classes, *The Courier-Journal* announced that "probably the main emphasis of the college will be on its business-administration department" and quoted Fr. Horrigan, who said its purpose will be "to train capable and virtuous men for the world of business, finance and industry." Indeed, 61 per cent of the first semester students enrolled in a business curriculum. The percentage would not stay that high. In fact, of the Pioneer Class of 1954, ten concentrated in business administration, eight in accounting, six in history, five in chemistry, four in English, four in psychology, two each in sociology and philosophy and one in economics. It was a ratio that would remain fairly constant throughout the history of the school.

Not only has the School of Business been fortunate in having willing, able and highly motivated students but it has also had good administration and a dedicated faculty. Leadership has been provided through the years by such people as the Rev. Henry B. Schuhmann, Stanley Zemelka, Richard Feltner, Joseph Horton and Edward Popper. An honor list of faculty in business and accounting would include Martha Oliver, David Collins,

Patricia M. Selvy, Ghouse Shareef, John Finnegan, Robert J. Fitzpatrick, Windell Bowles and Anna Jackey—all in accounting—and Frank O'Rourke, James Spalding, Walter Feibes, Bernard Thiemann, Norbert Elbert, Richard Dolin, John Byrd and Harold Koch—all in business administration. Members of the economics faculty have included Zemelka and Feltner as well as Brad Hobbs, John J. Bethune and Frank Slesnick.

Dr. Frank Slesnick

Dr. Norb Elbert

John J. Finnegan

Most of the students, an overwhelming majority of graduates, and most of the faculty are pleased and proud of the liberal arts curriculum required by the college. James "Bud" Spalding states it succinctly: "We don't narrowly educate students for business. Fewer than 40 of the required 130 hours for graduation are in business courses. We offer our students what I call a liberal arts core business major." John Oppelt, professor of mathematics, sometime academic dean and Acting President in the spring of 1999, states the liberal arts advantage somewhat differently: "At Bellarmine we try to educate the whole person, with all the professions addressing the whole person, whether accounting or nursing or teaching. A good business course is a good liberal arts course."

Timothy S. Swenson testifies to the quality of Bellarmine's accounting instruction. "Our accounting program," he says, "is still very good, but I was fortunate to be a student in the program when Bellarmine was dominant. For about 20 years, from the early '60s until the '80s, Bellarmine was the place to come if you wanted a good accounting degree. Now we have competition from the state schools." Nevertheless, Swenson says, Bellarmine's accounting program has the great advantage of being set in a liberal arts context. "I think I can illustrate the kind of accounting majors Bellarmine produces and how they are different from those in other schools. When accounting recruiters come to our campus, they say, 'At other schools we talk with accounting seniors about accounting practices almost exclusively. At Bellarmine we not only talk accounting but we talk about philosophy and business ethics and books and political science.'"

Dr. Edward T. L. Popper

While offering a professional dimension or an avenue to other professions, many of Bellarmine's departments serve as "service departments" for students in other fields. This is especially true in such main-line departments as English, history, philosophy and theology. Former professor of mathematics David O'Toole notes that Bellarmine didn't begin offering a major in math until the early '60s, after he joined Fr. Rusterholtz and James Leahy on the mathematics faculty. Nevertheless, he says, "we have been primarily a service department, with a core requirement and with service courses like statistics for students in business and accounting." Lee Bash, formerly of the music faculty, sees the arts as serving a double mission. "We serve Bellarmine and our discipline by instructing and producing professionals in music and art and by enriching life for all the students and faculty through choral programs, service courses in the core curriculum, as well as instruction in such popular courses as photography and instruction in piano and voice for the nonmusic professional. Overall, our vision is to have music and art leaven the entire campus loaf, whether a student is majoring in accounting or music or philosophy."

Bellarmine has accommodated thousands of students in summer school classes, seminars, workshops and in concentrated courses offered during a May short term. The three-week courses offered each May were begun in 1974 and have proved popular with students who want short, intensive instruction in one or two subjects. In addition to regular academic credit courses, the summer school has also offered review sessions for accountants interested in becoming certified public accountants, summer training programs for high-school students in chemistry, and college preparation courses for students with weak academic credentials. An unusual course was offered in 1961 when Dean Loftus approved a noncredit course during the summer session in cricket as a way of "training the whole man" and as a way to promote international understanding, he said, since cricket is played around the world. The instructor-coach was Major Raza-ul Haq (Bobby, to his friends), an insurance company employee and a veteran of the Pakistani Army.

Indeed, noncredit courses have always been popular in summer school. The list offered during the summer of 1996 included such traditional courses as creative writing, Spanish, rose-growing and photography. It also offered an introduction to the Internet, desktop publishing, spreadsheets, music software, a form of holistic slow-motion exercise called Chi Kung and an assertiveness workshop.

Programs of Concentration. . .

Now we come to the heart of Bellarmine's academic curriculum, the program of concentration, which differed from the conventional major-minor system of academic focus. In his 1961 President's report, Fr. Horrigan presented an overview of the

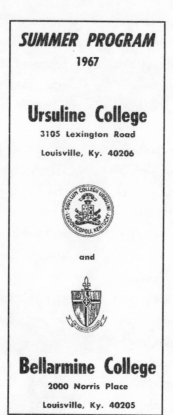

SUMMER PROGRAM
1967

Ursuline College
3105 Lexington Road
Louisville, Ky. 40206

and

Bellarmine College
2000 Norris Place
Louisville, Ky. 40205

college's first decade. He restated the intention of the college to be a liberal arts college offering a single degree, the bachelor of arts, and "to regard each course of study primarily as a means of imparting a liberal education rather than as a form of professional or career preparation; and to employ the plan of curricular organization known as the program of concentration, with its demanding requirements of seminar work and the final comprehensive examination."

Earlier, in an article in *The Record* of August 11, 1951, Fr. John Loftus, the college dean, explained that a concentration goes beyond the core liberal arts requirements to include "a rather thorough knowledge of some one particular field selected by the individual student." Such a system enables a student "to secure the maximum benefits of a liberal education through intensive study in the special field which he intends to make his lifework." A vital part of the program was the junior-senior reading lists and seminars which aided the student in integrating and comprehending a large body of knowledge from different fields.

In his President's report in 1961, Fr. Horrigan wrote that a concentration provided "maximum opportunity and incentive for the integration of the student's intellectual experiences and maximum encouragement of self-education." Under the concentration program (there were 11 in 1961, including accounting and business administration), students took from 24 to 36 credit hours in a single department and were required to demonstrate through a comprehensive examination the cross-relatedness of all their college courses and experiences. In Fr. Horrigan's words, it is not "improper to ask a student in the second semester a question about a topic he studied in the first semester" and it is not "unreasonable to expect him to apply what he has learned in philosophy and history courses to problems he encounters in business administration."

Before a student could be admitted to a concentration at the beginning of his third year, he had to demonstrate competence in written expression about what he had read, studied and discussed during his first two years. A typical sophomore comprehensive from 1960 was: "What are your reflections on the influence of the mass media of communication on the formation and influencing of minds and characters by these instrumentalities in the twentieth century?" Another question from the same year reminded sophomores that they were at the midpoint in their studies in a liberal arts college and were seeking permission to go into a concentration: "What is it about a liberal arts college and a liberal education that you find adding to mere professional competence as a preparation for your life in American society of the twentieth century?" Other sophomore comprehensive questions dealt with the role of Christianity in transforming society, the relationship of culture to career, conscience and civilization, the role of leisure in a well-lived life, the meaning and significance of *hamartia* or the tragic flaw as revealed in literature, philosophy and history.

During their junior and senior years students took required and elective courses in their chosen fields. In addition, they took a junior seminar to fill in gaps in their concentration and a senior seminar to relate their concentration to other disciplines.

Another feature of the liberal arts curriculum closely connected with the program of concentration was the senior comprehensive exam, which required students to pull together their knowledge and understanding from all the disciplines of the core curriculum as well as their own concentration. The exam had two parts, a question from the student's concentration and the dreaded "dean's question." The question for English concentrators in March of 1966 was: "How does the literature from the Middle Ages

to the present reflect the relationships and attitudes between man and God, between man and man?" A question from the history exam read: "Select any philosopher of history of the Age of Enlightenment and relate him to the French Revolution." The philosophy exam requested: "Comment on the statement, 'There is only one method of inquiry capable of producing reliable knowledge and it is the method of experimental science.'" Paul Davin, a member of the Pioneer Class, recorded his anxieties for *The Concord*. A concentrator in psychology, he was asked to write on such topics as the United Nations, the Popes, the Protestant Reformation, art and architecture. The exams, he said, were indeed comprehensive but fair. He also tried to put to rest the "misconception" among the freshmen and sophomores "that it's impossible to flunk." He added, ominously, "I say in all seriousness that it is not impossible." Needless to say, once a student had made it over Bellarmine's graduation hurdles, graduate and professional school must have seemed like level ground.

Special Programs...

A number of special programs have been developed at Bellarmine to accommodate special needs and requests. Here is a sampling. In the early '70s Bellarmine established the Religious Education Institute for Teachers, offering such courses as "Religious Formation of the Adolescent." In 1971 Bellarmine was the first college in the nation to offer a preschool training course in music for children 4 to 7 called the Bellarmine College-Yamaha Music School. Other special programs range from the Phoenix Program, an assistance plan for poorly prepared students, to the Small Business Development Center, established in the Rubel School of Business in the spring of 1983, with Deborra Clark Brand as its first director. The center provided counseling, training and research to small businesses and entrepreneurs. In early 1991 United Parcel Service relocated its Customer Service Account Executive Training Program to

Dr. Joan Brittain

Bellarmine and began holding training sessions in the Bonaventure Conference Center.

Another special program was the Bellarmine College Program for Women, begun in the fall of 1975 and located in the Center for Community Education. Headed by Dr. Joan Brittain of the English faculty, this program was designed to aid mature women to return to school. Dr. Brittain was an apt director and role model for the program. A married woman with four children, she had returned to college at 35 and earned her Ph.D. six years later. She told a writer for *The Concord* that "a woman's place today is any place where she is happy." The service had special programs for unmarried working women, working married women with no children, women with preschool children and divorced or widowed women. For several years the Philip Morris Corporation gave scholarship awards to women selected by the women's program.

Bellarmine has also offered many off-campus classes and programs for select groups.

In the fall of 1974, for example, the college offered a course in business management at the main post office in downtown Louisville. In 1988 the School of Business took undergraduate and graduate courses to a number of corporate sites in the Louisville area, including Philip Morris USA and Humana. In 1997 the Lansing School of Nursing was offering off-campus courses at Caritas and Baptist Hospital East. Such courses, usually restricted to corporate employees at each site, not only meant additional students for Bellarmine and optional work for faculty but also good community relations and enrichment for campus classes. Ruth Wagoner of the communications faculty has taught numerous off-campus courses and finds them rewarding: "I have usually taught courses for

business groups—courses like interpersonal relations, listening, public speaking—and I love it. I have learned a lot that I can take back to my students on campus."

Another type of off-campus academic program is the outreach to local and statewide high schools, ranging from Dr. John Daly's advanced chemistry courses for students from Catholic high schools in the 1960s to a program called EDGE in the mid-'80s, which stood for Encouraging, Discover, Growth and Excellence and attempted to interest young people in science. In the mid-seventies the Center for Community Education offered a spring credit series called "Early Start Program," a concentrated nine-week program of courses in English, math, western civilization and psychology. A very successful venture in extra-mural instruction was begun in 1971, when Bellarmine instituted the ACCP, the Advance College Credit Program (now called ACCESS), which allowed high-school students the opportunity to earn up to 30 college credit hours for certain courses taken in their junior and senior years. The courses were taught by qualified high- school teachers but supervised and approved by college faculty.

One of the most interesting of the outreach projects in which Bellarmine is involved is the Governor's School for the Arts, a three-week summer program for high-school juniors and seniors from around Kentucky. Bellarmine has been its home since its founding by Gov. Martha Layne Collins in 1986. In 1997 the 11th edition of the school was held at Bellarmine, with 160 student singers, instrumentalists, writers and dancers.

Bellarmine has been successful in various ways of introducing students to real life work experiences while completing their academic studies. Sometimes they were one-day field trips. In March of 1966, for example, Professor Henry Schoo took a class of senior business administration students to the annual stockholders' meeting of Reliance Universal, Inc. in Louisville, where they turned the meeting into a good-natured question-and-answer session on finance and economics.

Sometimes the professional contact was a semester-long internship. Charles Mattingly, who was a legislative intern in Frankfort during the 1970 General Assembly, told a reporter for *The Record* that he thought the experience would be

Kaelin Kallay Rybak, Class of 1974

useful in his later career as a lawyer—or a politician. "Politics is interesting," he said of his Frankfort experience. "It gives you an opportunity to do a lot for people." Although Mattingly did not become a politician, he became a close aide to one of Kentucky's congressmen, Romano Mazzoli.

Since the '70s internships have become a significant component of many courses of study, particularly in education, business, accounting, political science, computer science and management. Except for education, for which internships have long been a part of teacher preparation, most of Bellarmine's interns have come from business and accounting. Students have done internships with leading accounting firms and major conpanies, including Capital Holding Corporation, General Electric and Doe-Anderson. By the fall of 1997, there were more than 300 internships available to students.

According to news reports, Bellarmine's internship in accounting even helped to keep a major corporation from moving its headquarters from Louisville. In May of 1996, when Vencor, Inc., a Louisville-based hospital and nursing-home chain, was considering a move to Cincinnati, Vencor president W. Bruce Lunsford listed the Bellarmine-Vencor program as one of the factors that made him want to keep his company in Louisville. Lunsford, a member of the Bellarmine Board of Trustees, had originally

Accounting Professor Martha Oliver

suggested the program, which his company developed with business school dean Ed Popper and accounting professor Martha Oliver. The Vencor internships benefit both student and company. The students gain valuable professional experience and earn tuition money, while Vencor scouts talented students for permanent positions with the company.

Some of Bellarmine's outreach progams are international. Through the Kentucky Branch of the English-Speaking Union, since the '60s Bellarmine has sent dozens of students to study at various British universities' summer schools. Kaelin Rybak remembers her summer at Oxford University as "an incredible opportunity that made the summer a marvelous experience."

Most of Bellarmine's international programs have been campus administered and college supervised. One of the first faculty members to take students on study tours was Sr. Pat Lowman, who supervised groups of students to Europe or Australia every summer from 1968 to 1990. In the '70s and '80s Dr. James Dyar of the biology department led groups of students on study trips to study marine biology in such places as the Bahamas and the Galapagos Islands off the coast of Ecuador. By 1990 Bellarmine also had a summer study program at Oxford, consisting of 18 days of field trips and classes in such fields as English history and drama.

Indeed, according to the Institute of International Education in New York, rising numbers of American college students were studying overseas, reaching more than 85,000 by 1994. At that time Bellarmine had available more than 100 programs of study in 38 countries, for periods of one semester, one year or one summer. In 1994 Bellarmine also became a member of the International Student Exchange Program, in which students competed for study at member institutions around the world. In the summer of 1996, students were studying in such countries as Austria, England and Ireland; and in the fall they were studying economics in Hong Kong, history in Malta, marine biology in Australia, business administration in Japan and wildlife ecology in Kenya. Other study trips abroad are designed for honors students.

Enrichment Programs...

Bellarmine College was a beehive of activity from the first day, not only in the classrooms and labs but all over campus—on the sports fields, the chapel, the recital areas and beyond. Furthermore, faculty and students were busy thinking up projects for enriching the educational program. In April of 1962, the director of the college bookstore, Mrs. Alma Rademaker, chaired a five-day book fair, which featured special displays, readings, an art auction and the sale of books, records and art prints. Campus resources were used to enrich classroom work. A series called "Reading Writers" sponsored by the English department consisted of dramatic readings from the classics to the present, including Yeats, Twain, Flannery O'Connor and Thomas Merton. Students and faculty went across town and across the world to gain new experiences. Each year the honors students in the Cardinal Sections took a cultural trip under the supervision of Dr. Margaret Mahoney, visiting such cities as New York, Toronto, Chicago, Washington and New Orleans.

For about 10 years an enrichment program called Humanities Week took place each spring. Chaired by Wade Hall, the first week took place in April of 1975 and showcased the various departments of the humanities division to the campus and community. The events included a concert by the Crusade for Children Big Band, opera scenes performed by students, a jazz concert, a film talk and a student art show. Also featured each year were prominent speakers from off campus, including writers Marion Montgomery of the University of Georgia; Harriette Simpson Arnow, the author of *The Dollmaker;* James Still, author of *River of Earth;* and Sr. Therese Lentfoehr, poet and friend of Thomas Merton. Other events have included a Bicentennial Salute to Cole Porter, a concert of Aaron Copland works, a concert by folk musicians Dick and Anne Albin and an edible art contest in 1978, won by Helen Petrik, whose cake featured the current college slogan: "Bellarmine Is Vital to Louisville."

From its beginning Bellarmine has seen itself as a college that develops leaders. The roots of its emphasis on education for leadership may be traced to the founding fathers. The focus was on Catholic leadership at a workshop held at Lake Elmo in October of 1957 with 60 students from Bellarmine, Ursuline and Nazareth in attendance. The main speaker was Fr. Hilary Gottbrath, who gave his own definition of a leader: "A good leader is willing to take the initiative in improving a situation rather than waiting for some sort of natural law of adjustment to correct it."

In the fall of 1983, President Petrik announced the formation of the President's Leadership Society, composed of 20 students with leadership potential and interest. He said members, selected mainly from students on presidential scholarships, would have the opportunity to work with community leaders and thus develop their own leadership skills. Activities included off-campus visits with community and corporate leaders, special meetings with guests on campus and regular meetings with the President. Although the President was directly involved in the society, it was coordinated by Al Burke, assistant to the vice president for academic affairs. A recent addition is a student leadership and scholarship program, the Brown Scholars Program, funded by the James Graham Brown Foundation and featuring community mentors.

An umbrella program begun in the mid-'80s for high schools was designed to identify and nurture potential leaders. Called BILD, the Bellarmine Institute for Leadership Development, it included the Young Leaders Institute, Leadership Education, the Advanced College Credit Program and Classics in the Classroom.

One of the most successful—and inexpensive— enrichment programs was the Book-A-Semester, organized by Fr. John Loftus in the fall of 1958. A faculty committee from Bellarmine, Nazareth and Ursuline— later expanded to include the University of Louisville and Kentucky Southern College—selected a book for reading, discussing and writing about by students and faculty at the member institutions. The first book selected was *Frontiers in American Catholicism* by Fr. Walter J. Ong, who visited the campuses and lectured on his book. A headline in the *Louisville Times* read: "3 Colleges Gang Up On One Book." The focus book for the fall of 1961 was *The Liberal Education* by Mark Van Doren, who said during his visit to Louisville that no book should be censored or banned, not even Henry Miller's controversial *Tropic of Cancer*. "I never heard a censor admit that *he* has been corrupted by a book," he said. Furthermore, he said, "The principal function of a liberal education is to make us happy with our minds."

The Book-A-Semester program was open to the public and often reached out to the community for participants. In preparing for the visit of Clinton Rossiter, whose *American Presidency* was the selection for the spring of 1962, a discussion panel was convened which included Bellarmine history professor James P. Sullivan, Lt. Gov. Wilson W. Wyatt and publisher-editor Barry Bingham, Sr. Interviews and discussion of the books were often broadcast on local radio and television.

The Cardinal Sections and Program...

The best known enrichment program at Bellarmine has been the Cardinal Sections program started in 1961 by Fr. John Loftus to challenge gifted students. Its first director was Dr. John Ford, followed by Fr. Arnold Dearing. Beginning in 1965, Dr. Margaret Mahoney became director and headed the

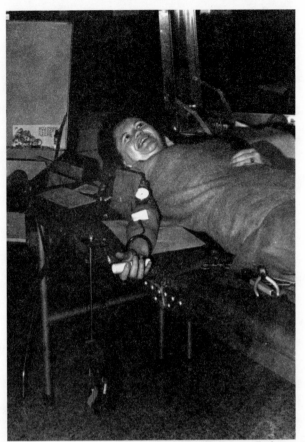

Dr. Margaret Mahoney donating blood at the Bellarmine Red Cross Blood Drive.

program until the early '90s. The program served the college well for more than a quarter of a century and paved the way for a new honors program headed by Dr. Bert Hornback.

According to Dr. Mahoney, Fr. Loftus named it Cardinal to mean "first" or "primary" or "top quality." Students were selected for the program, she says, based on their SAT scores, high- school record and interviews. Special Cardinal sections of approximately 20 students were established for the honors students in English, philosophy, theology and history. In these classes they were given more intensive instruction and standards were generally higher. Dr. Mahoney says that one of the signature features of the honors program was the weekly colloquium, which was an open discussion directed by faculty or community leaders. "The most memorable ones," she says, "were led by Dan Walsh, Thomas Merton's friend at Gethsemani, who brought us weekly news of Merton."

An important dimension was cultural enrichment, which involved attendance at performances by the Kentucky Opera Association, the Louisville Ballet, Actors Theatre of Louisville and the Louisville Orchestra. Cultural field trips were also made to nearby towns and cities like Bloomington, Indiana, and Cincinnati. In addition, students took one big trip each year to such cities as New York, Washington, Chicago, New Orleans, Toronto and Philadelphia. In these cities, Dr. Mahoney says, "students could learn to navigate a city and handle themselves, eating in foreign restaurants and getting a taste of cosmopolitan culture." For most of them, it was a totally new experience. Alumna Kaelin Rybak says, "Dr. Mahoney was determined that when we went to big cities we were given multicultural experiences in restaurants, in theaters, concert halls and museums that we couldn't have had in Louisville. It broadened all our horizons."

"Almost all of the Bellarmine faculty have been involved in the program," Mahoney says, "but especially Dr. Kathleen Lyons of the English faculty and Fr. Eugene Zoeller of the theology department. They were always willing and able to help with colloquia, special programs and trips. I don't believe I could have done it without them." Dr. Mahoney concludes, "I think the old Cardinal Sections program was highly successful, even though we operated it on a shoestring. But it's now time to re-form the program, and we've begun to phase in a new one, in which participants receive full tuition as long as they maintain a 3.5 grade point average. An important feature of the new Bellarmine Scholars program is that each student will spend at least one semester abroad." Hundreds of Cardinal Sections alumni can testify to the valuable experiences they had in the old program.

Dr. Bert Hornback's new honors program is tailored to provide for "a select group of dedicated students the best and most exciting education a liberal arts college can offer." It is designed to educate students for professional success as well as leadership roles in society. To achieve those aims, students take special seminars during their freshman and sophomore years, and as juniors and seniors they take independent studies that culminate in a research project and a senior undergraduate thesis. Up to three freshman students in the honors program each year are designated Bellarmine Scholars and are awarded full four-year tuition scholarships.

Other Programs. . .

Numerous workshops, clinics and institutes have been held on campus, ranging from a foreign language institute for elementary and high-school language teachers in the summer of 1959 to annual health fairs in the 1980s, with local hospitals and other health groups providing screenings for cholesterol, diabetes, vision, hearing and oral cancer. One of the first business management institutes sponsored by the business faculty was held on campus in 1960, with the support of the federal Small Business Administration. Clinics organized by the music department have been regular campus events, sometimes featuring a single instrument. In June 1996, for example, Jeff Sherman directed a Jazz Guitar Clinic and Concert. An event that signaled a sign of the times was a stop-smoking clinic held in the fall of 1983.

Summer schools have been a mainstay of the instructional program since the mid-'50s. In 1954 the first summer school enrolled 35 students in four classes. By 1957 there were 24

BELLARMINE COLLEGE

Summer Session
1958

Air Conditioned
Classrooms

LOUISVILLE 5, KY.

classes and 286 students. In 1955 summer night classes were offered for the first time. In addition to regular credit and noncredit courses, remedial work in such basic skills as math, English and reading have been offered in summer schools since the early '60s.

Bellarmine's Community Education Program for "nontraditional students" has been known by many names, including leisure learning, evening school, classes after hours, continuing education and adult education. Although credit and noncredit courses have been offered, the program was launched in October of 1951 as a series of noncredit adult education courses, with some 500 people participating the first year.

The classes were open to anyone "interested in the spiritual, intellectual, and practical values which flow from education as a continuing life-long process." Courses offered included Choir Clinic, Christian Parenthood, Social Justice, the Catholic Novel Today and Speaking in Public. Most of the courses were free except for a $4 registration fee and were taught by regular Bellarmine faculty, including Fr. Horrigan, the Rev. Joseph C. Emrich, Msgr. Felix Pitt and the Rev. Killian Speckner. The most popular course of the second series which began in January of 1952 was "Preparing for Marriage," with 140 enrollees. A course taught by Msgr. Pitt called "Morality in Politics and Business" attracted housewives, teachers, a printer and a refrigeration serviceman, among others, but, according to an article in *The Courier-Journal,* "no cigar-smoking politician." During a discussion period a

student asked, "If people see that General Grant didn't do a good job, why do they think General Eisenhower would?" Msgr. Pitt's politically correct response: "That's a good question."

The evening school has perhaps been the most elastic and imaginative creator of new courses, especially in the noncredit areas. Classes offered during the fall of 1953 included a course in Bible study called "The Book that God Wrote" and vocabulary building called "In Other Words," plus music appreciation and interior decorating (called "Beauty in the Home"). By then credit courses were being offered in commerce, business law and accounting. The list of noncredit classes offered for almost half a century in the evening is, however, much more colorful than the credit classes and it covers the academic waterfront, from the labor movement to belly dancing, from cartooning to assertiveness training for women, from real estate to beginning judo for women, from stress management

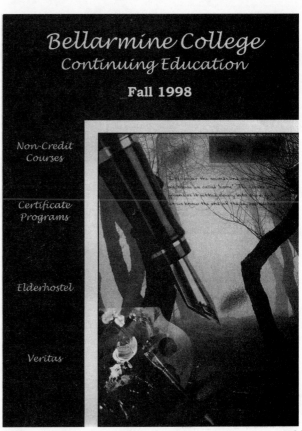

to divorce, from transactional analysis (it attracted 52 students in the fall of 1974) to loom weaving and fabric painting, from wine tasting to men's liberation, from macrame to options for the disabled.

In the mid-'70s the Center for Community Education was extending its outreach to include off-campus credit courses in banking through an agreement with the American Institute of Banking. In the 1976 May short term the center announced Dial-A-Course, which allowed a student to take a noncredit class in his or her own home and design his own class in speed reading, gourmet cooking or painting and use a Bellarmine faculty member to teach it. Indeed, the evening school curriculum was on the cutting edge of society. In the spring of 1998, non-credit courses included holistic slow-motion exercise, stress management, the Marx Brothers and alternative medicine.

Although Bellarmine was still technically an all-male college—at least in the day school—women were enrolling in increasing numbers in the evening school. Fr. Horrigan even admitted that women had been initially admitted to night classes to increase enrollment, with boys and their girlfriends and men and their wives attending classes together. It was a marketing technique that seemed to work, and by 1960 more than 5,000 students had enrolled in what was called the division of adult education.

The evening division, as it was being called, was growing in courses and students and needed its own director by the fall of 1957, when the Rev. Richard L. Friedrich, a Louisville native with a master's degree from Georgetown University, was selected. The first evening school students to receive Certificates of Competency from a program begun in 1954 were John T. Wessling in business administration and Louis A. Young in accounting. Soon the Bellarmine program was accepted for certification by the Association of University Evening Colleges. By the late '50s noncredit courses cost $5 each, and evening students were becoming an integral part of the college academic

program. In the mid-50s a column, "Knights at Night," in *The Concord* kept the entire campus informed on developments in the evening school. At the same time, some evening courses were being held at such off-campus locations as Holy Name School on South Fourth Street.

Adjunct faculty joined full-time day faculty in the night school classrooms. It was a practice that was not only economically beneficial to Bellarmine but made good pedagogical sense. Art museum directors lectured on art history. Lawyers brought the courtroom into their courses in business law. Practicing accountants taught accounting courses after work. Prominent interior designer Don Glaser taught a popular course in interior decorating in the spring of 1959. James Bentley, director of The Filson Club Historical Society, taught courses in genealogy. In the fall of 1976, Jim Bolus, racing writer for *The Courier-Journal*, taught the history of the Kentucky Derby. Fr. C. J. Wagner of Trinity High School taught a noncredit course in contemporary theater and took his students on a theater-train trip to New York over the Thanksgiving holidays.

The evening school was often a hotbed of experimentation. In the fall of 1959 the community education program offered parents and children the opportunity to learn French, Russian or Spanish together. The 10-week course featured classes devoted to practice in conversation, songs and games, plus a 20-minute period in the language laboratory. During the week family members were expected to practice their new language with each other. In the fall of 1960, 80 children and 40 adults enrolled.

The evening school students were sometimes as colorful as the classes they took. An unlikely student in Robert J. Fitzpatrick's class in accounting in the fall of 1952 was Br. Peter, a Franciscan lay brother who had taken the vow of poverty. His incongruous presence in the class was explained by Professor Fitzpatrick: "Brother Peter has been assigned to manage the house occupied by the Francisan friars on the faculty, and he needs to learn good management practices. Anyway, accounting is not foreign to Franciscan traditions. After all, the father of accounting and the first authority on double-entry bookkeeping was Friar Paciolo, a Franciscan from Venice."

As the evening school poises itself for survival in the 21st century, it continues to keep a little bit ahead of the times. In the fall of 1996, for example, the office of continuing education offered—in addition to traditional courses in languages, writing, art and music—courses in alternative medicine, money management, angels, marketing on the Internet and Cave Hill Cemetery. It's a curriculum that has something to educate and excite the most demanding and discriminating student.

Recent Developments. . .

Indeed, the entire academic program has been examined and reshaped in preparation for the new millennium, when the college would also be celebrating its 50th year anniversary. As the college approached the new era, it was offering bachelor's degrees in some 40 academic areas and graduate degrees in several areas. In 1995 several new initiatives were begun to guide and retain new students, including an innovative course, "Freshman Focus," which helped retain a record 95 per cent of freshmen from the fall to the spring semester. A new guidance and support program called Encore was begun in 1996 to aid drop-outs who want to return to college. Some structural changes were made that affected curriculum. In the early '90s art and drama were combined into a fine and performing arts department, which in 1996 began offering an innovative new degree in arts administration, with internships at Actors Theatre of Louisville, the J. B. Speed Art Museum, the Kentucky Center for the Arts, Kentucky Opera Association, and the Louisville Ballet. By 1996 a new department of foreign languages and international programs was offering courses in French,

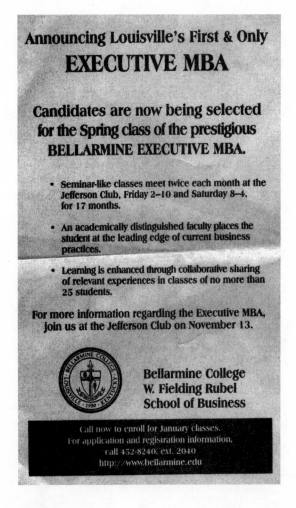

German, Japanese, Russian and Spanish as well as Latin and Greek.

In the fall of 1996, Bellarmine again led the way when the W. Fielding Rubel School of Business announced Louisville's first Executive M.B.A program, with classes meeting at the Jefferson Club on Fridays and Saturdays for 17 months. M.B.A degrees could also be earned in weekend and in week night programs on campus. A new program in nursing was also designed for people interested in a career change and holding a nonnursing degree. The following fall Bellarmine became the first area school to offer a Master of Arts degree in teaching in the evenings.

Neither was Bellarmine neglecting its older constituents. A new curriculum outreach program called the Veritas Society was founded in 1995 to meet the needs of people with a lifelong thirst for learning.

Fr. John Loftus lectures to a class in the "small" science theater.

Offerings have included noncredit courses in local history, diary-keeping, post-Soviet nations, novels and the movies made from them and one called "Girls of the '40's Meet Women of the '90's."

Computerization of registration radically changed the way students registered for classes. The '69 *Lance* described the old-fashioned way: "Registration was pure hell, waiting in line for an hour only to have that 'must' class close out." The computerized '80s and '90s did not do away with closed classes, but at least the waiting was reduced.

Perhaps the most revolutionary and forward-looking curriculum change occurred in the fall of 1997, when a new liberal arts core curriculum took effect. After several years of study, discussion and debate the new course of study was approved by the faculty, the

trustees and President McGowan, who hailed it as a program that "preserves and strengthens our Catholic identity and embodies the principles, goals and expectations passed in December of 1994," and provides "greater flexibility in program and course design, more student choice and better integration of core and major." The core requirements were reduced from 60 to 49 credits of the 120 required for graduation. Required courses in philosophy and theology were reduced from six to four. Requirements were also reduced by six hours in English and three in history. Additional options from these disciplines were added, however, in areas called "American Experience" and "Transcultural Experience." Four hours were added in freshmen orientation and seminar.

In his letter to the faculty approving their recommendation of the new general education core, President McGowan wrote: "With approval of this core curriculum, you have completed successfully an enormous, complex, difficult and important task. Now you have the chance to breathe new life into our curriculum." It was the culmination of the President's efforts to fulfill his promise to bring Bellarmine to "the next level" of its development.

Visitors. . .

Bellarmine's instructional program has always been connected to the work-a-day world and marketplace beyond the college walls. The connection is made when students go off campus for work experiences or for cultural enrichment. It has also been

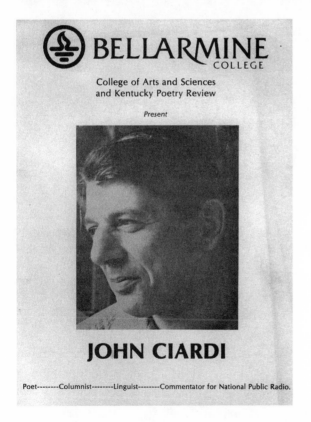

made when visitors bring their cutting edge— sometimes controversial—experiences to campus classrooms and lecture halls. Such curriculum

enrichment has been a hallmark of a Bellarmine education.

Fr. Horrigan saw such visitors as vital for students. "I wanted to have visitors come to Bellarmine," he said, "who would make us aware of their good works all over the world. I wanted our students to have meaningful contact with the people who were running the affairs of the world. That meant that we sometimes had men and women who were out of step with society. But I thought it was good for our students to get to know such people. Most of our visitors, however, have been people who have demonstrated in their lives the qualities that were outstanding in the life of Robert Bellarmine. That was the idea behind the Bellarmine Medal." Indeed, Bellarmine's first President set the standard for extramural guests. His secretary, Alma Schuler, helped to arrange their visits and met many of them. "I was always amazed that Fr. Horrigan was able to attract such prominent people to the college." It was truly remarkable, especially in its early years when it was too new to have a national reputation.

Another problem was the lack of adequate facilities. Except for several large lecture rooms and the gymnasium, there were few areas where large audiences could be accommodated on campus. The opening of Frazier Hall and Wyatt Hall in the mid-'80s provided additional, much-needed space for visiting speakers and performers. Campus visitors during the fall semester of the 1984 academic year, for example, included playwright Edward Albee, poet and critic John Ciardi and Merton biographer and poet Michael Mott. English professor Kathleen Lyons was heard to exclaim, "October has been a banner month at Bellarmine! I can't believe there is another college in the country that has welcomed the likes of Albee and Ciardi within the same month." So rich was the visiting talent that *The Concord* editorialized that perhaps the college had reached "the saturation point."

The heavy schedule of visitors continued into the '90s, when Bellarmine welcomed such notables as

Former British Prime Minister Sir Edward Heath, the 1994 Wilson and Anne D. Wyatt Lecturer, poses with the Hon. Wilson W. Wyatt, Dr. Bert Hornback and Dr. Joseph J. McGowan, Jr.

former British Prime Minister Sir Edward Heath, a soon-to-be Nobel Laureate in literature Seamus Heaney, presidential adviser David Gergen and Kentucky author and poet Wendell Berry.

Many of the visitors came to receive such college awards as the Bellarmine Medal and the Giovanni Martini Award or honorary degrees. When Mrs. Barry Bingham, Sr. spoke to students in the fall of 1953 on Bookmobiles, which were portable libraries serving the 47 Kentucky counties then without a public library, Bellarmine students volunteered to fill an entire Bookmobile, which took more than 600 books. Other visitors came as guests of two endowed lecture series, the Guarnaschelli Lectures in the Humanities and the

Anne and Wilson W. Wyatt Lectures in Public Affairs. The first honorary degrees were awarded in January of 1961 to the Rt. Rev. Felix N. Pitt, executive secretary of the Catholic School Board in Louisville, and Professor Alphonsus J. Lesousky of St. Mary's College in St. Mary, Kentucky. Other honorary degree recipients include Col. Harland Sanders, the founder of Kentucky Fried Chicken, in 1978 and Lyman T. Johnson, the Louisville educator and civil rights leader, in 1987.

The Giovanni Martini Award. . .

In June of 1962 the first Giovanni Martini Award was given to Robert Whitney, conductor of the

Photo by John Nation and Louisville Magazine

Rev. Jesse Jackson, Col. Harland Sanders and Dr. Eugene V. Petrik at the 1979 Bellarmine Medal dinner.

Louisville Orchestra and dean of the School of Music at the University of Louisville. The award, sponsored by the campus chapter of Delta Epsilon Sigma, the national Catholic honors fraternity, and named for the 18th century Italian composer, music teacher and Franciscan priest, recognized persons who render "distinguished contributions to the cultural life of the community." Other Martini awards have been given to such community leaders as businesswoman Mrs. Dann C. Byck; Moritz Bomhard, founder of the Kentucky Opera Association; Addison Franklin Page, director of the J. B. Speed Art Museum; Alberta Allen, civic volunteer and fund raiser; Clarence R. "Skip" Graham, head of the Louisville Free Public Library; Joshua B. Everett, president of the Kentucky Branch of the English-Speaking Union; Richard and Christina Munro, artistic directors of the Louisville Ballet; Melvin Dickinson, director of the Louisville Bach Society, and pianist Lee Luvisi.

When Richard Block, producer-director of Actors Theatre of Louisville, was given the 1967 award at the annual academic awards dinner, he gave a rousing speech calling for a return to national morals and values and warning that "nationalism will kill mankind unless

we kill it first." He received a standing ovation. The dinner, however, received a less-than-kind review in the humor column of *The Concord*, which was headlined: "8th Annual Dean's List Dinner or If the Curriculum Was as Tough as the Meat, Nobody Would Have Been There."

Two years later another culinary brouhaha occurred when *Courier-Journal* arts critic William Mootz received the 1969 Martini Award. The write-up in *The Courier-Journal* reported that Mootz had spoken to several hundred students, faculty and parents at a "poor dinner" honoring the critic for his contributions to the city's cultural life. The following day, a red-faced "Beg Your Pardon" printed this explanation: "A proofreader had written 'poor #,' which means 'poor spacing,' on the proof of the story. The typesetter took this to mean that the word 'poor' should be inserted." The apology continued: "Actually, the dinner prepared by Servomation Mathias Inc. was anything but poor. The menu included fruit cup, tossed salad, Swiss steak with burgundy mushroom sauce, boiled potatoes, green beans and apple pie." For the first and surely the last time, the menu was thus spelled out in detail for the world to read about.

The Book-A-Semester Program and Other Lecture Series...

In the early '60s Bellarmine hosted guests brought to campus by several series. In 1963 alone the Distinguished Lecture Series featured Alan Pryce-Jones, the former editor of *The Times Literary Supplement* in London, and Moira Walsh, movie critic for *America* magazine. Other guests in the '60s and early '70s included Michael Harrington, author of the best-selling book on poverty in America, *The Other America;* and Professor Helen Armstead Johnson, who spoke on African-American literature. In March of 1962,

Douglas Hyde, former Communist and former editor of *The Daily Worker* of London, spoke to a large Bellarmine assembly and called Communism "the Church's greatest opponent in Latin America." Equally dramatic but less controversial was Irish poet and storyteller Seamus MacManus of County Donegal, who called himself one of the last of the "shanachies"—that's Gaelic for storytellers—and proved it in November of 1957 by spinning tales for Bellarmine students and faculty dressed in a homespun suit made by a village tailor from cloth made on a hand loom in the old country. Another popular lecturer was Robert L. Short, the author of *The Gospel According to Peanuts,* who was the Town and Gown Week speaker in November of 1965. Sponsored by the Women's Council, the event the following year featured Frank Edwards, whose talk on flying saucers had to be moved to Knights Hall to accommodate the crowd.

Throughout the '60s many noted authors were brought to Louisville by the Book-A-Semester program, a consortium that included the University of Louisville, Ursuline College, Kentucky Southern College and Nazareth College and was chaired at Bellarmine by Jude Dougherty of the philosophy department. Participating schools agreed to promote the reading and classroom use of a book by the guest author recommended by the Book-A-Semester Committee. Some of the notable guests were Giorgio de Santillane, author of *The Origins of Scientific Thought;* poet and critic John Crowe Ransom; critic and biographer Cleanth Brooks; diplomat Walt W. Rostow, author of *The Stages of Economic Growth;* novelist C. P. Snow, author of *Two Cultures and the Scientific Revolution;* novelist Jesse Hill Ford, author of *The Liberation of Lord Byron Jones;* Richard Hofstadter, author of *Social Darwinism in American Thought;* Roger Shattuck, author of *The Banquet Years;* and William Hamilton, coauthor of *Radical Theology and the Death of God.*

One of the most popular and controversial authors in the series was Whitesburg, Kentucky attorney Harry Caudill, author of *Night Comes to the*

Cumberlands, who told his audience on November 9, 1964, that Louisville must pay the salaries of mountain teachers because mine owners "don't pay their share." He called Eastern Kentucky one of the nation's poorest, richest areas because absentee mine owners pay few or no taxes on the wealth of coal they were taking from the mountains.

Some visitors have come at the invitation of academic departments and classes and for special occasions. Early academic visitors included Dr. Laurence L. Quill, head of the chemistry department at Michigan State University, and Dr. George F. Carter, chairman of the geography department at Johns Hopkins University, who discussed Sputnik and other Russian developments in space exploration in December of 1957. Dr. Carter told a student assembly that World War III was "unavoidable," that flying saucers were probably already in our orbit and that American schoolchildren were no longer taught the fundamentals. At least he was right with one out of three. Space scientist and Louisville native William J. O'Sullivan, Jr. was the commencement speaker for the June 1962 graduation. Speaker at the 1997 commencement was poet Galway Kinnell, a professor at New York University and winner of a National Book Award and a Pulitzer Prize. St. Thomas Day celebrations included such guest speakers as Frank J. Sheed of the Sheed and Ward Publishing Company and French existentialist Gabriel Marcel.

Bellarmine has been fortunate, indeed, to have hosted a library of writers. In addition to those already mentioned, these nationally known authors have graced the campus: poet Philip Appleman of Indiana University; novelist and poet Guy Owen, author of *The Ballad of the Flim-Flam Man;* novelist and best-selling author of *Black Like Me,* John Howard Griffin, who conducted two-week seminars in 1972 on racism and Thomas Merton; poet Ruth Stone; poet and businessman James A. Autry; novelist and historian Tim O'Brien, author of one of the best books to come out of the Vietnam War, *Going After Cacciato;* novelist

(l to r) Dr. Bert Hornback, Dr. John Guarnaschelli, Nobel Prize Laureate Seamus Heaney and Dr. Joseph J. McGowan, Jr.

and historian Richard Marius; and such Kentucky writers as novelist James Sherburne; novelist Ben Lucien Burman; poet and essayist Wendell Berry; novelist Joe Ashby Porter; novelist and poet Barbara Kingsolver; and novelist Bobbie Ann Mason.

Before the establishment of endowed lectureships, such outstanding writers were brought to campus on very limited budgets through cost-cutting strategies devised by members of the various academic faculties. One frugal device was to have a member of the faculty host the visitor, thus saving lodging and food costs. Another strategem was to "piggyback" their Bellarmine visits with appearances at other nearby colleges and literary meetings. When it was announced, for example, that Reynolds Price, the renowned

novelist, poet and Duke University professor, would be the keynote speaker for an academic conference at Louisville's Galt House in the fall of 1981, the English faculty was able to negotiate a greatly reduced fee for his side visit to Bellarmine. The college has also benefited from the sizable seating capacity of Knights Hall. In March of 1977, the University of Louisville rented the auditorium for an appearance by Alex Haley, whose *Roots* had just smashed viewing records on television. While the University of Louisville paid Haley's fee, Bellarmine received most of the publicity when he spoke to an overflow crowd of more than 3,000.

The Guarnaschelli Lectures and the Wilson W. and Anne D. Wyatt Lectures...

Two endowed lecturerships, the Guarnaschelli Lectures founded in 1983 and the Wilson W. and Anne D. Wyatt Lecture Series founded in 1990, have provided the resources and the stability to attract prominent visitors in the humanities and in public service. The Guarneschelli Lectureship in the humanities was funded by an initial $100,000 endowment grant from Dr. John and wife Marty Guarnaschelli in memory of his parents. The first Guarnaschelli lecturer was poet and novelist James Dickey, author of *Deliverance,* who inaugurated the series in great style. The following year the series was given another boost with a reading from playwright Edward Albee, author of some of the most influential plays of the 20th century, *Who's Afraid of Virginia Woolf, The Zoo Story* and *The American Dream.* His campus visit also celebrated the foundation of the new College of Arts and Sciences and the opening of the new complex of buildings housing the humanities and fine arts. In 1989 the Guarnaschelli lecturer was Norman Mailer, the chunky, silver-haired, surprisingly avuncular author of the classic World War II novel, *The Naked and the Dead.* His wide-ranging 45-minute talk included a round-by-round description of Muhammad Ali's knockout fight against George Foreman in Zaire in 1974. Other guests in the series have included authors Joyce Carol Oates, Kathleen Norris, Richard Rodriguez and Peter Matthiessen, whose novel, *The Snow Leopard,* won a National Book Award, as well as journalist and author William L. Shirer, documentary film maker Ken Burns and former British Prime Minister Harold Wilson. The

Mike Mansfield, former Senator and U. S. Ambassador to Japan, presents the Inaugural Wyatt Lecture in March 1990.

Guarnaschelli Lecturer for 1998 was William Styron, winner of the Pulitzer Prize, the American Book Award and National Medal of Arts, who read from his novel, *The Confessions of Nat Turner.*

The first guest of the Wyatt Lecture Series in public affairs was former U. S. Senator and American Ambassador to Japan Mike Mansfield, who spoke on campus in March 1990. Other Wyatt lecturers have included Sir Edward Heath, former British Prime Minister, whose topic was "Europe in the 21st Century," and historian James MacGregor Burns, who spoke on November 11, 1996 on "Monday after the 1996 Presidential Election."

Actors, Athletes and Politicians Galore...

These lectureships and other sponsors have enriched campus life with visitors from many professions and vocations. In the '60s business-related speakers included Louis H. Pilie, president of the American Institute of Certified Public Accountants, NASA spokesman William J. O'Sullivan, who predicted in his 1962 commencement speech that soon there would be in place a system of global communication satellites, and J. Irwin Miller, board chairman of the Cummins Engine Company of Columbus, Indiana, who was awarded the Bellarmine Medal in 1969. In his acceptance speech he called for a second American Revolution of quality, which would bring social justice and material well-being to all Americans.

Predictably, many religious leaders have been campus guests. In the '50s they included such refugees from Chinese Communism as Bishop Cuthbert

O'Gara, who was expelled from China in 1953, and the Rev Harold Rigney, former rector of Fu Jen Catholic University in Peiping, who spoke on the horrors of Chinese prison camps.

In the '60s speakers on religious topics included Edward J. Kirchner, the United Nations representative for Pax Romana, an international movement for Catholic students and intellectuals; the Rt. Rev. Aloysius K. Ziegler, chairman of the history department at the Catholic University of America; noted poet and theologian Daniel Berrigan, S.J., speaker at the Baccalaureate Mass in May of 1965; the Rev. Andrew Greeley, author of *The Education of American Catholics;* the Rev. Ernan McMullin of Notre Dame University's philosophy faculty; and Sister Mary Luke Tobin, Superior General of the Sisters of Loretto and one of the 15 women auditors at the Second Vatican Council. Her address was part of the seventh annual Biblical Institute, cosponsored by Bellarmine College and the Passionist Fathers Seminary. In her speech she predicted that women would move into new positions of dignity and responsibility in the Church.

The presence of some religious leaders on campus sometimes led to considerable controversy. A writer in *The Record* attacked Bellarmine for hosting Dr. (Sister) Agnes Cunningham, president of the Catholic Theological Society and one of five editors of a hotly disputed study of contemporary sexuality, *Human Sexuality: New Directions in American Catholic Thought,* in which theologians took an open view on such sexual practices as masturbation and artificial contraception that were condemned by the church. In their response Dr. Petrik and Fr. Treece defended Bellarmine as a college where differing views are presented and discussed under the guidance of mature faculty. "Bellarmine College makes no apology for following the guidelines of Catholic education as set forth in the official documents of the Church," they concluded.

Another controversial guest was Hans Kung, whose liberal theology caused quite a stir during his 1981 visit to Bellarmine. According to Fr. Eugene Zoeller of the theology faculty, who was instrumental in bringing him to the campus, "The man should have been invited to this campus because he was an eminent theologian." Less controversial was Karl Rahner, professor of theology at the University of Munich and the brains behind Vatican II, who visited the college in April of 1979.

The music program at Bellarmine has been frequently enhanced by visiting performers and composers, ranging from vibraphonist Lionel Hampton and popular singer Glenn Yarbrough to composer Philip Glass and jazz pianist Marian McPartland. In April of 1972 Philip Glass lectured on his new oratorio based on John Milton's *Paradise Lost,* which was being given its world premiere by the Louisville Orchestra. Other visiting performers include The Brothers Four, jazz trumpeter Al Hirt and jazz legend Maynard Ferguson.

Fr. Clyde Crews and Karl Rahner.

Dr. Lee Bash, Dr. Steve Permuth, Lionel Hampton and Dr. Eugene V. Petrik

Orchestra leader Mitch Miller was guest speaker at an April 1967 Brotherhood Dinner sponsored by the National Conference of Christians and Jews at Bellarmine. Louisville liturgical musician and folk singer Joe Wise has played a number of campus concerts. When Wyatt Hall opened in the early '80s it became a perfect stage for such visiting musicians as drummer Buddy Rich and jazz pianist Dr. Billy Taylor. The Louisville Orchestra has played many campus dates, including an outdoor concert of Broadway musical selections in September of 1966, which attracted an audience of more than 3,000. A critic for the 1969 *Lance* wrote that a concert by folk singer Judy Collins "left you laughing, crying, applauding, quiet, feeling every innuendo of her music."

Sports figures on campus include numerous coaches and players from big-time teams. In March of 1968 two of the world's top tennis stars, Arthur Ashe and Manuel Santana, played tennis in Knights Hall. Ashe was awarded the Bellarmine Medal posthumously in 1993. Another sports highlight was the visit in November of 1974 by Jesse Owens, the American hero of the Berlin Olympics in 1936. In his address to the students he said he was encouraged by the new opportunities for black people, on and off the playing fields.

Actors and playwrights have often graced campus stages and lecterns. In January of 1958, Edward Brigham, a dramatic interpreter, gave a recital of selections from Shakespeare. Stage and film actress Irene Dunne returned to her hometown to receive the Bellarmine Medal in 1965. Dustin Hoffman spoke to an overflow audience in April of 1968 during a nationwide tour to promote Senator Eugene McCarthy's candidacy for the Democratic Presidential nomination. Knights Hall was the scene of a touring company's rousing production

of *1776* in the fall of 1975. Another memorable dramatic event was Natalie Ross's one-woman show, *The Belle of Amherst*, which brought poet Emily Dickinson to life on Bellarmine's stage.

And finally there are the politicians and political writers who have flooded Bellarmine's stages, halls and classrooms for almost 50 years. They have made Bellarmine a forum for rational discussion and debate

Irene Dunne Named 1965 Bellarmine Medalist

Actress Irene Dunne (Mrs. Francis D. Griffin), born in Louisville, and a United States alternate delegate to the United Nations in 1957, has been named 1965 recipient of The Bellarmine Medal.

In announcing the 1965 Medalist, Monsignor Horrigan made the following comment: "This year our Board of Overseers has turned to a new area of public life and achievement to select The Bellarmine Medalist. Previous honorees have distinguished themselves in the areas of government, industry, and diplomacy. Our 1965 Medalist has made her contribution to American society in the entertainment arts and in a variety of civic and philanthropic activities. Her personal and professional integrity throughout a long career in a field where standards of taste and artistic responsibility often are preserved only with extraordinary difficulty admirably illustrate the virtues which The Bellarmine Medal was established to honor."

The Bellarmine Medal is awarded each year by the college to a person "who on the national or international scene, exemplifies in a notable manner the virtues of justice, charity, and temperateness in dealing with difficult and controversial problems." Irene Dunne, the eleventh Medalist, will be in Louisville to receive the honor on Thursday, May 13, 1965, in Knights Hall.

Irene Dunne
Bellarmine Medalist

Bellarmine Foundation Raises $73,000

George M. Goetz prepares distribution of awards as the Foundation surpasses 100% of goal.

The 1964-1965 Bellarmine Foundation has surpassed its $70,000 goal by $2,978. Chairman of this year's drive is George M. Goetz, President of Falls City Brewing Company.

Memberships in the Foundation total 543, of which fifty-nine are family memberships, with individual memberships totaling 442. Company contributions comprise the remaining forty-two.

Awards presented at a special ceremony on February 18 were given to Al J. Schneider, John J. Martin, Charles C. Coy, and their respective team members for Best Team Performance. Arthur J. Deindoerfer received the Division Leader Award. Winner of the First-Year Worker award was Otto Knop.

Actress Irene Dunne wins the 1965 Bellarmine Medal.

on many of the crucial issues of the last half century, from the cold war to racism. One of the first nationally known speakers on campus was Dr. Bella V. Dodd, a reformed Communist, who had recently reclaimed her Roman Catholic faith and in April of 1953 told

Bellarmine students of the evils of Communism and its desire, as she said, "to swallow up our civilization." She also defended the Communist-hunting work of Senator Joseph McCarthy. "When the rancor has disappeared," she said, "we will think McCarthy has done us a service."

In March of 1955, Bellarmine was the site of a meeting of the Louisville chapter of Te Deum, which heard Louis F. Budenz, the controversial former editor of the *Communist Daily Worker*, predict that the Communists were trying to undermine the Democratic Party. He said that the Communist plea for "peaceful coexistence" is actually "a program to bring about peaceless nonexistence." Budenz, who had left the church in 1935 and returned in 1945, had recently appeared as "an expert witness" against "the Communist conspiracy" in court and before government committees.

Later journalists presented a more balanced view of political issues, ranging from television commentator Daniel Schorr in 1989 to presidential adviser David Gergen and *New York Times* columnist James Reston, who were Wyatt lecturers in the early '90s. During his lecture in March of 1992, Reston proved himself to be an equal-opportunity critic. Lamenting the state of national leadership, he compared the present state of affairs with the early years of the American republic, when with only twelve million people "we produced a George Washington and a Thomas Jefferson. Now we have a Bush leaguer and the playboy of the Western World."

On November 16, 1956, Douglas Hyde, a London journalist and former Communist, told Bellarmine students that the Hungarian revolt against Communism had been "heroic and inspiring but, if we are to be unemotional, it was ill-timed." During the same month a Requiem High Mass was held on campus for the victims of the uprising and a special

collection was taken to aid Hungarian students. Bellarmine Medalist Henry Cabot Lodge said in June of 1962 that the Cold War struggle was "a war of wills and ideas." He added, "In such a war, a strategy based on containment, a strategy which can merely react to the enemy's offensive . . . can lead us only to degradation and defeat."

Liberalism has also had its spokespersons on campus. The 1960 commencement speaker was Dr. Raymond F. McCoy, dean of the graduate school at Xavier University in Cincinnati, who told students they should fight conservatism and what it stands for. Conservatism, he said, is "more concerned with our material well-being than with solving the problems of the common good. It degenerates into selfishness. Look around you—the gray flannel suits, the affluent society, the organization man, the second car, the suburban home, the demand for lower taxes, the support of money for arms but not a cent for foreign programs—this is conservatism of the American frame of mind." What the nation needs, he said, is youthful "dash and vigor and commitment and desire."

William F. Buckley, Jr. and Dr. Eugene V. Petrik.

In April of 1961, two well-known New York Catholic journalists presented opposite sides of the ideological fence during two debates at Bellarmine. William F. Buckley, Jr., conservative television interviewer and author of *God and Man at Yale,* and William Clancy, liberal editor of *World View,* debated "The Catholic and the Modern World" and "Current Social-Political Problems and the Mind of the Church" to an enthusiastic, partisan audience in Knights Hall. Buckley called liberalism an atheistic movement and Clancy called conservatism blind to the problems of justice and politics.

In March of 1963, Dr. Jose Chaves, a Colombian educator and diplomat, spoke on political change in Latin America. In a speech at Ursuline College in January 1966, Fulton Lewis III, the son of the conservative radio and television commentator, spoke against Medicare, calling it "the greatest railroad job in the history of politics." His speech, which was part of the Bellarmine-Ursuline Coordinated Cultural Affairs Series, also attacked the war on poverty and proposed a more aggressive military policy in Vietnam. The featured speaker during Town and Gown Week in November of 1971 was Stewart Udall, who had served as Secretary of the Interior in the Kennedy and Johnson administrations. In the fall of 1988, vice presidential candidate Dan Quayle was represented on campus by his wife Marilyn.

The conservative side has also been ably represented by many other guests. In November of 1965, the principal speaker for Town and Gown Week was Russell Kirk, author, syndicated columnist and spokesman for the New American Conservatism movement. During his lecture on "The Future of American Conservatism," he defined his term: "The essence of conservatism is the belief in continuity, the great chain of being that binds the dead with the living and the yet unborn and which should not be altered at the pleasure of the reformer or the agitator." That same month conservatism was represented by Kelly Thompson, president of Western Kentucky State

College, who spoke against college students who were burning their draft cards and demonstrating against the Vietnam War. "When you hear of sit-downs and sit-ins and draft-card burners," he said, "please don't get the idea that they represent American college youths." Although campus surveys showed that many Bellarmine students opposed the war, very few of them burned their draft cards or resisted the draft.

Liberal partisans have also had their say on all the issues. In March of 1971, for example, the campus student government invited Dr. David E. Smith, medical director of the Haight-Ashbury Medical Clinic in San Francisco, to present his views on the worsening drug epidemic. And so he did. Tax dollars were being wasted to enforce laws against marijuana, he said; instead, he recommended that money be used to arrest heroin pushers and to treat addicts.

Another forceful liberal speaker was Fr. Robert Drinan, former U. S. Congressman from Massachusetts, who spoke on American foreign policy in February of 1983. He attacked the U. S. government's policy maintaining the status quo in Latin America. He supported the priests serving in the revolutionary government in Nicaragua, where, he said, the Roman Catholic Church was not only saving souls but fighting for social and economic justice.

One of the chief standard-bearers for liberalism in the '70s and '80s was on campus in March of 1989 as the Guarnaschelli lecturer. George McGovern, the seasoned and mellowed former Democratic candidate for President, tried to take a broad historical view of clashing political philosophies and chided Ronald Reagan and George Bush for trying to turn "liberal" into a dirty word. Both liberal and conservative positions are needed for democracy to work. "The creative tension between liberalism and conservatism," he said, "is an important part of the genius of the American system."

In addition to nationally known political visitors, Bellarmine has also hosted numerous local and regional politicians, active and retired. Such a list is a roll call

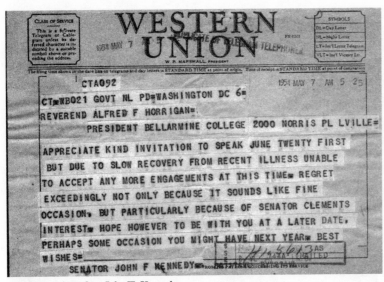
A telegram from Sen. John F. Kennedy.

Senator John F. Kennedy at Bellarmine in 1956.

of prominent men and women, from former Louisville Mayor and Kentucky Lt. Gov. Wilson W. Wyatt, Sr. and Senator and Vice President Alben W. Barkley to a gallery of Kentucky governors and a host of senators and congressmen, including John Sherman Cooper, Thruston B. Morton, Frank W. Burke, Romano Mazzoli and Eugene Snyder. When Republican Snyder was running for re-election to the House of Representatives in the fall of 1964, he appeared at Bellarmine before a mostly hostile student and faculty audience of about 100 people. He noted, moreover, that a recent campus poll had turned up only 22 Republicans out of a student body of some 1,700.

One of the most important visitors to Bellarmine College came early—in October of 1956. He was still a young senator from Massachusetts and had just lost his campaign to become Presidential candidate Adlai Stevenson's running mate to Estes Kefauver. Kennedy was proving himself to be a gracious loser by campaigning for Stevenson-Kefauver and, as it turned out, positioning himself for first slot on the Democratic Presidential ticket four years later. Fr. Horrigan remembered John F. Kennedy's great sense of humor. "He told the joke about the old Indian scout who had been saved from an attack by Indians, who had filled his body with arrows. His rescuers asked, 'Does it hurt?' and he said, 'Only when I laugh.' That's the way

I feel about losing the second slot on the ticket to Kefauver.'"

When Kennedy arrived on campus October 5, he was not only helping his party's bid for the Presidency but he was also honoring a rain check he took several years before when he had to cancel a speech for a Bellarmine graduation. During his whirlwind 23-minute visit, he told an overflow audience that Catholic youth must get involved in politics, despite its disappointments. In explaining his loss of the vice-presidential nomination at the Democratic Convention earlier that year in Chicago, he discounted religion as a major factor. "I received as much, or more, support from states with few Catholic voters," he told the more than 700 Bellarmine students and faculty. "Things have come a long way since 1928, when Al Smith's Catholicism was the central campaign issue. The South, in particular, has progressed a long way toward maturity."

At the end of his speech he was given a standing ovation, even by students wearing "I Like Ike" buttons. The students—most of whom were eligible to vote because of Kentucky's voting age of 18—were enthusiastic about Kennedy but not about the ticket he was supporting. Just before the November election, a mock election on campus favored Eisenhower-Nixon over Stevenson-Kefauver by 180 to 105. It was prophetic of the national election results.

Kennedy himself, however, was on the road to triumph and, sadly, tragedy. Just before the Democratic Convention in 1960, Fr. Horrigan moderated a panel discussion on campus of the role that Kennedy's Catholicism would play in the nomination and election. The panelists agreed that it would be a factor but not a decisive one. Vincent Tortora, a news commentator from New York, said, "Once a Catholic becomes President this entire issue will be put to bed." And so it was.

Bellarmine's academic dean was with the President in Washington two days before the assassination. On November 20, 1963, Fr. John Loftus attended a ceremony in the Rose Garden of the White House at which President Kennedy accepted a peace citation from the Eighth Armored Division Association, of which Fr. Loftus was chaplain. He told newsmen that during the ceremony he congratulated the President for his bipartisanship when he told a Catholic youth organization in New York a few days before that bishops and monsignors were all Republicans and the nuns were all Democrats.

On November 25, 1963, during a Requiem Mass in St. Robert's Chapel for the slain President, Fr. Horrigan said: "We Americans are a vigorous and demanding people. We think for ourselves and fight hard for what we believe in. Often we are much more conscious of the tensions and conflicts among us than we are of the things that unite us. The death of

President Kennedy has revealed to us with a splendid new clarity all the things that we love together and believe together."

James Stammerman—later to be a Bellarmine student and staff member—was still in high school when Kennedy paid his 1956 visit to Louisville, but he has a treasured memento of it. "I was with a bunch of guys down at WAVE taping a radio program for Junior Achievement. We had just finished and were walking by the TV studio when I looked in and said, 'Isn't that guy in there the senator from Massachusetts? Let's wait and get his autograph.' When he came out from his interview, we talked with him for several minutes and he signed his autograph, which I still have: "To Jim, With best wishes, John Kennedy."

Bellarmine Medalists...

About halfway between external fund raising and curriculum enhancement is the college's oldest and most effective system of bringing visitors to town and gown, the Bellarmine Medal. Sponsored by the Board of Overseers, the Bellarmine Medal has been awarded since the spring of 1955 to the person "who has shown

JEFFERSON CAFFERY

First Bellarmine Medal Recipient Jefferson Caffery

outstanding qualities in dealing with the problems, conflicts and controversies of modern times," a person who has also "illustrated in a notable manner those virtues which distinguished the public life" of St. Robert Bellarmine. The medal, three inches in diameter and cast in silver, bears the seal of the college under which is inscribed the school's motto, *"In Veritatis Amore."* The award is given to a recipient at a public dinner, held either on campus or at a Louisville hotel.

The first medal was awarded to veteran American diplomat Jefferson Caffery, a former Assistant Secretary of State and Ambassador to Cuba, Brazil, France and Egypt. During his 44 years of diplomatic service he participated in many important events, from the Paris Peace Conference following World War I to the discussions over the disputed Suez Canal Zone and the Anglo-Egyptian Sudan. The dinner honoring Ambassador Caffery was held on May 23, 1955, at the

Crystal Ballroom of the Brown Hotel with some 350 guests attending. Tickets were $5 each.

The second medalist was Carlos Romulo—editor, journalist, soldier, author, lecturer, diplomat and at the time of the award, Philippine Ambassador to the United States. In 1949 and 1950 he had served as president of the Fourth General Assembly of the United Nations. During World War II he was MacArthur's aide-de-camp at Bataan, Corregidor and in Australia. Before the war he had won the Pulitzer Prize for a series of articles about the Far East. Fr. Horrigan was not exaggerating when he called him "one of the noteworthy Christian statesmen of our day."

The dinner honoring Romulo was supposed to have been held on May 16, 1956, in the Kentucky Hotel but had to be delayed until June 26 when he fell victim to shingles, an inflammation of the nerve endings. Finally, before an audience of 700 in the Crystal Ballroom of the Brown Hotel, Romulo attacked incompetent American diplomats as well as certain Asian nations who, he said, were ungrateful recipients of American aid and had become easy prey to Communism, which, he warned, "has developed the science of terror, of mass murder, of tyranny unequalled in history." The dinner and the lecture were still only $5.

The third Bellarmine Medalist was Congressman John W. McCormack of Massachusetts, "the fighting Irishman" who was the first Roman Catholic ever elected majority leader in either the U. S. House or Senate. As chairman of the first House Un-American Activities Committee, he was called a Communist by right-wingers and a Fascist by left-wingers. In Louisville Fr. Horrigan praised him for "his breadth of vision and powers of conciliation." The 65-year-old statesman was accompanied to Louisville by his wife of 37 years, the former M. Harriet Joyce, a former member of the Metropolitan Opera Company. McCormack explained that since their marriage they had never been separated overnight. In his speech on

May 13, 1957, he cautioned against a national policy of peaceful coexistence with the Soviet Union. Closer to home, he called St. Robert Bellarmine "one of the great figures of history against the absolutism of his day and a great advocate of the 'consent of the governed.'"

The 1958 winner was Frank M. Folsom, former chairman of the board of the Radio Corporation of America. Before a sold-out audience of 600 in the Flag Room of the Kentucky Hotel on May 13, Folsom was praised for his "justice in dealing with competitors, fair treatment of employees, government service during World War II and advocacy of interracial justice." The prominent Catholic layman responded: "No matter how many nuclear reactors stand out against the sky, they will never supplant the spire of the church and the cross."

The 1959 medalist was Robert D. Murphy, an Under Secretary of State and the nation's number one diplomatic troubleshooter. His acceptance speech, however, almost caused a serious international incident. After praising the "spirit" of Robert Bellarmine as "the only road to durable peace," he attacked the Chinese Communists' military aggression against the Tibetan people. A later radio broadcast monitored from China said that he had "slandered China" in a speech from "an agricultural college" in Louisville. Murphy sent a translation of the broadcast to Bellarmine with this comment: "Perhaps we should let the Chinese know that when they talk of slander, they had better be careful about describing Bellarmine as an 'agricultural college.'"

On May 13, 1960, then celebrated as the feast day of St. Robert Bellarmine, James P. Mitchell, the Secretary of Labor in President Eisenhower's Cabinet, received the sixth Bellarmine Medal. He was a major figure in labor-management relations and had played a crucial role in settling the national steel strike earlier in the year. His citation called him a man who had tried "to follow the social principles of the Gospel and the great Christian thinkers." An audience of 625 heard

him urge federal assistance for school construction. In addition to his Bellarmine Medal, Lt. Gov. Wilson W. Wyatt conferred on him what he called his "second Kentucky Colonelcy." He had been given the first one a few hours before.

The 1961 medal winner was Frederick Henry Boland, the president of the United Nations General Assembly, who had presided over some of the stormiest sessions in UN history, including a session in which he smashed a gavel to silence several impassioned Communist speakers in the fall of 1960. The press reported that one of his favorite Latin quotations was from Horace: "Aequam mememto rebus in arduis servare mentem" or "Remember to keep a cool head in difficult circumstances." As several dinner guests noted, it was a motto that also fit the college namesake, who was frequently called upon to calm the turbulence and controversies of his day.

Boland was followed in 1962 by Gen. Alfred Maximilian Gruenther, president of the American Red Cross and formerly Supreme Allied Commander in Europe. He was accompanied to Louisville by his wife, Grace Elizabeth Crum, of Jeffersonville, Indiana, whom he had met when he was stationed at Fort Knox in the early 1920s. At the dinner in Knights Hall congratulatory messages were read from President Kennedy and former Presidents Eisenhower, Truman and Hoover. One telegram message was not read because no one could identify its sender, Charles H. Green. Later the general identified the name as bridge authority Charles H. Goren. One of the nation's top bridge players, Gruenther was a close friend of Goren. In his acceptance speech before 650 people, Gruenther said: "The main problem we have to face in the world now and for a considerable time in the future is not the level of armaments. It is how to run a civilization. We think it should be by stressing the dignity of the individual. The Communists develop the loyalty of the individual to the state, and the state decides what shall come back to the citizen."

Other medal winners in the '60s included R. Sargent Shriver, Jr., director of the Peace Corps and special assistant to the President, actress Irene Dunne, former U.S. Ambassador to the United Nations Henry Cabot Lodge, Senator Everett M. Dirksen, U.S. Attorney General Nicholas Katzenbach and comedian Danny Thomas, who told an overflow crowd in Knights Hall that what the country needed to combat juvenile delinquency was a return to "good old cornball Americanism."

Senator Dirksen was five months late in receiving his award because of an accident. Scheduled to be honored at the usual dinner on May 11, 1966, he fell at Walter Reed Army Hospital in Washington and broke his right hip the day before he was to leave for Louisville. Fr. Horrigan's secretary, Alma Schuler, remembers the event: "The telephone caller said that the senator couldn't come. Well, it put us in a near panic. We had no choice but to cancel the dinner. We notified the media and they reported the cancellation. Then we quickly sent out letters to all the ticketholders telling them that they could have a refund or could choose to donate the cost of their tickets to the college. Very few people requested a refund."

The senator did, however, receive his award. In early October of 1966, Fr. Horrigan, Fr. John Loftus and a delegation from the Board of Overseers, headed by George Goetz, flew to Washington to make the presentation. The ceremony was held in the Vandenberg Room of the U.S. Capitol at a luncheon given by Senator Thruston B. Morton of Kentucky.

The first woman and the first actor to be honored with the medal was Louisville native Irene Dunne in 1965. A star of stage, screen, radio and television, she was also noted for her philanthropic and religious work. In her acceptance speech she asked her audience to give their "supernatural gifts" of faith, love, goodness, truth and beauty to the poor, whom she defined as "everyone."

Recipients in the '70s included the Rev. Theodore M. Hesburgh, Senator John Sherman Cooper, the Most Rev. Fulton J. Sheen, William F. Buckley and the Rev. Jesse Jackson. Fr. Hesburgh, president of the University of Notre Dame, delivered a very optimistic acceptance speech in 1970, predicting that the new technology could feed the six billion people in the world of 2000 and that by then all Christians would be reunited into one Church of Christ. At the award dinner for Bishop Sheen in 1975, Archbishop McDonough praised the author, educator and television personality as "our Archbishop for all seasons." A special feature of the award dinner in October 1977, when the medalist was author and television host William F. Buckley, Jr., was an after-dinner harpsichord recital by him in Knights Hall. Afterwards he quipped, "I wish I had spent less time in the search for truth and more time on finger technique."

The 21st recipient of the Bellarmine Medal— and the first African American to win—was the Rev. Jesse Jackson, a former aide to Dr. Martin Luther King, Jr. and the head of PUSH for Excellence. *The Concord* called him "an electrifying and charismatic speaker." Mrs. William Mapother said of him: "He's saying something both blacks and whites need to hear."

Although many worthy men and women have received the Bellarmine Medal since 1955, there are some who stand out in bold and beautiful relief. Perhaps the high point of the awards was reached with the selection of Mother Teresa as the medalist for 1981, when President Petrik and film maker and Bellarmine alumnus Michael Nabicht traveled to Calcutta, India, to present the award to her. Following the simple ceremony, she said, "Our futures are now tied together." Petrik replied, "If that is so, then you must come and visit Louisville and the Bellarmine community soon." She said she would. And in June of the following year she did.

Mother Teresa's visit to Bellarmine was easily the most widely covered event in the history of the college. On June 22, 1982, the 71-year-old founder of the Missionaries of Charity delivered her simple, profound

Mother Teresa of Calcutta on her visit to Bellarmine in 1982.

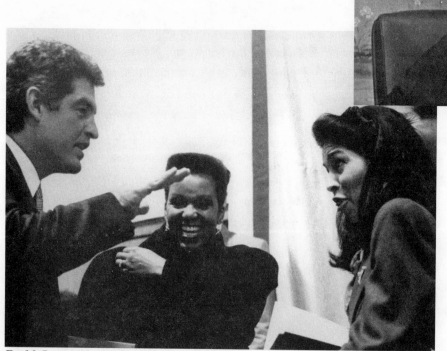

Dr. McGowan with trustee Rita Phillips and Jeanne Moutoussay Ashe, widow of Arthur Ashe, the 1993 Bellarmine Medalist.

Michael E. Nabicht, '68

message of love to a standing-room-only crowd of over 4,200 in Knights Hall. Two thousand tickets had been given to the public free on a first-come, first-served basis, with some people waiting in line all night to get their seats. "It takes so little effort to love," she said, "and the results are so beautiful. You should love everyone, little children and big children, wives and husbands. That alcoholic man roaming the street is Jesus. Love him." In response to the medal award, she said, "I am most unworthy, but I accept in the name of God and in the name of the poor, so you and I and everyone in this college may share in the joy of loving."

Susie Hublar, secretary to Dr. Petrik, remembers the tight security that surrounded her visit. "During a private meeting with her in his office," Mrs. Hubler says, "I had to go downstairs to get some work in the duplicating room, and I almost didn't get back. I had to convince the security police that I was the President's secretary so they would let me get back to my desk." She adds, "Mother Teresa's visit was very important to Dr. Petrik personally. It was one of the high points of his Presidency."

Michael Nabicht's half-hour television documentary, "Work of Love," which included her visit to Bellarmine, premiered in January of 1983 to critical acclaim. A *Courier-Journal* critic called it "a study in joy" and said the film "managed to convey the beauty and spirituality of Mother Teresa's ministry to the poor, the sick and the dying."

Other medal recipients of the '80s and '90s included newscaster Walter Cronkite, American diplomat Philip C. Habib, former UCLA basketball coach John Wooden and Polish trade union leader—and later President of Poland—Lech Walesa. As Cronkite rose in the ballroom of the Seelbach Hotel to speak to his audience of some 500 in May of 1982, the lights went out. Fortunately, someone found the right switch and the ceremony continued. Since political conditions in Poland would not permit Walesa's visit to Bellarmine, President Petrik, his wife

Helen and Congressman Romano Mazzoli flew to Warsaw to present the medal to him. In addition to the silver medal, Petrik presented Walesa with a quilt, a monogrammed bottle of Maker's Mark, a mint julep cup and Easter candy for Walesa's eight children. Petrik also carried a message to the youth of Poland from Bellarmine's students: "We earnestly hope that by conferring this medal upon Lech Walesa we will at the same time affirm with you our common goals of free citizenship, visible expressions of faith and prosperity for all." A posthumous award was made to tennis professional Arthur Ashe, whose widow accepted the medal in 1993.

Such a galaxy of visitors to Bellarmine has not only introduced students to some of the twentieth century's premier achievers and role models but it has also enlarged their classrooms to include the world. These campus visitors are a part of Bellarmine's many-limbed learning tree that seeks to educate a diverse student population for personal fulfillment, professional success and leadership in the new century.

Diversity and Controversy
Minorities and Women

The 43rd Annual Commencement of Bellarmine College in 1996 seemed to be an all-Irish affair. The two recipients of honorary degrees were the Most Rev. Charles G. Maloney, Auxiliary Bishop Emeritus of the Archdiocese of Louisville, and Dr. Arthur H. Keeney, Distinguished Professor of Ophthalmology at the University of Louisville. The speaker was Sr. Mary Kathleen Sheehan, SCN, executive director of the St. John Center for the Homeless in Louisville. The chancellor was the Most Rev. Thomas C. Kelly, Archbishop of Louisville. The President was Dr. Joseph J. McGowan, Jr. The names on the commencement podium were deceiving. In addition to people of Irish descent, Bellarmine has always welcomed faculty, administrators, students, staff and visitors of diverse backgrounds.

In November of 1996, when President McGowan appointed a Blue Ribbon Task Force on Diversity, chaired by Dr. Lucas Lamadrid, therefore, he was continuing a tradition as old as the college. When the panel reported the following spring, one of its main suggestions was that the President appoint a staff member to oversee institutional diversity. Appointed as assistant to the President for

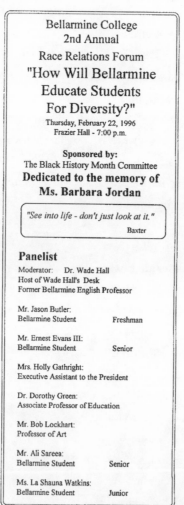

Bellarmine College
2nd Annual
Race Relations Forum
"How Will Bellarmine Educate Students For Diversity?"
Thursday, February 22, 1996
Frazier Hall - 7:00 p.m.

Sponsored by:
The Black History Month Committee
Dedicated to the memory of Ms. Barbara Jordan

"See into life - don't just look at it."
Baxter

Panelist
Moderator: Dr. Wade Hall
Host of Wade Hall's Desk
Former Bellarmine English Professor

Mr. Jason Butler:
Bellarmine Student   Freshman

Mr. Ernest Evans III:
Bellarmine Student   Senior

Mrs. Holly Gathright:
Executive Assistant to the President

Dr. Dorothy Green:
Associate Professor of Education

Mr. Bob Lockhart:
Professor of Art

Mr. Ali Sareea:
Bellarmine Student   Senior

Ms. La Shauna Watkins:
Bellarmine Student   Junior

institutional diversity in October of 1997 was Dr. Dorothy Green of the education faculty.

In a memo announcing the appointment, McGowan stated that "improvement of diversity in all areas at Bellarmine has been a goal of my presidency since my appointment in 1990." Although progress had been made, he said, it "has not been as compelling as I wish." Therefore he said he had asked Dr. Green to develop "a strategic plan proposal," which will contain "strategies for improving our recruitment and hiring of a more diverse faculty, staff and administration as well as plans for improving and retaining a more diverse student body in our traditional and nontraditional student areas."

Diversity, a buzzword of the '90s, had become institutionalized at Bellarmine College. It was not, however, the first time diversity and openness had been practiced on campus. Indeed, Bellarmine's inclusive policies were in place from the beginning. While proud of its Catholic origins and orientation, its classrooms have always been open to faculty and students of all faiths. Although founded as a male college, its evening and free classes and programs have welcomed people regardless of sex, age, race, disability or religious affiliation. In a May 1971 report to the college, Fr. Horrigan wrote: "The college helps to safeguard the cherished heritage of diversity and freedom of thought and choice in American life."

In the beginning the faculty was all-Catholic and a majority were priests; however it has since become broadly diverse. In 1955 Henry Wilson became the first black and the first Baptist to serve on the faculty. Before his retirement in 1967 he was made Bellarmine's first full professor. Another move toward more openness occurred in 1968, when the Rev. Raymond Bailey, a Baptist minister, was appointed to chair the communication arts department and to be a member of the theology faculty. In the fall of 1980, Nancy Howard, also a Baptist, became Bellarmine's first non-Catholic and first lay academic dean to be single.

The list of non-Catholic faculty is long and includes Jewish and Islamic members. Louisville native Gail Henson of the communication arts faculty came from a "heavily academic" Presbyterian family to Bellarmine during the Petrik administration because, she says, "not only did I like Gene's leadership style but here I could teach the whole person—mind, body and spirit. I could affirm the spiritual dimension of life openly."

Perhaps the best example of diversity on the faculty, however, was the presence of Dr. Margaret Celeste Jackson Nichols from 1993 until her death in 1996. Her short tenure was long on influence. A native of Tulsa, Oklahoma, she once wrote that she had "walked gracefully in high heels through doors kicked open by my barefoot ancestry." She was remembered as an extraordinary educator and woman of God at her campus memorial service, with participation by President McGowan, Dr. Theresa Sandok, dean of Arts and Sciences, Dr. Anthony J. O'Keeffe, chair of English, Ms. Betty Winston Baye, columnist for *The Courier-Journal,* and Ms. Ernestine Hayes, president of UMOJA, an African-American student organization.

Dr. Kathleen Lyons, Seamus Heaney and Dr. Celeste Nichols

From day classes filled with young men in the fall of 1950, the Bellarmine student body, though predominantly white, has evolved into a rainbow anthology. The publication of Bellarmine's "Student Non-Discrimination Policy" in the fall of 1980 prohibiting discrimination because of race, color, handicap, religion, age, national origin or sex only made official policies long practiced.

In fact, Bellarmine College is perhaps the only predominantly white college in Kentucky that has always opened its doors to African-American students. A headline in *The Courier-Journal* of April 19, 1950, announced: "3 Catholic Colleges Here Open Doors to Negroes: Nazareth, Ursuline and Bellarmine to Accept Colored Students in All Their Departments." A statement signed by Fr. Horrigan of Bellarmine, Sr. Charles Mary, dean of Nazareth, and Sr. George Marie, dean of Ursuline, announced that blacks would be accepted in all classes "from this time on." The three colleges had used a legal technicality to admit blacks.

The 1950 Kentucky General Assembly had recently approved an amendment to the 1904 Day Law, which prohibited interracial education in public or private schools in the state at any level. The amendment permitted the attendance of blacks in colleges that offered courses not available at the Kentucky State College for Negroes in Frankfort, provided authorities at each institution approved. The

Bellarmine-Ursuline-Nazareth statement noted that, in addition to standard college courses, they also offered courses not available at Kentucky State, namely courses in religion and philosophy. "It seems evident to us, therefore" they wrote, "that we are now legally permitted to accept Negro students in all departments of our colleges since none of our courses can be said to be offered in a complete sense at the Kentucky State College for Negroes."

The college academic heads further emphasized the religious and moral grounds of their decision, stating their "thorough satisfaction that the legal barriers against the full application of the principles of Christianity and democracy in the field of higher education in our state have now been removed." They added: "The doctrines of the fatherhood of God and the consequent brotherhood of all men must be given unqualified expression in these days of universal crisis if the values we cherish are to remain a significant factor in the world of affairs. We wish also to reaffirm our faith in the basic principle of Christian social philosophy that all human rights derive from man's spiritual nature and his supernatural destiny as a child of God. When the right to the intellectual and spiritual development which is the proper concern of higher education is curtailed by the physical accident of race, there is implicit in such curtailment a materialistic philosophy of life which is intolerable in a Christian and democratic society."

An editorial in *The Courier-Journal* on April 20 praised the actions of the schools and noted "the special place in community life filled by church-sponsored educational institutions" because "state schools and universities supported by tax money cannot too far outrun the prevailing prejudices of taxpayers in such matters as segregation." Such schools "based in religion," however, can "act as a spur to the community conscience in such matters. The tax-supported school must follow policy. The denominational schools in their smaller and more

sensitive field may make a policy which is based consciously on the Christian tradition."

Indeed, the Catholic schools' action had spurred the local conscience. Later, on the same day as their announcement, according to an editorial in the April 20th *Louisville Times*, following "the lead of the community's three Catholic colleges," the University of Louisville trustees voted to admit blacks to its graduate and professional schools in the fall and to the undergraduate liberal arts school in the fall of 1951.

As an editorial in *The Record* of April 22, 1950, pointed out, the action of Louisville's three Catholic colleges followed a resolution passed the week before by the College Department of the National Education Association at its annual convention in New Orleans. The resolution called upon Catholic colleges everywhere to make every effort to end the pattern of racial segregation in education and for Catholic colleges to "spearhead" the efforts toward integrated education. In Louisville, they had taken the lead. Their leadership was recognized in February of 1952, when the Kentucky chapter of the National Conference of Christians and Jews awarded the Louisville colleges citations for their acceptance of all students regardless of race.

Windell Bowles, editor of *The Concord,* in an editorial on Brotherhood Week in February of 1956, also noted Bellarmine's leadership: "In 1950, Bellarmine College opened its doors to those who wanted education. From the outset, it mattered not the color of the man's skin, the religion he believed in, or his nationality as long as he was in search of truth through education and was willing to work for it. Following Bellarmine's example, many of the schools in the State of Kentucky have admitted Negroes and much to the surprise of those ignorant persons who foresaw inevitable disaster, nothing has happened. No schools were burned down. None were bombed. None collapsed."

Aggressive recruiting of blacks has been a Bellarmine policy since the early '50s. In May of 1952, for example, Bellarmine awarded scholarships to three honor graduates of the Catholic Colored High School—Evelyn Morton, Perry Jean Thompson and Freeman Franklin. Three African Americans were in the Pioneer Class in 1950, and three more were enrolled in the freshman class in the fall of 1951. Five black students were enrolled in the fall of 1952.

Indeed, Catholic schools led the way in integrating schools at all levels in Louisville, in Kentucky and throughout the South. In the December 1952 meeting of the National Catholic Education Association in Memphis, Fr. Horrigan predicted that the U.S. Supreme Court would soon "demolish the whole segregation pattern" in the South. Several segregation cases were scheduled to be heard by the court, he said, and he predicted that the cases could not be settled on the basis of the "equal but separate" doctrine, which he described as "a sham and a fraud." The whole structure of segregation was crumbling, he said.

Calling on Catholics to take a leadership position, he said, "The times challenge the capacity for leadership of our Southern Catholic colleges. It would be an irreparable tragedy if Catholics in the South, either at the personal or institutional level, would be guilty of dragging their feet and fail to exercise the positive leadership that the times so urgently demand." His prediction was fulfilled when the Supreme Court issued its decision against racial segregation in 1954. Soon after the decision the Southern Regional Unit of the National Catholic Education Association, representing all Catholic colleges and universities in 17 Southern states, met in Louisville at Nazareth College and strongly endorsed the court action.

Catholic schools were already in the vanguard. One year before public school integration, Catholic elementary schools were integrated. On June 5, 1951, Nazareth College awarded degrees to two black students, the first time since 1904 that a black student had received a degree from a predominantly white

school in Kentucky. The first black student was graduated from Bellarmine in June of 1955.

Leadership in civil rights at Bellarmine was not limited to admission of black students. As African Americans began demanding their full rights as Americans, Bellarmine administrators, faculty and students provided support. In the April 24, 1961 *Louisville Times* a large advertisement headed "For Integration" called for "immediate desegregaton of public accommodations." Some 115 singles and couples signed the declaration, plus two lines that read, "Bellarmine College Faculty Association" and "Bellarmine College Student Government." They were the only signators identified specifically with a local college. On October 3, 1962, John W. Dillo, president of the student executive committee at Bellarmine, wrote a letter to the student body president at the University of Mississippi, indicating the support of the Bellarmine student government for the intervention by federal troops during riots over the admission of black student James Meredith. In a December 1962 speech to the Louisville Rotary Club, Fr. Horrigan stated that "we can no longer tolerate the exclusion of any American, regardless of the color of his skin, from full and unhampered participation in the economic, political and educational life of our country."

The active support of many members of the Bellarmine community continued throughout the '60s. When Bellarmine played the University of Louisville on December 6, 1960 at the dedication of the new Bellarmine fieldhouse, the only African-American player on either side was John McGill. He was a 5 feet, 10 inch guard for Bellarmine. On December 14, 1960, *The Concord* editorialized that "Negro students living in the dorm are experiencing difficulty finding a place to eat on holidays" and recommended a boycott by all Bellarmine students of restaurants that refused service to blacks. In February of 1964, 35 faculty members signed a letter to Kentucky's congressmen urging them to support the federal civil rights bill then in Congress. In November of that year dorm students fasted one night and donated the money to buy food for poor black families in the South. In December of 1964, three Bellarmine students and a philosophy professor, Fr. Roland Mullen, spent a week in Mississippi renovating community centers for blacks in Hattiesburg and Meridian and encouraging them to register and vote. In October of 1965 the Rev. C. T. Vivian of the Southern Christian Leadership Conference and one of the organizers of the Selma to Montgomery March spoke on campus.

Throughout the explosive decade of the '60s members of Bellarmine's administration played leadership roles in the civil rights revolution, promoting issues that ranged from open housing to the integration of public accommodations. At a convocation in October of 1962 marking the 12th anniversary of the college, Fr. Horrigan called racial segregaton "an evil thing" and stated that colleges like Bellarmine "must function as the conscience and the beacon light of society." He said that Bellarmine was, therefore, pledging its "unqualified support in eliminating completely from our community all forms of compulsory segregation." On December 31, 1963, he was designated Jefferson County's second prophet-laureate as a reward for a prophecy he had written one year before. His was judged the best of some 200 that had been sent to Father Time, in care of the Jefferson County Playground and Recreation Board, then buried for a year in the Jefferson County Forest. It read: "I prophesy that the Mayor's human-relations commission will recommend to the Board of Aldermen the passage of an ordinance outlawing enforced segregation in all public accommodations in the city; and that such an ordinance will be passed by the aldermen and accepted without serious difficulty by the vast majority of Louisville citizens."

In the mid-'60s Fr. John Loftus chaired the Urban League Housing Committee and, with Fr. Horrigan, was a leading advocate of open housing. Fr. Loftus was, in fact, in the center of a controversial lobbying expedition to the 1964 General Assembly when he and some 30 civil rights advocates went to Frankfort in early February to ask the legislators to vote for a bill requiring businesses to serve customers regardless of race or creed. Outside the legislative chambers, Fr. Loftus signed a note sent to key legislators which said, "A small group of clergymen would like to speak with you briefly concerning the public accommodations bill. If you could leave the floor for a few moments we would be grateful." Although most of the legislators were cordial to them, some protested that he was violating a prohibition against lobbying in the chambers and had to be stopped. And so they were.

On March 5 many Bellarmine faculty and students joined in a March on Frankfort to press legislators to pass the accommodations bill. Fr. Horrigan stated publicly that students and faculty had been given permission to skip classes to take part in the march. In a letter to students published in *The Concord,* he said: "I am pleased to learn that many students have expressed a desire to participate in the March on Frankfort planned for March 5, 1964, as a peaceful and dramatic demonstration that their state should accept full responsibility in the solution of the greatest domestic problem of our time. As a member of the Louisville Commission on Human Rights, I have pledged my support to the announced purposes of the March 5 program at Frankfort and plan to participate in it." In February of 1965, Mayor William O. Cowger appointed Horrigan chairman of the commission.

In March of 1965, Fr. John Loftus joined some 50 other Louisvillians for the final two days of the civil rights march from Selma to Montgomery. They joined the marchers on the highway west of Montgomery, spent the night with them at the City of St. Jude, a small Catholic hospital and school near Montgomery, and completed the march to the capitol of Alabama the next day. Near the end of the line going into Montgomery was the gray-haired dean of Bellarmine College, wearing thick-soled shoes and his

Roman collar, who told a reporter for *The Louisville Times:* "I had felt ever since Selma that I should be down, taking part. I think it's a civic movement, and I'm a citizen. I think it's an educational movement, and I'm an educator. I think above all it's a religious movement. Because of my religious convictions, I need to make use of every opportunity that comes my way to make a public demonstration of my belief."

In March of 1966, 66 Bellarmine students joined other area college and seminary students in a campaign for open-occupancy housing. They urged residents to sign pledge cards that they would sell or rent their property to anyone regardless of race, color, religion or nationality. As chairman of the Louisville and Jefferson County Human Relations Commission, Fr. Horrigan told the Louisville Rotary Club in December of 1966 that open-housing legislation should be enacted not because it was expedient "but because it is the right thing to do." During his tenure as chairman of the commission, he presided over a number of stormy sessions. In January of 1967 he urged the Board of Aldermen to pass an enforceable open-housing ordinance. "We are looking to you. . .for statesmanlike leadership," he said. "In God's name, gentlemen, let's

Graduation Day

not get backed up under pressure on those things we believe in."

In many ways Fr. Horrigan became the conscience of Louisville as he prodded and stung recalcitrant community leaders like a gadfly—but to no immediate success. The Board of Alderman by a 9-3 vote defeated an open-housing ordinance in April of 1967. Bellarmine students, however, backed their President. A poll of almost 300 students showed that three-quarters of them wouldn't object if a person of another race moved into their neighborhoods.

Fr. Horrigan and his supporters were down but not out. He said the aldermen's rejection of open housing was "a very serious setback" in race relations and harmony for the community, calling it evidence of "a complete vacuum of business and civic leadership." Church leaders as well as politicians, he said, were responsible. For his unpopular stand, he was frequently attacked. A letter writer to *The Courier-Journal* suggested that he "take care of Bellarmine College" and keep out of other people's business. But Fr. Horrigan was not the only churchman to be criticized. Another letter writer criticized the participation of nuns, who, she said, were seen kneeling on the sidewalk in front of city hall. "How can children respect them after seeing them kneeling in the grit and dirt for no apparent reason?" she asked. "There are plenty of churches in Louisville, so no one has to kneel in the streets."

Almost 30 years later, Fr. Horrigan reflected on his and Fr. John Loftus' controversial activities. "I was pleased that we often had large numbers of students involved in civil rights and peace activities off campus, but I'm sure some students and others were opposed to our work. I know we were somewhat ahead of most people. One consequence of our activities was that we never had a campus-wide crisis, as happened on so many other campuses during the unrest of the '60s. It was as though our work defused student criticism. Of course, most of the opposition to my activities came from the adult community. In the mid-'60s three or four members of our Board of Overseers resigned in protest of my work. I always thought, however, that I was doing one of the missions of the college in trying to promote human rights and social justice. I thought Bellarmine should not only be a place of education for our students but an example to the entire community. Fr. John, in particular, was an ideal witness to our mission. He became so controversial he had to have his telephone number changed to avoid crank calls late at night." In the long run, the principles of these two men prevailed. They helped to prepare the way. Fr. Horrigan earned the plaudits of *The Louisville Times*, which called him in May of 1968 "a voice and a symbol of enlightened human relations—between races, between sects, between age groups."

The ground-breaking work of the '60s also continued to bear fruit in succeeding decades on campus. In January of 1969, for example, a columnist for *The Louisville Defender* described Bellarmine's recent homecoming dance. "There were approximately six couples of us [blacks] there. With the 'Soul Society' and another group furnishing the sounds, everyone had a swinging time. According to the word around campus, it was something nice. Whites and blacks dropped the color barrier and blew their minds on an out-of-sight time."

The recently organized Black Student Union planted a tree on campus in the spring of 1969 in memory of Martin Luther King one year after his assassination. With offices in the Student Activities Building, the BSU became an important influence for diversity on campus. Books and magazines on black history and culture were added to the library, and courses in black studies were added to the curriculum. In the fall of 1971, *The Concord* ran a series of articles on racial discrimination. By the early '70s Black Awareness Week was being celebrated annually, with singer Josh White, Jr. as special guest in February of 1974.

One of the proudest members of the class of '82 was Chester Jones, the 56-year-old retired manager of the Fern Creek Post Office, who earned a degree in business administration. Jones had graduated from Central High School when it was an all-black school back in 1944 and spent two years in the Navy. Then he had begun a succession of extension courses, correspondence classes and classroom lectures at five colleges and universities over some 35 years, culminating finally in his Bellarmine degree. The high cost of tuition had motivated him to do well, he said. Indeed, he did, making A's in most of his courses.

In the fall of 1989, the Student Association for Equality was formed for minority students. By the decade of the '90s Black History Month was being celebrated with month-long events, including visiting speakers, seminars, concerts and special exhibits. Recent highlights have included a lecture by Julian Bond in 1994 and the African-American Literature Read-In Chain begun on campus by Dr. Celeste Nichols. In 1994 UMOJA was organized to offer a cultural home for minority

1962 - 63 Men's Basketball Team

students and a platform from which African American culture could be shared with people of other races. In 1995 an annual Race Relations Forum was started.

For a college founded for Catholic young men and with no female teaching faculty, Bellarmine has made impressive strides on many other diverse fronts. By the fall semester of 1997 there were 805 men enrolled in the college and 1,431 women. At the same time there were 50 men on the full-time faculty and 38 women. Women had been enrolled in evening classes from the beginning, but it wasn't until several female employees began taking day classes that opposition erupted. In fact, it wasn't until Jeanne Smith, 23, enrolled in courses in theology, history and sociology in the fall of 1957 that male students apparently took

Students from the 1994 African-American Leaderhsip Institute.

notice and objected. Responding to a student senate resolution objecting to "the admittance of a female," Fr. Horrigan explained that her admission to classes was "a fringe benefit" for Ms. Smith, who worked part-time as a secretary and cashier in the college business office. Fr. Horrigan promised that the school "has no intention of going co-educational."

But the walls had been breached and women's numbers continued to increase. Mrs. Frances Callahan, who began taking classes in 1957, was graduated in June of 1965 as the third woman and the first mother and the first grandmother to receive a Bellarmine degree. This mother of four and grandmother of eight was a long-time secretary to Fr. John Loftus.

In 1968, with the Bellarmine-Ursuline merger, what had been a small number of women on campus soon became a majority. Women also began to be recognized in various ways. In 1963 Mrs. Virginia

Sternberg, secretary to Fr. Hilary H. Gottbrath, became the first woman to have the yearbook dedicated to her. In June of 1972, Natalie Jeanne Stewart became the first Bellarmine woman to be commissioned a second lieutenant in the Women's Army Corps. Since the '70s women have dominated the numbers. Marge Wesolowski, director of the Bellarmine Women's Resource Center, reported that in the fall of 1979, women were aging the student body to the point that one out of every four students was a woman over 25.

Older women—who were sometimes women of color—were no longer novelties on campus when Joanne Grube, a Fern Creek mother became a freshman at 40. She said at first she felt "like a Geritol bottle out with the Pepsi generation" but soon found her college experiences "exhilarating beyond my wildest hopes." She recorded her impressons of life as a nontraditional college student for *Womens World News* in October of 1979. "There are also moments of coming to grips with reality," she wrote, "like when the student in front of you is RUNNING up the stairs and you know—there's no way. But there are other moments, too, in the midst of a lecture when a new idea bursts upon you and you realize that whatever the bodily limitations, the mind is ageless." Consider also Judith Wiedenhoefer, 36 and the mother of 6, who in the fall of 1979 was a student at the Kentucky Baptist Hospital School of Nursing at the same time she was in the BSN program at Bellarmine. She said of women like herself that "the limitations they have are the limitations they put on themselves. The doors are wide open."

In fact, by the early '90s "adult learners" made up more than 50 per cent of the student population, and the FLEX Plan (Flexible Learning, Educational Excellence) provided programs and services to meet the unique needs of adult learners. In addition to Saturday classes and accelerated programs, there were contract courses, credit for armed services courses, credit for training programs, for competency and for independent study. The adult outreach program was dubbed Encore in the mid-'90s. Even language was affected by the changing student and faculty make-up. During the '80s "chairman" was gradually replaced by the nonsexist "chairperson."

By the '90s the college was celebrating Women's History Month. Women's athletics also became a force on campus, especially after 1972, when the federal law known as Title IX, which prohibits sex discrimination in schools that receive federal funds, became law. In 1996 *The Concord* had male and female sports editors. By the 1996-97 academic year women were not only equal partners in campus life but were providing much of the leadership, with women holding four of the six positions on the Student Executive Committee, which was headed by Christa Spalding.

Nowadays it's hard to imagine Bellarmine without women faculty and students. Still, it's easy to imagine what Bellarmine is like to a student who has never sat in classes with students of the opposite sex. It was thus so with Donna Olliges. "I have been to Catholic schools all my life," she says, "and even in grade school the boys and girls were essentially separated. And Assumption High School was, of course, an all-girls school. So it was a bit scary for me when I came to Bellarmine and had boys sitting next to me in class." She adds with a gleam in her eye, "But I quickly adjusted."

Although steeped in the traditions of Roman Catholicism, Bellarmine has, indeed, become a campus

of great religious diversity among students and faculty, from Catholic to Muslim to Jewish to all colors of the Orthodox and Protestant rainbow of denominations.

Bellarmine also has a good record of meeting the special needs of its disabled students. Even before affirmative action for the disabled, the college was making accommodations for its special students. Of the dozens of special students to attend Bellarmine, several can be easily singled out. As far back as 1953, a student named Thomas Lutes, a 21-year-old man from Bardstown, was using a pocket-sized Braille writer to take notes in class. Two special students who helped each other were also on campus in the fall of 1953. They were 19-year-old accounting student Gerald Harlan Geiser, a polio victim paralyzed from the waist down and confined to a wheelchair, and his buddy, 21-year-old John Hackel, a Korean War veteran, who lost one of his eyes during the Battle of Heartbreak Ridge. Hackel picked up Geiser every morning at his home and the two attended classes until noon, when Hackel took Geiser home.

In 1971 a blind couple, Larry and Freda Crowe, were enrolled at Bellarmine. As a student of computer technology, Larry Crowe was well ahead of most of his classmates. In the '80s Ted Lisle, though blind, was not only busily involved in extracurricular activities but he was busy making the honor roll. In September of 1978, the campus held a Handicapped Awareness Day, during which students and faculty learned firsthand the difficulties encountered by disabled students in wheelchairs. Disabled men and women are now counted among Bellarmine's most distinguished alumni.

By 1995 the college had expanded services for students with disabilities to the point that it was in full compliance with the Americans with Disabilities Act.

It was a part of a long humanitarian tradition at Bellarmine begun by its first President. In a letter Fr. Horrigan wrote to *The Louisville Times* in October of 1974 in support of expanded public transportation, he stated what could be considered an unofficial college manifesto in human rights. "It is fine to talk about our aspiration to become 'The City of the Seventies,'" he wrote, "and to compete with Cincinnati, Atlanta and Denver in our expansion plans. But we need to keep our priorities straight. Cities are for people. The true greatness of a community cannot be measured in terms of the amount of chrome and glass and concrete that can be assembled in dazzling new patterns. A community is great—in fact, it is a community at all—only when its first concern is for the basic human needs of all its citizens, including the most handicapped and underprivileged."

For the past 50 years Bellarmine College has matured along with the rest of the country in terms of human rights and social justice. In fact, it has usually stayed a few yards ahead of most other institutions. In February of 1996, the Race Relations Forum topic was, "How Will Bellarmine Educate Students for Diversity?" Diversity was no longer merely a buzzword at Bellarmine. It was a part of the front-line agenda. At Bellarmine it has been a policy that not only set a moral high ground but has benefited the educational environment. Jack Daly singled out one of his own students as an example of the success of African Americans at Bellarmine: "Mike Cowherd was not only a good track star but a good chemistry student." Numerous other examples could be cited from the army of "nontraditional" students that Bellarmine has been privileged to welcome.

The Bellarmine-Ursuline Merger and Other Inter-Institutional Cooperation

From its inception Bellarmine College has cooperated with other colleges and universities and institutions promoting education at all levels, public and private. In a commencement address to Ursuline Academy graduates on June 1, 1953, Fr. Horrigan touted the value of both Catholic and public school systems, which, he said, "provided friendly, stimulating competition for one another." During the '60s when plans were being made for a state-sponsored community college in Louisville, Horrigan said he would welcome such a school. "We need a college like this here," he said. "It will enable anyone who wants to attend college." This cooperation has been so much a part of Bellarmine's outreach that only a few representative instances can be given.

An early example and an appropriate symbol of these harmonious relationships is a choral program sponsored by Bellarmine, Ursuline, Nazareth and the University of Louisville and performed by their faculty and students at the University Playhouse during the Christmas season of 1952. Another musical outreach occurred in the spring of 1961, when the 50-member Glee Club announced a series of concert swaps with the St. Mary of the Woods chorus at Terre Haute, Indiana. In April of 1962, Bellarmine's first choral festival was held in Knights Hall and attracted six colleges and high schools. There have also been frequent exchanges of art works by faculty and students with sister institutions. The Book-A-Semester was a Bellarmine-originated program that eventually would involve five colleges in the Louisville area. Each series began with the selection of a book to be read and discussed on member campuses and culminated with the visit of the author to Louisville.

Another kind of educational cooperation took place in February of 1961, when Bellarmine was one of ten colleges nationally asked to participate in a Youth Corps Program study to determine student opinion about President Kennedy's plans to send American young people to underdeveloped countries for educational and economic development. Other schools participating in the study included Yale, Swarthmore, and the universities of Michigan and North Carolina. It was the beginning of a program that would become the Peace Corps.

Intercollegiate cooperation has included not only such vital parts of the Bellarmine program as athletics and debate, discussed elsewhere, but curriculum agreements with other institutions. In the summer of 1969, for example, Bellarmine-Ursuline signed a cooperative pact with the Louisville School of Art, providing for a cross-town exchange program, with the art school becoming in effect the art department for Bellarmine students. In return, the art school students took academic courses at Bellarmine. Another local pact was approved in 1988, when Bellarmine and the Louisville Presbyterian Theological Seminary began to offer a dual-degree program that allowed students each a Master of Divinity degree and an MBA degree at the same time.

The most extensive and long-lived of Bellarmine's local collegiate alliances, however, is Metroversity. It was the brainchild of Fr. Horrigan, who in October of 1966 proposed hiring a consulting firm to study the feasibility of "inter-institutional cooperation" in programs and classes. It was formally established in the fall of 1969 as a consortium to coordinate certain courses and activities in the five participating schools: Bellarmine, Indiana University Southeast, Southern Baptist Theological Seminary, Spalding College (now University), and the University of Louisville. The schools agreed to share their libraries

and to allow students to take certain courses on each campus without paying additional tuition.

From the beginning Metroversity had an identity problem. It was a consortium with no campus, no classrooms, no faculty and no students of its own. Its offices were shifted around, first to the University of Louisville's Shelby Campus, then to Gardencourt on Alta Vista Road, and later to the Ursuline campus. Its mission was to encourage and coordinate cooperation among the member institutions, eliminating

unnecessary programs and enlarging the curriculum and programs for all students through sharing. During its first year, however, it drifted without a full-time head. Joseph F. Maloney of the University of Louisville was appointed part-time director, but it wasn't until the appointment of Jack Ford, a former Bellarmine philosophy professor, as director in the early '70s that meaningful activities began. As he said to a writer for *Louisville* magazine in September of 1973, "A consortium should encourage colleges to undertake things together they wouldn't do alone."

Ford became an effective facilitator. The first Metroversity venture into drama was a summer 1974 production of *Oklahoma*, directed by Bekki Jo Schneider and staged at the Spalding College Auditorium. Later summer productions, including *Kiss Me Kate* and *Camelot*, were staged at Iroquois Park. Students could earn credit for set design and construction, costume design, acting, singing and dancing. There were social events—like dances and Metroversity Night at Champ's Roller Dome in the Mid City Mall—which brought students together from the widely separated campuses. Bowling tournaments, ice-skating parties, chess tournaments, leadership conferences, creative writing contests and even annual medieval conferences were other activities coordinated by Metroversity. In the '80s Metroversity had its own cable television channel and developed such local programming as "Reader's Choice," a discussion of books hosted by Bellarmine's Don Osborn and Tom Kemme.

Bellarmine's closest cooperation, especially during its first two decades when it was a male college, was with the Catholic women's colleges of Nazareth (later Spalding) and Ursuline. The cooperation among the three colleges was motivated not only by a desire to provide male-female social activities but by a practical objective—to attract more students. Noting that some Catholic young people choose "secular" colleges for their social advantages, *The Concord* in January of 1954 called for an increase in the tri-college activities. "When one considers that about one-third of last year's Catholic high school graduates of Louisville who chose to continue their education are doing so in secular institutions," the writer said, "there is an awareness of the need for a revised emphasis on the advantages, if not the necessity, of our Catholic colleges."

Robert Pfaadt remembers fondly the social activities with students from Nazareth and Ursuline. "We had a lot of chances to be with female students," he says, "on such occasions as plays, variety shows, mixers, dances and dinners." As Jimmy Ford, director of alumni affairs, would point out later, "Years before the merger of Ursuline and Bellarmine, there were mergers of a different kind, the marrying kind. Dozens of Bellarmine, Nazareth and Ursuline alumni had already pledged themselves to each other at the marriage altar." On one of those social occasions Barbara Emrich, Ursuline class of '55, met Alvin Cassidy, Bellarmine class of '54. It was the beginning of a lifelong relationship and, in the words of Barbara Cassidy, "a fantastic marriage." She adds, "He must have learned a lot about women at Bellarmine!"

A Bellarmine student and an Ursuline student become husband and wife.

It was a natural consequence of the close ties promoted among the three schools. The Catholic Inter-Collegiate Council, made up of student government representatives from the three colleges, planned cooperative activities, including leadership camps, Masses, literary contests, College Bowl competitions and frequent mixers. The winner of the 1963

Monsignor Felix N. Pitt Award given by the Bellarmine department of philosophy for the best student essay in philosophy, for example, was Maureen McNerney, a sophomore English major at Nazareth College. Her topic was "Does the Same Order of Causality Apply to the Microcosm as the Macrocosm?" Her prize was $35.

Without an official female student body until the merger with Ursuline in 1968, Bellarmine even chose its homecoming queen each year from either Ursuline or Nazareth. A 1959 photo in *The Louisville Times* shows a happily indecisive Joe Reibel, co-captain of the basketball team, trying to select his favorite of four beautiful candidates from Ursuline and Nazareth. The queen would be actually chosen by vote of the male student body and announced at the homecoming game at Columbia Gym with Georgetown College. In the fall of 1962, Ursuline and Nazareth selected by vote of their student bodies three candidates each for Bellarmine's homecoming queen. The six candidates were then voted on by the Bellarmine students and crowned at half time ceremonies at the Bellarmine-Transylvania basketball game on December 8, 1962. The winner was Mary Beth Jepson, a sophomore at Ursuline. The winner of the game was Bellarmine, 74-55.

Or was the real winner Joe Reibel, who later married one of the other candidates for queen?

A milestone in cooperation among the three colleges was reached in the fall of 1962, when they agreed to open certain credit courses to each other's students. The first males to attend Ursuline were Bellarmine students John Young and Boyd Hanke, who took a course in statistics. On the other hand, 10 students from Ursuline and one from Nazareth were visiting students in philosophy and chemistry classes at Bellarmine. According to Fr. John Loftus, academic dean, the arrangement in no way was "a threat to the autonomy of the cooperative institutions," but rather, he said, a way of improving efficiency while expanding options and eliminating needless duplication and overlapping facilities.

In the fall of 1964, cooperation between Bellarmine and Ursuline became even closer. In a joint venture led by Fr. Horrigan of Bellarmine and Sister M. Angelice Seibert, Acting President of Ursuline, the two colleges established a new agency called the John XXIII Institute of the Church in the Modern World, which sponsored courses, lectures and workshops on topics covered by the Second Vatican Council. At the same time the men of Bellarmine and the women of Ursuline agreed to share their cultural events in a coordinated program of more than 25 lectures, art exhibits, musical programs and movies. By July of 1967, Catherine Spalding College was considering some sort of closer cooperation with Bellarmine and Ursuline, though as Mother Lucile Russell, chair of the Spalding board said, "Merger is a rather strong term." Indeed, nothing came of it—at least as far as Spalding was concerned. With Ursuline, it was a different matter.

Women had been admitted to Bellarmine's evening classes from the beginning. But it was a male college and any hint of women breaching its walls in broad daylight was met with stiff opposition. In the fall of 1957, the student senate passed unanimously a resolution mandating that the student council president, Cletus "Sonny" Roppel, investigate the presence of a female day student in several classes and requested that in the future the administration inform the senate of any changes in college admission policy. After all, the resolution noted, the college catalogue stated unequivocally that "Bellarmine is a Catholic college for men." In response, Fr. Horrigan rejected the resolution as inappropriate but advised the group

YOUR DAUGHTER AND URSULINE COLLEGE

that college admission policy had not changed. The female student in question, he said, was a college secretary and had been admitted to day classes as an exception to the policy. The senate, he suggested, should concern itself with student programs.

It was small wonder that male students were nervous about an invasion of females. Earlier that year, an April Fools' Day headline in *The Concord* read: "BELLARMINE GOES CO-ED: 800 Females Clutter Campus in Fall Semester." The article reported that several departments were to be added to accommodate the new students and such courses as home economics, rug making and martini mixing were being offered. Several prospective "Bellargirls" were interviewed, including Inez Potrzebie, Ophelia Furshlugginer and Hecuba Pastafazool, whose only comment was "All those men!" Why, any red-blooded BellarMan would wither in fear and trembling at such prospects! Of course, Bellarmine students welcomed co-eds from Nazareth and Ursuline on their own terms.

Indeed, Ursuline women and Bellarmine men seemed to like each other on the dating field from the start. In early October 1950, members of Ursuline's junior class sponsored a freshman mixer to which Bellarmine students were invited. Following a wiener roast and Cokes, a throng of students, including Peggy Pike, Bob Doyle, Carol Stratman and Joe Burke, headed for the Ursuline gym to do some slow dancing to juke box music. Less than a week later, Ursuline held its College Daze Hop with Bellarmine students as guests of honor. The dance decorations were collegiate—complete with megaphones, mortarboards, pennants, footballs and cowbells adorning walls and windows.

Relations between Bellarmine and Ursuline would become even closer during the following two decades.

Sr. M. Concetta Waller, who was President of Ursuline between 1962 and 1964, remembers that she raised the question of inter-institutional cooperation at a meeting of the Ursuline Board of Trustees in October of 1963. Later that month at a board meeting with Fr. Horrigan a decision was made to retain the services of consultants to study the feasibility of closer cooperation between Ursuline and Bellarmine. Apparently, the original plan was to include Spalding. According to minutes of the meeting, "Mother Salome asked if we could proceed with our plans if Catherine Spalding College does not participate," and Fr.

Sr. Angelice Seibert

Horrigan responded that plans could proceed "if we can find a way to do so."

Because of Sr. Concetta's illness, Sr. M. Angelice Seibert was named Acting President of Ursuline, and she worked with Fr. Horrigan to set up committees for the Ursuline-Bellarmine coordination, which

eventually led to merger. Two later studies—the Booz, Allen & Hamilton Study and the Raymond F. Hart Study—would recommended an all-out merger for financial and academic reasons. According to Fr. Horrigan, the studies predicted that a merged school would enjoy reduced expenses and expanded academic programs. "At that time," said Fr. Horrigan, "we were seeing the disappearance of single-sex colleges. At Bellarmine we had also had experience with inter-institutional cooperations by providing core courses for both the Passionist seminarians and for students at the Louisville School of Art. Institutional cooperation was in the air. So with the strong support of the majority of both faculties, we entered into the merger, with Fr. Frederick serving as the coordinator in working out the details." It would be four more years, however, before the merger would be accomplished.

A headline in *The Concord* of January 7, 1964 read, "Bellarmine Goes Co-ed?" and announced that day and evening classes as well as the summer session would be open to women. In early November of 1964, Sr. Angelice and Fr. Horrigan released a statement of coordination, which began: "We are pleased to announce at this time that the boards of control of Bellarmine and Ursuline colleges have authorized the institutions to proceed with plans for a program of coordination for the purpose of minimizing operating costs and strengthening the quality of academic

offerings. We deliberately employ the term 'coordination' to describe the new program. 'Coordination' is something less than 'merger' and considerably more than 'cooperation' as this term is usually employed in references to relations between colleges." Furthermore, the consultants recommended that all departments be grouped into four major divisions—humanities, natural sciences, social sciences and theology and philosophy—headed by a faculty member drawn from one of the two colleges.

Opposition to the new relationship surfaced quickly, and the 1965 April Fools' issue of *The Bellarmine Concord* predicted an eventual disaster. Projected to a date of April 1, 1985, and renamed *The Bellarmine University News,* the spoof's lead story was headlined, "Coordination Dropped; Unqualified Flop." It read: "President Arnold Dearing announced yesterday that the University is taking immediate steps to disassociate itself from any formal relationship with Ursuline College, long the University's partner in a program of coordination. Although the announcement really surprised no one, the student body rose to the occasion and warmly expressed their approval of the proposed move. An informal gathering of dorm students gleefully ripped the laced Cape-Cod curtains off the cafeteria windows, burned a hundred and fifty table cloths and scattered fourteen pounds of cigarette butts over the floor.... Fr. Arnold reported that the decision had been in the offing for a long time. Student and faculty dissatisfaction with the coordination program had been prevalent over the years, Fr. Arnold noted, but it had been hoped that the problems would correct themselves in time. 'Well, we tried,' Father remarked, 'but everybody's had about enough. The report of the consulting firm leaves no choice but to drop the

URSULINE COLLEGE

whole mess.'" Fortunately, it was a prophecy which did not come to pass.

In the fall of 1965, Fr. Horrigan announced that 121 Ursuline and Bellarmine students were involved in coordinated courses on the two campuses. Ursuline began the semester with 173 freshmen, its largest in history, and a total enrollment of 555. The two colleges shared much of their faculties, facilities and special events, such as classical guitarist Basil Gural, who gave concerts on both campuses. At the same time the colleges operated on a coordinated schedule with identical registration dates, holidays and exam periods. They also announced a trimester schedule, which cut summer vacation by two weeks in order to complete a fall semester before Christmas vacation. By the fall of 1965, a campus column was appearing in *The Concord* called "Ursuline Utterances." Earlier in the year Bellarmine students had helped Ursuline students raise money to allow an Eskimo student, Elizabeth Beans, to visit her family in St. Mary's, Alaska, for the first time since she became a student at Ursuline. In November Fr. Horrigan appeared before the student senate to dispel the rumor that the purchase of the Collings estate across Newburg Road from Bellarmine was tied to the relocation of Ursuline on an adjoining campus. He said there were no immediate plans to bring the two colleges closer together, although he stated that two such similar colleges so close together were not likely to survive.

In the fall of 1966, both Sr. Angelice and Fr. Horrigan hailed the coordination program as a success. Sr. Angelice termed it "a rewarding and satisfying record" of coordination, and Fr. Horrigan said the success of this venture was a first step in a proposed cooperative plan among all of Louisville's colleges and seminaries. In her annual report to the Ursuline Board of Trustees, Sr. Angelice applauded the coordination plan for strengthening the education program and improving the economic status of Ursuline. She also noted that during the year the board had approved the establishment of a corporation that would separate Ursuline College from the Ursuline Society. Yet there were negative voices heard, some trivial and some serious. A letter from Mary Linda Lee to *The Concord* on November 24, 1965, commented on the attempts by the student senate to address the issue of wearing high-school letters on jackets. "You may not be wearing a letter jacket," she complained, "but you will still stand in the corner at mixers—just like you did in high school." In October of 1966, an Ursuline student griped about a "cold war" between Bellarmine and Ursuline students. In a letter to *Counterpoint,* she wrote:

PLAN FOR INTER-COLLEGE COOPERATION

URSULINE COLLEGE
BELLARMINE COLLEGE

"As of yet, I have found only smirks of sarcasm from the boys and looks of indignation from the girls." The war of the sexes was heating up!

Despite occasional murmuring and some opposition, in June of 1967 the boards of both schools approved a resolution which endorsed the recommendations of management consultant Raymond Hart that the colleges should merge. During the 1967-68 "transition" year, the pages of *The Concord* were filled with pro and con opinions about the impending merger. The paper reported on September 22 that Sr. Angelice and Fr. Horrigan might have different understandings of what the newly approved merger meant. According to Sr. Angelice it would be "a merger in the true sense of the word," with a new institution that would be "different from any other college now existing." Indeed, controversy over the name of the new institution suggested deep-seated differences over exactly what the merger would be. During the transition year the merger steering committee hammered out a "Statement of Intent to Merge" for approval by the governing boards of both institutions, including one recommendation, believe it or not, that for a period of three years the name of the institution would be Bursuline College. Sr. Pat Lowman of Ursuline's history faculty remembers that the meetings and deliberations were sometimes "heated."

In an October 20 article Barbara Lega of Ursuline noted that many people believed that Ursuline would gain everything and Bellarmine nothing. On the contrary, she wrote, Ursuline had much to lose— their honor system, their closeness to each other and their Ursuline traditions. "I only hope that Bellarmine is prepared to do a little giving-up and compromising too," she concluded. In a later article she profiled the "UGABers," the Ursuline Girls at Bellarmine. Some of the girls, she said, having attended girls schools for as many as six years, were finding it hard "to get used to all of those boys around." They all liked, however, not having to open doors; and one girl admitted that

Counterpoint

Vol. 39, No. 6   URSULINE COLLEGE, LOUISVILLE, KENTUCKY   January 31, 1968

At Last! It's Bellarmine-Ursuline College

"going to Bellarmine is like going to a big mixer in which the odds are in favor of the girls."

In April 1968 the Bellarmine board voted itself out of existence, and a new Bellarmine-Ursuline board was appointed. Fourteen of the 21-member board were laymen, and four were not Catholics: Robinson S. Brown, Jr. of Brown-Forman Distillers; Samuel H. Klein, president of Bank of Louisville; Mrs. Irvin S. Rosenbaum and T. Ballard Morton Jr., of WAVE, Inc. Fr. Horrigan recalls the forming of the board: "We constituted a new board made up of members of both of the old boards. Every member of each board was invited to join the new board, though some chose not to. The first chairman of the new board was Kenneth Barker, who had been chairman of the Ursuline board as well as a member of the Bellarmine board. He was the perfect symbol of the merged institutions."

The new board then selected Fr. Horrigan to be the first President of the new college. He had previously announced that he would not accept the presidency except on certain conditions, namely, that the Bellarmine and Ursuline faculties approve and that students be allowed the freedom to protest orderly. "I was President for five more years," he said after his retirement, "but I made it clear that I would not stay unless the faculties were polled and decisively wanted me to stay. I had been President for almost 19 years, and I was ready to hang up my spikes. But the faculty overwhelmingly, though not unanimously, asked me to stay on."

Sr. Angelice remembered later her own hopes for the new school: "My dream for the college was that we'd have a President who would be neither Fr.

Horrigan nor myself, with a new name, a new shape, a new form—taking the best from both institutions, all done in a way that neither college would feel that it was submerged."

In the spirit of new beginnings, *The Bellarmine Concord*, which had been the campus paper's official name since 1962, was changed in the fall of 1968 back to its original name of *The Concord*. Even the humor column, AKOH, gave the merger a warm, enigmatic endorsement: "A lot has been said recently about the effect the merger will have on the academic atmosphere of the college. Lest we forget, gentlemen, the ladies possess qualities men have been seeking for years." In the next issue, however, the satirists were back to their old tricks with an announcement that the Bellarmine-Ursuline social committee had promised "an exhibit of the remains and relics of St. Robert Bellarmine-Ursuline," including "autographed photos and a memento or three."

The full impact of the merger was felt in the fall of 1968, when some 550 co-eds began attending classes on the former Bellarmine campus. Most of the male students seemed to like the influx of women. Don Poppe, a senior, said women in the classrooms made "classes more exciting." The new year brought a new concentration in communication arts as well as raises in tuition and dormitory rates. The combined faculties from the two colleges meant some overstaffing and a subsequent financial squeeze. A $200,000 deficit was forecast at the beginning of the new academic year because of the larger faculty and smaller than expected freshman class. The deficit was reduced by releasing some faculty and by curtailing some programs.

Indeed, the 1968-69 year was one to remember. Playtex tampon ads began to appear in *The Concord*. John Jacob Niles appeared on campus in November with a cycle of songs based on the poetry of Thomas Merton. Women won three of the four freshman class offices, though a male, Bob Thurmond, became class president. Judy Collins entertained a capacity crowd in Knights Hall in April. Student government was revamped. In his final editorial of the year, *Concord* editor Bob Sleezkowski summed up the year just passed at international and campus levels in one word—"Frustration." One optimistic note at the end of the year was the news that under the terms of his will, Thomas Merton, who had been killed in an accident in December of 1968, had made Bellarmine-Ursuline College the beneficiary of most of his works.

Perhaps the increasing numbers of women on campus and their increasing presence at ball games gave the basketball squad a boost. The sports editor of *The Concord* summed up the year by contrasting it with Jim Spalding's first two years as basketball coach, when his teams had 25 wins and 25 losses. "This year's edition displayed no resemblance to the two preceding squads. They set numerous team and individual records; filled Knights Hall to overcapacity; defeated Middle Tennessee State University, one of three pre-season favorites of the O.V.C.; broke a 21-game winning streak at Central State, the NAIA 1968 defending champions; knocked Tampa out of the national rankings . . . and gained much publicity and recognition as the No. 1 Un-Ranked Team in the College Division with its 'damn band' and 'those damn screaming students.'. . . No longer do we play Bible colleges at grade school gyms but the nation's best in a famous coliseum."

With merger came women playing competitive sports—something new under the Bellarmine sun—or as worded by the '69 *Lance*, "Girls Basketball?" It surely was, and it was at Bellarmine to stay. Coached by Don Baron, the first team roster included a new set of Bellarmine pioneers, the first set of female cagers:

Fall 1998 Women's Volleyball Team posing with a touring team from Russia.

Sharon Boone, Connie Byron, Cindy Cecil, Martha Edlin, Mary Jane Englert, Judy Gossman, Joyce Jeffers, Ann Morton, Molly McGrath, Mary Lane McNamara, Margaret Pierce, Mary Ellen Schnurr and Marilyn Steinmetz. Their first-year record was not exactly star quality, but it would improve greatly.

For another year some classes and college activities continued to be held on the Ursuline campus. The February 1969 production of Jean Anouilh's *Antigone* took place in the Ursuline auditorium. But the '69 Lance called the merger, in the parlance of the period, "a new happening" with great opportunities for a new cornerstone and identity for both colleges. Finally, in the fall of 1969 for the first time all classes were held on the Bellarmine campus, with the opening of expanded facilities in the New Science Building and the addition of facilities for women's physical education classes in Knights Hall.

For the first time in the fall of 1970, men and women lived on the same campus. Until then, the merged colleges used a dual campus setup, with the male resident students living on the Bellarmine campus and the female residents living on the Ursuline campus and commuting by bus to the Bellarmine-Ursuline campus. After a $91,000 renovation, the women had their own residence in Kennedy Hall. Improvements included rest room revisions, the installation of kitchenettes, sewing machines and a color TV set. The men had a more comfortable building as well when Newman Hall was carpeted and centrally air-conditioned. Each dorm had its own lounge plus a jointly shared recreation room in Newman.

Bellarmine not only gained a large female student body but a rich academic tradition from Ursuline, as alumna Joan Riehm testifies. A former *Courier-Journal* staff writer and former deputy mayor of Louisville, Riehm is the recipient of "16 years of Ursuline nuns," she says, from grade school through college. She pays tribute to the values she received from the Ursulines, who, she realized much later, were "the first feminists in my life and taught me that women can be somebody." She adds: "I've always thought of myself as an equal person, and when I traced it back, I realized it was a result not only of the influence of my parents but the nuns who taught me all those years. Yes, it was a different time and they wanted us to be good wives and mothers, but they also trained us to think and not be just vegetables turning out dinners and babies. They taught us philosophy and theology and mathematics. They encouraged us to go out into the world and be good citizens and take part in society and speak our minds and do our parts to save whatever parts of the world needed saving. Of course, now I can laugh and admit they taught me some things I've had to unlearn, but I also have to confess that some of that unlearning was a lot of fun."

Indeed, the Ursulines have a long history of service. Founded November 25, 1535, by Angela Merici in Brecia, Italy, at the Church of St. Afra, the order immediately attracted women who did charity work from their homes, devoting themselves to instructing young girls, comforting the sick, admonishing the sinner and setting a true example of Christian womanhood. In the Louisville Archdiocese

they have served as teachers in schools and colleges, including Angela Merici High School, Sacred Heart Model School and Ursuline, Bellarmine and St. Catharine colleges.

Sr. Consetta Waller, archivist and former President of Ursuline College, is well aware of the Ursuline heritage in Louisville, which goes all the way back to 1858. "Bellarmine could gain some age and academic prestige," she says, "by using Ursuline's heritage. In academic processions like presidential installations where institutions are arranged in the order of founding, Bellarmine could move up in line." Ursuline College, says Sr. Angelice Seibert, was originally formed in 1922 as a junior college to educate the sisters but was soon opened to other women students. It became a senior college in 1939.

Bellarmine College has been enriched also by the Ursuline faculty who joined the merged school. According to Fr. Horrigan, every full-time faculty member wanting to stay on was welcomed into the new school. A number of Ursuline faculty moved to the Bellarmine campus, including chemistry professor Thomas E. Kargl, communications professor Raymond Bailey, education professor Mary Ann Fueglein and Sisters Clarita Felhoelter, Patricia

Sr. Frances Marie Andriot

Lowman, Vera Del Grande, Frances Marie Andriot and Anna Marie Trance. Other prominent members of the Bellarmine faculty with close Ursuline connections include librarian Marquita Breit of the Ursuline class of '64.

Sr. Clarita, who became one of Bellarmine's most respected and beloved professors, began teaching at Ursuline in 1956. Her presence on the Bellarmine

Bellarmine - Ursuline College

∞

1968-69

Louisville, Kentucky

campus provided a great deal of Ursuline continuity. "Even though the transition was smoothed for me," she says, "because I taught some night classes at Bellarmine before the formal merger, I still felt a great deal of sorrow and grief over the merger and what we had to give up, especially at the beginning, though I soon learned to accept it. In fact, I soon began to love the coed environment. Now I know that although we had a very good college at Ursuline, the merger was right and necessary."

Sr. Pat Lowman, who taught at Sacred Heart Academy from 1958 to 1965, when she became a full-time professor of history at Ursuline College, joined the Bellarmine-Ursuline faculty in 1968 and quickly became a popular presence in the classroom as well as on the athletic field, where she became an important liaison between student athletes and faculty. She remembers the rancor felt by some Ursuline people

over the merger. "I know that the merger was necessary because both colleges were in an economic bind, but it left a lot of bad feelings with the Ursuline side, especially among the alumnae, who felt that it wasn't a merger but rather a submerger. Many of the women felt that the men had taken advantage of us. At the least, they thought that the college should have taken a new name and that both Presidents should have resigned and a new one appointed." Nevertheless, she says, "Teaching at Bellarmine has been a wonderful experience for me. I have loved every second of it."

Sr. Consetta Waller expresses her reservations about the merger. "During the merger negotiations," she says, "a lot of us at Ursuline feared that our women wouldn't have the leadership opportunities that they had at Ursuline. I also felt at the time that it was more of a take over than a merger, but I feel much better about it now. We've had a hard time winning the alumnae over to Bellarmine, but I think we have largely succeeded."

Sr. Angelice Seibert, who was President of Ursuline during the merger, has worked hard to combine the two alumni associations. In a May 1980 open letter to the Ursuline alumnae, she urged the pre-merger alumnae and alumni associations to merge. She stressed that the combined labors of Ursuline and Bellarmine had germinated and it was time for the associations to become one. "At this moment in its history," she wrote, "Bellarmine College (our college) needs the strength and vigor that a single, vibrant alumni association can give it." After the merger she took a Fulbright Fellowship to teach biochemistry at the University of Galway in Ireland, followed by periods at Smith College and Jefferson Community College, where she set up a division of allied health professions. At the 1975 Bellarmine graduation she gave the commencement address, the first female commencement speaker in Bellarmine's history.

Fr. Horrigan was sensitive to all the factors involved in the merger, from the retention of faculty to choosing a name for the new college. In July of

1967, a writer for *The Record* speculated mock-seriously on names for the soon-to-be merged colleges. Among the offerings were Ursabell, Bellsuline, Catholic College of Louisville and Bellarmine-Ursuline, which at least rhymed. In September of 1967, the Bellarmine Student Senate passed a resolution calling for the retention of "Bellarmine College" as the name for the combined institutions. The new board chose Bellarmine-Ursuline for a three-year period, beginning on June 1, 1968.

Horrigan expressed this and other merger issues succinctly. "Mergers are, of course, always emotional," he said, "especially if one side feels that it's giving up its identity, as many on the Ursuline side did. Indeed, after the interim period when the college was known by the hyphenated name, the board chose to use the Bellarmine name for the institution, effective on June 1, 1971. At that time many Ursuline faculty and alumnae felt betrayed, and I was sympathetic to their views because whoever names a thing controls it. Before the final name decision was made, I was personally very open to the use of a completely new name. But it was a position that the Bellarmine alumni vehemently opposed. One name I thought of as a candidate for the school was Spalding, to honor Bishop John Spalding, but it was later chosen by Nazareth College to honor their founder, Catherine Spalding. There was some sentiment for retaining Bellarmine-Ursuline or for naming the college after Thomas Merton, but I was less enthusiastic for these two possibilities."

Most of the college community had gotten used to the hyphenated name, despite some confusion by outsiders. A package received at the college in February of 1970 was addressed to "Bellarmine Vaseline College." The final decision to return to the original Bellarmine name was apparently a popular choice on the campus. A poll of faculty, students and alumni showed a four to one preference for "Bellarmine College."

Some Bellarmine faculty and administrators also had reservations about the merger, which not only made Bellarmine College co-ed but also changed its legal status and governance as it became a private, independent college with a self-perpetuating Board of Trustees. Alumnus and long-time business manager Jack Kampschaefer was concerned about all the changes and initially opposed the merger. At the time of the merger, as the newly appointed finance officer, he was on the hot seat. "I didn't have enough information to make an informed decision," he explains, "but I now know that it was the right thing to do. It has greatly enhanced this college."

Fr. Hilary Gottbrath, who was Bellarmine's dean of students during the merger, felt that "We brought too many faculty from Ursuline, and that helped bring on the financial bind we found ourselves in during the late '60s and early '70s." Some 20 years later, however, he found it "a good union for both schools." For several years, however, financial problems plagued the newly combined college, with a decrease in enrollment and an increase in faculty. Total enrollment of the merged school for the fall of 1968 was 2,021, compared to 1,870 enrolled at Bellarmine College alone before the merger. Costs were rising. Hundreds of potential Bellarmine-Ursuline students were choosing to attend the new Jefferson Community College. For two years following the merger the college ran a considerable deficit. In the spring of 1970, therefore, the school announced that it would reduce the faculty by 10 members (a 17 per cent reduction) for the following year and make similar reductions in the administration and cut library and other expenses to reduce the budget by $200,000 and thus bring it into balance.

Despite the obstacles of pride and prejudice and finances, the merger was, indeed, a grand success. The evidence is the students and the committed alumni they have become. Evelyn Williamson Poppeil, who had studied two years on the Ursuline campus, became a member of the first Bellarmine-Ursuline graduating class in 1969. This is her testimony: "We knew we needed to merge, but we loved our identity and our name. I remember a skit we did about a woman marrying a man and losing her name and it bothered her. It was a lover's quarrel that resolved itself the way lovers do. You are antagonistic for a while, like a rubber band that gets stretched far apart but when you do come back, there is a wonderful love that lasts forever. Although we feared it, by the time of the actual merger, it didn't seem like a jolting experience at all. The opposition that had popped up before the merger, evaporated as we got used to it. I think we Ursuline women have learned to love Bellarmine. I know I have."

Sr. Angelice's vision of Catholic higher education in Louisville was broad and reasonable and at least part of it came to fruition. In the mid-'90s she restated it. "My dream was that all our Louisville Catholic colleges—Bellarmine, Ursuline and Nazareth—would come together and form a single college with a new name, taking the best from all three schools and becoming a first-rate Catholic university of Louisville. It was apparent to me that Louisville wasn't big enough for three Catholic colleges. Nazareth decided not to go with us. At Ursuline we had a good college but we were too small. We needed at least 1,000 students to survive and we never got much above 600. We were putting a lot of Ursuline Sisters' money and resources into the college and finally decided that we should spend it elsewhere.

"We didn't have to merge with Bellarmine in 1968. We could probably have lasted another 10 years or so before we had a real crisis, but we wanted to make the decision before we had to make it. We have brought much to Bellarmine. We strengthened many departments, especially the education department, which we revitalized. There were some hard feelings for a few years among our faculty and alumnae. There were some problems created by changing a male college into a co-educational college, beginning with inadequate rest room facilities; but those were addressed and most have been effectively dealt with. For a while I was afraid that the Ursuline Sisters wouldn't be able to maintain a high intellectual level without a college to service, but that hasn't happened. We still have young nuns who go on to get their graduate degrees and teach on the college and university level. I can still envision sometime down the road a single Catholic university in Louisville, with a suburban campus and a downtown campus. It would be a strong institution with a new name—perhaps Thomas Merton University. But as for what happened in 1968, I have no regrets. The merger was the way to go."

And what has happened to Ursuline? As the new school Ursuline helped form faces the new millennium on its expanding campus between Norris Place and Newburg Road, Ursuline is still very much in the business of education at its campus on Lexington Road. The Ursuline campus is now home to five schools: Sacred Heart Academy, Sacred Heart Model School, Ursuline Montessori School, Ursuline Child Development Center and the Ursuline School of Music and Drama. Education is, indeed, thriving on both campuses.

The Bellarmine Difference

What set Bellarmine apart from other colleges at the beginning? In other words, why should a young man in Louisville in the 1950s choose Bellarmine and not some other college? In an open letter to prospective students in *The Record* on August 11, 1951 on the eve of its second year, from "The College Faculty," but probably written by Fr. Horrigan, five reasons were given "that make Bellarmine the logical choice." The first reason was that "Bellarmine College is a Catholic college. . . and has as its primary principle of integration the truths of Divine Revelation entrusted by Christ to His Church." The other reasons were that "it belongs to you" as a part of the local Catholic community; that Bellarmine is an adventurous new college with the latest facilities and equipment; that this new college has a rounded academic program and that the cost is reasonable.

In an article in the same issue of *The Record*, Fr. John Loftus buttressed these arguments by stressing the advantage of "college at home." For the first time in Louisville, he said, young Catholic men wanting a Catholic education would not have to break family ties

Bellarmine's 1998-99 National Championship Mock Trial Team

by going to college out of town. Furthermore, he said, students living at home would have lower costs. He also emphasized its small size as "one of its finest attractions." Bellarmine, he wrote, "is not an impersonal diploma mill." Students are not lost in the crowd. "Bellarmine students are not strangers." Students and professors know each other, he concluded, and work together toward the one end, the development of well-trained Christian gentlemen." Former student and present faculty member Ruth Wagoner implies the value of a small student body, when she says, "I not only found my professional career at Bellarmine College but I found my husband, James Wagoner, in the cafeteria."

So what kind of new college was about to be founded in 1950 on the 100 acres of neglected pastures and woods along Newburg Road? According to Edward Malloy, the president of Notre Dame University, "A Catholic university is the place where the Church does its thinking." But how is this objective spelled out in a real institution like Bellarmine? Each person who has had a part in the shaping of Bellarmine through the years has had a vision of what he or she has wanted the college to be. Indeed, it has been many things to many people. It was not founded to turn out cookie cutter, look-alike graduates. To say that we are all made in the image of God does not mean that we are identical robots. But a college founded with a mission that includes the development of a right relationship of creation to our Creator will have a certain, unique vision to guide it—a vision that will find many dimensions and many expressions. Invitations to the March 1995 groundbreaking for the new W. L. Lyons Brown Library were headed, "Realizing the Vision." Indeed, that's what had been going on at the college for 45 years and more in classrooms, lectures, chapel Masses, committee meetings, social gatherings, athletic contests, dormitory rooms, library carrels, board meetings, fund drives and private prayers—wherever Bellarmine people have been.

It is difficult, therefore, to try to sum up the uniqueness of Bellarmine College. Perhaps the people who have lived the vision should describe it, beginning with the first class. When *The Concord* polled members of the Pioneer Class for their "most lasting impression" of their Bellarmine education, here are some of the words they used: good liberal arts education, high intellectual level, the learning of humility, close relationship of students and professors, a Christian education, friendliness and concern of faculty for students' academic and personal problems.

Fr. Horrigan, the founding father, stated his views in an article he wrote for *The Courier-Journal* in August 1972 after leaving the Bellarmine presidency: "Probably the most distinctively American institution is the independent liberal arts college. It is the original ancestor of all American colleges and universities. It is found on a broad scale nowhere else in the world."

But, like the first liberal arts colleges founded in this country, Fr. Horrigan's college would be built upon the solid rock of the Christian faith. Bellarmine would also be different from most Catholic colleges that are operated and staffed by orders of nuns and monks. With major support from the Franciscans, this college would be owned and operated by the entire Archdiocese. This Diocesan dimension meant that most of its students—at least in the beginning—would come from the Louisville area and that most of its graduates would remain and work in the area following graduation. An early survey showed that some 75 percent of the first three graduating classes did, in fact, remain near home. Although this figure has been reduced as the college has extended its outreach far beyond the Archdiocese into other states and countries, the college continues to provide Louisville and the surrounding areas with a highly educated and motivated alumni who have assumed leadership positions in business, politics and the professions.

In a series of articles he wrote for *The Record* in the spring of 1950, Fr. Horrigan projected his vision of what the college would be: "The College will recognize, and seek to discharge completely, the obligation to teach young men how to make a living in our complex 20th century world. But it will always insist upon giving first attention to the obligation of teaching its students how to live and die in the light of eternal truths." Furthermore, he wrote, the college will not teach students "tricks to make money" or "that the only important values in life can be measured with the dollar sign." Neither will the college teach students "to fit into the world" but rather "to evaluate this world and. . . to change it where and when necessary." Finally, he promised, "From the day that Bellarmine opens its doors, it will be dedicated to the proposition that it is obligated to impart wisdom to its students; to give these students a sense of values and an insight into the culture and history of their civilization, and a clear and intelligent grasp of their responsibilities as Christian citizens." Elsewhere, he stated that the college did not intend to train young men simply how to "slither" into society, knowing the tricks of their trade, but to inculcate in them a sense of social responsibility.

Bellarmine's second President, Eugene V. Petrik, brought a different style and more businesslike approach to college management; but he maintained a vision of its special calling. In appealing to the business and professional community for support, Petrik used such words as "partnership" and "vital" to show how the college and the community could work together for mutual benefit and development. At the same time he called upon the college to honor its moral and spiritual roots.

Near the end of his presidency, he wrote in a promotional brochure directed to prospective students what he believed to be Bellarmine's uniqueness: "Our distinction is mainly, I believe, in the mix of our superb faculty, our highly motivated students, our sound curriculum and our grounding in Christian principles. It's a combination that works." After listing "the things we do well"—like teaching the intellectual traditions of Western culture, producing people with marketable skills and leadership potential and respect for all kinds

of people, he added: "Finally, we want to develop in our students what I call 'greatness of heart.' We not only want to give students the intellectual equipment to earn a good living and the cultural equipment to know how to live well. We also want our students to have another dimension to their lives, a quality that causes them to reach out unselfishly in love and service to other people."

He concluded: "When you become a Bellarmine student, I believe you will soon feel yourself part of our common educational adventure—one shared by students, faculty, administration and staff. It is this camaraderie, this fellowship of learners united in the love of truth, that produces the Bellarmine dimension." All Bellarmine people—students, alumni, faculty, administration, staff, support groups, indeed anyone who has been touched by the Bellarmine experience—can amen Dr. Petrik's words.

Bellarmine has, indeed, been fortunate in the three Presidents who have led it through its first half century. Each one has had a clear mission, understanding, dedication and remarkable energy in leading the school. President Joseph J. McGowan, Jr. articulated the importance of the school's uniqueness from the beginning of his tenure: "Bellarmine has to be clear about who it is, about where it is going and how it will get there." During his decade McGowan has spelled out the college mission in innovative as well as traditional ways. New words like diversity, inclusiveness and community have become a part of the campus vocabulary.

Wendell Berry, perhaps Kentucky's most vital author and an occasional campus visitor, emphasizes loyalty to community in his books and in his life; but he laments that "the educational system doesn't educate people to be members of communities," because, he says in the spring 1996 *Kentucky Review,* "the idea of community loyalty removes the whole glamour of ambition from education, and it makes education a desperate undertaking." From its beginning, Bellarmine has had a mission, a faculty and a curriculum dedicated to Berry's ideal way of living—the developed individual who cares for and nourishes others, whether they are in his family, his interest groups like church, school or civic clubs, his town, his county, his state and nation—indeed, all the many communities in which he holds an allegiance.

Bellarmine's emphasis on community has been enhanced by McGowan's policies and example. The Opening Convocation and the Rite of Matriculation, instituted by McGowan in the fall of 1991, impresses upon all students new to the college the importance of belonging to the Bellarmine "community" with a Matriculation Oath, which states: "I promise to observe the statutes of Bellarmine College; to obey all its rules and regulations; to discharge faithfully all scholastic duties imposed upon me; and to maintain

and defend all the rights, privileges, and immunities of the college, according to my station and degree in the same." Furthermore, the entire orientation program has been revamped to introduce students to the community which they are joining, not merely for four years but for life.

Making it possible for all members of the college to participate in this community has been a long-term goal. With the new awareness of disabled students and their needs in the '80s and '90s, Bellarmine has developed a number of initiatives to meet their special needs. An undated questionnaire sent to all "handicapped students" in the '80s was prefaced: "A college community, as any community, is only as good as its component parts; it cannot function at the optimum level if any of those involved are not allowed

Bellarmine's Class of 1995

to perform at their highest level of achievement." Indeed, in many new and innovative ways McGowan has dedicated to making Bellarmine, in his words, "a human scale institution."

Despite the best intentions and efforts of Presidents and public relations officers, however, Bellarmine has been plagued throughout its history by public misunderstanding of its identity. At the beginning many people thought it admitted Catholics only or that it was a seminary to train men for the priesthood. Incredible as it may seem, some people thought it was a school for barbers, and in September of 1954 *The Louisville Times* reported that someone had called it "Ballerina College."

Bellarmine has attacked such ignorance and misinformation on many fronts—through efforts in public relations, various outreaches to the community and by asserting its identity through its public displays and symbols. The college coat of arms, designed by Sister Thomas, O.S.U., formerly head of the Ursuline College art department, and adopted in May of 1953, for example, portrays the religious, cultural and intellectual spirit of the college. One large stone panel, 4 feet by 7 feet, containing the coat of arms is located on the south side of Horrigan Hall.

After someone asked Professor Leonard Latkovski the significance of "that hand grenade" on the panel in the upper left field, he explained that the coat of arms of the Bellarmine family included six pine cones, which were ancient symbols of strength and fertility. In the lower right field is a torch, representing learning and wisdom, taken from Archbishop Floersh's coat of arms. The fleur-

de-lis in the center is a symbol of the Trinity and was taken from the City of Louisville flag. It represents the college tie to the city, which had borrowed it from France, where it was an emblem of the French kings. The Cross of Faith is stretched over a scarlet background and honors the college patron, St. Robert Bellarmine. Finally, from the Collect of the Mass of St. Robert come the words, "In the Love of Truth," in banner form at the bottom of the crest. The dominant colors of the coat of arms are the college colors, scarlet and silver.

Another visible reminder of the college motto is built into Horrigan Hall, with five quotations relating to truth inscribed on five stone panels placed on various parts of the building's exterior: "And you shall know the truth and the truth shall make you free"; "Everyone who is of the truth hears My voice"; "I am the way, and the truth, and the life"; "He will teach you all truth"; and "O God, Who didst endow blessed Robert, Thy bishop and doctor, with wondrous learning and strength, grant through his merits and intercession that we may grow in the love of truth."

A fuller and more academic description of truth was contained in the dedicatory address by the Very Rev. Paul C. Reinert, S.J., for the new administration building on June 19, 1954. Of Bellarmine College Fr. Reinert said: "Truth will be searched for in this institution, but any presumed discovery of new truth will be postulated on the most solid of evidence; it will not be the product of whims, or of emotions, or of preconceived notions. Here in the students and faculty members will reside a deep intellectual humility and intellectual honesty—a humility which will require that emotion, prejudice, and personal preferences must always yield in the face of evidence, and an honesty that demands that truth be recognized and given full respect and acceptance whenever and wherever found."

From 1971 to 1974 Bellarmine had a new logo, a large capital B composed of two stacked books. It was called a new logo for a new age and was designed for use in a fund drive, "Campaign for the Seventies."

Fall
1971

BELLARMINE COLLEGE

2000 Norris Place • Louisville, Kentucky

Before the ink on the new logo was dry, however, writers for *The Concord* were using words like "baffling," "confusing" and "curious" to describe the new Bellarmine symbol. An editorial called it "a miscarriage of a frustrated mind." Soon after he became President, Petrik declared it obsolete and retired it. Then in the late '70s his public relations experts came up with another logo and motto, a flame inside a circle, with the slogan, "Lighting the Way." When he became President in 1990, McGowan returned to a slightly modified version of the original coat of arms.

The school colors of scarlet and silver also conveyed an image to the public. Scarlet, the fire of the color spectrum, was chosen for the significance it had in the life of St. Robert Bellarmine; and silver, the sparkling reflection of light, was chosen because it was the traditional color of the Franciscan Fathers, who had provided much of the early faculty.

School songs have also reflected a positive image of the college. In early 1954, Frank Knoop wrote a sports fight song, "On Knights of Bellarmine," and Frederic Jarman wrote an alma mater which was used until President McGowan wrote a new one after his arrival.

Despite the many twists and turns that the college has taken during its first half century, there has seemed to be general agreement as to its objectives. The visitation committee from the Southern Association of Colleges and Secondary Schools in April of 1956

reported an impressive unity among college officials as to the college mission: "The committee found the administration and faculty of Bellarmine were very clear in their understanding and their statements of the purpose of the institution."

Another Bellarmine quality that is often cited by present and former students, faculty and staff is the feeling of community, of camaraderie, of togetherness they experienced while on campus. It was a tradition that started early. Alma Schuler remembers an incident that occurred during the first year of classes. "The mother of one of the boys called the office one day and said her son had left home without his lunch money. She asked, 'Please see if Fr. John will lend him lunch money so he won't go hungry.'" And, of course, he did.

As the busy first President Fr. Horrigan lamented in later years the fact that he didn't get to know the students as closely as he wanted. "I attended basketball games and dances when I could, but I was never able to teach a class; and I never got to know students one-on-one as well as did Fr. John and Fr. Hilary, whose positions as academic dean and dean of students brought them into closer contact. Fr. John had a string

Students visit the home of Dr. Wade Hall.

of students running in and out of his office all day, usually with smiles on their faces."

It was a camaraderie that occurred all over campus but nowhere so persistently as in the cafeteria. Rosalie Baker of the library staff remembers the periods when all of the administrative staff, the maintenance workers and faculty ate together at one table. Students and faculty mingled freely at tables throughout the cafeteria. On one occasion when a separate faculty dining room was proposed, the students complained of elitism and *The Concord* ran an editorial opposing such an egregious example of segregation.

Faculty camaraderie has become almost legendary, especially among those who were on campus during the college's first decades. Jack Daly: "When I came on the faculty, everyone knew everyone else. We were very close socially. There was a wives club, several informal men's groups, frequent potluck dinners and picnics for everyone." Indeed, Dan Sweeny remembers the close-knit faculty of the early days. "I was a member of a pinochle-playing group—or rather, I should say, a drinking group that played pinochle." That closeness has been somewhat dissipated as the college has grown larger and especially after the academic programs were divided into three colleges with their own faculty meetings. "I think we lost some important faculty communication when we stopped having one big faculty meeting," says David O'Toole, "though the recent formation of one faculty assembly has brought us somewhat back together."

The Bible says that "You shall know them by their fruits." The best measure of Bellarmine College is its alumni. They make all who served them while they were students proud. The December 26, 1995 issue of *The Courier-Journal* published an essay on his five-year service as a family court judge in Jefferson County, Kentucky, by Bellarmine graduate Steve Mershon. In clear and forceful language Judge Mershon discussed the ways he had tried to help mend broken families during his tenure on the bench. Not only did he reveal a thorough knowledge and understanding of the legal parameters of his profession but he displayed something more important—a concern for and dedication to the common good that is the goal of any good citizen. His essay also revealed a liberally educated man whose vision reflects the mission that Bellarmine College has set for itself from the beginning, to educate the total person in the love and pursuit of truth. Moreover, a professor of English and humanities would be pleased to count buttressing references to a wide range of sources—from the popular singer Eric Clapton and the Beatles to Socrates, Hamlet, the Golden Rule, Goethe and Walter Lippmann. It was an impressive testimony to Bellarmine's mission and its success in achieving it.

What made Bellarmine special for Beverley Ballantine, a nontraditional student in the late '70s? "I loved Bellarmine for many reasons. It was a comfortable environment. I loved the whole ambiance of the school and the sense of family between faculty and students. I made a number of lifelong friends with faculty and students, young and old. Oh yes, it was such a joy to be able to park my car close to my classrooms."

While individuals have doubtlessly felt underappreciated, most of the Bellarmine community have seen themselves as an important part of the whole. When Donna Olliges was assistant vice president for business affairs, she said: "I think most of us feel a part of one community. We are all on the college team—faculty, students, staff, administrators, trustees—and all players are interdependent. We know that the college could not survive without any one of these groups."

From President and dean to classroom instructor and cafeteria worker, from clerical assistant and mailroom clerk to work-study library assistant and housekeeping employee—all Bellarmine people have been made to feel wanted and necessary. Take Cecil Mingus, former assistant superintendent of maintenance, who says, "I feel we do important, necessary work at Bellarmine. Working here is more to me than just a job. I feel a part of this college. It has been an important part of my life."

Or take Nell Crews, switchboard operator, unofficial counselor to dozens of students—and occasional matchmaker. After working in the Louisville City Hall under eight Democratic mayors, she came to Bellarmine in 1980 and was still greeting people by telephone and in person from her booth in the lobby of Horrigan Hall 18 years later. She has seen her two sons, Clyde and Stevens, attend Bellarmine and return to teach. She says, "I enjoy meeting people and I have made a lot of dear friends here among the faculty and students. Once I saw a young girl walking into the library crying. I motioned for her to come over. She told me that she and her boyfriend had broken up. I hugged her and said, 'Don't worry, honey. You're young and pretty and there are many other boys to choose from.' About that time I saw a young man I knew coming down the stairs. I called him over, introduced

them and suggested he take her to lunch. They are now married. You see, I try to be a friend to anyone who needs a friend."

Of course, intelligent, active, thinking, productive people are going to disagree. But after a thorough airing of contrary opinions, Bellarmine people have usually come together for the common good. That is also part of the Bellarmine difference.

Camaraderie, newness, Catholicity and all the other Bellarmine distinctives are well and good; but alumnus Michael Steinmacher takes us back to the college's primary reason for being. "Most of Bellarmine's students are serious about learning because they know that Bellarmine is serious about education." Carole Pfeffer, '74, and now a member of the English faculty, was more direct in testifying to the value of her Bellarmine education: "I fell in love with Bellarmine from the start, and I'm still in love."

Mrs. Nell Crews

The Religious Dimension

The world of 1950 was very different from the world of today in just about every way imaginable—economically, racially, scientifically, socially, sexually, politically, even religiously. The United States is much more openly diverse today. Closet ecumenists have come out into the open and proclaim universality and brotherhood in the quest for meaning through religious dialogue. While Bellarmine's origins in Catholicism have always played a vital role in the college's identity, its public image today is broad and inclusive.

In the beginning, however, the college was parochial. Bellarmine was proudly established as a Catholic college for men. The college celebrated its maleness and its Catholicity. Most of the men who enrolled at Bellarmine in the early days were influenced by its Catholic connection. The first college catalogue of 1950-51 states unashamedly and boldly its parochial origins: "Bellarmine College is a Catholic college. It is Catholic not merely in the sense that courses in religion are included in its curriculum, but in the much deeper sense that its whole curriculum is organized around, and has as its principle of integration, the truths of Divine Revelation by Christ to His Church."

The religious core of the college was proudly proclaimed in the May 7, 1950 issue of *The Courier-Journal* in an ad signed by Fr. Horrigan and Fr. Treece: "The college recognizes, and intends to discharge completely, its responsibility to teach young men how to make a living in the complex modern world. But it will always insist upon giving first attention to the task of teaching these young men how to live in the light of the truth of Christian principles." At the end of a letter he sent to parents of prospective students in February of 1953, Fr. Horrigan wrote: "I do want to say the most important thing of all in closing: A <u>Catholic</u> college is the place for a <u>Catholic</u> boy." At a meeting of the Southern unit of the National Catholic Education Association at the Brown Hotel in Louisville in November of 1959, Fr. John Loftus said, "It is best for a Catholic student to be in a Catholic school."

The first issue of the college yearbook, *The Lance*, had also echoed its primary mission as a Catholic college. In fact, throughout the '50s the ritual of

Blessing of the Administration Building by Archbishop John Floersh.

graduation each year included the kissing of the Archbishop's ring.

Other college publications also proudly asserted their Catholicity. Throughout the '50s and beyond, the editorial stance of *The Concord* on moral and political issues was generally Catholic. Indeed, the newspaper won an "All Catholic" rating from the Catholic School Association for the 1953-54 academic year. The award was based on editorial content, style and make-up as well as its Catholicity and diffusion of Catholic thought.

Indeed, the college's Catholic identity was evident in all aspects of its operation, from crucial Diocesan financial support to course requirements to such campus community events as a religious pageant dedicated to Mary in October of 1954 as a part of Marian Year celebrations. Campus religious organizations and observances were numerous. In March of 1952, Fr. Jeremiah Smith helped to organize a Bellarmine chapter of The Militia of Mary, whose mission was "to help men sanctify their souls and convert all sinners to the Church through Mary Immaculate." Its activities included Masses and processions in honor of Mary. By 1954 it was the largest religious organization on campus with more than 150 members. In the 1950s the major religious event of the year was the annual retreat led by a carefully selected retreat master. When the administration building opened, it included a chapel with three altars and seating for 350. Mass was offered by a priest member of the faculty and students recited the rosary each day at noon and attended Benediction each Friday.

The absence of an honor system at Bellarmine was justified by the assumption that the students didn't need one. As Windell Bowles stated in a January 1956 issue of *The Concord:* "Bellarmine College simply places

St. Francis of Assisi

its confidence in the spiritual honor system of each and every Knight." His advice in preparing for exams: "Do not worry, do not cheat, do not cram, and do not forget to pray!"

Bellarmine's Catholic dimension was important to most of its students. In the early years the student body was overwhelmingly Catholic. In the May 8, 1952 issue of *The Concord* it was noted that during the previous school year the college had only two non-Catholic freshmen, both of whom were baptized into the Catholic faith in April. Finally, in April, 1953 the only non-Catholic on campus was baptized. Indeed, most students could echo James Sohan, '59, who said simply that he had enrolled at Bellarmine "because it was a Catholic school." Anthony Banet, Jr., editor of *The Concord,* in an interview in the fall of 1958 gave this as his motivation for coming to Bellarmine: "If you are a Catholic and want to be an educated man, it is logical to want a Catholic education." The close ties between the college and the Archdiocese are seen in the generous financial support from the church. In his annual letter in *The Record* the Archbishop wrote in November of 1964: "Due in large measure to your past generosity, Bellarmine College has extended the scope of its services to the Church in the Archdiocese year after year." By the end of its first decade, a writer for *The Louisville Times* could proclaim its success: "Bellarmine College is one of the proudest achievements of the Catholic Archdiocese of Louisville and of the Most Reverend John A. Floersh, the Archbishop."

In August 1951 Fr. John Loftus wrote in *The Record* that while Bellarmine is not a theological seminary "the influence of the Faith is felt in every classroom, through all personnel, in every college undertaking." He concludes: "Bellarmine could have no purpose apart from the furtherance of the Faith." An early promotional brochure emphasized its priest faculty: "Most of the professors at Bellarmine are Catholic priests. For them teaching is not a job, but a vocation. Their lives belong to their students."

Religious services were regular and often. At the beginning of each academic year the Mass of the Holy Ghost was celebrated for students of Bellarmine, Ursuline and Nazareth colleges at the Cathedral of the Assumption, often with a prominent speaker, such as the Very Rev. Comerford J. O'Malley, president of De Paul University in Chicago, in the fall of 1959. Mass was followed by a student breakfast, usually on the Ursuline campus. At the opening Mass, in the words of the '69 *Lance,* "we dedicated ourselves to the Christian commitment of a Christian college."

Masses were held daily at 7 and 7:30 a. m. and on Monday, Wednesday and Friday at 10:30 a. m. and on Tuesday and Thursday at 12:05 p. m. Confessions were heard daily from 11 to 11:30 a. m. and from 12 to 12:30 p. m. Fr. Clyde Crews remembers a time when they were popular with students: "There were confessionals in the old chapel on the second floor of the administration building, and on the day following the beginning of the Cuban missile crisis, I saw a long line of students waiting to attend confession. We thought we all might die in a nuclear war and we wanted to be ready."

Special Masses and other religious observances were often held. The beginning of the Christmas holidays was marked by the blessing of the nativity crib and the Christmas tree by Fr. Horrigan, with Christmas carols sung by the Glee Club. On May 13, 1951, Bellarmine observed for the first time the feast of St. Robert Bellarmine, with Mass offered in the chapel by Fr. Horrigan and the sermon delivered by Fr. Treece. In February, March and April of 1954 Bellarmine participated in the celebration of the Marian Year with eight public lectures, "In Praise of Mary." The death of Pope Pius XII in October of 1958 and

the election of Pope John XXIII were both appropriately observed on campus with Masses, lectures and convocations. St. Thomas Day was celebrated annually in March and included the announcement of the Msgr. Pitt Philosophy Award. The speaker for 1960 was Dr. Francis J. Collingwood, a philosophy professor at Marquette University. Memorial services were held following the death of Dr. Martin Luther King, Jr., and memorial concerts in his honor have become a fixture on the campus music calendar.

The Catholic connection was evident not only in the credit curriculum but in numerous noncredit, adult-education courses, in lectures by off-campus visitors and in special observances. Each February the library celebrated National Catholic Book Week with exhibits and speeches. In the fall of 1961 the college sponsored a six-session lecture series of noncredit courses based on Pope John XXIII's recent social encyclical, *Mater et Magistra.* In February of 1962, a Pre-Lenten retreat for married couples was held on campus. In March of 1962, the adult education division sponsored a Joyce Kilmer Forum of four sessions on Catholic beliefs for servicemen and women and their dependents at Fort Knox. In March 1975, the New Science Theatre was the site of the Archdiocesan observance of World Peace Day, with speaker Bishop Carroll T. Dozier of Memphis.

The campus religious dimension is also seen in the hundreds of students who came to Bellarmine to begin preparation for a church vocation—some of them individually and some as members of seminary classes. Pioneer Class member John J. Ford enrolled at Bellarmine with plans for a religious vocation: "My original reason for going to Bellarmine was that I was planning to be a Dominican priest, but the Good Lord had other plans for me. I fulfilled my vocation as a lawyer and have had the privilege of being Bellarmine's lawyer for a quarter of a century."

In December of 1964, the college announced that beginning in the fall of 1965 the college-level unit of the Passionists would shift from Chicago to Louisville and that more than 100 students preparing for the Catholic priesthood would be studying at Bellarmine under a cooperative program with the Passionist Fathers of the Holy Cross Province. (At the same time the Passionists' four-year theology program was moved from Louisville to St. Meinrad Seminary in Indiana.) The announcement stated that the new students would live at the Passionist House on Newburg Road, attend most of their classes on the Bellarmine campus and receive their bachelor's degrees from the college. Bellarmine officials noted that this new venture was designed to reduce costs, raise quality and exploit advantages from closer association between ecclesiastical and lay students. Several of the Passionist Fathers from Chicago were to join the Bellarmine faculty along with the students.

Although only 31 novices from the Passionist monastery actually began classes in September of 1965, they soon felt at home with the other students. They dressed not in the traditional Passionist black vestments but wore what Fr. Roger Mecurio, rector of the monastery, decided was more practical apparel—black trousers, white shirt, black tie—all of which complemented the Bellarmine red and white freshman beanie. The nearby monastery and academic experiment both were victims of changing times, and by the fall of 1974, only 17 members of the Passionist community lived at the monastery—seven priests, four brothers and six students who attended Bellarmine. In a few more years the monastery was closed and the Passionist students at Bellarmine were no more.

Another Bellarmine-seminary venture was with the St. Thomas Seminary, which had been founded in 1952 by the priests of the Society of St. Sulpice and located on Brownsboro Road. Because of falling enrollments and rising costs, the seminary closed at the end of the spring 1970 term and the 15 college students were moved into three apartments near the Bellarmine campus, where they were supervised by the Rev. Nick Rice, rector of the seminary's college

department. The formation house for these college seminarians was later moved into Bonaventure Hall. In addition to course work, the seminarians took their meals in the college cafeteria and were involved in student life.

In the fall of 1957 the college received from Mr. and Mrs. Thomas Nolan, Sr. a set of carillon bells, which could be played manually or set to play the Angelus automatically three times a day. In the words of Fr. Clyde Crews: "When I was a student we had the Angelus, and when the bells rang, you stopped where you were for the recitation of the Angelus—on the sidewalk, in the cafeteria line or talking to someone in the lobby. If you were sitting down, you stood up, shut up and prayed along with the leader on the public address system." The observance inspired a poem by retired staff member Norma Ryan, "The Angelus: Noon on Campus," which commemorates the daily

Fr. Joseph T. Graffis

devotion as a quiet time when footsteps stop, speech is suspended and a hush descends through hallways and breezeways, a time when "Ivy halls and Bethlehem walls meet."

For most of its history, the religious life of the campus has been directed by the college chaplain and the campus ministry staff, which has evolved from an almost exclusively Catholic focus to an ecumenical ministry with many non-Catholics participating. By the late '70s the typical campus ministry staff included two Catholic priests, a Catholic sister and an ecumenical minister, usually a Baptist. In the early '80s the ecumenical minister was Ms. Barbara Prince, a student at Southern Baptist Theological Seminary. Increasingly, the campus ministry program encourages students to become involved in social service programs, including Circle K, the Chapel Singers and Vital Voices. In addition to serving as leader in campus liturgies, the campus minister became a kind of college ombudsman, or as Fr. Joe Graffis was described in the '81 *Lance*, "a friend and counselor."

Although Mass was said on campus from the beginning, it was not until December of 1955 that St. Robert's Chapel housed the Most Blessed Sacrament. At that time the Rev. John Lyons became resident chaplain and took up quarters on campus. He and the Rev. John Clancy, college registrar, began their "life in the tower," as they called their residence in the tower rising above the administration building. The college has been fortunate in having many excellent priests to follow in Fr. Lyons' footsteps. In the late '50s and '60s, it was the Fr. J. Howard French. In the early '70s it was Fr. John D. Deatrick, followed in 1974 by the Fr.. Joseph T. Graffis, who served for seven years and was succeeded by Fr. Jack Conley, whose title was campus ministry coordinator. During Fr. Conley's tenure he developed a strong relationship between the campus ministry and the Highlands community. In

St. Robert's Chapel in Horrigan Hall

the '80s and '90s campus ministers or "coordinators" included Fr. Peyton Padgett, Fr. Robert Stuempel, Fr. Paul Joseph McGuire, Fr. Leonard Callahan and Fr. Nelson Belizario.

Religious services have been held in St. Robert's Chapel in various locations—first in Pasteur Hall, then on the second floor of the administration building and later the first floor of the same building, then finally, a prominent location and more space in Wyatt Hall, when it was opened in 1984. Masses and other services have generally been well attended—sometimes too well attended. In the fall of 1973, the city fire marshal ordered Fr. Deatrick to limit attendance at Mass to those that could be seated. Standees along the walls and in the aisles were no longer permitted. Most of the overflow were accommodated, however, when Fr. Deatrick had the chairs rearranged, increasing the seating capacity from 240 to 283. Adequate space should be provided in the new freestanding chapel, Our Lady of the Woods, in the wooded area above Newburg Road near Bonaventure Hall. Ground for the chapel, which will be dedicated to the memory of Bellarmine's founder, Archbishop Floersh, was broken on June 14, 1998. It should be completed and ready for use in 2000.

In one form or another and under various names, special days of discussion and prayer, called Days of Recollection or Days of Reflection, have been a feature of the campus religious scene. Often held for a full day each semester, they replaced classes and focused on such topics as prayer, family, war, death, judgment, the search for meaning, sexuality and violence. In 1988 the principal speaker was novelist Susan Dodd, whose fiction has been commended for its religious themes. Although usually planned and promoted by the campus ministry office, in the spring of 1960 the Faculty Wives Club sponsored an evening of recollection in the college chapel.

St. Robert's Chapel in Wyatt Hall

Bellarmine's religious life has also been freely shared beyond the campus boundaries, usually by priest members of the faculty who have conducted religious services, written articles and columns for *The Record* and other religious publications, delivered church-related lectures, pastored churches and provided commentary for the media on religious issues and events. Faculty and students have often added an academic flavor to the religious life of the community. In October of 1960 Fr. Treece spoke at the ninth annual Living Rosary Devotion in Freedom Hall. Indeed, Bellarmine played a central role in the Rosary devotions throughout the '50s and '60s, when as many as 20,000 people attended the services. In May of 1967, Fr. Treece emceed the installation ceremonies at Convention Center for Archbishop McDonough. In the early '60s he also conducted a popular Sunday morning Bible study program on WHAS radio, called "Your Sunday Visitor."

The religious outreach has also touched secular organizations and institutions. In the early 1950s Fr. Richard O'Hare, a professor of psychology and sociology, served as a chaplain for the Louisville Fire Department, and in 1962 Fr. Kevin Cole of the theology faculty was appointed chaplain of a local unit of the Kentucky Air National Guard. For several

HOLY THURSDAY

APPLIANCE PARK – MARCH 30, 1972

years beginning in 1962 priests from the faculty celebrated Lenten Masses at the General Electric plant. In the same year, the Flaget Forum, a five-week lecture series on Christian thought and current affairs, was directed by Bellarmine professors in the Knights of Columbus Hall in Bardstown.

Fr. Horrigan's ministry beyond the campus extended far and wide. In February 1965 he gave the benediction at the University of Kentucky's centennial celebration at which President Lyndon Johnson was the principal speaker. Like Fr. Horrigan, Fr. John Loftus was a popular speaker, especially at ecumenical forums in various churches and institutions, including the Louisville Presbyterian Theological Seminary and the Southern Baptist Theological Seminary. The secular faculty have also played signficant roles in Bellarmine religious outreach, serving in important positions in their local churches and ecumenical organizations such at the Highlands Community Ministries. English professor Thomas Sheehan and his wife exhibited their religious devotion on a European trip, when they were received by the Pope in a private audience at Castelgandolfo in the late summer of 1957. Following the Second Vatican Council's decision that Mass should be said in the vernacular language, Professor Leonard Latkovski, a prominent campus conservative, became active in the Lay Apostolate for the Traditional Catholic Mass, which received permission from Archbishop Thomas J. McDonough for a Latin Mass to be celebrated in at least one church. Priest and secular faculty have also been active in liberal and antiwar movements.

From its beginning Bellarmine has served as a meeting place for numerous Catholic and non-Catholic religious groups, ranging from the Catholic Physicians Guild of Louisville in 1957 and the Catholic Business and Professional Men's Club to a temporary home for a local Jewish congregation; from a 1955 Knights of Columbus-sponsored Cana Conference on Marriage to the Priests' Parents Club in 1975; from Te Deum, a Catholic men's organization devoted to adult education to a class reunion for St. Xavier High School.

Indeed, in addition to its central mission of preparing young people spiritually as well as academically and vocationally for a fully dimensioned life, the college has served the Church directly in numerous ways. Archbishop Floersh's 1954 Christmas reception for the people of the Archdiocese was hosted by Bellarmine faculty. In the spring of 1965 the college hosted a Preachers' Institute, which was designed to

Exploring the Light

improve preaching among priests of the Archdiocese. To everyone's surprise, the institute attracted 127 priests, who were instructed on how to prepare and deliver sermons. Later in the same year, the college sponsored a Pastoral Psychology Institute, chaired by Fr. Joseph Voor and Dr. Robert Munson of the psychology faculty, which aided clergy in recognizing and counseling people with serious emotional problems. In 1972 the campus office of continuing education developed the Parish Religious Education Program (PREP), a training program for religious education teachers.

The college continued its close relationship with the Archdiocese under President Eugene Petrik. In June of 1974, the college served as the site of a conference to instruct priests about the role of deacons in the life of the local church, and later that year a Bellarmine-based, two-year course of study for prospective deacons was begun under the leadership of Fr. Nick Rice. In 1978 the Merton Studies Center offered a series of service courses for the religious community, including "Money Management for Church People."

A number of Bellarmine people were involved in the renovation and rededication of the Cathedral of the Assumption in 1975. Fr. Clyde Crews, who had earlier written a history of the Cathedral, led the planning and design for the Cathedral Museum, which presented a visual panorama of regional Catholic history. He also planned the program for the rededication, which took place in April. Bellarmine art professor Robert Lockhart designed and executed new statues of Christ on the cross, the Virgin Mary and St. Joseph for the sanctuary. At the dedication ceremony, the homily was delivered by Fr. Raymond Treece, Bellarmine's executive vice president. In his commentary for *The Record,* Fr. Crews wrote: "It speaks to us of simplicity, solemnity and solidarity. In short, it stands as a Cathedral religiously right for our time."

In the early '60s the college demonstrated perhaps its most signficant testimony as a Church-related college during the series of meetings of the Second Vatican Council, which helped to update the Church to face contemporary challenges, including issues of social justice and ecumenism. Indeed, in October of 1962, Fr. Horrigan accompanied Archbishop Floersh to the opening of the Council in Rome, where some 2,800 Church leaders had convened at the call of Pope John XXIII. Although Fr. Horrigan was a nonvoting observer and returned early with the ailing Archbishop of Louisville, he brought away many views and insights of the Council, which he shared often with college and community groups. At a campus assembly in January of 1963, he noted that "Pope John has done much to end the myth that the 13th century was the Golden Age of Christianity which modern Christians can only wistfully sigh after."

In October of 1965, Fr. Horrigan was again in Rome as an observer of the Council. A report he sent to *The Record* that fall ended with this optimistic but realistic appraisal: "Vatican II has accomplished far more than most of us could even have imagined three years ago. But over and over again as it draws to an end Council Fathers remind one another and the world that all this is just the beginning. Everything depends not upon the words on paper but on the faith and love with which they are made to come alive in today's world." During a lecture at Ursuline College in December of 1965, he stated that the Council had fulfilled its aim of addressing the Church's dialogue with the world in "a most stunning way." He added: "We do not have the answers, but we do have new hope, new humor, new patience, new tolerance, new humility. The old defensiveness is gone and the old apologetics is dead."

In March of the following year Fr. Horrigan was selected by the Archbishop to chair the newly established Commission on Ecumenism, formed to implement locally Vatican II's Decree on Ecumenism. Another indication of strong campus support for the Council's recommendations was a collection of essays, *Impact of Vatican II,* edited by philosophy professor Jude P. Dougherty and including contributions by Fr. Horrigan, Thomas Merton, Fr. Jeremiah Smith and Dr. John Ford. At the death of John XXIII Fr. Horrigan paid him this tribute: "We cherish the hope that all of us may preserve the ideals and spirit which he has left as one of the great legacies of modern history."

Bellarmine's close ties to the Church are also seen in the religious vocations of its numerous priests, nuns and former seminarians as well as many others who have been "called" to their vocations at the college. Fr. George Kilcourse, for example, believes that his vocation as a priest is being fulfilled as a professor of theology. "My vocations as priest and teacher mutually reinforce each other," he says.

A number of Bellarmine's faculty and staff started on the road to priesthood but instead fulfilled their vocation in other ways. William J. Stewart, a sometime dean of students and general utility infielder, became a student at Bellarmine in 1955 after leaving the St. Meinrad Seminary in Indiana "when I decided that the priesthood was not my vocation." Hundreds of Bellarmine students through the years can testify, however, to the value of his secular vocation at the college. A long-time employee on the maintenance staff, Cecil Mingus, who spent a year at St. Thomas Seminary, believes that he has served his church by helping provide a safe and comfortable physical plant for the college community.

Jack Kampschaefer, whose long relationship to Bellarmine is unrivaled, states his commitment to the college convincingly: "Much of my life, I believe, has happened by Divine Providence, from my decision to enroll at Bellarmine as a student to my later decision to return as an administrator. I believe I found my vocation at this college. That's why I've stayed all these years, despite lucrative offers from other institutions and businesses. It hasn't all been smooth sailing. I've been ticked off by people and disapproved of some policy decisions. I've even been chewed out a couple of times. But I've never, ever regretted the day I cast my lot with Bellarmine College."

The religious dimension also includes courses in the curriculum, conferences and visitors to campus. Students are required to take core courses in theology and philosophy, but these courses are among the most demanding and rigorous in the college catalogue. As Fr. George Kilcourse says: "As a theologian I teach my students to think critically. I use no indoctrination in class. In fact, I see the role of theology at Bellarmine as making students literate in the discipline of theology. We want to engage them in conversation on faith and ethics. Our students will know the Catholic view and tradition, but we also want to expose every possible view on every question. We want our students to have a liberal education, and by that I mean an education worthy of the free, inquiring mind in all disciplines."

Of the many conferences, seminars and other forums that have religious implications, one of the cutting-edge areas is medical ethics. Often led by philosophy professor Fr. Fred Hendrickson, meetings have included a symposium on religious ethics and medical experimentation in the spring of 1985.

One of the most eminent theologians to appear on campus was Karl Rahner, a professor of theology at the University of Munich and respected Catholic spokesman. He was persuaded by the Bellarmine theology faculty to visit Bellarmine in April of 1979, when he was in the United States to speak at Marquette University in Milwaukee. During his visit to Louisville he met with students at Bellarmine and monks at Gethsemani. When he was made an honorary captain of the Belle of Louisville, he made his only public speech when he said, "We are all on a ship which is the Church, which is carrying us to the shores of eternity."

From its founding Bellarmine College has not only been Church-centered but ecumenical-minded.

A statement issued in November of 1949 by Fr. Horrigan and Fr. Treece and published in *The Record* emphasized the broad outreach of the new school: "While our college has as its specific purpose the education of Catholic young men, it is our confident expectation that it will serve the best interests of the entire community and that it will identify itself with every laudable program of community activity. We feel that its accomplishments in the course of time will prove a source of gratification to all the people of Louisville of whatever faith."

Indeed, Bellarmine in time became a place of free inquiry and discussion where students and faculty of many religious and cultural traditions could meet in mutual discourse and respect. Through the years many Protestant and Jewish and Islamic voices have been heard on campus—from the faculty and staff, from visitors, among the students and in the administration. In the fall of 1983, for example, the college's ecumenical minister was a Canadian graduate of the Southern Baptist Theological Seminary, Faye Summach, whose principal mission was to minister to non-Catholic students on campus. Ruth Wagoner, a member of the Disciples of Christ denomination who has been a student and faculty member, says that "Bellarmine has always been careful about other people's rights and beliefs." In 1963 a guest of the theology faculty was George Hakim, Archbishop of the Eastern Catholic Church. He returned in 1967 and celebrated a Mass in the Greek Orthodox rite at St. Agnes Church.

Bellarmine faculty and administrators have been leaders in ecumenical projects in Louisville. Perhaps the first time in Louisville that Catholics and Protestants worshipped together in a regular church setting was on November 29, 1964, when Fr. John Loftus of Bellarmine participated in an Advent service at St. Paul United Methodist Church, along with Dr. Wade Hall, a Baptist layman and English professor at Kentucky Southern College, the Rev. John Payne, pastor of Douglass Boulevard Christian Church, the

Rev. Andrew Anderson, rector of St. Andrew's Episcopal Church, and the Rev. Ted Hightower, pastor of the host church.

Bellarmine's relationship with Jewish groups has been especially warm. For several months in the fall and winter of 1979 and 1980, Temple Shalom, a Jewish community, used St. Robert's Chapel for services until they moved in their new building on Lowe Road. Fr. Joe Graffis, the college chaplain, said that not only had there been no complaints but that the arrangement "has given us all a chance to learn more about each other's religions." One member of the Jewish congregation told a *Courier-Journal* reporter that "I've never received this feeling of fellowship and welcome before." In the fall of 1979, the Jewish Chautauqua Society endowed a lectureship in Judaica at Bellarmine. The first lectureship was given by Rabbi Dr. Herbert Waller of The Temple. Other Jewish-oriented courses included "The Literature of the Holocaust," which featured such writers as Anne Frank, Elie Wiesel and Hannah Arendt in the fall of 1989.

Faculty and students have generally acclaimed the Catholic traditions and the ecumenical outreach. Robert Wittman, the Bellarmine academic dean, told *The Record* in the fall of 1975 that the college was "unashamedly Catholic" in its outlook "but not to the exclusion of others." In the words of alumnus Alvin Cassidy: "Bellarmine has had a large ecumenical impact on this community and has opened its doors to all religions and races; and I think this has been done without watering down its Catholic foundation."

When college ties to the Archdiocese began to loosen in the late '60s, many Catholic laymen and women were critical. In an interview published in August of 1975 in *Louisville* magazine, President Petrik described the situation which he was attempting to correct: "Many local Catholics felt for a while that Bellarmine was moving counter to traditional Catholic values. The college was referred to as a 'Christian institution' and the student newspaper ran some abortion-counseling ads." In 1972 Dean Robert

Preston published an essay in which he cited Fr. John Loftus's preference that Bellarmine continue to be called "Catholic" rather than "Christian," since the term was a statement of the college's founding mission. Preston, however, suggested that the college should "provide" its students with "a knowledge of the Catholic tradition of Christianity with its special values" but not "require" it. He concluded: "We have a responsibility to develop students who are critical, not students who are skeptical."

Because of his close ties to the business and non-Catholic community, many people assumed that Petrik's commitment to the college's Catholic heritage had weakened during the '80s. Fr. Horrigan thought otherwise. "Petrik had strong Catholic commitment," he said. "There was some criticism among faculty and alumni that the college's identity was becoming a bit fuzzy during his last years as President, especially with the expansion of the trustees to include about half non-Catholics. Some people were afraid that the next President might not even be Catholic. But I felt that the momentum of tradition would preserve the Catholic tradition and presence. Indeed, it did. I feel sure that the work of Petrik and McGowan will ensure its continuance in the future."

In August of 1989, the college created the position of vice president of religious affairs and named Fr. Leonard Callahan to the office. President Petrik noted that one of the benefits of having the new position was that it made possible the naming of the best people as administrators, regardless of their religion. Archbishop Thomas Kelly applauded the move: "Maintaining the Catholic character is something they are deeply committed to, and that's what this position is all about." The office, however, has since been dropped and its mission accomplished more effectively by other means.

Indeed, as the college faces a new century, its Catholic character appears solid and intact. In August of 1996, President McGowan announced that funds were being raised by Fr. Horrigan and Bishop Charles

G. Maloney and plans were being designed for "a freestanding chapel to honor the memory and contributions of Bellarmine's founder, Archbishop John A. Floersh." Furthermore, although by the 1990s the college was governed by an independent, self-perpetuating Board of Trustees, it retained a strong Catholic identity, with the instigation of Bellarmine Day to commemorate the birthday of the college patron that included a Catholic liturgy and community lecture and supper. In addition, to show the centrality of its religious dimension, President McGowan relocated the Thomas Merton Studies Center to the new Brown Library and established the Thomas Merton Center Foundation to plan programs and provide support for the center.

The Catholicity of Bellarmine has indeed changed over its first 50 years, but it is nonetheless central to the college mission. In February of 1968, the Swiss-born liberal Catholic theologian Hans Kung spoke in Knights Hall on "Sincerity: The Future of the Church" to an audience of more than 1,300. "The future," he said, "belongs to a thoroughly truthful Church." Alumna and faculty member Carole Pfeffer can echo Dr. Kung's sentiments by citing her experience at Bellarmine: "I lost my simplistic way of looking at my faith, but I knew it was a part of my growing experience, a necessary preparation for the important journey that Bellarmine helped equip me to take. I knew that the spiritual life was important on campus, but I never felt that I was being indoctrinated. The feeling that I had gotten from my parents and from my teachers at Assumption High School was reinforced and strengthened intellectually at Bellarmine. It was a sense of mission, the belief that we are here on this earth to accomplish something."

It is appropriate that a priest should have the final word on this subject. Fr. Clyde Crews in an essay in *The Concord* celebrating the silver anniversary of the college in September of 1975 recalled the omnipresent evidences of religion on campus when he enrolled as a freshman in 1962: "The Angelus was celebrated each day. A priest was President. A priest was vice president. A priest was dean. Over 20 priests, in fact, made up a large bulk of the faculty ranks. Everyone took four theology courses (no electives) from a series of red textbooks called *The Bellarmine College Theology Series.*" While there had been many surface changes, the religious dimension remained strong, he concluded: "So the style of faith shows a new face to a different generation as Bellarmine enters another quarter century as a distinctly religious institution." And thus it is as the college enters yet another quarter and begins its second half century.

Our Lady of the Woods Chapel   Bellarmine College   Nolan & Nolan Inc.

Our Lady of the Woods Chapel groundbreaking (L to R) James P. Ford, Bishop Charles Maloney, Dr. Joseph J. McGowan, and Alumni Board President Carl Heger

Alumni

Al Alvey, starting guard of the 1962-63 basketball team under Coach Alex Groza, moved to New York after graduating with a degree in accounting. After stints with a Big Eight accounting firm and with *The Wall Street Journal,* he ended up with a top management position in a leading investment house. At a class reunion he said, "When I went to New York, I always knew I could compete on the same level with everybody else because of the way I had been prepared at Bellarmine." It is a testimony that thousands of Bellarmine alumni could echo. If a tree is judged by its fruit, a college is judged by its alumni. In its half century of preparing young men and women for worthwhile lives and careers, Bellarmine has been exceptionally successful.

The Pioneer Class of '54 set the standard. At the 10th Anniversary Reunion held at Bellarmine on May 30, 1964, the class roll of 42 already included two medical doctors, a doctor of dentistry, a Ph.D. in history, a Ph.D. in chemistry, two attorneys, one priest, numerous business leaders, two CPAs and several alumni with master's degrees. The first and most immediate influence was felt in the Louisville community. The first graduates began taking responsible positions in business and the professions. Small

Joseph P. Clayton '71 receives the Alumnus of the Year Award from Dr. Joseph J. McGowan at the 1996 Alumni Awards Dinner.

wonder that Fr. Horrigan, when asked some 40 years after he became the college's first President what he was most proud of about the college, said, without hesitation: "I am proudest of the wonderful alumni that we have produced who have gone out into this community and other communties all over the nation and world and become productive, responsible, moral leaders. In particular, they have helped to integrate the Catholic presence into these communities as an influence and force for good." Before the decade of the '50s was over, Bellarmine graduates began appearing routinely on lists of those who passed state bar exams and CPA exams, and were recipients of advanced academic, medical and dental degrees.

After almost 30 years of glowing reports of alumni achievements, in the spring of 1980 the college announced the establishment of the Gallery of Distinguished Graduates to be installed in the administration building lobby, now Horrigan Hall. The first honorees were Maurice Buchart, Jr., '56, an executive with *The Courier-Journal* and *The Louisville Times;* Dr. Morton Kasden, '59, a renowned plastic and hand surgeon; Emil Graeser, '59, a construction company executive; John E. Tobe, '62, an executive with Jerrico, Inc.; Sr. Angelice Seibert, Ursuline '47, president of the Louisville Ursuline Community; and John Habig, '58, an executive with

Kimball International. In an interview with *The Concord*, Kasden remembered Bellarmine as "a small school that really cares about you." Dozens of other officially designated "Distinguished Graduates" have been honored since then, as Bellarmine's graduates continue to excell in their professions and communities, including Charles Ricketts, '65, Sr. Sarah Stauble, '59, Paul Browne, '69, and Fr. Clyde Crews, '66. In 1974 another distinguished graduate, Dr. Joseph C. Burke from the Pioneer Class, '54, became president of Plattsburgh State University College in New York State.

Bellarmine has also honored her graduates with other awards. Beginning in 1961 the Bellarmine Pride Corps, a service organization, gave an Alumnus of the Year Award. The first two awards went to John O. Kampschaefer, '54, a Louisville accountant, and Dr. Henry G. Ellert, '54, a research chemist with the Esso Research Laboratories at Baton Rouge, Louisiana— both of them members of the Pioneer Class.

Alumni have performed lives of service locally and around the world. The Peace Corps has claimed many Bellarmine graduates, especially in the '60s, when Elias David Meena, '64, taught biology and chemistry in Tanzania, Africa; when Creighton Mershon, '63, taught physical education and history in Venezuela; when Joseph Rogers Dickinson, '61, volunteered to go to Bolivia and James R. Skelton went to Ecuador. Other graduates were sent by religious orders. Brother Joseph Weissling, who joined the Franciscan order in 1950, completed his degree at Bellarmine in 1958 and took a job teaching English at a boys' school in Northern

Hank Ellert '54

Rhodesia that summer. Few graduates can equal the versatility of Ralph Crews, '67, who, while serving as a district manager for General Electric in Mobile was also winning national contests in figure and dance roller skating.

The majority of Bellarmine's graduates, however, have established themselves in the Louisville area and enriched their home community. In the fall of 1961, the college reported that some 80 per cent of its alumni were living and working within 150 miles of Louisville. In the local community they may be found in dozens of professions, in the board rooms and executive offices of industry, in government and education. Here is a random sampling of some of them. Burt J. Deutsch, '66, was appointed director of the City Law Department in 1974. Ken Clay, who was in the class of '60, has been a social activist, television personality, promoter of the arts and programmer at the Kentucky Center for the Arts. Robert Scherer, '63, who went to work for WHAS the day before he was graduated from Bellarmine, became vice president and general manager of the seven Clear Channel Communications radio stations that dominate the Louisville area, including WHAS and WAMZ. David Thurmond, '71, who was a basketball player and president of the student body, became a member of the Louisville Ballet. Tom O'Hearn, '65, graduated to manage the Galt House. Jim Vargo, a 1982 honor graduate, who teaches mathematics at Assumption High School in Louisville, is a competitive runner and a guide runner for blind athletes. In 1998 the Louisville Board of Aldermen included two members who had attended Bellarmine College, Bob Butler and Barbara Gregg, '72. Moreover, the board president, Steve Magre, is a Bellarmine graduate in accounting, class of '72; and furthermore, Magre's wife, Judy Simpson Magre, is also a Bellarmine graduate, class of '72.

Graduates in local educational institutions are legion. The first lay principal of a Catholic high school in the Louisville Archdiocese was James H. Brown, '60, who became head of the Elizabethtown Catholic

Members of the Class of '56 at the 40th Reunion Celebration during Jubilee 1996.

High School in 1967. The first lay principal of a Catholic high school in Jefferson County was John Moll, '55, who became head of Bishop David High School (now Holy Cross) in 1972. One of the first lay principals of an elementary school was Albert J. Luckett, '60, who became principal of Guardian Angels Grade School in 1967. James Paul Clark, '63, became principal of Sacred Heart Academy in 1973. At 31, Fr. Thomas Batsis, '63, was one of the youngest high-school principals in Kentucky when he was appointed principal of De Sales High School.

Dozens of Bellarmine graduates have also staffed classrooms in Catholic and public schools at all levels. William P. Bradford II, '67, has had a long and distinguished career teaching theater to students at Trinity High School and elsewhere. In the late '60s not only was Carl A. Nett, '63, principal of Guardian

Angels School but he was serving in the Kentucky General Assembly. Indeed, in 1977 Bellarmine had seven alumni serving in the General Assembly, compared to a total of nine for all other Kentucky independent colleges.

Bellarmine graduates have also been active in social and civil rights projects. A prominent example is Tom Hogan, '66, who was elected chairman of the Kentucky Civil Liberties Union in 1977. As an attorney he was a leader in civil rights litigation, filing the lawsuit which led to busing to eliminate segregation of Jefferson County schools in 1974. He and another Bellarmine alumnus, Mark Chmiel, '82, traveled with an ecumenical action group called Witness for Peace to the war-scarred country of Nicaragua in opposition to U. S. policy in that country. As a Bellarmine student he had been editor of *The Concord*. He died of cancer in September of 1984. Alumni have attended and excelled in dozens of distinguished graduate schools. Jack Daly, who nurtured his students not only while they were at Bellarmine but also when they went on to do graduate work, pointed with pride to his "legion of outstanding graduates in chemistry," including Hank Ellert, '54, Bellarmine's first alumnus to earn a Ph.D., and Jim Heck, '72, who earned his Ph.D. at Harvard. Ellert was issued a patent by the U.S. Patent Office in 1961 for a process to refine shale oil. Another of Daly's graduates was Chuck Thiemann, '59, who became president and CEO of the Federal Home Loan Bank of Cincinnati.

Three of the University of Louisville's Medical School graduates in 1962 were from Bellarmine's Class of '58: Stuart A. Fink, Bernard D. Greenwell and Michael Greenwell. Another of the medical graduates that year was Robert R. O'Connor, '54, a member of Bellarmine's Pioneer Class who changed careers. Many of the alumni have achieved status by publishing articles and books in their fields. A book by Gene Logsdon, '61, *Wyeth People,* was called by *Courier-Journal* art critic Sarah Lansdell "engaging, heart-warming."

According to Jimmy Ford, '86, director of alumni affairs, one of Bellarmine's best known graduates is John MacLeod, '59, an all-around sportsman who won 10 letters as a student athlete, became head basketball coach at the University of Oklahoma, then became head coach of the NBA's Phoenix Suns, and in 1991 became basketball coach at Notre Dame. Ford is one of the many Bellarmine alumni who have returned to their alma mater to teach, coach or work in administration. In addition, alumni have become members of various Bellarmine boards and active in fund raising. Al Cassidy, '54, while

still an executive with Anaconda Aluminum, served as chairman of the Finance Committee of the Board of Trustees.

As director of alumni affairs since 1989, Ford calls himself "an ambassador of good will" for the college. His mission, he says, is to bond Bellarmine graduates and former students to the college and to ask their continuing support for the college that helped prepare them for life. It is, he says, "a sometimes tough but fun job." With more than 12,000 Bellarmine and Ursuline alumni, he has a mailing list of some 10,000 and a Phon-a-Thon list of more than 6,500.

Ford is uniquely qualified for his job. Both his father and mother were members of the Class of '54, his father, John, at Bellarmine and his mother, Mary Lloyd Alford, at Ursuline. He obtained his Bellarmine undergraduate degree in 1986 and completed his graduate studies in the MBA program in 1997. "With these connections," he says, "I feel that I know the history and traditions of Bellarmine inside out, and as a result can genuinely relate to alumni of all ages.

Bellarmine alumni are not only good contributors to the college—they helped build Alumni Hall, the humanities building—but they are important recruiters

Cindy Cain Huber, '69, Linda Dunn Meir, '69, and Dr. Steven Kirn, '69, help entertain classmates at their 30th reunion in May of 1999.

Windell Bowles (left) and John A. Nold (right) served as president and vice president of the Alumni Board from 1965-67.

basketball team. His favorite memory, he says, was the game in the mid-'70s when Bellarmine beat Kentucky Wesleyan by a score of 72-64. At the time Wesleyan was ranked nationally at the top of its NCAA class.

Much of alumni support has been channeled through the Bellarmine College Alumni Association, whose first president was John O. Kampschaefer of the Pioneer Class. Founded in 1954 with a membership of 42, the group had increased to more than 300 by the summer of 1956. Other early presidents included Robert Lincoln, '54, Ben Erskine, '54, and Joseph R. McDevitt, '56. By 1966 membership was up to 1,400 when alumni

of new students. A timely letter from a successful Bellarmine grad will often persuade a prospect to come here.

A favorite alumni association event is the golf scramble held each year on campus.

The Nelson County Alumni Club presents a scholarship check to Alumni Director James P. Ford. From left, are Jodi Haydon, '67, Jack Barnes, '61, Byron Corbett, '68, George Ballard, '71.

Indeed, Bellarmine alumni have been remarkably loyal and supportive of their alma mater in a number of ways. John O'Regan, '54, the first student to enroll at Bellarmine, served for 33 years as the volunteer official scorer at the home games of the Knights

president Windell Bowles, '57, listed some of the organization's achievements: annual alumni fund drives which had raised more than $75,000, with 68 per cent contributing; Easter Sunday Mass and Egg Hunt; New Year's Eve dances; a newsletter; bimonthly alumni meetings; a joint session with the Board of Overseers; annual meetings with Fr. Horrigan; a reception for each graduating class; career counseling for students; and providing a close liaison between alumni and college. The 1966 Easter Egg Hunt for some 300 children of alumni yielded one surprise. One little fellow returned from his egg search with a small rabbit, explaining, "It was just sitting under a tree."

Other activities have included the sponsorship in 1988 of Kentucky Harvest Night on campus, featuring a celebrity vs. faculty basketball game to collect food for the area's hungry. Also an annual Bellarmine College Alumni Golf Tournament has been held for over 20 years. In the fall of 1974, the association sponsored a daylong symposium on child health and safety. In 1965 the association formed the Alumni Forum, which met monthly at the home of an alumnus or at the college. In June of 1992, the association sponsored, under the direction of Robert Stallings, "Center Court with Rick Pitino," the University of Kentucky head basketball coach who had just completed his third year. The event netted $25,000 for the Alumni Association Scholarship Fund.

As the number of alumni grew and graduates became more numerous outside of Louisville, alumni clubs and networks were formed. By the fall of 1996, organizations were being formed in Indianapolis, Chicago, Nelson County, Kentucky, Cincinnati/ Northern Kentucky, Washington D.C./Virginia/ Maryland and Southwest Florida.

Perhaps, however, Bellarmine alumni are most supportive when they send their sons and daughters, brothers and sisters, nieces and nephews and friends to the college as students. In May of 1989, two members of the Pioneer Class, John O'Regan and Pete Korfhage, were in the audience as their daughters received degrees from their own alma mater. They watched as Dianne O'Regan was given her associate's degree in political science and Linda Korfhage her bachelor's degree in elementary education by the Bellarmine Chancellor, Archbishop Thomas C. Kelly.

The first alumni newsletter, January 1956.

The current alumni publication, Bellarmine Magazine, in 1998.

Speaking for two generations of his family, Al Cassidy, '81, says, "I feel good that I went to Bellarmine and that my son Joseph Cassidy, who is now director of student activities at Notre Dame, went to Bellarmine. It prepared us both for a good life."

Indeed, the Bellarmine alumni and the Bellarmine Alumni Association are continuing to foster good will between the college and its once and present students, faculty and administration. No one could describe the role of the alumni better than Fr. Horrigan in the first issue of the *Bellarmine Alumni News*. In January of 1956 he wrote: "An alumni association is not merely a casual sort of social group operating on the edges of a college's program. It is an integral and vitally important part of the college itself. It is the carrier of the college's traditions and identity. Faculty and student bodies come and go with the years. The alumni association is the stable and continuing unit which preserves and grows one generation after the other."

Perhaps an alumnus should have the final word. W. James Lintner, Jr., B.A., business administration, '71, co-founded CompDent Corporation in 1977, became the founding chairman of the National Association of Prepaid Dental Plans in 1989, and in 1996 organized River Hill Capital, LLC, a venture capital firm. He is currently vice-chair of the college Board of Trustees and president of the Alumni Board. This is what he says about the importance of Bellarmine's alumni to their alma mater: "The key to the future growth and realization of the college's potential rests with alumni. We are the ones who helped build and shape the tradition by which current and future students are measured. We must lead by example and continue to strengthen our base of support so that future alumni will follow." No one could have said it better.

W. James Lintner, Jr., '71

Mission and Performance, The End and The Beginning

And so Bellarmine has almost completed its first half century and looks forward to the promise of the new millennium. In 1961, after more than 10 years as President of Bellarmine College, Fr. Horrigan looked optimistically to the future: "At Bellarmine and at all similar colleges today there are more things to be done than ever before, but they can be done. It will be difficult to find all the money we must have, but it can be found. Good teachers are even more difficult to find, but even they can be found if we are sufficiently determined. I do not believe the prospects of the Catholic colleges and the other independent colleges of the country are fatefully limited by either money or personnel. The only mortal threat is a possible limitation of our own convictions about, and dedication to, the essential mission of the colleges."

Such faith and dedication have guided Bellarmine through its first 50 years. From first to last, Bellarmine has stood for vision and values. David O'Toole says, "I think the basic mission of the college has been constant during my years here—a strong liberal arts education, with a strong component of philosophy and theology, in the Catholic tradition."

Neither has the mission changed of graduating virtuous, decent, educated persons from the opening of the school. Using the rhetoric of Bellarmine's infancy, Windell Bowles, editor of *The Concord,* in December of 1955 listed his set of qualifications for Bellarmine "knighthood": meaningful religion, cleanliness in body and clothes, articulate expression without profanity, respect for campus and buildings, responsible drinking and driving, wise use of

intelligence and knowledge, obedience to the rules of etiquette, a sense of humor, proper respect for women, a wise counsel seeker, a desire for leadership and the ability to know when to work and when to play. Of his last knighthood trait, he wrote graphically: "The halls of a school building are not the place to hold wrestling matches or hog calling contests." Still using the metaphor of the medieval knight, Bowles concluded: "The day you entered Bellarmine, you became, automatically, a squire. But there is no reason why you should remain a novice. Your armor, lance, shield and helmet are waiting for you. But no one shall wear the armor of a knight who does not qualify. Earn your armor, wear it proudly and remember, chivalry is a philosophy of life, not just a word in the dictionary."

Perhaps President Petrik defined the goals of the college as well as anyone in his fall 1978 welcome to students, published in *The Concord,* when he asked, "Welcome to what?" and then answered, "To a community which enjoys and covets your presence. To a place where you can expand your spirit. To the opportunity to transcend time and place through your studies in general education. To the chance to sharpen your knowledge and skills."

By the fall of 1996, under the McGowan administration, a working motto was: "A modern experience in the Catholic tradition." Promotional materials echoed earlier promises: a broad range of degree programs, a close-knit academic environment with personal attention from the faculty, a beautiful and safe campus, an internship program and the social and cultural advantages of living in Louisville.

As chairman of the Association of Independent Kentucky Colleges and Universities, Dr. McGowan published a letter in *The Courier-Journal* of August 1, 1998, in which he affirms the value of the liberal arts education offered at schools like Bellarmine College. "It is in the area of adaptability and responsiveness that the liberal arts-prepared graduate shines brightest. Today's college graduates face a work scenario that in all probability will entail multiple job (and even career) changes as technology makes traditional ways of doing things obsolete. The liberal arts learner is well equipped to survive—even thrive—in this environment because an understanding that learning is a lifelong process is at the core of a liberal arts education. Rather than train for a specific job—one that may or may not exist in the years ahead—students educated in the liberal arts tradition are prepared to adapt to new environments, to think analytically and conceptually, to integrate broad ranges of experiences, and to assume leadership roles."

In conclusion, he wrote: "The liberal arts have been and will continue to be the most effective preparation for the leaders of tomorrow. It is primarily through the liberal arts that a human being is educated to think clearly, communicate effectively, work collaboratively and develop the framework that allows him or her to succeed in the maelstrom of change that is contemporary life." These eloquent words of Bellarmine's third President are a reaffirmation of the bedrock principles upon which the college was founded and has continued to thrive.

Indeed, even with occasional adaptations to the changes in the *zeitgeist,* the Bellarmine mission has been constant. Now, as the college looks to the future, President McGowan affirms the rich tradition on which he is building for the next century. Faculty, administration and students look ahead. As he prepared to retire after some 30 years of association with the college, Jack Kampschaefer offered this advice

and this hope: "I'm very optimistic about the future of Bellarmine. We must keep our priorities straight, continue to improve our programs and facilities — and from time to time expand them carefully—and remember that this school is bigger than any of its parts." Alumnus Michael Steinmacher speaks from experience: "Bellarmine prepares Renaissance people for the future—graduates who will be able to change and adapt and survive." Kaelin Kallay welcomed President Petrik to his new job in September of 1973 with an editorial in *The Concord.* "Maybe Petrik's way . . . is just what will put Bellarmine among the few private Catholic colleges which will still be part of the educative process in the 21st century." Her hope has become prophecy.

"An institution is the lengthened shadow of one man," wrote Ralph Waldo Emerson some 150 years ago. At Bellarmine the institution is not only the lengthened shadows of Horrigan, Petrik and McGowan but of all the people who have guided, taught, studied and supported this institution. When he retired in 1976 Professor Leonard Latkovski was asked how he wanted to be remembered. This refugee from war-torn Europe and the political chaos and despotism that followed in his native Latvia said the question reminded him of a poor Spaniard who resisted the Communists who tried to separate him from his church by saying that he had nothing in common with it. He pointed to a magnificent cathedral and said, "When this cathedral was being built, I carried bricks to build it. My work is in that cathedral that I helped to build." Latkovski said, "Like that poor old Spaniard, I'd like to say that I helped to build something. In my 25 years with Bellarmine College, I hope it can be said that I put some bricks in."

The achievements of Bellarmine College have been recognized in numerous ways—from its outstanding alumni to its standing in national rankings. In the fall 1990 issue of *Money Guide: America's Best College Buys,* Bellarmine was ranked 10th—just behind Indiana's Hanover College and just before Yale—on the list of the country's top 100 private college buys by *Money* magazine. President McGowan said, with controlled elation, "We're not surprised by this article, but we're delighted to read about it."

Indeed, Bellarmine has a proud legacy to take into the new century. There have been problems and disagreements over finances and policies. Bellarmine has been no educational utopia. People who know the college well want to see it become better. This is Robert Pfaadt's vision: "I'd like to see Bellarmine become the school of choice for the best students. I'd like for them to see that attending Bellarmine is a privilege. We are already a good school, but I think we can be even better. Several years ago a young Harvard graduate with a 4.0 grade average, a 1600 SAT and a law degree from the University of Louisville enrolled in our MBA program. In his first class under Stan Zemelka he made his first B ever. When the young man told how he made his only B, he used it as an example of Bellarmine's high standards and academic excellence. In the not too distant future I'd like for us to have more residential students, a full-time enrollment of about 1,500 and a total enrollment of around 3,000. I'd like for us to be to Louisville what Xavier is to

Cincinnati, what John Carroll is to Cleveland and what Duquesne is to Pittsburgh."

Marilyn Staples' vision has more women and minorities on the faculty and administrative staff. She would also like to see "a true student union" and a wellness building, with a pool and a gym. John Oppelt has already seen much growth at Bellarmine since he arrived as academic vice president in 1981, but he sees more growth possible: "When I came here, I saw Bellarmine as a kid not completely formed, but one who knew its parents. Like other faculty and administrators, I have tried to help it develop toward adulthood. In the mid-'90s Bellarmine is still in its lengthy teenage, searching years. It is an institution on the make, trying to grow up. A model that we can look to is Notre Dame, which is an adult, mature institution that knows what it is and is still growing. Indeed, it is vital that Bellarmine define itself and know what it is and what it wants to become. When the school reaches that state, it will command the loyalty of students, faculty, alumni and others who support our concept of higher education. The college is in a crucial period of its life. Its adolescence is ending. If it is well formed by the year 2000—and I believe it will be—it will grow into a productive adult."

Others are hopeful that the religious underpinnings will continue to be in place. Former academic vice president David House said: "As the college evolves and approaches the new millennium, I hope the spiritual dimension will not be ignored." Fr. Fred Hendrickson reiterates that desire: "I hope that with the changes that will inevitably come, Bellarmine College will be able to maintain its vision of what a Christian liberal arts college should be." Fr. Eugene Zoeller is realistic and optimistic: "We're like a cat. We land on our feet. We've been through some dark periods, but we have a strong survival streak in us. And as Christians we have hope." The most valid testimony of Bellarmine's past and its promise comes from its alumni. Pioneer Class member John O'Regan says of his Bellarmine experience: "I have zero regrets about enrolling in this new, untried college in 1950. After more than 40 years, I still can't get the smile off my face."

In December of 1996 the U.S. Department of Education issued a report, *Building Knowledge for a Nation of Learners,* which looked toward the 21st century in education. In summary, it said: "In order to meet new challenges in the workplace and in civic life, America's learners will need a firm grasp of basic competencies, a broad general knowledge of their world and the skills to respond to the rapid generation of new knowledge." It was coincidentally what Bellarmine has been saying and doing for almost 50 years. Indeed, at a certain time in a certain place, certain groups of people have come together to make a college. Bellarmine College is the college these people have made. This is the college we now take into the new century.

More specifically, the college we take into the new century is the one being shaped and envisioned by its third President, Joseph J. McGowan, Jr. Hear his charge and his vision. "When I became President of Bellarmine College in 1990, I was charged by the Board of Trustees with providing the leadership to bring the college 'to the next level.' I, therefore, initiated a visioning and strategic planning process. In order to determine the next level, I needed to understand where we had come from and where we were. I determined that the college had gone through two cycles, the first one being its foundation in 1950 as a Catholic liberal arts college for men by Archbishop Floersh and its construction led by Fr. Horrigan and Fr. Treece. When it merged with Ursuline College in 1968, it became completely co-educational and a legally secular institution in the Catholic tradition and developed an independent, self-perpetuating Board of Trustees.

"The next cycle was begun in 1973, when Eugene Petrik became President and was immediately faced with a serious financial crisis. He responded by centralizing authority, connecting to Louisville through a powerful and prestigious Board of Trustees and by building and diversifying the college through a School of Business, a School of Nursing, a Department of Education, a strengthened summer session and continuing education program. Both the number of students and campus facilities increased during his presidency. Bellarmine's connection with the business and governmental communities in Louisville improved significantly. Bellarmine had become a diverse, comprehensive university. It was in reasonably good financial health. It had built an increasing number of loyal alumni. And it had good visibility in the community. Each of my predecessors had done his work well.

"I realized, however, that the college was ready to enter another cycle and faced a number of serious challenges. Here are some of the problem areas I identifed. Student enrollment and retention were declining. To make the college more attractive to newcomers, student life and residential life needed improvement, and much work was called for in facilities, programs, policies and personnel. The college was over-organized for its size. The core faculty in arts and sciences were concerned about the emphasis on professional programs. There were internal divisions within the School of Business and enrollment was declining. There was turmoil in the nursing area. Overall, faculty development was weak.

"The core curriculum was antiquated. The governance of the college was complex and unclear. Faculty groups were often unrepresentative. Few alumni and minorities served on the Board of Trustees, and members were often unaware of college weaknesses and problem areas. Although some progress had been made, technology was still in the Dark Ages. While the annual balance sheet had been in the black since 1973, there was still an internal debt of over $2 million. Tuition and financial aid levels were low. Endowment stood at a low $7 million. Petrik Hall, a new student residence, opened in 1990, but renovation was badly needed in the older residence halls. Fund raising had stalled in the middle of a capital campaign, and no hard plans existed for a long-planned library. It seemed to me that the crisis mentality and bottom line decision making that had been necessary during the financial exigencies of 1973 were still governing the college in 1990. In addition to these challenges, I found, of course, many positive programs to build on.

"In my 1990 inaugural address, I outlined my vision for Bellarmine College and began to work on a plan to take the college to the next level. With help from other administrators and input from faculty and students, we developed a strategic plan based on academic excellence in the liberal arts. A first-rate professional education would be informed by the liberal arts as the core. We would become a more residential campus and attract more students from the region. The plan we developed had the following specific objectives: more and better students; better faculty and staff; increased faculty development; diversity at all levels and in all areas; maintaining our core Catholic identity; a new classroom building; a new library with state-of-the-art technology; a better informed and more engaged Board of Trustees; more shared information and governance; increased alumni involvement; accreditation for programs in education, nursing and business and, finally, a new core curriculum.

"I am pleased that by 1998 we are achieving great success in improving academic excellence on many fronts, including notably these: faculty development through a grant from the Knight Foundation; curriculum reform in general education; the development and implementation of a master technology plan; and the planning and construction of the W. L. Lyons Brown Library. Our new library has become a transforming facility and resource and a visual statement of the new level of excellence throughout the college.

"As we approach the new century and as a part of the celebration of our 50th anniversary, I am proposing a very ambitious $70 million Plan of Advancement for Bellarmine College. Many of the details of this Master Plan, as we are calling it, remain to be worked out; but the first-stage plans call for a new Campus Center with meeting spaces, a bookstore and a cafe in the old library space in Horrigan Hall, an Academic Resource Center in the Brown Library and, very importantly, the construction of a separate campus chapel on the hillside overlooking Newburg Road near the residence halls.

"The next stage includes a major renovation and expansion of Pasteur Hall for our science programs and the development of Wyatt Hall into a performing arts center. The Brown Activities Center will be expanded and redesigned as a lifetime sports/ recreation center. Early in the next century our plans call for the expansion of Alumni Hall and the Norton Music and Art Buildings around a terraced amphitheater. There are also plans for a piazza at the Horrigan end of the quadrangle, including a fountain or an open pergola.

"Finally, I think it important that, from time to time, we pause to consider and articulate our mission and vision in a formal and concise manner. As a part of our institutional self-study for reaffirmation of accreditation with the Southern Association of Colleges and Schools, concluded successfully in 1998 under the expert leadership of Dr. Nancy Howard, we agreed on the following statement of mission: 'Bellarmine College serves Kentucky and the region by providing an educational environment of academic excellence in the Catholic liberal arts tradition, where talented and diverse persons of all faiths and ages develop the intellectual, moral and professional competencies to lead, to serve and to making a living and a life worth living.' Our vision statement reads: 'Bellarmine College aspires to be the premier innovative, independent Catholic liberal arts college in Kentucky and the region for preparing diverse persons to become dynamic leaders to serve, live and work in a changing, global community.' Our intention now is to become a first-class regional college connected to the rest of the world. We must know and honor our past, but we cannot live there. Students are changing. The world is changing. As a living, growing institution, Bellarmine is an organic college—always changing, always incomplete.

"As Bellarmine's third President, I have a wonderful opportunity to build on what Horrigan and Petrik did. You could say it this way using a food metaphor. Msgr. Horrigan opened the dining room. Gene set the table. And now I am allowed to prepare the feast."

In a 1958 special report Fr. Horrigan proclaimed the bedrock on which the college was founded. "The motto of Bellarmine College is *In Veritatis Amore*—'In the Love of Truth,'" he wrote. "I think this motto cuts to the heart of the educational problem in any age or place. Truth is most of all to be loved and searched for because in itself it is something incomparably good. And because, in all its forms, it has its origin in God and, faithfully served, will always lead back to Him." With the words and deeds of such men and women who founded and guided Bellarmine College through its first 50 years as our manifesto and our calling, we look forward confidently, exuberantly, to the next 50—and beyond.

Perhaps *Concord* editor Ray Tillman's conclusion to his May 1954 tribute to the Pioneer Class is an appropriate way to conclude this history-in-the-making. "Bellarmine College is a living organization," he wrote. "The splendid buildings and campus are only symbols of the spirit which is Bellarmine—the spirit of the faculty, the student body and of the thousands of people outside the college who have unselfishly contributed toward its advancement. May it retain always the spirit which it has come to know during these first few years." Forty-five years later, it is also our wish.

****

Fr. Clyde Crews poses with the historical marker on Bellarmine's campus.

Computers are located throughout the W. L. Lyons Brown Library, with connections available for over 400 lap-top computers.

A POSTSCRIPT IN JEST AND
SERIOUSNESS
WITH A LOOK TO THE PAST AND
FUTURE:

Dr. McGowan's Address
On the Occasion of the First Knight of Knights
September 12, 1998

To All Assembled Here This Evening, Lords and
Ladies, Princes and Princesses, Warriors, Peacemaker,
Knaves, Jesters, and the Few Assorted Low-Lifes:

*My Queen Maureen and I Bid You a Warm Welcome to
the Castle Del Bellarmino and to This Noble and Historic
Gathering of the Knights of the Bellarmine Round Table.*

This evening, we join together in festival, song
and merriment to give honor and blessing to one, as
well as to all.

One of the many things enjoyable to me this
evening, as we recreate in this recreated medieval
environment, is that not only did knighthood find its
origin in these times almost a thousand years ago, but
so too did universities as we know them today.

As so much of the western world was Catholic
in those days, so too were the great original universities
like Bologna and Salerno. Because of universities like
Bologna and Salerno in those days, through to
Bellarmine College today, the Catholic tradition in
higher education is the oldest continuing education
tradition in the history of the world.

With its continuing emphases on the liberal arts
and the professions, on great cities like Louisville, and
on academic excellence in the teaching of each
individual as a creature of God and whole person, with
its unabashed affirmation of an education in which a
religious faith in God is fully compatible and consistent
with knowledge and the power of reason, Bellarmine
College is clearly in the great educational tradition of
Bologna and Salerno.

But just as the Middle Ages gave birth to
knighthood and to universities, so too do the people
in this castle hall tonight continue to give birth and life
to the distinguished university in creation that is
Bellarmine College.

Because of you, members of the President's
Society, and people like Owsley Brown Frazier and the
many families, corporations, foundations, and alumni
here tonight, Bellarmine College not only has a past
that finds its roots and its mascot in the Middle Ages,
but because of you and with you, it has an enormous
and exciting future as we move toward our 50th year
and into the 21st century in the year 2000.

The freshman class that just entered, historic in
its size and academic power, is the class of *2002*. It is
made up of students, most of whom were *born* in 1980
and were ten years old when I became President eight
years ago!

The invitation and enormous opportunity that
the history of Kentucky is providing Bellarmine at this
very moment is the invitation and opportunity to be
for Kentucky what Vanderbilt is for Tennessee; to be
for Kentucky what Notre Dame is for Indiana; to be
for Kentucky what Emory is for Georgia; to be for
Kentucky what Case Western Reserve is for Ohio; to
be for Kentucky what Duke is for North Carolina—
not that we should be or try to be Vanderbilt or Notre
Dame or Emory or Case Western or Duke, but that
we can and should become Bellarmine in all of its
potential, the premier private university in Kentucky.

Governor Patton, the state legislature and the
economic leaders of Kentucky want and need to
dramatically improve the quality of life and the
economic life of Kentucky. And they know that to do
that we need excellent universities in both the public
and private sectors. The University of Kentucky and
the University of Louisville in particular appear to have
been offered an opportunity for leadership in the public
sector.

Many of us believe, and I invite you to believe
with us, that Bellarmine has the invitation and

opportunity to be the premier *private* university in Kentucky—and thus, if you know how much easier and faster excellence can be achieved in the private sector, I also believe that Bellarmine has the opportunity to be the premier Kentucky university—period.

As citizens of Kentucky and Louisville we all take much pride and pleasure in the great new football stadium recently built and opened at the University of Louisville. I celebrate that stadium and love football, but I believe that what Kentucky needs even more deeply, more importantly, more enduringly is a first-rate stadium of the mind, heart and soul for the brightest students in the region. That is what I would like Bellarmine to be for Kentucky. And that is what Kentucky and the region needs Bellarmine to be!

I will be developing this vision more fully and completely for you in the weeks and months ahead. But now let us return to our roots to celebrate Bellarmine as a great university in a long and distinguished education tradition and as knights. Let us enter, through our imagination, into the magic and majesty of the Middle Ages, into a grand and sumptuous medieval feast and festival at a great roundtable within the dramatic main hall of Castle Del Bellarmino.

It is here that we will rest and recreate a while, close to our roots, as we gather energy and inspiration for our courageous journey into the future and toward our compelling destiny as Kentucky's premier private university.

Bellarmine's campus was magically transformed into a medieval township at the inaugural Knight of Knights.

President Joseph J. McGowan, Art Professor Bob Lockhart and Bellarmine's first Knight, Owsley Brown Frazier pose for a picture at the inaugural Knight of Knights.